GANGSTER SQUAD

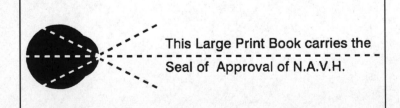

This Large Print Book carries the
Seal of Approval of N.A.V.H.

GANGSTER SQUAD

COVERT COPS, THE MOB, AND THE BATTLE FOR LOS ANGELES

PAUL LIEBERMAN

THORNDIKE PRESS

A part of Gale, Cengage Learning

GALE
CENGAGE Learning·

Detroit • New York • San Francisco • New Haven, Conn • Waterville, Maine • London

GALE
CENGAGE Learning®

LIBRARY OF CONGRESS CATALOGING-IN-PUBLICATION DATA

Lieberman, Paul, 1949–
    Gangster squad : covert cops, the mob, and the battle for Los Angeles
/ by Paul Lieberman. — Large print ed.
      p. cm. (Thorndike press large print Crime Scene)
    ISBN-13: 978-1-4104-5344-0 (hbk.)
    ISBN-10: 1-4104-5344-8 (hbk.)
    1. Cohen, Mickey, 1914–1976. 2. Los Angeles (Calif.). Police Dept.—
History—20th century. 3. Gangsters—California—Los Angeles—History—
20th century. 4. Organized crime—California—Los Angeles—History—
20th century. I. Title.
HV8148.L55L54 2012b
364.106'60979494—dc23   2012034542

Published in 2012 by arrangement with St. Martin's Press, LLC.

Printed in Mexico
1 2 3 4 5 6 7 16 15 14 13 12

For Heidi

CONTENTS

7

PRELUDE:
A VIOLIN CASE
UNDER THE BED

"Willie Burns called," Connie O'Mara said when her husband, Jack, came home.

"What did he want?"

"He wants you back at the station."

"OK, boss."

It was a cool fall evening in Los Angeles so Sergeant John J. O'Mara retrieved his topcoat from the closet and his snap-brim fedora from the rack by the door of the garden apartment they had been renting since he got back from the war. His revolver still was in his shoulder holster.

Their old Plymouth was parked across from Saint Anselm Catholic Church, whose priest already had roped him in as an usher, finding the young Irish sergeant ideal for passing the collection basket — Jack O'Mara would give 'em his withering blue-eyed stare and that was it.

Their apartment was only three miles from the Los Angeles Police Department's 77th Street Station, on the edge of Watts, so the drive didn't give him much time to ponder why Lieutenant Burns might be calling him in after hours. O'Mara had been getting grief in the department for busting a burglary ring that included the teenage son of a police commander. Some old-timers thought he should have let the case file disappear. He hadn't.

When O'Mara reached the station house, eighteen men were gathering in the squad room, many of them enormous, the largest cops he'd ever seen. This wasn't about any burglary case. Most all wore topcoats and hats just like his. Lieutenant Willie Burns kept his hat pulled down low, over his eyes, like the bad guys.

Burns was waiting at the far end of the squad room. He was a tough little fellow who had been shot early in his police career and had served as a gunnery officer in the Marines. He was standing behind a bench. On it sat a Thompson submachine gun.

"We've been asked by the chief to form a special detail," Burns said as his hands effortlessly took apart the Tommy gun and reassembled the pieces.

That's all he called it then, the *special detail.* Burns later told a grand jury, "My primary duties were to keep down these gangster killings and try to keep some of these rough guys under control." Now he gave these eighteen men the particulars: If they joined him, their targets would be the likes of Benjamin "Bugsy" Siegel, the playboy refugee from New York's Murder, Inc., and Jack Dragna, the Sicilian banana importer who quietly lorded over Los Angeles' illegal gambling and related rackets. Most of the cops had never heard of Dragna, the man they were told ran the rackets in their city.

Most had at least heard the next name, if only because Mickey Cohen had killed a man the year before, a fat bookie. Mickey was almost a local boy too. Born in Brooklyn, as Meyer Harris Cohen, he had been brought west by his mother as an infant and had grown up in L.A.'s poor Boyle Heights neighborhood. He fought first for street corners as a newsboy then moved away to fight for pay, as a flyweight, five foot five at most. Mickey was a little man, but one of the breed who learned that a gun could make him bigger. He gravitated from boxing to running dice games and sticking up joints around Cleveland and Chicago until he drew the attention of the old Capone mob, becoming "the Jew kid" to them. They encouraged him to take his moxie back west where he might learn some style from the cashmere-suited Ben Siegel, and perhaps help Bugsy muscle aside L.A.'s second-tier hoods. But Mickey had gained little notice until 1945, when 250-pound Maxie Shaman stormed into his thinly disguised gambling parlor in a

Santa Monica Boulevard paint store. Mickey said big Maxie had come at him with a .45, the one found by the body, so he had no choice but to plug the burly bookie with the .38 he kept in his desk.

Since then another bookmaker, Paulie Gibbons, had been shot seven times on a Beverly Hills street. Next to fall, in 1946, were Chicago natives Bennie "The Meatball" Gamson and George Levinson, that dual execution generating the GANGSTERS IN GAMBLING WAR headline that was the last straw for Los Angeles officials — and the reason Lieutenant Willie Burns assembled eighteen hand-picked candidates for a secretive new squad that October.

"You'll be working with these," Burns told them as he hoisted the Tommy gun and slid in its circular 50-round drum.

The deal was: If they joined him, they would continue to be listed on the rosters of their old stations while operating out of two rusted old Fords. They would not make arrests. If someone had to be booked, they'd call in Homicide, Vice, or Robbery. They would also be available for *other chores*, as Chief C. B. Horrall saw fit. They would have cash at their disposal, a Secret Service Fund to pay informants who might help them gather intelligence on the likes of Bugsy, Dragna, and Mickey Cohen. But they would have no office. They'd meet on street corners, in parking lots, and up in the hills. In effect, they would not exist.

Burns gave the eighteen men a week to ponder his invitation and some advice from an old lieutenant at the 77th who said an assignment like that could get you in good with the chief, or even make you a hero, "Or you could end up down in San Pedro, walking a beat in a fog." Sergeant Jack O'Mara puffed on his pipe as the old lieutenant cautioned them, "Whatever you do, keep your nose clean."

After the week to think it over, only seven came back to join Willie Burns, making a Gangster Squad of eight. One was O'Mara, who had to explain to his wife, Connie, what was in thc stylish black violin case he began keeping under their bed.

Sergeant Jerry Wooters came on board later. He was not a church usher or a pipe smoker. He went for cigars or cigarettes, which he dangled from the corner of his mouth. Gerard "Jerry" Wooters was lean and angular — he was all about playing the angles. He was the son of an itinerant gold miner who had come to California following its oldest get-rich-quick fantasy, but mostly stayed poor. Jerry tried to avoid the war but couldn't, then got shot down over the Pacific and was left floating in a raft. If a Japanese boat found him first, he was dead. If an American ship found him, he'd come home with medals. After he came home with his medals, he kept photos of himself with the comely nurses who helped him recover. As a policeman he displayed the same screw-you defiance to the crooks and his bosses alike. On his first case for the Gangster Squad, he led the investigation that changed the ground rules for policing in California.

Jerry Wooters and Jack O'Mara had nothing in common except for their rank as sergeants, and their shared obsession with Mickey Cohen.

In time, O'Mara set a trap for Mickey, using his own guns, to prove he was a killer.

Wooters forged an alliance with Mickey's budding rival of the 1950s, Jack "The Enforcer" Whalen, a powerhouse of a man who took pride in never needing a gun — his fists were enough — and had dreams of making it in Hollywood.

Neither cop told the other what he had done.

On the job a decade before J. Edgar Hoover's FBI acknowledged the existence of the Mafia, the Los Angeles Police Gangster Squad took an anything-goes approach to making life hell for Mickey Cohen and his ilk. Squad members faked drive-by shootings to confound their targets and took out-of-town hoods up to Mulholland Drive for *chats* designed to scare them back home. They posed as termite men and telephone repairmen to plant hidden microphones — to hell with warrants. They bugged TV sets and a mistress' bed. They neutralized a pesky newspaper columnist and did hush-hush favors for Jack Webb, who glorified the LAPD with his *Dragnet* television show. They stole guns and address books from mobsters and left anonymous messages, not loving chocolates, on their pillows.

There were close calls — grand jury investigations, lawsuits, and a skeptical police chief or two — but they endured through the '50s. That's when one of their cases reached the State Supreme Court and one of their own, the defiant Jerry Wooters, got a bit too reckless, setting the stage for the deadly night in the Valley when a bullet between the eyes signaled that the Gangster Squad's time was over, and so was a defining era in Los Angeles' history.

They operated at a time and place where truth was found not in the sunlight, but in the shadows, and justice found not in marble courthouses, but in the streets. That was their Los Angeles, the sun-washed city of palm trees and self-invention, the city that spent a long century pretending that evil came from afar.

■ ■ ■ ■

PART I
THE WHALENS
MOVE WEST TO THE
CITY OF ANGELS

■ ■ ■ ■

CHAPTER 1
THE DUSTY ROAD CON

Fred Whalen learned to scam along the Mississippi, the river that divides America, at pool halls and revivals. He was born in 1898 in Alton, Illinois, just upriver from St. Louis, and by the time he was a teenager he had figured out the traveling evangelists who set up shop in tents, barns, and occasionally, even, in real churches. He saw the people writhing in divine ecstasy out in their congregations and sensed immediately what was up: they were phonies, plants, shills for the preachers. Little Freddie was barely able to see over the pews but he knew they were fakers, those folks writhing in the aisles. So he'd take his coat and cover them up and spoil the show . . . until the preachers began paying him $5 to stay away.

Freddie had another tactic for evangelists who didn't have Holy Rollers shaking with the spirit. He didn't need a hymn book — he knew all the words to standards such as "Are You Washed in the Blood?" so he'd rise with the crowd and belt it out, through the closing lines,

Are your garments spotless?
Are they white as Snow?
Are you washed in the blood of the Lamb?

The evangelist then would signal everyone to sit, eager to get down to business, and the flock would do as told, except for Freddie. He'd remain on his feet and start it again, "*Are you washed in the blood?*" and everyone would rise back up and join him, singing it over, first verse to last. Then the preacher would gesture once more for all to be seated, only to have Freddie launch into the refrain once more, "*Are you washed in the blood?*" His deal with those preachers was the same, five bucks and I go away.

As for pool, he was a true prodigy — there was nothing fake about him being able to beat anyone in Alton by fifth grade. An old shark known as Tennessee Brown saw the Irish kid toying with some pretty fair players for a jar full of pennies and begged Freddie's parents to let him tutor the boy. Freddie's father worked as a railroad switchman for the Illinois Terminal but had grown up in Ireland amid the potato famines, and he knew the value of a little extra money. So little Freddie soon was giving trick-shot exhibitions in which he wowed the crowds by hitting balls

22

off the top of Coke bottles. But the real payoff wasn't in showing off. It was in looking as bad as possible while still beating the other guy, making him believe it was his fault he lost. Freddie dropped out of school to hit the road with his cue and his mentor, who guided him through the pool parlors and dives along the river, perfecting his hustle. Sometimes Tennessee Brown would offer to play people using one pocket, they got the other five. Once he took their money he would treat himself to a 25-cent cigar and tell the loser, "Bet you can't even beat that kid."

Freddie's childhood officially ended when his railroad worker father got consumption and couldn't shake the cough. John Whalen took off without his family for that beautiful and distant place called California, having heard of its miracle cures, only to return to Alton four weeks later, homesick and still coughing. Freddie was fourteen when his father passed in 1912.

He moved up to Chicago to put all that he'd learned about human nature to work as a door-to-door salesman. He was slender but close to six feet tall and looked grown-up in a gray suit and vest. He had an oversized smile, a natural salesman's smile, and if it looked fake to some people, so be it — most liked how he lit up a room. Freddie convinced two rival photo studios in the Windy City to let him represent them. For $1, families got a certificate they could bring in, good for an 8-by-10-inch formal portrait. He never let either studio know he was selling for the other.

In no time Freddie was peddling a more elaborate product, a check writing machine. People were fearful that someone would alter checks they wrote to raise the amount, so the typewriter-like device punched down and perforated the paper to form the number. It literally *cut a check*, the origin of that phrase. He found it easy to convince customers they were in great peril if they didn't have one of his check protectors. Before long, the company that made the machines offered to send him to New York, to sell there. He declined because of a girl.

Whalen family lore offers two accounts of how Freddie met Lillian Wunderlich. One version was pure Americana, sweet, romantic, and innocent. In this telling, his selling took him back down to St. Louis, where he'd stop at a teeming boarding house run by Lillian's mother. The Wunderlich clan was huge, with sixteen kids, many raised doing chores on a family farm in Pacific, Missouri. Perhaps that's why the boys were so strong — one, Augustus, "Gus," could hoist the heaviest wooden chair in the house with one hand. But the eldest girl was why Freddie kept coming back. Born in 1899, the year after him, Lillian was just fourteen when they went out for the first time, with several Wunderlichs along to chaperone, eager to keep an eye on the pool-playing salesman with the oversized smile.

But the other account of their meeting suggests that the Wunderlichs understood exactly who they were letting into the family. Young Gus also loved the spectacle of the revivals on the sawdust circuit and attended one in a barn, then dragged two of his sisters back the next night, telling Lillian and Florence, "You gotta see this." They sat up in the loft, looking down on the preacher imploring the crowd, "I KNOW there's a sinner out there — a gambling, drinking, womanizing sinner. And if we all bow our heads, he's gonna come to the lord TONIGHT. Come forward, sinner, COME FORWARD!" With that, a lanky young man, dark-haired and duded up, jumped to his feet. "It's me!" he shouted while marching up front to be saved, on his knees, in tears. It was Fred Whalen, of course, and after the service Gus guided his sisters to the back of the barn and again said, "Watch this" as Freddie and the preacher shook hands and something green passed from the man of the cloth to the night's repentant sinner, no longer the enemy of the traveling evangelists.

Lillian Wunderlich was smitten on the spot. She liked to point out that her grandmother had gone to dances with the train-robbing

James boys, Frank and Jesse, in the mid-1800s. It was in her blood, an eye for a certain kind of man. She was sixteen when she married Fred. He was seventeen. They honeymooned at the Mineral Springs Hotel in Alton, which touted the therapeutic powers of the waters bubbling up below its basement and sold the stuff by the bottle.

The couple had a daughter first, Bobie, then a son, Jack. Decades later, the family insisted that the baby boy was huge, ten pounds out of the womb, or maybe fourteen pounds, or sixteen. Family legends vary that way. But the State of Missouri birth certificate did not list a weight, reporting only that Jack Fredrick Whalen was born just after midnight on May 11, 1921.

The next year, Fred Whalen led the clan's migration west, he and his young wife, their two kids and a slew of Wunderlichs. He showed up at their boarding home with $26, his pool cue, his fancy clothes, and two vehicles. "Everybody that wants to go to California, pack your stuff, we're leaving," he announced, and a dozen of them stuffed into two cars waiting outside. One was a let's-hope-it-works black sedan made by the Dorris Motor Car Company of St. Louis ("Built Up to a Standard. Not Down to a Price."), soon to go defunct. But the other was eye-popping, a Marmon Touring Car made by the Indianapolis company whose yellow one-seat speedster had won the first 500-mile race in that city. Now Marmon offered discerning motorists "The Major Car of the Major Class" featuring a large rear seating area set well back from the driver, running boards on each side, the first rear-view mirror, and a front grill topped by a silver ornament you might see on the car of a millionaire company president, which is exactly what Fred pretended to be in the small towns en route.

They'd stop at a dusty roadside camp on the outskirts of Anywhere U.S.A., where everyone got out but Fred and his young wife and the iron-muscled Gus. An aunt would take charge of baby Jack, who traveled in a makeshift cradle they suspended on a rope inside one car, hanging down behind the front seat. While other Wunderlichs wandered off to find a nearby farm, searching for a stray chicken to poach, Fred put on his three-piece suit and Lillian her frilliest dress, with a hat to match. Gus got ready in a white shirt and vest . . . and a chauffeur's cap. Then they rode in toward Main Street in the imposing Marmon, the couple in back, Gus up at the wheel. Fred called him "kid" and "palie," but Gus was an ideal chauffeur, having driven farm vehicles, and rebuilt their motors, from the day he quit the sixth grade.

In each town, Gus would look for the busiest tavern and stall the Marmon in front of it. By the time he got out and lifted the hood, a crowd would be gathering to gawk at the car that sure wasn't a Ford and at the regal-looking couple inside, dressed to the nines. Gus would examine the engine and shake his head and ask if anyone knew where he could find tools. Then he'd walk back to tell Fred, "Excuse me sir, it's going to take a while to fix. Why don't you go inside where it's cool and have some refreshment?"

Fred would take Lillian's hand and stride into the tavern and as soon as they disappeared a local would ask, "Who's that?" Gus-the-chauffeur then would tell of the finance company Fred ran, consolidated or associated something-or-other, and then he'd asked the locals, "Do you have any pool tables in there?"

"Yeah, sure."

"Well, my boss fancies himself a pool player. He thinks he can play."

Gus would glance side to side to make sure his boss was gone then confide that if anyone knew what they were doing, and stayed sober, they could beat him easy. All Gus asked was that they share some of their take with the kindly servant who had tipped them off, slip him a token of appreciation after they took his boss to the cleaners. The news spread quickly that there was a rich, easy mark in town.

That's how the Whalens and Wunderlichs

financed their trek west, with Fred's winnings from all the suckers in America's heartland.

CHAPTER 2
THE CITY WHERE EVIL COMES FROM WITHOUT

The fear of invading evildoers had been a refrain in Los Angeles since before the turn of the century. The nation's burgeoning railroad system did not reach the young city until 1876, when the Southern Pacific linked up to it from the North, and that same year a new position of Chief of Police was established to supervise six officers. By 1891 Los Angeles was a scattered community of 65,000 with a police force of seventy-five, counting the matron, clerk, bailiff, and secretary. If you discounted the two men who drove the horse-drawn Paddy wagons, Chief John Glass had 48 patrolmen to watch over thirty-six square miles and combat the nagging problems of the day. "There are some (too many) poker games kept running in the back of cigar stores and saloons, and they do great damage to the young men of this city and furnish a living for a lot of wretches who are too lazy to work," Chief Glass told residents in his annual report. "Lottery gambling is not easily eradicated . . . The number of pawnbrokers and other dealers in second-hand goods has increased." The good news for Los Angeles was that the tally of houses of prostitution had held steady and "war has been made on the pimps," the chief said. "I believe that there now are less of those vile human beings in this city than in any time in years past." Other good news was the $1,867.10 in savings achieved by having inmates cook their own food, rather than pay a restaurant to furnish prison meals. But Chief Glass had an ominous warning for the sun-drenched outpost that fancied itself America's Garden of Eden: "One very serious cause of annoyance and danger to the residents of this city is yearly growing: Each winter brings us an increased number of burglars, safe-blowers and other skilled thieves from the large cities of the East." While there had been some important arrests of "Eastern crooks," Glass said it was time to furnish his officers with more than a rosewood club and leather belt and not count on them to buy their own handcuffs and revolvers. The chief called upon the city to provide each officer with all that plus a "police whistle, fire key . . . and a first-class repeating rifle."

With the onset of the twentieth century, shootouts erupted among L.A.'s immigrant fruit cart vendors — first hints that the notorious Black Hand might be in town —

and the unwelcomed outsiders were upgraded to "Eastern gangsters." After George Maisano was shot three times in the back on June 2, 1906, he lived long enough to tell police that the gunman was a fellow immigrant fruit peddler, Joe Ardizzone, the "Iron Man" of the city's small Italian quarter. But Ardizzone quickly "disappeared in the darkness," noted one account at the time. "The case is a difficult one, because other Italians in the colony here are doing all they can to aid the criminal in escaping and refuse absolutely to talk about the case, saying they never heard of it."

A few months later, a man on a bicycle shot Joseph Cuccia, a father of three, as he drove his wagon along North Main Street, his horses then spooking and the cart careening for two blocks. When a witness tried to run after the fleeing cyclist, the man turned with his gun and said, "Let no one try to follow me." Next to go was a barber, Giovannino Bentivegna, who was shot through the window of his shop. Authorities said a letter found in his pocket was written in Sicilian and had "a crude drawing of a clown and a policeman," the Black Hand's warning to a stool pigeon. Those were the sort of incidents that had plagued New York's Little Italy following the 1890s' wave of immigration across the Atlantic. But Los Angeles? A new name was suggested for one street in its Italian quarter, "Shotgun Alley."

In 1913, the LAPD announced that it was hiring twenty-five new officers to repel what were now described as "Eastern hoodlums," spurred in part by a jewelry store heist on South Broadway. Unknown parties cut a two-foot hole in the roof, lowered themselves down a rope, avoided several alarms, and made off with a tray containing dozens of diamond rings worth $6,000, the most lucrative criminal haul in the city in a year. The culprits were pros, clearly, but Los Angeles officials were sure it was more, evidence of an influx of Bunco men, porch climbers ("ding-bats"), pickpockets ("dips") and safe crackers ("pete blowers"). "A thousand thieves are headed for Los Angeles," police told the *Los Angeles Times*, adding that the grim news had come directly from law enforcement agencies in the know. "The eastern departments recently sent word that nearly every thief caught said he would leave for Los Angeles if released and, further, that every man that was wanted was reported to be in Los Angeles or headed for the city."

As if to punctuate the warning — and quiet any skeptics — one of the twenty-five rookie police officers hired to repel the invasion almost immediately got into a shootout with two gunmen. Days on the job, Frank "Lefty" James became an overnight hero by taking a slug in his left shoulder while killing one of his assailants and wounding the second, who promptly told officers he had shuffled into town only the day before . . . from Buffalo.

Then two Los Angeles County sheriff's deputies were caught in a nighttime car chase and shootout on a lonely stretch of West Temple Street and one of the gunmen left behind a hat with a .45 bullet hole in it and a label from a store in . . . Chicago.

It was all leading to the nightmare scenario, the arrival of Al Capone. Word spread quickly that the nation's most feared hoodlum had slipped into L.A. under an alias and checked into the Biltmore, the ornate new hotel with an aquamarine tile swimming pool in the basement. Detective Ed "Roughhouse" Brown led a delegation of cops over there to ceremoniously escort Capone and his bodyguards onto the first train back to Chicago. Just twenty-eight, yet rumored to be worth $2 million from the beer and booze trade, Capone took the bum's rush in good humor, noting that his crew had at least gotten to tour a film studio. "I came here with my boyfriends to see a little of the country," he quipped. "Why should everybody in this town pick on me? . . . we are tourists and I thought you folks liked tourists. Whoever heard of anyone being run out of Los Angeles that had money?" But the city evidently was a dangerous place, even for a Capone — someone stole his jug of wine en route to the train station. "Now I won't have a drink," he said, "between here and home."

So L.A. had an early glimpse of a hoodlum who turned everything into a goof — there would be another to come. The city also had a second celebrity cop guarding its borders. First "Lefty" James and now "Roughhouse" Brown. What a glorious headline Roughhouse earned. Glorious! Glorious!

"Scarface Al" — Came to Play
Now Look — He's Gone Away!

By then the Whalens had settled in a small apartment above a dry goods store they opened with the last of Fred's earnings from the trip out. They'd come in through the desert along the Old Santa Fe Trail, fixing the inevitable flat tires on the Dorris during the day and camping nights in tents as coyotes howled outside. There were few other Marmon Touring Cars on the roadway soon to be anointed Route 66, but it was crammed throughout 1922 with fellow Midwesterners in their Model Ts and jalopies, on their way to swelling Los Angeles' population past San Francisco's, making it the largest city in California. One hundred thousand people a year were migrating to the area, primarily from the heartland states and no longer drawn west by the last century's fantasy of riches from gold. Though some were entranced by the fantasy that replaced it — of fame in the movies — for most it was enough to dream of a fresh start in "the city where there is everlasting sunshine," in the words of Cornelius Vanderbilt Jr., not to mention the free lunches that real estate developers served up to anyone visiting their new housing tracts. With no less than 631 subdivisions in the works the year the Whalens arrived, one builder was preparing to erect an enormous sign in the hills touting HOLLYWOODLAND, his housing tract below. Another adorned his lots with images of houses-to-come on false fronts supported by wooden braces, the real estate version of Hollywood sets. Another offered a free rooster for your backyard — you could still feel like a farmer, just like back in Iowa. A fellow Midwesterner-émigré to L.A. meanwhile was redefining the cemetery as a *memorial park* with none of those morbid monuments sticking up, just stones laid flat along peaceful sweeping lawns, so the bereaved might find hope and solace. Missouri native Herbert L. Eaton vowed that his Forest Lawn would be "as unlike other cemeteries as sunshine is unlike darkness, as Eternal Life is unlike death." In Los Angeles, the cemetery would become "God's Garden!"

The Whalens set up shop a mile west of downtown, well beyond its commercial clutter and the intersection already touted as the busiest for traffic in the nation, though development was edging their way. The castle-like Ambassador Hotel had just gone up on Wilshire Boulevard, with 500 guest rooms and a nightclub, the Cocoanut Grove, where dancers waltzed "under the spell of the (artificial) palms." But Wilshire remained unpaved in the other direction, away from the city, passing dairy farms and fields of lima beans as it headed toward the ocean. The Whalens also were within walking distance of Westlake Park, a favorite setting for the colorized postcards that were all the rage, with pastel-enhanced scenes of gents and ladies strolling in their Sunday finery by cypress and palm trees to a boathouse by the lake, an American-flag topped gazebo looking down on young couples paddling their canoes. You'd find such idealized images for sale next to the Whalens' cash register, amid all the merchandise they stole.

Fred and Lillian were arrested after Christmas, 1924, charged with swiping three sweaters from another store across town. With Fred waiting in the getaway car, Lillian had reprised her Jesse James heritage by carrying off the sweaters while a clerk was helping other customers. Then Los Angeles police put more of the Whalens' merchandise on display at the Central Station — stockings, dresses, women's silk unmentionables — and merchants from around the city came by to examine the items and announced, "That's mine!" or "That's ours!" By the time of the

Whalens' trial, prosecutors had a dozen witnesses to their far-flung petty larceny.

When Fred had his turn on the witness stand he flashed his salesman's smile and swore all the bras and nighties were gifts, given to them at a "birthday shower." But jurors took all of twenty minutes to find the couple guilty. Lillian fainted when the verdict was announced and Fred had to endure a night in jail, plus the indignity of the local newspaper calling him a "*self-professed* champion billiard player."

It was an unpleasant start to life in L.A., but at least no one pegged them as outsiders. In a city of refugees and wannabes, being ma-and-pa shopkeepers with two toddlers was enough to qualify the Whalens as bona fide Angelenos. There even was an upside to having the idiots doubt Fred's ability with a cue.

He preferred straight pool, where you had to sink 125 balls, the no-nonsense tournament test. But the money still was at bars and parlors where the rubes liked quicker games such as Eight-Ball. A player of Fred's caliber often could sink all the solids or stripes in one turn, but he'd never earn a buck if he did — even drunk, most pea-brains would take their money off the table after seeing how easily he ran out the rack. What he'd do instead, then, is barely miss his opening shots, lagging his balls — whether the stripes or solids — to the edge of the pockets.

More importantly, he'd leave the white cue ball in a spot that gave the other guy no good shot, no opening at all. After the fellow's futile turn, all Fred had to do was knock in his balls sitting on the edge of the pockets, duck shots anyone could execute. The other guys thought he was lucky, that's it. They might start out playing for quarters, but a frustrated loser soon could be betting dollars, or more, to get even.

That was Fred Whalen's MO as he made the rounds of upscale pool parlors favored by the beneficiaries of the area's two booming industries. The oil people had cash in their pockets from the newly gushing Signal Hill field down by Long Beach, where one well alone spewed 1,000 gallons a day. The Hollywood folks were flush too, by 1927 spending $100 million a year making movies.

But Fred didn't ignore the lowlier neighborhoods where pool was a staple of life, and a test of manhood. One such community was Boyle Heights, a slum on the east side of the Los Angeles River made undesirable by its proximity to factories and the rail yards. That neighborhood got groups proper L.A. didn't want — or banned by real estate covenants — the Mexicans, Italians, and especially poor Russian Jews, often ones who had sampled New York first and now were refugees a second time. Boyle Heights was a classic survival-of-the-fittest slum, typified by the action each night at Art Weiner's pool hall. It attracted guys with names like Matzie and Dago Frank who could roll any number they wanted with the right pair of dice and fancied themselves primo pool hustlers too. The tough local kids competed for their favor, including a pint-sized newsboy, proper name Meyer Harris Cohen, whose mother Fanny, an immigrant from Kiev, had brought her six children west after the death of her husband Max. They helped in the small grocery she opened, stacking cans, though her youngest preferred the streets or the pool hall, where he often racked balls and kept score for the local hustlers Matzie and Dago Frank. "Gimme the chalk!" they'd say and he'd do it, the little kid they called Mickey for short. But there's no way of knowing if young Mickey Cohen ever saw Fred Whalen wander in to play his idols for fools, or whether their eyes locked across one of the green felt tables at Art Weiner's pool hall, as they would in a Los Angeles courtroom, decades later.

Sometimes Fred wanted to show off — he got tired of holding back — so the family would road trip out of L.A. to smaller communities reminiscent of the ones they'd victimized on their cross-country trip. Lillian sewed him a bright blue satin costume with a Russian Cossack–style top and a mask and they would post flyers advertising an exhibition by "The Masked Marvel." Fred performed the tricks he'd learned as a kid, including hitting balls off Coke bottles, plus new ones using pairs of cue sticks as ramps — the cue ball went up one ramp and down another, then knocked three or four balls into pockets. Or he'd hide balls under a handkerchief and sink them, or make them disappear. There was an exhilarating honesty to the shows, and not only because his skill was unleashed. It was one time he could announce who he was. "I'm going to cheat you," he could say, "but even after I tell you, you still can't see me cheat you." Then he'd make the red ball vanish, steal it right from under their eyes.

Understand, he hadn't given up on cons like the chauffeur bit, not at all. He loved that sting, loved it. In fact he'd do it again, just not with Gus putting on the cap to play a fake chauffeur in the St. Louis version of a rich man's car. Fred Whalen soon would be able to afford a genuine chauffeur, and a genuine Stearns-Knight Touring Car, and how he got those had nothing to do with pool.

CHAPTER 3
YOUNG JACK WHALEN
TAKES A PLANE RIDE

The cops who'd run off Al Capone sounded no such alarm when a large group of locals — by L.A. standards — held a banquet ten days before Christmas, 1929 to celebrate the city's Italo-American Welfare League. Much of it no doubt was old-fashioned politics, playing to the ethnics. But the mayor, district attorney, and county sheriff were among the guests at the Flower Auditorium who applauded tributes to Italian opera and the courage of Italian-Americans in the Great War, undaunted by the program listing the evening's chairman as "J. Ardizzone" and its vice chairman as "J. I. Dragna."

J. Ardizzone was Joe Ardizzone, the Iron Man of the Black Hand during the fruit cart wars, back when drive-by shootings were done on bicycle. He indeed had disappeared after the 1906 killing of a rival, fleeing to Louisville, Kentucky, disguised as a military officer, Captain J. D. Fredericks. But he returned to California unnoticed a couple of years later, bought a ranch in the hills above the San Fernando Valley, and turned it into a vineyard. Authorities insisted they did not realize that Ardizzone was back until 1914, when they surrounded the property and maneuvered by two armed guards to arrest him. But their attempt to nail him for the old murder proved futile, "case dismissed, insufficient evidence, no witness that would talk," a police report summed it up. A few years later, when another Italian fruit dealer was killed in a more modern fashion, by a shotgunner in a Buick, Ardizzone called the hospital to find out where the body was taken and then laughed when asked who might have done such a thing. He was perfectly positioned when Prohibition arrived in 1920 promising big profits for anyone who could supply hard liquor to the thirsty masses and perhaps use a shotgun to grow his market share.

Ardizzone's vice-chair for the banquet, J. I. Dragna, was Jack Ignatius Dragna, originally from Corleone, long before the Sicilian city was made famous by a movie's Don Corleone. When Dragna first appeared on a Los Angeles police blotter in 1914 for extortion he looked fresh off the docks in his booking photo, a starched white collar pinching his neck and a round-topped hat tilted back above his moon-shaped face. Now he looked like just another middle-aged businessman with his large eyeglasses, gray suit, and a decorative handkerchief in his breast pocket. Dragna too was developing a vineyard in the hills, on 538 acres, and owned a large ship, the *Santa Maria*, supposedly for carting bananas up from Central America. Dragna also had a piece of what was being billed as "the finest pleasure barge on the coast."

He and five others had bought an old five-mast sailing ship built for service in World War I but used since then mostly for fishing. They transformed the main deck into a casino with eight craps tables, sixteen for blackjack, fifty slot machines, and four roulette wheels, those rigged to prevent anyone from winning too much. There was a polished wooden floor for dancing and a restaurant promising "the best $1 fish dinner in California." In 1928, the football-field–long *Monfalcone* became one of the first of a fleet of gambling ships operating off the coast in what were believed to be international waters, beyond the law. Water taxis shuttled to and from the mainland carrying patrons well advised to watch their wallets — if they defied the odds and won, someone might follow them to their cars. Dragna himself thought it prudent to take precautions. Two policemen made the mistake of stopping his sedan early one morning after he came ashore with three of his men, prompting one to point a sawed-off shotgun at the officers. Dragna calmly raised his hand, ordering his guy to back down, and explained that they needed the shotgun — along with four pistols and two knives — to protect the weekend's profits from the *Monfalcone*. Dragna did not volunteer that one of the crew in his car was a cousin of Los Angeles' favorite Chicagoan, Scarface Al Capone. Later, when Dragna applied for U.S. citizenship, a judge said it wasn't quite time, but he should keep trying — he seemed to have "a fine family."

Fred Whalen had no such illusions about these crude characters from the Old Country, the so-called Moustache Petes, for he, too, ran boats off the coast, reputed to be the fastest out there. One with a mahogany-walled cabin was named *The Bobie*, after his daughter, and had dual Liberty engines, like some aircraft used, so it could outrun the amply armed vessels of Dragna and his ilk and the patrols of the Coast Guard as well. But the great innovation of the Whalen boats was a feature that Fred's brother-in-law worked up.

Gus Wunderlich looked like a dolt with his snaggletooth grin and one of the squarest noggins ever seen on a human being — he literally was a blockhead. But he was a genius with anything mechanical, as good as Fred with his cue, and his idea for the rum-running speedboats was this: After they picked up a haul from the mother ship, or from an intermediary tender craft, he used a thick rope to lash all the barrels together at the rear of their speedboat. Then he placed the first barrel at the back edge, almost over the water and right above a hydraulic lift he built under the deck, the key to his system. If the feds got on their tail, they merely had to push a button and the front part of the deck rose and the back tilted down, so the lead barrel slid into the sea and then pulled the other barrels into the water behind it. The contraption came in handy after one large pickup of whiskey, close to two hundred barrels, slowed them down enough for a Coast Guard cutter to gain on them, despite their twin Liberties. Fred had to push the button and dump the damning evidence into the ocean, only to see the tops of the barrels floating above the surface — the containers apparently were less than full, a shortchange by the supplier on the mother ship. The swindle proved to be a savior, however, when the bobbing barrels created a minefield for the Coast Guard ship, shearing off the bottom of its wooden hull and leaving it dead in the water.

When authorities nicknamed the Whalen patriarch "Freddie the Thief," his family thought that all wrong. Their moniker for him was "Mile-Away," because that's where he'd be, a mile away, when the you-know-what hit the fan. But nothing was that simple in the bootlegging trade. As an independent and an

Irishman, Freddie tried to steer clear of Italians such as Dragna and Tony "The Hat" Cornero (born Stralla), who by the age of twenty-five had a chauffeur-driven Cadillac thanks to the large network of rum-running trucks he'd assembled and his control of mother ships, including a lumber schooner capable of carrying 7,000 cases from Canada down to Mexico. Yet even Cornero and his brother had to fear hijackings when they weren't pulling them on rivals. It could happen at sea or during nighttime landings at remote coves, when the speedboats cut their engines, and the whiskey was unloaded to dories, which were rowed onto beaches where law enforcement was friendly for a price. There was peril at every step, though one contemporary description may have been a bit melodramatic:

> Stuttering machine gun fire in the fog. Murky lights of waiting trucks. Muffled voices on the beach and the wind-born coughing of marine motors. Creaking car locks and dories shooting the pounding breakers . . . Hard men, tough men, sometimes desperate men ready to kill.

Fred Whalen allowed himself only one bootlegging partnership, down in Mexico with Percy Hussong, whose family owned a popular cantina in Ensenada, the tavern that later would claim to have invented the margarita. The Hussongs had a perfect arrangement with a mother ship, getting their whiskey for skiffs full of fruits and vegetables in addition to a little cash. When the Hussongs headed back toward shore, the Mexican Navy would only shoot over their heads — the sailors were not about to jeopardize their chance of having a drink the next evening. It was different up the coast when the Whalen-Wunderlich gang found itself under fire while approaching a beach one moonless night — they did not get the impression that the gunmen atop the cliffs were trying to miss.

Freddie's other significant business relationship those days was with a cop in Santa Monica, the beach community with a carousel on its pier. Lieutenant Thomas Carr was the Sherlock Holmes of local law enforcement, using a professional makeup kit and closet full of costumes to disguise himself as everything from a tattooed sailor to an English dandy in order to mingle in waterfront bars and pick up scuttlebutt on the bootleggers. The newspapers called him "The Man of a Thousand Faces," after the silent film actor Lon Chaney, who transformed himself into the Phantom of the Opera and the Hunchback of Notre Dame. The remarkable Lieutenant Carr also was an Olympic-caliber marksman, underscored when the supposed

48

deadeye sheriff from Twin Falls, Idaho, strutted into Los Angeles with his pearl-handled pistol and buckskin jacket, touted as the winner of a six-gun competition staged by the Idaho Frontier Club. After a challenge was issued, they stuck an ace of spades on a post at a police shooting range to see who could hit the little black spot most frequently . . . and the California beach cop blew away the Wild West lawman in the cowboy hat.

Carr became a minor celebrity through episodes like that, but when the newsmen went away and his English derby hat went back in the closet he was just another bloke who liked a few drinks and a few extra dollars to spend. Freddie Whalen kept him happy on both counts and served him up a few lowly bootleggers to nab — having a cop on your side was a safer way to deal with rivals than hijacking their loads, or blowing their brains out.

As for Los Angeles police, they were a joke. When Freddie arrived in town their chief was distinguished-looking Louis D. Oaks, soon caught in his official car with a half-empty bottle and a half-dressed woman not his wife, prompting his actual spouse to complain (in divorce papers) that he was the captive of both intoxicating liquor and a Follies dancer. A couple of years later the department got a chief originally from Texas, James "Two Gun" Davis, a proud onetime cotton-picker who was nearly as expert with a pistol as Santa Monica's Lieutenant Carr. Never mind that Davis enjoyed daily massages and manicures, he soon formed a Gun Squad headed by Lefty James, the hero cop wounded as a rookie in 1913. Davis also talked big as Texas. "The gun-toting element and the rum smugglers are going to learn that murder and gun-toting are inimical to their best interests," he said. "I want them brought in dead, not alive, and will reprimand any officer who shows the least mercy to a criminal." Tough words, indeed, but once the Depression descended on top of Prohibition the leaders of Los Angeles seemed less concerned with rum-runners than with the vagrants drifting into town. New task forces swept up those invaders by the dozens and gave them a choice — jail or the first freight train east, the pokey or Yuma, Arizona and points beyond. Eventually the LAPD dispersed its officers all the way to the state's borders to stop the *hobo hordes* there, launching what became known as the Bum Blockade. Communists and other radicals also diverted police resources and a Red Squad soon was competing with the Gun Squad for center stage, doing its part by seizing the muckraking writer Upton Sinclair at one rally of supposed subversives.

All the while, Los Angeles police never could stop the violence tied to the Prohibition liquor trade, which finally turned on its leading practitioner. The Black Hand's old strongman, Joe Ardizzone, survived one wild shotgun shootout then vanished after leaving his vineyard at 6:30 A.M. to pick up a cousin just in from Italy. His wife had to wait years to have him officially declared dead but there was no waiting period for his banquet vice-chairman, J. I. Dragna, who was in line for a promotion right away.

The remarkable Fred Whalen made it through that era virtually unscathed. He did have one speedboat smashed against the rocks and a mahogany-adorned cruiser sunk by a leak. But the worst part of that was getting sunburned on the beach of San Clemente Island before he and Gus were rescued by a foul-smelling whaling ship. Authorities never caught on to their method of transporting their whiskey over land, using trucks decorated exactly like those of the Mayfair Markets supermarket chain, maroon with fruits and vegetables painted on the side. For direct sales, Fred took over a recently closed dry cleaning shop in the lower level of a hotel, next to a back alley, where he invited customers to drive up to a window and get their illicit refreshment handed to them in a paper-wrapped bundle. Not surprisingly, some naive neighborhood residents brought in actual clothes to be cleaned, so Freddie had to hire a man to set up an off-site plant to do that work . . . and soon they had three locations serving as drop-off points for the legitimate dry cleaning business, in addition to distributing their booze. When drive-through dry cleaners became commonplace years later, the Whalen clan wondered whether their site, in the hotel, had been the first.

Fred dutifully gave his occupation as "dry cleaner" when the 1930 census taker came by the South Alvarado Street home he shared with his wife Lillian and their children, Bobie, who was thirteen by then, and Jack, listed as eight. But few dry cleaners took their family for Sunday drives in a Stearns-Knight Touring Car, a luxurious tank that made their old Marmon seem like a heap — this car really was meant for a CEO. Gus Wunderlich also embraced their dry cleaning front when the census taker came by his home, listing himself as the "tailor" at the shop. His younger brother had some fun, though, when he was surveyed by the census — George Wunderlich gave his profession as "aviator." In 1928, the National Air Races had come to the city's Mines Field, which eventually would become Los Angeles International Airport but then was a mere cluster of runways amid wheat, barley, and bean fields. Two hundred thousand spectators drove through the farms to see demonstrations of the latest military aircraft along with races around pylons that drew a Who's Who of flyers including Charles Lindbergh, a year past his solo flight across the Atlantic. The risks were on display, too — John J. Williams, one of the Army Air Corps' "Three Musketeers" of aviation, was killed during a practice run. But many in Los Angeles got the flying bug and a fortunate few bought their own planes. Fred Whalen's was a two-seat Alexander Eaglerock, a single-engine biplane favored by the barnstormers who set down in rural areas and offered the wide-eyed locals ten-minute flights for fifty cents.

The biplane was neither big enough nor sturdy enough to carry much booze — it was just another showy plaything for the Whalen clan's patriarch. Freddie had one lesson from the salesman before inviting Gus to join him on his maiden flight as the whole family gathered to admire his new toy. But someone else clamored to come along, Freddie's young son, Jack. The boy's mother gave a dirty look as the boy pleaded, "Me, too!" but Freddie flashed his salesman's smile and waved for his son to join them. There was barely room in the tiny passenger compartment for the youngster and his uncle Gus to stuff themselves in before Fred took off like a pro and guided the plane through the Sepulveda Pass and over the orange orchards of the San Fernando Valley.

Their destination was a new airstrip in Van Nuys — after making a few lazy loops over the Valley they were going to land, take a breather, and come back home. The problem was, Fred hadn't mastered the altimeter. The biplane hit down too hard on the new runway and bounced back into the air. Then Fred tried landing again and miscalculated again, bashing into the ground once more before catapulting back into flight. That's when Gus began to panic. After the second failed landing, he gestured madly from the passenger seat like he was gonna jump, while Fred waved for him to climb over the divide and try the damn stick himself. They were screaming back and forth but unable to hear each other over the engine. Freddie Whalen may have thought his wits and his smile put him above all peril but now he was going to crash and burn and kill them all.

The third time he made it. He still came down roughly on the new airstrip, but the wheels stuck and they landed and were safe. Only then did Fred realize that one person on the plane had not panicked. His little son had remained calm, even delighted, through everything. Gus said the boy had squealed "Wheeee!" one of the times they nearly crashed and died. Freddie Whalen couldn't be prouder — he told everyone how fearless his boy had been, the child who would grow up to become known as Jack the Enforcer.

So one lesson they should have learned was that Freddie's wits and smile did not place him above all peril. Another lesson was in the danger of messing with the wrong people — that could kill you, too. Gus Wunderlich learned as much in the episode that sent him to prison.

Gus could blame his ice cream bar machine for his foolhardy decision to become a modern-day pirate. After years of using his mechanical wizardry in the cause of Freddie's rum-running he invented a device to churn out frozen desserts. But with the lifting of Prohibition at the end of 1933 it wasn't easy to find funds to patent and market an invention, so Gus turned to an alternate means of raising capital.

Another member of their bootlegging crowd came up with the insane idea of robbing one of the gambling ships. There already had been a couple of mysterious fires on the pleasure barges and two murders, one victim proving to be not the croupier he claimed but an East St. Louis hood who used the ship-top gambling as a cover to fence stolen jewels — that was a rough crowd on the seas. But the former rum-runner Harry Allen Sherwood had an inside tipster, a former cook on the *S.S. Monte Carlo*, and he was convinced that a band of modern-day pirates could make a big score on that boat. The *Monte Carlo* had been an ugly concrete-hulled tanker during the decade it hauled oil and it still was ugly after new owners built a warehouse-sized structure on the deck, with a curved roof, to serve as a casino. But all you saw at night were the twinkle lights. On one Saturday alone 1,736 patrons took the 25-cent water taxis to and from the gambling ship where the dining area had linen tablecloths and a sign above the craps tables promised, "These Dice Are 100% Perfect."

The six-man gang struck after the busy Fourth of July weekend, 1935, when the ship's safe figured to be loaded. Several of the pirates headed out in a 48-foot gray speedboat, the *Zeitgeiste*, while others left shore in a stolen wooden fishing boat, the *Nolia*. They picked a foggy night, so no one would see their boats meet up mid-ocean where all the men got into the quieter fishing craft. By 3:30 A.M., the last gamblers had left the *Monte Carlo* and its main deck had gone dark. The pirates had stocking masks over their heads, gloves on their hands, and two sacks full of handcuffs, leg irons, and chains. They glided the fishing boat alongside the gambling ship and climbed up, everyone armed.

The pirates surprised the *Monte Carlo*'s crew down below, in the kitchen, playing poker. The men being robbed later said someone called out, "Down on the floor, all of you," then, "Do as you're told and no one gets hurt." The gang made them empty the safe of cash and an assortment of trinkets,

$10,000 worth of necklaces, rings, and watches left by gamblers who had fallen in debt or were desperate for more chips. One loser that weekend had hocked a large diamond solitaire in a platinum mounting, a ring worth $1,000. He was offered just $50, and took it, and that ring too was snatched by the thieves along with stacks of wrapped bills and silver dollars from a wall rack, $22,000 cash in all. One of the pirates told the chained victims "Take it easy boys. See you in church."

They carried two sacks of loot to their stolen fishing boat and motored away from the *Monte Carlo* and what looked to be the perfect robbery. "A boat leaves no trail," noted the highest-ranking local detective soon put on the case, Long Beach Inspector Owen Murphy.

But their fantasies of an easy life were undermined by an age-old mistake of the foolish criminal, suspicious spending. One of the pirate crew was veteran jailbird Frank Dudley, recently paroled from San Quentin. He believed in living it up during his interludes of freedom so he played the big shot at a downtown bar, giving the waitress a keep-the-change $5 bill and $10 to two women of questionable repute who came to sit by him. "More where this came from," he boasted, and at that point two undercover detectives at a corner table had heard enough. Dudley asked only that they let him see his girlfriend, a redhead, before he said, "Ever hear of the *Monte Carlo*?"

He quickly led officers to the address south of town where the gang had met to divide the cash, a bandbox house wedged between two cypress hedges on E. 116th Street. The raiders found Gus Wunderlich inside with his kid brother George, along with a loaded .38 wrapped in cloth under the dining table, a .38 under a pillow, and a .45 in a dresser. Still, it took a while for the raiders to discover the hidden chamber. They had to connect two wires virtually invisible in the bedroom's baseboard, setting off a groaning in the closet — its concrete floor shifted, part of a perfect counterweight system, to expose a room below with a bar and several barrels, remnants of the glory days of Prohibition. All that was left was for the cops to stumble onto Gus' hollowed-out bedpost full of jewelry, including a telltale diamond solitaire ring in a platinum setting.

It's not often there's a federal trial for piracy and plundering. Augustus "Gus" Wunderlich swore at his that he was at the movies the night of the robbery, but he couldn't describe the film he'd seen — he slept through it, he said. He got eight years for conspiracy and was signed into the federal penitentiary right behind a white slavery suspect and a murderer.

There was some consolation for the family. The feds on the piracy case never found any evidence to prosecute George Wunderlich, the runt of the old bootlegging clan. And Gus fared better than the man who'd gotten him into that mess. Harry Allen Sherwood also was sentenced to federal prison, but didn't live long after he got out. He stumbled into a hospital with a bullet by his spinal column, a form of justice for a high-risk life of crime that the courts did not hand out — and a reminder that the streets of the City of Angels could be just as perilous as its seas.

. . . .

PART II
THE GANGSTER
SQUAD'S SERGEANT
JACK O'MARA SETS
HIS TRAP FOR
MICKEY

. . . .

CHAPTER 4
ORIENTATION IN AN ALLEY

Los Angeles was supposed to have been transformed and cleansed by World War II, its scandals of the past erased by the time hordes of heroic servicemen returned home and streamed off their ships at the port, ready for a new start in life. The city was supposed to have bottomed out before the war. It wasn't being a Pollyanna, or a Chamber of Commerce booster, to believe that everything had to be heading up-up-up for Los Angeles after one particularly horrible day, January 14, 1938.

That was when private investigator Harry Raymond got into his car, turned on the ignition and a black-powder bomb went off under the hood. Raymond miraculously survived the 150 fragments doctors had to remove from him but the force of the blast carried far beyond his body. A former San Diego police chief, he had been helping expose local wrongdoing on behalf of the city's unlikely civic reformer, Clifford Clinton. Clinton owned two cafeterias that served comfort food at low cost to the masses and often at no cost to the poor — under a policy of "whatever you wish to pay," he gave away 10,000 free meals one summer during the Depression. The son of two Salvation Army captains, Clinton was a true Good Works soul who had been shocked by his service on a grand jury, which gave him a glimpse of the city's underbelly. He personally funded CIVIC, the Citizens Independent Vice Investigating Committee, to ferret out the sickening specifics: Los Angeles was home to 1,800 bookies, 600 brothels, 200 gambling parlors, and 23,000 slot machines, all operating under the nose of Mayor Frank Shaw.

Shaw had won office with the slogan, "Throw the grafters out" but it was an open secret that his own brother was L.A.'s most accomplished of grafters. Joe Shaw had been elected to nothing but used a City Hall office as a perch to collect bribes of up to $1,000 from cops seeking promotions and much more from vice lords seeking protection. The most outrageous of those was a former LAPD Vice captain, Kansas-born Guy McAfee, who during his days on the force supposedly warned racketeers of raids by calling them up and whistling over the phone. Figuring that being a gambling czar paid better than being a cop, McAfee married a madam and then a starlet and ran "The World Famous Clover

Club" on the Sunset Strip where the black-jack and roulette tables could flip over to be hidden, just in case.

When Clifford Clinton's do-gooder committee began raising a stink about the gambling parlors and brothels, the Shaws and their friends gave the crusader just what he wanted, an investigation — city inspectors swarmed into his cafeterias in the name of public health. When a bomb exploded at Clinton's home, destroying his kitchen, they accused him of staging the episode himself, for publicity. "I'll never stop now," Clinton was said to have responded. Then his private investigator, Harry Raymond, tried to start his car and KABOOM!

James "Two Gun" Davis, serving his second stint as L.A.'s police chief, was traveling in Mexico when the bomb exploded, so the head of his Special Intelligence Unit phoned him with the news. Captain Earle Kynette offered the chief a theory about who might have wanted to blow up the private eye, "I said that he had such a score of enemies in the underworld that possibly the enemy came from Las Vegas." Unfortunately for Captain Kynette, evidence pointed closer to home, to his own squad. He and six of his men had been renting a house across from Raymond's for $50 a month to watch him, eavesdrop on him and finally shut him up. They all took the fifth when called before a grand jury looking into the bombing, but Kynette did offer an alibi — he was at home nursing an eyeache while his wife and in-laws played cards downstairs. "I made a compress out of boric acid and went to bed," he said. Harder to explain was the detonating wire found in his garage. Kynette was convicted of attempted murder and sent to San Quentin.

"It was a lousy, crooked department," summed up Max Solomon, who knew about crooked L.A. from serving as defense attorney for many of its toughest characters of that era and for decades to come. "You know, in Chicago the gangsters paid off the police but the gangsters did the job. In Los Angeles, the police were the gangsters."

At least the city had reached its nadir — that day had to be it — and could start its climb. Captain Earle Kynette shouted "It's a travesty of justice!" but he was behind bars. Chief "Two Gun" Davis was forced to resign. Mayor Frank Shaw was recalled, the first mayor of a major American city to be ousted that way, and in his place the city elected a more convincing reformer, a judge no less, Judge Fletcher E. Bowron. The new mayor was about sobriety, not sizzle, a man of gray suits, black shoes, rimless glasses, and a fondness for the dusty Los Angeles of his childhood before all the cars ("chug wagons," he called them) and clutter. The scoundrels were not going to ruin the Los Angeles he remembered — more than 200 police commanders and officers were fired, demoted, retired, or transferred, including the head of another infamous detail, the Red Squad. The past was past, as they say, and the future finally was at hand, under the shadow of war.

What had been the nation's thirty-sixth largest city at the turn of the century boomed into fifth place after the hostilities broke out in Europe and the Far East. Six aircraft factories soon were operating within ten miles of downtown and vast shipbuilding facilities at Los Angeles County's ports. With much of the male population called away into the Armed Forces, including 983 members of the city police and fire departments, warm and willing bodies had to be found and recruited. A decade after the LAPD spearheaded a Bum Blockade to keep migrants out of California, even the Okies from the Dust Bowl were welcomed with semi-open arms. By October 1943, the county had 569,000 new residents and a year later the aviation industry alone needed 230,000 workers to keep mammoth plants such as Lockheed's in Burbank and Douglas' in Santa Monica churning far beyond 9:00 to 5:00. More than 40 percent of the workers were women whose bandanas became almost as iconic to the war effort as the helmets of the GIs abroad. Earning 60 cents an hour at minimum, mothers on the assembly line could park their children in one of 244 nursery and daycare centers established by the National Aircraft War Production Council, while single women could go from their shifts as riveters to shifts as volunteer dance hostesses at the USO's Hollywood Canteen, dreamed up by film stars John Garfield and Bette Davis to lift the spirits of servicemen on leave. The movie crowd also was waving the banner by selling war bonds on the road, adding to the positive pictures L.A. was sending to the world.

The inevitable housing boom provided vivid visuals of its own as it echoed the real estate frenzy of the '20s, when the Midwesterners came to town. Especially at the war's end, scores of remaining orchards and ranches were sacrificed in the outlying San Gabriel and San Fernando Valleys to make room for rows of two- and three-bedroom starter homes, yours for just $150 down in one development. The bottom line was that Los Angeles was overflowing with nearly a million newcomers who had little inkling of the city's sordid past and with returning vets and their wives eager to start families and pursue the American Dream in a city that promised to deliver just that.

There were a few glitches, of course, like the Zoot Suit Riots. The newcomers in the latest migration were not all pale-skinned farmers (or pool players) from Illinois or Missouri. This wave of transplants included tens of thousands of blacks from Alabama and Georgia for whom it was harder to blend in, along with Mexicans and other Latinos, some of whom chose to stand out. Teen-age Mexican-American boys began wearing frock jackets with exaggeratedly padded shoulders and pleated pants pulled high up on their waist, a look-at-me style enhanced by swinging key chains, wide-brimmed hats and hair slicked into ducktails. It was unclear how they began clashing with young sailors on leave, or who beat up on whom, but the situation got out of control by the time a throng of servicemen piled into twenty-nine taxis to seek out zoot suiters to pound on. As police swooped in amid the rumbles, they naturally sided with the men in the government's uniforms, not those of the streets.

When Mayor Bowron went on the radio to discuss the mess, he said most criticism he heard was that the police were not brutal enough, letting the zoot suiters "run wild and ruthlessly attack servicemen." As the mayor saw it, his city fell under a spotlight no matter what it did. "What it will be next week or next month, I cannot guess," he said, "but the Hollywood section of Los Angeles is always good for some spicy domestic scandals, and divorce cases of movie stars rate a headline in any newspaper from Maine to Florida." Like any politician, he pleaded for more good news, pointing out how the area had produced one-tenth of America's war goods and most all the oil used by the forces in the Pacific. The most miraculous news, however, was how his city had transformed its law enforcement over those same years it was helping to save the world.

"It's high time that Los Angeles should be given the reputation it deserves, that of a modern, progressive great city," Mayor Bowron told the radio public. "The nation should know this about our Police Department: It has enforced the law. There is no widespread commercialized gambling or vice in Los Angeles, no pay-off. It is the cleanest large city in America."

But soon his cleanest large city in America would have to explain the bullet-riddled bodies of guys named Maxie, Paulie, Georgie, and The Meatball.

The "paint store" at 8109 Beverly Boulevard wasn't really a paint store, but neither was 250-pound Maxie Shaman the "produce broker" he claimed to be, or so his family described him after he barged in there on May 15, 1945 and was shot dead by the proprietor, Mickey Cohen. Shaman and his two brothers were well-known bookies and it wasn't hard to figure out that Mickey's place took bets on the horses too, regardless of what its sign said. The store was a sorry-looking one-story box set in a patchy, weedy lot, not the best advertising for a product that was supposed to beautify your home. Kon-Kre-Kota, "The Wonder Paint," was touted on a billboard and on the sides of the store as a cement coating that would not peel, chip, leak, or burn. "Lasts Years Longer," the signage promised, and Kon-Kre-Kota was "Vermin Proof," too — the rats wouldn't get it. There even were a few displays of paint, or whatever the stuff was, inside the narrow screened door. But beyond them was a back office with three phones and a pay window, along with scratch sheets listing the horses withdrawn in races at various tracks and the odds on those still running. There also was a desk with a .38 in the drawer, which is where Mickey sat waiting that afternoon, well aware of who was coming his way.

The beef of the moment began at another place Mickey ran, a café on North La Brea. It also had two sides, or levels, the downstairs serving food like any restaurant while the upstairs hosted high-stakes craps games, took bets on sports events, and invited bookies to come in, settle accounts, and compare notes with their peers. Mickey ordered 5,000 chips at a time for the marathon poker sessions staged there, games in which the uninitiated might learn what could happen if you played with a (very subtly) shaved deck. A trusted customer calling in might be told, "We've got

71

craps, roulette, everything."

The gambling area was adorned with photos of Mickey's boxing idols — the tough little guys who'd done big things. They were fighters such as Bud Taylor, the bantamweight champ known as the "Terror of Terre Haute" who had killed two men with his fists, and Jackie Fields, a Jew from Chicago, born Jacob Finkelstein, who twice won the welterweight crown. Mickey was proud of having won a title himself as a five-foot-three flyweight when he lived in the Russian Town section of Boyle Heights, fighting in the newsboy championships at the American Legion just a few years after he was racking balls at Art Weiner's pool hall. Soon he was headed east to go pro, first settling in Cleveland, where a brother lived, then spending stretches in New York and Chicago while segueing into other endeavors. Scrawny as he was as a teenage fighter, he entered the ring like a gladiator with only a towel over his shoulder and no robe, his shorts displaying a Star of David. While he put on a good enough show to be matched with a future champion or two, there wasn't a great future for him in that racket — his official record had him losing nine of his last ten fights. No matter. These days he strutted about the city's nightspots as if he once held a belt.

The spat at his La Brea Social Club the night before involved Max Shaman's brother,

Joe, who had misbehaved among the boxing pictures. Joe's version was that he was leaving on his own when Mickey and some others in a car tried to run him down. "They caught me in a vacant lot and really gave me a working over," Joe said. But accounts of events leading to a shooting are like family lore, the details get tweaked by the telling. Mickey at first said it was Joe who kept bothering other patrons and got rough, until "he ripped me over the head with a chair" . . . only to rethink, later on, who had wielded the furniture. Under Mickey's subsequent account, his right-hand man Hooky Rothman warned Joe good, "Look it, behave yourself in here or get the fuck out," but Joe didn't cooperate. "So Hooky broke a chair over his head and bodily threw him out of the joint, slapped the shit out of him, you know, gave him a deal, gave him a going over." That telling made more sense because it was Joe who needed the six stitches in his scalp.

The next morning, the two other Shaman boys, Izzy and big Maxie, set out to get even. They stopped twice at Mickey's social club on La Brea, then drove to Santa Anita racetrack and asked around for him there. By then it was no secret that they were on the prowl, and why.

They finally tried the paint store on Beverly, where Izzy kept their car idling while twenty-eight-year-old Maxie went in. Izzy heard the first gunshot, rushed to the door and was warned not to enter. "Then I heard two or three or four more shots, so I ran to the car and got a pistol, walked back to the office and found nobody there but my brother, dead."

Mickey insisted that big Maxie pulled his gun first, so he grabbed it and, "I blasted him with a piece I had in my desk." Mickey didn't see any reason to stick around and see if Maxie, sprawled on the floor, was still breathing. "I didn't stop to say, 'Are ya dead?' when I banged him out."

Mickey was thirty-one and no longer a flyweight. Though he had added a couple of inches to his listed height since his newsboy days, that may have been the (elevated) shoes. They already were describing him as pudgy and his face was puffed too, accentuated by a nose flattened from his time in the ring and by an unnaturally small, rounded mouth that was perpetually pursed, or pinched, in the classic "sucked-a-lemon" look — his standard look was *displeased*. They called Mickey "swarthy" also, but there was nothing he could do about that. His dark, bushy eyebrows grew like weeds, and he could shave in the morning and his face started to shadow by the time he got dressed and out the door. Of course, it took him longer than most to get ready given how he scrubbed himself in the hot shower for an hour at least before powdering his body. Then he washed his hands dozens of times each day. Mickey scoffed at any notion that his obsession was like the crazy lady's in Shakespeare who kept seeing something on her flesh and pleaded, "Out, damn'd spot! Out, I say!" and that was supposed to be her guilt from killing. Bullshit. Mickey simply had one of those compulsions. He feared that germs, not bullets, would get him.

He finally showed up at police headquarters with his lawyer and told how the big fat bookie, Maxie Shaman, had come at him with a .45, the one found by the body. Detectives knew it might be a drop gun, planted next to the corpse, but there were no witnesses to contradict Mickey's tale of self-defense.

"It was me or him," Mickey said. "I let him have it."

The captain of Homicide, Thad Brown, tried to reassure the public that the shooting at the paint store had nothing to do with bookmaking. It was just a personal dispute among lowlifes, better forgotten.

Maxie Shaman at least had been shot behind closed doors. Paulie Gibbons got it May 2, 1946 on an all-too-public street, as he returned home from a card club at 2:40 A.M. Paulie had just $1.92 in his pocket — he had not had a good night at the card tables —

but his gold watch and gold ring with his initials, in diamonds and sapphires, were still on his body, indicating that the gunman had something other than robbery in mind. The killer had been sitting in an Oldsmobile in an alley, waiting for Paulie to return to his apartment just off Wilshire Boulevard in Beverly Hills. Neighbors heard him cry "Don't! Don't!" before the first shots, and one looked out the window as Paulie called out again, "Please don't kill me!" before the final two shots to his head. The gunman got back in the Olds and drove off.

The forty-five-year-old Gibbons had a rap sheet with thirty arrests going back to 1919 and was known for being slow to pay off on bets while casing gambling joints looking for lucky winners to rob — he was, in the lingo of his peers, a "gabby guy with plenty of front but few buckeroos in the kick." A police report was more clinical, listing him as a "known gambler, bookmaker, pimp, muscleman, etc." and speculated that he had been killed "for welching or pulling a shady deal with associates." In other words, the cops didn't know nothing. They pulled in for questioning: A liquor store owner to whom Gibbons owed money; a dog track operator; the proprietor of a Central Avenue café; a wrestling promoter from Long Beach; a nightclub hat check concessionaire; and Mickey Cohen, operator of the La Brea

Social Club. Mickey said he'd never heard of the man, which was odd because Paulie once was caught in a raid at his place and still carried a membership card from the La Brea Social Club.

The final suspects questioned and released were a pair of gambling figures originally from Chicago, Georgie Levinson and Benny "The Meatball" Gamson, who supposedly had gotten into a black market nylon deal with Paulie. Before long they were dead, too.

The round-faced meatball, a bookie and a card cheat, had been shot at already, weeks before Paulie. His car was struck five times, though he denied that the holes in the side or the smashed back window were from gunplay. He also refused police protection — vandals must have drilled the holes, he said. But Gamson might have had an inkling he was a target because he was living away from his family in an apartment with Levinson, who was newer to town and described in police ledgers as "a Chicago trigger-man." Authorities believed the pair had made enemies while trying to squeeze some unaffiliated bookies around Los Angeles into working with them. Meatball's wife and three-year-old daughter were staying across town, while Levinson had his wife and two children, a boy and a girl, in the same building as the late Paulie Gibbons. The men themselves were holed up in an apartment house on Beverly Boulevard where another unit facing the front was set up for a phone clerk or lookout, adorned only with a portable radio, empty whiskey bottles and highball glasses. Neighbors this time heard no warning shouts or scuffle, suggesting that The Meatball and Georgie willingly opened the door for someone they knew at 1:30 A.M. on October 3. The killer must have come in blasting, though, for Georgie was dropped on the spot, hit in the shoulder, back and head. He had no time to get the Mauser automatic under the sheets of their pull-down bed, the .38 Colt under a blanket in the closet, or the two sawed-off shotguns in a brown suitcase. Meatball was shot five times in the stomach but managed to stumble away as the gunman fired twice at him in the hallway. Clutching his midsection, he made it out the front door and down a grassy slope just as a police cruiser was driving by, carrying a drunk to the station. The patrol officers got to him right as he died.

A few years later, when authorities knew much more, a state crime report would link the killings of Paulie, Georgie, and The Meatball, saying "Their deaths automatically removed three potential obstacles in the path of Cohen's plans for building his gambling empire." But at the time about all they had were the headlines, OUTBREAK OF UNDER-WORLD WAR FEARED, UNDERWORLD

GRILLED, GANGSTERS IN GAMBLING WAR.
Mayor Bowron said, "We must rid ourselves
of gangsters."

The mayor's first instinct was to import cops
from New York who were experienced in
crimes like this. Someone else mentioned
bringing back old "Lefty" James, reincarnat-
ing the past. But the city's police chief had
another idea. Clemence B. Horrall was a rar-
ity on the force by having both a college
degree and a Wild West pedigree. After studying animal husbandry at Washington State
University, he moved to Montana to work for
the cattle country version of a Savings &
Loan, riding the range on horseback to
investigate whether ranchers had all the stock
they claimed as collateral. Monitoring that
rugged crowd was almost a law enforcement
job, which is how C. B. Horrall described it
after frostbitten toes sent him south to
warmer Los Angeles, where he joined the
LAPD in 1923. Even then, he kept true to
his roots by buying five acres in the Valley to
keep pigs, chickens, horses, and cows, which
his wife milked each morning. Horrall became chief in 1941, not long before Pearl
Harbor, and put a cot in his office so he'd
never have to leave if the city was attacked —
that did not seem far-fetched after a Japanese
submarine snuck into Santa Barbara Channel
and fired shells onto the mainland up the

coast. But Horrall was no longer a young man. He had served as a lieutenant back in the First World War and his heart gave him problems. Word was he used the cot to nap during the day, with a trusty sergeant stationed outside to buzz him awake if anyone important came by. Horrall even toyed with rewarding his gatekeeper by making him the head of his new *special detail* until his chief deputy, Joe Reed, talked him out of that foolishness. They didn't need an office guy. They needed a street cop, like that tough little sergeant at the 77th Street Station, Willie Burns.

Burns had been another traveler in the great Midwestern migration, coming from Minnesota, where he worked as a tree-topper as a teenager. Figuring that any profession had to be safer than timbering, he came west, joined the police force and got himself shot . . . by evil outsiders. The Starr brothers from Detroit had pulled a dozen grocery store and gas station robberies in their first month in L.A. before Burns confronted them outside the Western States Grocery on San Pedro Street and took a slug in his shoulder. Four years later, he was one of the LAPD officers dispersed to guard California's borders against Okies and other Depression refugees looking for fruit picking work that usually wasn't there, "thieves and thugs," the police chief called the itinerant job seekers.

The hobos responded with a song,

I'd rather drink muddy water
Sleep out in a hollow log
Than be in California
Treated like a dirty dog.

Burns did not necessarily buy into the Bum Blockade — he basically was a good soldier who did what he was told. But he was a good soldier with skills that belied his small (five-foot-seven) stature. He had been a gunnery officer in the Marines — that's how he knew about machine guns, learning on the Browning Automatic — and he had won a welterweight boxing title in Pacific Fleet competitions. In a department of sometimes undisciplined brawlers, he earned a reputation for being the opposite. He was light on his feet and quick and accurate with his fists, as he demonstrated as a watch sergeant when his officers brought in a struggling suspect. Without a word, he clocked the guy on the jaw, sending him sliding across the polished wood floor, all the way to the far end of the booking room. Only then did he ask, "OK, what'd the asshole do?" That was Willie Burns at work. Off the job, he lived in a small house near the station, 900-square-feet, where he and his wife poured their heart into caring for a daughter crippled by polio. He was in line for a promotion from sergeant to lieutenant when Chief Horrall and Joe Reed called him in and asked if he'd head their new *special detail*.

Another team had just been assembled in Los Angeles, the pro football Rams, and that was Burns' model. A good football team started with the line, with the giants. So atop the list of cops Burns invited to his mysterious after-hours meeting was James Douglas "Jumbo" Kennard, a native of Grand View, Texas. Jumbo went six foot four, 245 pounds, and was the son of a small-town constable who kept the peace while sporting a tin badge atop full Western regalia. Jumbo left Texas at sixteen to find work as an oilfield roughneck in neighboring Oklahoma, where someone snapped a picture of him in his coveralls, looking as towering as the wells. Oilfield labor took him most of the way through the Depression before he moved to Los Angeles and briefly wasted his time as a parts man in an auto plant, fetching carburetors and batteries, before he discovered the LAPD. His fingers were so long, and strong, he could clamp them atop the heads of misbehaving suspects and lift them up out of a chair. He carried an intimidating 6-inch revolver, too — anything smaller would look puny in those hands. Willie Burns rejoiced when Jumbo Kennard was one of the seven cops who came back after their first meeting and said, "I'm in."

Benny Williams was in too. He was an old-timer born at the turn of the century, with a gimpy leg and crow's-feet eyes. But he might have been a pro football player for real if the sport paid more than pennies back in its leather helmet era. After growing up in Indiana, Benny had joined one of the early traveling teams on which you played offense, defense, everything, while scrounging for a few bucks. He proved to be so skilled at drop-kicking, in particular, that he got a letter from George Halas in 1921 inviting him to come out for the Chicago Bears, Halas' team about to join a new circuit called the National Football League. But Benny had already become fascinated by Southern California after the Army sent him there to learn balloon reconnaissance during World War I. So he became a policeman rather than a Chicago Bear, and the brass placed him on a Prohibition liquor-fighting squad. He promptly was shot, like Burns — that happened a lot to cops in those days. In Benny's case, he and his partner were struggling with a pimp who snatched the partner's gun. Benny was wounded in the knee but Officer Vern Brindley was killed. The only time Benny's wife saw him cry was at the hospital when he got the news. "He's got two boys just like us," Benny said. As if he wasn't born strong enough, Benny built himself up doing construction work, volunteering as one of the

83

officers who in their spare time built the Los Angeles Police Revolver and Athletic Club, better known as the Police Academy. In tussles with suspects, Benny's trademark was a closing kick to the fanny that sent them flying. Once a drop-kicker, always a drop-kicker.

Archie Case's specialty was the rabbit punch to the back of the head. Archie carried 250 pounds on a six-foot frame and earned his rep in the black community once known as Mud Town and now called Watts, an area annexed into Los Angeles in 1926. For a beat officer on foot, it was not simple to transport a suspect — to get a patrol car you had to find a street-corner Gamewell call box, a fire-alarm–sized container that flipped open to reveal a phone connected right to the station house. Going to the box one time, Archie sensed that a young fellow he'd collared was antsy, itching to flee. Archie warned him, "You take off, I'm gonna shoot you in the ass." The guy ran, naturally, and Archie shot him in the ass. When he got back on the Gamewell phone, he told the watch commander back at the station, "Never mind sending a pickup — send an ambulance," and from then on Archie was known as "The Mayor of Watts."

That was the start of Willie Burns' squad, the muscle. Jerry Thomas and Con Keeler were big enough too, both a shade over six feet, but they were not around for head-knocking. Others dubbed Thomas "The Professor" for his photographic memory — he could mingle in a bar for hours, then come out and recite every name and every address anyone mentioned, letter perfect. Keeler was a red head from Iowa farm stock who'd come out of the war with an iron brace on his leg, making him useless for most police work. Except if you needed to pick locks. Or plant bugs.

But the muscle guys and specialists were worthless without tough, wily quarterbacks, and Burns himself was one. The other was square-jawed Jack O'Mara, the Sunday church usher who'd knock you on your ass if you crossed him. As a condition of joining, Jack insisted that Burns invite his partner from the 77th, Dick Hedrick. That completed the squad to start, the original eight. Others would join them down the line, including the roguish Sgt. Jerry Wooters, but these were the pioneers.

The challenge was getting them to work together, the bruisers and the brains. Enter the theater pickpockets.

Chief C. B. Horrall agreed it might be good training, tackling the young thieves who targeted the servicemen still returning from overseas by the shipload. That was an unfinished chapter amid L.A.'s post-war celebration and it enraged military and civilian officials alike. The weary veterans spent just one night in the city before boarding trains to their hometowns, often passing the night in the dime movie houses downtown. The theaters had begun staying open twenty-four hours to coincide with the round-the-clock schedule of the defense plants during the war — workers could go from their shift, whenever it ended, and see a film. Now America's returning heroes could do the same. The enormous movie palaces along Broadway showed the new releases, but the smaller theaters along Main were cheaper, in a district that included a few tattoo parlors and burlesque houses. So what if those theaters ran second-run films? Many of the vets just wanted to snooze. The problem was, they were used to being jostled in trucks or boats, making it easy to lift wallets or pouches, flush with their separation pay, even from sailors' thirteen-button trousers. The pickpocket would plunk down next to anyone he saw sitting alone and give 'em a nudge, making sure they were asleep. Then he'd lift their wallet, pouch or roll, or slice it out, if necessary, with a knife. In the time-tested modus operandi of the trade, the thief often had a partner walking up the aisle for a handoff no one could see. The evidence was gone.

The plan, then: Keeler and Thomas, or O'Mara and Hedrick, would sit up in the projection booths with binoculars, watching for any suspicious civilians sidling up to a vet. When they suspected a theft, they'd give a hand signal to big Archie or Benny, waiting by the exits. No culprit would get by those two, no way. But nabbing them was the easy part. The reality was that none of the servicemen wanted to hang around to testify against the pickpockets, none. A court hearing could be set in two or three days, but after years away at war the servicemen wanted to get home, right away.

That's how the squad came to use Winston Alley and James Douglas "Jumbo" Kennard. Understand, off the job Jumbo was a normal, quiet man. At home, he mostly wanted to plunk down on his easy chair and eat his bowl of chocolate ice cream. After his father died, Jumbo and his wife took in his kid sister and he watched over the teen-age Betty in the extreme, even inspecting her ears before she went out to make sure they were clean. Jumbo always kept his own hair brushed and the wide-lapel jacket on his suit neatly buttoned. He was totally civilized off the job — but on it he could go berserk. It didn't take much acting for the son of a Texas constable to start waving his six-inch and ranting about what they should do to those punks when the guys delivered them in the middle of the night to the L-shaped alley by the railroad tracks. O'Mara would plead with Jumbo not to shoot, "they're still investigating the body from last week," and Jumbo would turn away from the young thief to argue the issue, still waving his giant gun while shouting, "I'm gonna kill the motherfucker!" At that moment O'Mara would whisper to the panicked kid, "Get out of here — now!" and the kid would flee down the alley in the dark and turn left and the cops would not bother to chase him. They'd just wait for the crash, for there was a chain around the corner, stretched across the alley, knee-high. One after another, the Main Street pickpockets plunged head-first to the pavement, until the guys got tired of that routine and moved to a bridge over the railroad tracks, where Jumbo held them by their feet, upside down . . . and finally Chief C. B. Horrall said, "Enough!" — maybe a body wouldn't get up.

Two nights later they were down at the bars by the harbor, where the ships came in. At a few places girls were slipping Mickey Finns to the returning soldiers and sailors and leading them outside, toward dark alleys, where their boyfriends would roll the drugged vets. It was the same routine down there, except that Jumbo held them over the edge of a dock.

At one joint where they thought the bar owner was in on it, they took the cash register's money tray, just lifted it out and announced, "The business is closed! Everyone leave!" and the guy said, "You can't do that." Willie Burns was along for that one and he said back, "Yeah, good luck — have your attorney call us." But he didn't leave a card.

Chief C. B. Horrall again said "*Enough*," and this time it was. There wasn't much pickpocketing in those theaters and bars anymore.

L.A.'s new Gangster Squad was ready for the gangsters.

CHAPTER 5
O'MARA'S MULHOLLAND DRIVE SNEEZE

Their first real assignment: the visitors shaking down Hollywood restaurants and nightclubs, "hoodlum types from Rhode Island," in O'Mara's words, "what we called 'dandruff.' " The hoods — from Detroit actually, an echo of the old Purple Gang — were demanding a percentage of the take at such places as the Brown Derby, where the gossip columnists hung out, and the Mocambo, where the rail-thin band singer Frank Sinatra had begun his solo career a few years earlier. The law enforcement problem was the same as with the servicemen victimized by pickpockets — the club owners did not want to go to court, in their case fearing what might happen to their families. "What are you gonna do?" asked Sergeant Jack O'Mara.

The nightclub managers did not even report the squeeze themselves, they didn't dare to — a couple of bookies had witnessed an episode and quietly passed the word. All the squad had to do was disperse in pairs to the various Hollywood hotspots and wait. Jumbo and his partner came up with one hit, sitting at a bar, sipping a few drinks to blend in. Right in front of them, like out of an underworld comic book — they swore it was this brazen — two guys come in, one says:

"We're here for the protection money."

"Protection from what?" asks the bartender.

"Protection from this," says the second Detroit guy, and punches the barkeep. Then he reaches into the till to take the cash, with the walk-away line, "See ya next week."

The owners of the joints still would not testify. As O'Mara said, "What are you gonna do? Are you gonna leave it or are you gonna take action?" He had an action in mind.

John J. O'Mara was not a native, either. Who was? He wasn't sure how his family got from Ireland to Portland, Oregon, but that's where he was born in 1917 and spent his toddler years. Then the record winter of 1919–20 dumped 40 inches of snow in one day above the Hood River, followed by 1922's "silver thaws," where the rain fell through a layer of frigid air and came down as ice ready to kill, each drop like a bullet from the sky. "My dad said, 'California here we come, where the streets are paved with gold.' " His father piled the seven children into the Model T and off they went to join the great migration, reaching Los Angeles the same year as the Whalens, except the O'Maras came from the north.

Jack's dad found work with the power company, believing a weekly paycheck to be the foundation for survival. It also was enough to buy a small two-bedroom house in working class South Los Angeles then build another bedroom for the three boys in the back. The kids all started in the parish school at Nativity Church, which crammed eight grades into four classrooms and taught that heaven and hell were real, not abstractions. There was good and evil and not much between. Perhaps fighting fell in the middle, though — the boys sure did a lot of it, that's how Jack's nose got broken. He was a scrawny boy with jet black hair and piercing turquoise eyes that the family saw as a badge of the true-blooded Irish — he could easily be mistaken for an innocent fresh off the boat. But those same wide blue eyes had a way of looking through people, and intimidating them, long before he realized it.

When it was time for high school, the O'Mara girls were sent to parochial Saint Agnes while the boys were unleashed on public Manual Arts, known for its shop classes in printing, auto mechanics, and blacksmithing, and its football and track teams. Though Jack gave hints of his strength in his sturdy neck and gnarled hands, he was five foot nine and chicken-chested and relegated to running cross-country and middle distances, like the half-mile, where sheer determination could carry the day — he basically went as fast as he could until he conked out. His social life revolved around an unapproved fraternity spearheaded by Frank Bruce, a Memphis, Tennessee, boy destined to become an aerospace millionaire. Calling themselves *Delta Tau Sigma*, they rented the bottom of a house in Hermosa Beach with just enough room for eight of them to put on suits, run down to the water and later crash on the floor, or have boxing matches. That's when Jack discovered he could knock down bigger guys, "I surprised 'em," is what he'd say. They entered a team in the semi-pro Municipal Football Association, which staged games at a field where up to 10,000 spectators were invited to drop a token of appreciation into a hat, usually 25 cents. The "two-bit football" drew one team of rugged San Pedro Longshoremen and another that was all black, the Ross Snyder Bulldogs. Filled out to 135 pounds, O'Mara told his teammates, "Give me the ball, I'll run right through them," and *Delta Tau Sigma* won the league title in '39, you could look it up.

But the fraternity's most popular activity was girl-hunting on Catalina Island. The boys saved up to buy $3.95 tickets that included a round trip on the big white steamer and a night in "villas" that were little more than tents. During the day, they spear-fished out of a makeshift diving bell built from an old water heater, the air hand-pumped into it through a sixty-foot garden hose. Their prime destination, however, was the island's famous Casino, not the gambling type, the dancing one. The massive art deco ballroom in Avalon Harbor drew the big bands of Glenn Miller and Harry James and hordes of young ladies eager to let off steam doing the jitterbug.

Connie Paegel was sixteen when he noticed her calves across the room. She was a Saint Agnes girl like his sisters, dark-haired with pale hazel cat eyes, a golden under-glow to her skin, and curves all over. She was a lively dancer too, an early bobby-soxer, yet clearly sheltered — she would never drive a car in her life. What she noticed about him was equally profound, "He was the skinniest guy, the smallest and the toughest. He had muscles." More than seventy years later, one of their daughters sized up another era's boy-meets-girl this way:

> You married a woman because she had great legs and big tits and she was pretty and fun and you wanted to get her into the sack. And you married a man because he was handsome and he'll be a good provider and you wanted to get out of the house. It wasn't like a huge amount of thought or existential angst went into selecting these mates, right?

Before the wedding, Connie went with her mom and sister to check out dresses at I. Magnin and tried on one that the elegant actress Myrna Loy might have worn, with layers of silk and lace. Then they went home and got on the old foot-pedal black Singer and sewed up a perfect replica. Connie kept a little photo-diary book chronicling "Our Wedding Journey" and "Our Honeymoon" in which she duly noted how she and Jack took the winding road up into the San Bernardino Mountains, a drive that was spooky but fun.

Got to Big Bear about 7 in the evening — found a nice cabin & then went for dinner & what a dinner . . . we bought rums, cokes & lime and went back to the cabin. Had a few drinks and retired — !

When they awoke the next morning, it was snowing. A day later, they had to shovel themselves out.

He told her he wanted to be a cop the night they met. He already was out of high school, scrounging jobs at the gas company and joining some of the frat crowd in unloading freight trains that came down overnight from San Francisco. In the Depression, you took whatever work you could get. He was considering applying to the FBI, but Los Angeles needed bodies more in the wake of its scandals. With so many men fired or retired, the new Bowron administration was ready for an influx of fresh blood. The future Connie O'Mara said that sounded great — maybe he'd rise to chief someday — and she stuffed him with bananas and ice cream to make sure he met the minimum weight. John J. O'Mara entered the Police Academy on September 3, 1940 and became part of the generation that was supposed to forge a new LAPD. Of course, he foolishly kept challenging the fastest recruit at the Academy to race, never understanding why he couldn't beat Tom Bradley, a former UCLA track star poised to become one of just 100 black officers on the force and eventually the first black mayor of Los Angeles.

He worked traffic and patrol before the war, with only one complaint against him, from a drunk he pulled out of a car. He once got a call that his kid brother had been picked up for causing a ruckus in a bar, so he took off his gun and asked to be left alone in a cell with Paul — Jack's knuckles ached for days after that. He fired his gun one time, when he caught a burglar breaking into an apartment of two old ladies. The man took a slash at him with a knife then ran off and started climbing a fence — Jack got him in the ass, like Archie with the guy in Watts. In those days they didn't question why you shot someone running away, they congratulated you on your aim.

After Pearl Harbor the Coast Guard sought out policemen, thinking they might be valuable in helping to protect ports and other critical installations. But they gave them all aptitude tests first and ordered O'Mara to an Aleutian Islands cryptography unit working to intercept Japanese communications, part of the effort to break the Japanese code. Who knew he had brains? The hush-hush work at times had him on desolate Adak Island, but he twice snuck Connie up there and rented a small room in someone's house on the mainland, all against regulations — even then he was willing to break the rules for a good cause.

When he got out of the service, he was a pipe-smoking 165-pound Spencer Tracy look-alike, and just the sort Willie Burns wanted for his secretive squad that was going to protect Los Angeles from evil invaders.

O'Mara and Jerry Thomas, "The Professor," were staking out a nearby nightspot when Jumbo and his partner seized the two strongarm assholes from Detroit. Thomas was great on such assignments because he could reproduce every word your suspects said without using a notebook — they thought you were shooting the breeze but he was getting it all down in his head.

"Where should we take 'em?" Jumbo asked

when the two Gangster Squad teams met to decide the fate of their evening's catch.

"Why not the desert?" Thomas said. "Strip 'em down, leave 'em there."

"City Hall no good?" Jumbo said — there were empty rooms in the basement they could use at night with no one around to see or hear what they did.

"No, let's take 'em up," O'Mara said, and that was it.

The view was great from Mulholland Drive, the winding road atop the hills that divide Los Angeles, so why not show it to the hoods muscling in on the Hollywood hotspots? It was a five minute drive up from the Sunset Strip, no one saying a word, all squeezed together, the cops and the hoods.

Los Angeles policemen had taken suspects up into those hills before. O'Mara was hardly the first to suggest it. But the new assignment called for a new approach.

I'd emphasize the fact that this wasn't New York, this wasn't Chicago this wasn't Cleveland. This is L.A. and we're not going to put up with this crap and get the word out to your people back East. And we leaned on 'em a little, you know what I mean, up in the Hollywood Hills, off Coldwater Canyon, anywhere up there. And it's dark at night, and we'd talk to them man to man.

O'Mara liked the darkness of the hills, with the city twinkling in the distance, to make his point. Amid the darkness, to drive it home, he put a gun to one guy's ear. He didn't plan what he said. It just popped out.

You wanna sneeze?

And that became the O'Mara signature, the gun in the ear and a few suggestive words.

Do you feel a sneeze coming on? A . . . real . . . loud . . . sneeze?

CHAPTER 6
MICKEY MOVES UP, BUGSY MOVES (SIX FEET) DOWN

The columns called Benny Siegel a "Hollywood sportsman" or some such nonsense when he was seen with another B-starlet or his old friend George Raft, the smooth cabaret dancer turned movie tough guy. Los Angeles was a playground for Bugsy, who had come of age on Manhattan's Lower East Side as part of an alliance of real-life Italian and Jewish tough guys including Lucky Luciano and Meyer Lansky, the latter eventually giving him the Mafia version of the old pep talk, "Go West, young man."

No one was sure exactly when he arrived for good — '34, '35, '36, or '37 — but he didn't come out to hide out. He could be found along the Sunset Strip or holding court in a box at Santa Anita racetrack, waving to other bettors while jotting down his Ws and Ls in a little black book. You also might find him taking meetings at the steam room at the Hollywood Athletic Club or yukking it up at Hillcrest, the Jewish golf club whose members included the Marx Brothers, Milton Berle, and many of the studio moguls — that may explain why they were willing to deal with him when he moved in for a time on the union that represented screen extras, trusting him to deliver labor peace for a price.

Mickey Cohen laid out the qualities he admired in the man quite succinctly, "money, clothes, and class." When it came to capturing the look, Bugsy was up there with the aptly named Joe Adonis and with Frank Costello, the New York mob boss who mixed comfortably with the powerful squares of the world. In Mickey's eyes, Bugsy's cashmere-suit style was the opposite of the old Moustache Petes, who often dressed like rag pickers. He wasn't necessarily referring to Jack Dragna, who dressed OK. But Dragna was "lackadaisical," Mickey said, and that was a prime reason the organization sent Bugsy out, and him later on. Dragna may have been working L.A. since 1914 but "he wasn't able to put a lot of things together to the satisfaction of the eastern people." So there was some tension, you know? Bugsy's main ties were to New York, Dragna's to Chicago. Plus the Italian-Jew thing — such an alliance may have made sense on the Lower East Side but not every Sicilian bought into being upstaged by those people. "Fuck Dragna," Bugsy basically said to that.

Fortunately, there was money to be made

for all in the new enterprise of choice. As if to hand the racketeers a timely gift, Santa Anita Park opened on Christmas Day almost exactly a year after the end of Prohibition cut off their main revenue stream. The races fueled a demand to place bets legally on the track and illegally off of it, and also provided a simpler way for Bugsy and his friends to get legions of bookies to cut them in on their take, through a racing wire. The wires provided the essential information — track conditions, jockeys, etc., along with results — directly to customers over telegraph-like tickers or through regional distributors, who printed up the data on the daily scratch sheets neither bettors nor bookies could do without. One local distributor boasted that he was a leg of a loop that "circumvents the United States." He was asked if he really meant *circumvents* as in *circumvents the laws?* "Circumcises, I don't give a shit what you call it," he said. "It goes coast to coast."

Bugsy's top priority on the West Coast was pushing the mob's Trans-America wire, and he worked wonders in Nevada, where gambling was legal — he gained a monopoly at many of the gambling houses, sending an estimated $25,000 a month his way. While not the most faithful husband, he was able to build a 12,000-square-foot home for his wife and two daughters in Los Angeles' exclusive Holmby Hills neighborhood and enrolled the girls in a private school and riding academy. The mansion had a recessed bar flanked by slot machines, a large pool, and more powder rooms than most houses have rooms. Bugsy wasn't just flash, he had the cash.

He was listed as "Siegel, Benjamin" in the notebook Con Keeler began keeping on the Gangster Squad's targets: height, weight, address, aliases, hangouts, car type, plate number, and so on. Keeler used a fine-tip pen and precise, compressed handwriting because the book was so slender, able to slide into his breast pocket. Regular files were not an option if you had no office, if you didn't exist. "Damn fine print," Lieutenant Willie Burns told him. "I can't see it."

There quickly were dozens of names in the little book, but Bugsy was of special interest because he validated the darkest visions of city officials. The squad got the lecture from Assistant Chief Joe Reed, who with his paunch and balding head fancied himself resembling the British leader Winston Churchill. Reed gathered them after hours at City Hall to talk about . . . New York. He warned that underworld figures in that state were feeling the heat because their governor was Tom Dewey, who had made his mark as a prosecutor and mob fighter, up there with Eliot Ness, the Treasury agent. "Trust me, they'll be looking for fertile ground," Reed said. "They're comin' out."

It may have sounded like paranoia, but one other Murder, Inc. figure already had done that, with fatal consequences. George Harry Schachter, aka "Big Greenie," had snuck out west for his safety after foolishly hinting to mob associates in New York that he might cooperate with authorities if they didn't pay him more. How dumb was Big Greenie? They pumped five shots into his head and neck after he eased his Ford convertible to the curb in front of a Hollywood rooming house. When the LAPD pulled Bugsy in on suspicion of murder, he asked to borrow a comb and necktie from the detectives who escorted him to the jail. "I'm Ben Siegel and I'm not gonna look like a bum," he said.

The case went nowhere when a key witness in New York plunged to his death from a hotel window, but at least Bugsy was described with a little less naivete in L.A. after that. He now was in the columns as a "one-time New York police character" or even as "a man who lived by the bluff of his good connections." The hardest part for Bugsy was having to resign, with a boot at his rear, from Hillcrest Country Club. "I missed the golfing," he said.

Mickey cringed when anyone suggested that he was brought out to be Bugsy's gofer and mindless muscle. In his first years in L.A. he fancied himself still the wild young buck who didn't need anyone's permission to stick up bookie joints, nightclubs, even one of Dragna's gambling places. At the same time, "Benny was trying to put some class in me and trying to evolve me," Mickey said, and he did study the New Yorker's dress and lifestyle. For one thing, he followed Bugsy's lead in avoiding alcohol — it paid to keep a clear head in their line of work, as when the operator of a competing racing wire needed to be sent a message. Mickey did a characteristic verbal dance when asked later about the visit he and Joe Sica paid to Bugsy's uncooperative rival.

Q: Were you convicted of administering a beating to Russell Brophy?

Cohen: No, sir.

Q: Let's start at the beginning. Russell Brophy managed the wire service in Los Angeles, is that right?

Cohen: That is right.

Q: Giving racing wire service to bookies?

Cohen: That is right.

Q: You and Joe Sica entered the place and beat him up, isn't that correct?

Cohen: There was some kind of thing there, yes . . .

Q: Who hired you to do the beating?

Cohen: Nobody.

Q: Where was the assault?

Cohen: There was no assault, really. It was just an argument.

Q: Two of you hit him . . .

Cohen: I know I hit him. I don't know who else hit him . . .

Q: The court apparently did think you both hit him. You were fined $100 and he was fined $200.

Cohen: Then I must have hit him less.

Bugsy Siegel was a great mentor, indeed, for Mickey Cohen. Bugsy had the whole class act nailed to the last, when they laid him out in a $5,000 bronze coffin lined with silk, candelabras at each end.

The gangster squad had little time to build its dossier on Bugsy. He often was away in Las Vegas directing construction of his Flamingo hotel-casino, which was supposed to transform the Nevada city. Bugsy was there a lot because his dream project was way behind schedule and over budget, plagued by a misguided design that gave each room its own sewer line and created a penthouse suite with a beam down the middle so a man had to duck to avoid conking his head. When Bugsy was in California he increasingly stayed outside the squad's jurisdiction, at the Beverly Hills mansion rented by his mistress Virginia Hill. Though generally described as a party-loving Alabama oil heiress, she was hardly a prototypical Southern Belle, having used some of her money to back a prominent Chicago bookie, earning a piece of his action. The *Los Angeles Mirror* columnist Florabel Muir was at a beauty salon when a package addressed to Virginia Hill was delivered with ten $1,000 bills in it. "She was a hey-nonny-nonny sort of gal," Florabel wrote, but also "knew all the Boys."

On the morning of June 20, 1947, Bugsy flew back from Las Vegas and stopped at his barber shop before meeting his lawyer. He also may have squeezed in a visit with Mickey, though Mickey once said it was the day before that Bugsy asked him, " 'Ya got armament?" and he replied, "Whatever ya' want." That night, Bugsy and his friend Allen Smiley decided to try a new restaurant in Santa Monica, Jacks-at-the-Beach, and ordered the trout. On the way out Bugsy picked up the early edition of the *Los Angeles Times* and they returned to the Moorish mansion, where Bugsy sat at one end of the living room sofa, bright white with a floral pattern. For some reason the curtains on the window were drawn back, giving anyone outside a clear look in. The bullets came from a .30-caliber military carbine. When the columnist Florabel Muir heard the news she rushed over and discovered "perfume pervaded the room from the night-blooming jasmine clustered outside the window through which the deadly shots had been fired. The *Los Angeles Times* was lying across his knees and on it was stamped: 'Good Night. Sleep peacefully with compliments of Jack's.' Bloody sections of his shattered brains partially blotted out the eight-column headline telling of another fatal shooting in a poorer section of Los Angeles." Florabel got the best words, but the competing *Herald-Express* got the best picture, showing the body on a slab at the morgue, the big toe protruding from under a sheet with a tag hung on it, "Bugsy Siegel."

Jack O'Mara and Willie Burns rushed to Beverly Hills police headquarters to get in on the investigation, but the profusion of law enforcement agencies in Los Angeles County could frustrate anyone, even the crooks. By the late 1940s, forty-six different agencies were policing parts of the sprawling county's 4,000 square miles. For the crooks, the problem was whom to bribe — a police official might be able to offer you protection on one side of the street but not the other. For honest cops, the problem was who to trust. The Gangster Squad would not share information with many agencies, but Beverly Hills police were considered OK so the two men offered their services to that city's chief, hats in hand. Chief Clinton H. Anderson said, "We don't need any help," O'Mara recalled. "I said, 'Well screw you. It's your case — you take the heat.' "

108

And Beverly Hills cops did just that. O'Mara watched the inquest from a back row and came up with his own theory. He didn't go for the conventional wisdom that the mob's higher-ups had enough of Bugsy's wasteful spending on the Flamingo, some of it their money. He didn't believe Dragna did it, either. From the back of the inquest, O'Mara kept eyeing Virginia Hill's brother, Chick, who lived upstairs in the mansion and might well have heard Bugsy's famous temper play out on his sister. The brother was a veteran too, he knew how to use a carbine. But finding the truth was a mind game you couldn't win — this was a murder they'd never solve, the living room slaughter that created a vacancy in the hierarchy of organized crime, such as it was, in Los Angeles.

"I took over from Benny right away, on instructions from the people back east," Mickey said later. "To be honest, his getting knocked in was not a bad break for me."

CHAPTER 7
THE FAKE DRIVE-BY

Sometimes five men piled into one of their rusted '40 Fords to head out on a Gangster Squad stakeout, several smoking cigars, and by the end of the day their suits stank so badly their wives had to hang them outside on the clothesline at night. Connie O'Mara held her husband's coat at arm's length with two fingers while her other hand held her nose. The cars themselves were pathetic, going on their third or fourth engines, with 200,000 miles on the odometers. They had no floor mats and had plugs in the floorboard to pour fluid in the master cylinder. If you saw a puddle ahead, you had to put a foot over the hole or you'd get sopped, the water splashing up into your face. If there were three men in back and the car hit a bump, the middle guy's head would bonk into the roof. That's how it was until they got a third car so they could split more sensibly into teams.

Before they got radios in the cars they assembled at a street corner they agreed upon the night before. Then Burns would say, "OK, you two will be following . . ." and name their target for the evening. Once they got the radios, he'd still give them directions in a way only they would understand, "OK, meet me two blocks east and one block south of last night."

The Tommy guns were great — they could intimidate anybody — but they were a pain. The men couldn't leave them anywhere for fear they'd be stolen, even in the trunks of their cars. If they had to go into a store or a house to question someone, they dragged the Tommy along and put it where they could watch it. The circular fifty-round drums were available but those were a nuisance, too, because they couldn't easily hide them under their overcoats. Most of the men opted for the 20-round clips they could stash in a pocket. There was no SWAT team then, no special training, no lightweight bulletproof vests. The Tommy gun cases were beautiful, though, about three feet long and a foot wide and deep, each with a handle. You really could imagine there was a violin inside.

Within the LAPD there were rumors about what the shadowy new squad did, with most of the gossip pegging them as internal spies, headhunters, and not without reason. The chief's office had them quietly follow a number of fellow cops under suspicion, including one pretending to be from the state Attorney General's Office in order to shake down a juke box company up the coast, looking for bribes. But there was nothing quiet about their actions after a beat officer confided that a bookmaking barber on 6th Street had made him a brazen offer, "Why don't you get on the take?" Chief Horrall instructed Willie Burns, "That son of a bitch, take the bastard out," so the squad caravanned over and demolished the barber shop, ripping out the chairs, smashing the mirrors, and tearing down the display shelves. They did it in minutes, with barely a word while Jumbo held the barber in his giant arms, making him watch. Then they lathered the fellow's head and shaved it, with his own razors, a touch they dreamed up on the spot.

Things did not go as smoothly when O'Mara was asked to tail a notorious member of the Los Angeles County Sheriff's Department, Al Guasti, its captain of Vice and protector of the most blatant bookmaking operation in the L.A. area. Guarantee Finance maintained a series of front businesses as excuses to have seventy-four phones on its ledgers, one enterprise supposedly selling magazines, one making loans, another a wake-up service — the place even had a few phones taken out in the name of "Stone's Service Station." Guarantee Finance had a collection arm too, an excuse to have 118 "agents" on the streets. When naive outsiders approached it looking for loans, they were told, sorry, we're out of money. Guarantee Finance operated from behind blackened windows in a two-story building on East Florence Avenue, in an unincorporated area of the county, the sheriff's turf. But the LAPD's higher-ups had reason to be interested in this outrage beyond city borders — they got rumblings that one of their own sergeants might be helping Guarantee Finance make collections. So a plainclothes contingent went to check it out, sneaking through a skylight to get into the upstairs loft area, where a pit boss was supervising a dozen phone clerks amid racks of betting markers. The L.A. cops had no formal authority to make arrests but ripped up the betting records, spoiling a day's work. When they were about done a sheriff's deputy stumbled in, thinking they were part of the regular bookmaking crew. "Has the smoke blown over yet?" he asked. Soon after, Sheriff's Captain Guasti stormed into the LAPD's nerve center in City Hall and hand-delivered a letter to Reed, essentially saying: "STAY AWAY. THAT'S OURS." So Reed asked the Gangster Squad to follow this guy and O'Mara and his partner got the job.

They tailed Sheriff's Captain Al Guasti for an hour, through a circuitous route that ended at Schwab's, the drugstore on Sunset where starlets were said to be discovered. Guasti took a seat at the lunch counter. They did too, at a safe distance. He waved them over and said, "You know fellas, you can tail just as well from the front. You go first and I'll follow you."

It was obvious the squad could use someone who spoke Italian, so O'Mara suggested a young LAPD officer he'd met during the war, Lindo "Jaco" Giacopuzzi, a 230-pound former all-Valley football lineman who bulked himself up carting milk cans at his immigrant family's dairy — Jaco's father spoke about ten words of English in his entire life. Jaco was an easygoing bruiser who had hoped to become a fireman and took the police exam first only because he wanted practice taking a civil service test. The job was a job to him, not a crusade. He was on routine uniformed duty in a patrol car in the Hollywood Division when O'Mara and Burns tracked him down to sell him on the perks of the Gangster Squad. "Oh yes, it sounded good," Jaco recalled.

Let's face it, every Friday night we'd have to go to the fights in the Hollywood Legion Stadium. And every Tuesday night we'd have to go to the fights at Olympic Auditorium because that's where all these bums hung out. Then we'd have to go to the football games. All we'd have to do is just walk in — we never had to buy a ticket or anything, just go in and see who was there with who. That's what we'd do.

Hell, yeah, he wanted in — you or your partner even got to take home the unmarked car. Jaco kept some horses in the Valley and the other guys swore they found hay in the back seat after he got to use it. "I loved the detail," he said.

They found Jaco a partner during another *ex officio* job, like the one at the barber shop. Some roughnecks in West L.A. were giving their neighbors and the beat cops a hard time while hanging out on a hill. Assistant Chief Joe Reed told the squad, "Tame 'em down a little bit," so they made like a wrecking crew again. But this time their caravan stopped first at the LAPD's local station to get a couple of extra men before storming the hill and kicking the crap out of the troublemakers, leaving them sprawled on the ground. Willie Burns was impressed with one of the West L.A. cops who joined in the pounding, a guy nearly as large as Jumbo, their Texas shit-kicker. Jerry Greeley looked goofy with his hair parted in the middle but he'd been a Navy commander in the war — he was smart plus scary big. Screw the haircut. They invited him out for a few drinks to explain about the nights at the fights and all that.

■ ■ ■ ■

You could keep such an operation secret only so long. The squad made news for the first time on November 15, 1947, with a report that an LAPD contingent had rousted six Midwesterners in a limo on Wilshire. The six — all Italian — were booked on suspicion of robbery though there was no evidence they had as yet committed any crimes in Los Angeles. Photographers were invited in to snap the six seated on a bench in the Wilshire Station, with heads bowed, before the squad escorted four to the state border, including a Cleveland fight promoter in a blue suit found to have nineteen $100 bills in his wallet, a Detroit "roofing salesman" who said he'd come west "for my health," and a self-described trucker who admitted having served 6 1/2 years for a murder "I never committed." Secrecy sometimes had to go out the window because the public needed reassurance that something was being done about what a state report soon called the "Invasion of Undesirables." The *Los Angeles Times* wrote, "Led by Lt. William Burns and Sgt. J. J. O'Mara, the flying detachment apprehended the six men in a New York-licensed limousine at Wilshire Boulevard and Burnside Avenue. Check of the expensive black vehicle showed its owner to be an ex-convict from

116

New York."

The registered owner was identified in another account as Edward "Eddie" Herbert, but that reporter heard wrong because "Eddie" wasn't right. *Neddie* Herbert was the house jokester and most trusted courier of messages between the coasts for a certain ex-boxer. Neddie was Mickey's best munitions man, as well, reputed to be able to reassemble a machine gun like a Marine, or Willie Burns. But Neddie wasn't in the black '47 Caddy stopped on Wilshire, only the six Midwesterners. The squad members intentionally didn't give the first three quite enough time to pack, so news photos showed clothes slung over their arms as they were led off for the drive out of state — in this mission, images mattered in a way they didn't teach you at the Police Academy.

The 5-cent final edition of the *Daily News* sent exactly the message city fathers wanted, "Three shady characters from the East left town today in a convincing heave-ho designed to rid Los Angeles of its growing gangster element." The fourth visitor was sent packing the next day. "Los Angeles doesn't want your kind of characters," Assistant Chief Reed declared. Willie Burns even got a quote in after one of the hoods griped that someone had written them a parking ticket on top of everything. "Give me the ticket, boys," Burns said. "I'll fix it for you."

Of course, no one knew then what would become of the two Midwesterners allowed to stay on promises of good behavior: that self-described used car salesman James Fratianno, a parolee from Ohio, would become the L.A. mob's most feared button man, the infamous "Jimmy the Weasel"; or that James Regace, years later, would rise to head the local mob himself, under his real name Dominic Brooklier. During the roust Fratianno hid his face when the photographers neared and let police portray him as just another over-matched buffoon. "I know these other ex-cons," they quoted him as saying. "I met them at a nightclub here." Regace acknowledged serving nine years for robbery but emphasized that he was gainfully employed in town, having lined up a job at a new store on Santa Monica Boulevard, a clothing shop run by this fellow Mickey Cohen.

The initial entry in Keeler's notebook for "Cohen, Mickey" had him driving a " '46 Cad. Sed Blk. Shiny 3T9 364." But by the end of 1947 Mickey was leading a caravan of three Caddies that sped about town for nights of club-hopping with his men — they made for quite a spectacle. They no longer operated out of a ratty paint shop, either, since he opened the haberdashery selling imported suits, silk ties, and smoking jackets, a more appropriate inventory for a man of his stand-

118

ing. Mickey took pride in having gotten his education on the streets and flaunted his dese-dems-and-dose lingo. "I hadn't gone to no school," was how he phrased it. But he had *evolved* himself, as his betters urged, into an aficionado of French lisle socks and $275 Panama hats, allowing an occasional departure from the pro forma gray fedora. It was astonishing to look back at his first booking photo after his return to Los Angeles as an adult — the 1933 shot showed him with his top shirt button undone, tie askew, and in a plain wool jacket that was wrinkled and soiled. Now "The Mick" was the peacock in unlined pastels and a pinky ring and his boys declared that mustachioed Adolphe Menjou, the dapper actor who played rich executives in the movies, was no longer the best-dressed man in town. His crew was a mix of Jews who'd been with him for years, such as Hooky and Neddie, and Italians such as Regace, Jimmy the Weasel, and especially the Sica brothers, whom Mickey knew when "we were just kids, hustling around." All and all there were a lot of guys to list as salesmen at a clothing store.

The haberdashery was a natural testing ground for the Gangster Squad's newest team, Greeley and Giacopuzzi. When that duo got their Tommy gun, they showed they understood the rules of the gig — that there were none in making life unpleasant for the likes of Mickey Cohen. Assigned to stake out the new store, Greeley and Giacopuzzi figured they would leave Mickey's boys guessing whether they were cops or fellow hoods, and why not from Chicago? Jaco's account:

Before we went down there we took the plates off our unmarked police car and we went to the DMV there in Hollywood, where we looked in the garbage pail and found some plates from Illinois, and we put those on. Then we went up and we parked one block down from Mickey's place. I was on the driver's side and Greeley was on the other side. We had our hats and overcoats and just parked the car there. Well, they didn't know who we were and they'd send one guy out and he'd walk up to check us out and every time he'd pass by us we'd pull our coats up and pull our hat down. And so then, this was about 5 or 6 o'clock, it came time for us to leave. And so when we left, I was driving towards Mickey's place and when we got there all the men in Mickey's establishment came out on the sidewalk to look . . . And as we were going by, I took the car and I swerved it in and Greeley leaned way out of the passenger window with the Tommy gun. And you should've seen 'em hit the deck. All of 'em went down. He had one fellow that was quite fat and he tried to go underneath a car and he couldn't get underneath it, you know. Then I gunned the car and off we went.

It was a great prank to share with the squad afterward, the fake drive-by, at least until the double-barreled shotguns started firing for real. But before those blasts echoed across the Sunset Strip, Jack O'Mara would meet the man whose future would intertwine with Mickey's, and his, in ways he could not imagine.

CHAPTER 8
O'MARA MEETS THE WHALENS

O'Mara got the word when he arrived for the night shift April 16, 1948: "Freddie the Thief" Whalen had been kidnapped by three Fresno men who said he had conned $2,900 from them and a bookie friend. Fred Whalen was taking a stroll near his Hollywood home with his twenty-month-old grandson — the son of his daughter Bobie — when the trio descended and handcuffed him, then shoved him in the back of a car and drove off, leaving the toddler on the sidewalk. Family members saw the abduction and ran after the fleeing car, then called the Hollywood station, setting in motion an all-points bulletin that helped police seize the culprits in Burbank. They had been threatening to take Freddie up in a plane and drop him from the skies if he didn't return the money he'd suckered from them as "Dr. Harry Moore."

The general public still had no idea who Fred Whalen was unless they were hard-core pool players who knew of his trick shot exhibitions or his challenge match with the great Ralph Greenleaf a decade earlier. But Freddie the Thief was a legend among Bunco and gambling detectives, who considered him the cleverest con man Los Angeles had seen in years, or perhaps ever, if you discounted the fellow who'd stung half the city with an oil stock swindle in the '20s. Then again, C. C. Julian fled the country and killed himself — Freddie Whalen was still around, topping himself with one new scam after another. When many bootleggers foundered after Prohibition, he had simply started buying cheap drug store whiskey and reselling it as expensive Johnny Walker, in look-alike bottles. But this current scam — the reason three Fresno guys wanted to drop him from an airplane — was something else, pure genius.

Freddie would go to a hospital posing as a visiting doctor, wearing the white coat and stethoscope around his neck. First thing, he'd carry a break-the-ice bouquet of roses to the receptionist and switchboard operator and introduce himself as doctor-so-and-so, Dr. Harry Moore up in Fresno. He would explain that he'd be around a week checking on a couple of patients as a favor to one of the hospital's regular physicians who was away on vacation, then give the phone operator that oversized smile and say, "I'm expecting a call, dear, and if you'd page me I'd appreciate it." Next Freddie would spread the word around the hospital that he had a passion for the ponies and did anyone know where he could place a bet? He would be connected to the local bookie in no time and place a few small wagers to start, sure losers. After that, he'd make the bookie a proposition — how about if *he*, Dr. Moore, collected bets from people at the hospital? What an offer — an amiable doctor volunteering to solicit wagers for you! And from fellow physicians, nurses and patients! What bookie could resist? Few could, though they might do their due diligence and call the hospital to check if he was legit. "Oh, Dr. Moore, certainly," the hospital operator would say. "Let me page him."

At midmorning, the horse-happy Dr. Moore would arrange for the bookie or his runner to meet him at a nearby motel so he could hand over the bets from the hospital — written on index cards — just as the day's races were to begin on the East Coast. Freddie would offer the guy a drink and tell a few jokes, filling a little time. His mark had no way of knowing that an associate or two — sometimes his brothers-in-law, the Wunderlichs — were in the adjoining room, getting the results over the phone as the races were run. They used a thin curved wire to slide additional index cards under the door with new bets, except these were winning wagers, often on long shots. The furniture in Freddie's motel room had been rearranged so that the desk was in front of the door between the rooms, blocking the mark's view of the cards being slid underneath on the wire, then up to him, seated at the desk. Being a pro with his (pool shark's) hands, Freddie effortlessly slipped the new cards into the stack he was handing the bookie, one at a time. The dupe had no reason to suspect a con — the doc had been alone with him since before the tracks opened. It was classic past-posting that took one bookie after another to the cleaners in communities around California and beyond. "Daddy didn't get above the fifth grade," his daughter said, "but he didn't need it."

This time, Freddie had outdone himself by convincing a bookie in Merced that he could gather bets from three hospitals in nearby Fresno. The bookie rounded up several associates to back the venture, only to quickly lose $2,900 because of a series of seemingly lucky winning wagers. That's when the stung trio got suspicious and followed the good doctor, then decided to help him skydive without a parachute from a private plane out of Burbank airport. But after they snatched Freddie off the street in Hollywood and roughed him up a bit, he volunteered a way to pay them back — with his wife's two diamond rings, 10 carats and 5 carats, worth $12,000 at least. The trio bit and called Lillian from a pay phone to tell her to bring the jewelry, fast, to a Burbank drug store. The police showed up instead.

O'Mara hoped to learn, for starters, who stood behind the stung bookmaker. The trio who snatched Freddie appeared to be low on the gambling food chain, one describing himself as a former plumber, another as a stud poker dealer and sheet rock finisher. But many bookies were paying someone like Mickey up the ladder, if not for the racing wire then for protection, whether from his own goons or from (bribable) authorities . . . or from past-posting scammers. It made sense to have muscle behind you that could administer painful punishment to people who dared to cheat you. One state report estimated that Mickey had 500 bookies in his network, charging them by the phone. Dragna no doubt had a slew paying him. So O'Mara headed over to Fred Whalen's place in Hollywood, playing a long shot himself.

Freddie lived now in a garden apartment in the flats, on Lodi Street, across from the Hollywood Studio Club, the sorority-like rooming house for young women in the entertainment industry, or trying to crack it. A twenty-one-year-old wannabe named Joan Cory was coming out of the club just as Freddie was walking his grandson and witnessed his abduction — "It looked like a scene from a movie," the dark-haired actress said. Another young aspirant living at the rooming house that year was the former munitions plant worker Norma Jeane Baker, who posed nude for the first time to earn $50. "I was behind in my rent," explained the roomer who would become better known as Marilyn Monroe.

Freddie Whalen let Jack O'Mara in, no problem, like he had nothing to hide. They talked turkey, too, the two Irishmen — Whalen and O'Mara. Only one other person was present, Fred's son, Jack, though O'Mara never would have guessed they were related. The elder Whalen was of average build and dressed in a short-sleeve white shirt and looking incredibly relaxed for someone who'd nearly been dropped from a plane — he had ultimate confidence in his wits. His son, in contrast, was pure physicality. O'Mara's hand disappeared when he shook Jack Whalen's massive mitt. Photos around the living room showed the younger Whalen in uniform — Freddie proudly reported that his boy had been a pilot in the war. The kid looked the part, too — dashing, as they say, with thick, wavy, jet-black hair. He resembled the darkly brooding bad-boy actor Robert Mitchum, only he was much broader and thicker than Mitchum. Shaking his hand was enough to unsettle you.

But the son, Jack Whalen, said little. He mostly paced about, grim-faced, as his dad finally said, no — he didn't know much about the trio who had come down to kill him and certainly wouldn't testify against them.

O'Mara didn't argue. He understood the code among thieves. Plus, Freddie could hardly get on the witness stand and explain what he was doing in a Fresno hospital in a white coat and stethoscope. They parted with an agreement, then. If unsavory visitors tried that again, Freddie would let his new friend on the Gangster Squad know. Freddie wouldn't have to worry about going to court. Sergeant J. J. O'Mara would take 'em up into the hills for a chat.

CHAPTER 9
A BUG IN MICKEY'S TV

The Gangster Squad finally was given an office, albeit a cubbyhole in the ancient Central Station, which still had horse stalls from the 1800s and a circular turnaround where the old horse-drawn Paddy wagons had been pivoted about. When they got the go-ahead to get a secretary, she was picked carefully — Sally Scott had top security clearance during the war, when she worked for the Navy in Washington. She helped Keeler transfer data from their breast-pocket notebooks to five-by-seven cards. She took out mail subscriptions to newspapers from around the country so she could clip any articles about the hoodlums and file them in a small cabinet next to their spittoon. They still received their paychecks as if they were in their old jobs, but they had a place now, complete with a hat rack by the door.

Their greater reward was the knowledge they were getting to Mickey — the bug in his home made that clear. The day after their limo roust on Wilshire, his henchman Neddie Herbert was overheard saying, "I can't meet you at the Mocambo, I'm afraid they'll pick me up." At 3:30 A.M., Neddie rushed into Mickey's bedroom to update him, "Somebody else got picked up. Jesus Christ. I'm getting out of this. I want to live to be a grandfather."

"They can't make anybody leave town," Mickey insisted. "It's against the Constitution."

Later he was overheard grumbling that some LAPD officers were harassing customers at his haberdashery, sometimes smearing their new clothes with red chalk. "For god's sake, some of these guys got on $200 suits," Mickey said. "It's ridiculous — anybody they see leave the store they take right downtown."

Another of his crew was overheard wondering whether Willie Burns was campaigning to be "the next Mayor of Hollywood."

So the Gangster Squad could take pleasure in getting Mickey's goat. But it couldn't take credit for the eavesdropping that proved it — or be blamed when that turned into a fiasco. The bug in question had been planted by a Vice crew back when the squad was getting organized, right at the time Mickey's rising fortunes enabled him to buy and renovate a ranch home in Brentwood, an upscale suburb he assumed was outside Los Angeles' borders. It wasn't — Brentwood was part of the city — and the Vice detectives posed as construction workers on a rainy day, when the real ones took off, putting on hardhats and work boots and nonchalantly going in and out of the torn-apart house. They hid their microphone between the fireplace and wood box in Mickey's living room then ran a thin wire under the lawn to a telephone pole and from there to a listening station. The bug was set to go by the time Mickey and Lavonne Cohen moved to 513 Moreno Avenue with their dog Tuffy, a Boston bull terrier.

It was a wonderful coup, but for one mistake, the Vice team's use of a private electronics expert. Russ Mason was paid for helping them get the bug going, and he expected to be hired to monitor the wire, also. When he wasn't given that job, he secretly ran a second line to his own listening post, setting the stage for the eventual public disclosure of 126 pages of notes chronicling conversations overheard in Mickey's home.

But that scandal came later. For a year, from April 13, 1947 to April 28, 1948, the bug by the wood box gave a group of LAPD officers a pretty good idea of what Mickey was up to.

He was up to a lot, whether plotting to fix a prizefight being staged for charity, lamenting that "We need a shotgun in this outfit" or gossiping with the boys about an old friend back in Cleveland who bought an estate for

$120,000 and had "gone for society — maids, butlers, cooks, chauffeurs." The year's worth of conversations also made it clear where Mickey was doing most of his business, namely in the nearby city of Burbank and in unincorporated portions of the county, the Sheriff's turf. Perhaps the LAPD once was the logical place for racketeers to secure protection for gambling, but not now. In Burbank, Mickey built a full casino on the Dincara Stock Farm, out past Warner Bros. studios. He and his boys occasionally rode horses out there in full western regalia, and put their first craps table in a shed used by stable hands. Before long they had four craps tables, five for blackjack, three for *chemin de fer*, and slot machines, as well. The gamblers were offered free drinks and grub — turkeys and ham — served by Filipino house boys. Mickey thought it was a scream, the film crowd they drew, "there'd be guys in Indian suits or dressed up like cowboys, or girls dressed up like doing a dance. They'd just come over from the set."

One of Mickey's pals laid out the potential take from the casino, "if that joint can go for 90 days, it'll be worth over half a million." They did have to worry about occasional raids by the Los Angeles County District Attorney's Office, but not by Burbank police — the chief there, Elmer Adams, earned $8,500 a year yet was able to buy a 56-foot yacht largely with cash. Adams once received $100 from a bookie in the mail while attending an FBI training program outside Washington, D.C. He enjoyed his suits from Mickey's store and dinners at Mickey's house.

But Los Angeles police could not gloat too easily about the comical level of corruption in Burbank and on the county's turf — a retired LAPD captain, Jack Dineen, was running Mickey's ranch casino. And Mickey griped about how L.A. cops kept hitting him up to buy tickets to their annual show, a fundraiser featuring professional talent like the young song-and-dancer Sammy Davis Jr. Mickey calculated that he had forked over $1,600 for all those damn tickets.

Los Angeles had a bona fide gangster on its hands. The Mickey Cohen overheard by that bug was more than a pint-sized peacock putting on his own show by leading a procession of Cadillacs about town. Yet it wasn't easy to get the goods on him, for he'd be puffing one day about having books at five racetracks doing $8,000 to $15,000 in business, then remark, "I haven't booked a horse in four years . . . Hooky is leaving Cleveland tonight. He is bringing me $45,000 so I can finish this house." One reassuring visitor was Allen Smiley, the man on the other end of the sofa the night Bugsy was killed. Smiley marveled at how Mickey stood up to all the setbacks, the headache moments. "Some men are born to have ulcers," Smiley told him, "and some men are born to give ulcers." Everyone in the room knew which one Mickey was born to be.

Thank goodness for Lavonne Cohen. She would be up waiting when Mickey got home at 3:00 A.M., put out coffee and pie for the fellas and entertain them by showing all the tricks Tuffy could do. She was training their birds to talk, too. The Cohens' marble-topped coffee table always had a vase full of flowers and she kept two dozen crystal containers of scents and potions on the mirrored vanity in her boudoir. So what if she chided Mickey about the phone bills that ran to $300 on a month when he was laying off bets for that guy in Florida? She could cook "in t'ree languages," Mickey boasted, "Jewish, Italian, and Irish."

They met in 1940 at a party at Billy Gray's Band Box, a club that drew a lot of comedians in the Fairfax District, an area populated with Jews moving up from Boyle Heights. But Lavonne was not of the tribe — she was a twenty-three-year-old Irish Catholic who wore her red hair primly up, worked as a dance instructor at the studios, had an aviator's license, and golfed. She was anything but a gun moll, another way Mickey was *evolving* himself. She was "a lady from her toes to her head," Mickey noted. "You could take her anywhere." That didn't mean he always took her out on the town, of course, for the trade-off was the usual one in such marriages — she could help herself to the cash he kept in the dresser but she wouldn't ask about other women who might have been at his table on any particular night.

The gangster squad often had a car outside the Cohen house in those days. Mickey was understandably suspicious of any cops — "Who's behind you?" he'd ask — but he generally was a good sport about their surveillance. Lavonne once sent out chocolate cake to two of the guys in the unmarked car. On one hot day the Cohens' faithful maid, Willa, came out and asked if they wanted a beer. Hell yeah, they did.

But Willie Burns, Jack O'Mara, and the rest only learned of the Vice bug with the rest of the public, when the scandal broke — such were the turf wars and secrets and tensions within a police department. Mickey himself apparently had sensed what was up because he could be heard warning callers, "these phones are no good, so take it easy." Or sometimes he turned the radio way up when he was having a conversation. Later on Mickey said, "I knew all the time the cops had a bug in my rug. I gave them fine music, nothing but the best Bach and Beethoven."

His gardener discovered the wire outside

while digging up fence posts. Mickey then had his property swept by his own electronics expert, 304-pound J. Arthur Vaus, who used a metal detector and current sensor to find the bug by the wood box. Still, Mickey kept quiet about it until the *Los Angeles Times* and *San Francisco Chronicle* published pages of purported transcripts under headlines that blared, COHEN'S BIG DEALS or more stingingly, COPS HAVE BEEN SITTING ON THE DATA.

While Mickey's own words drew much of the focus, so did the fact that the LAPD had overheard them and done nothing, or so it seemed. An angry county prosecutor said he had never been informed of the bugging and given a chance to determine if a criminal case could be made from the overheard nuggets — that outburst became, D.A. BLASTS/COP COVERUP/ON COHEN. To City Councilman Ernest Debs, it smacked of a return to the crooked old days in L.A. when the Vice Squads might get the goods on criminals merely to extort payoffs. "They must have gotten the information to shake down Mickey Cohen," the councilman said. A grand jury called in every Vice officer who had monitored the bug amid reports that their transcripts were for sale along the Sunset Strip — you could enter Mickey Cohen's inner sanctum for $2,500! It was one giant nightmare for the LAPD.

Luckily it was not hard to determine how the bugged conversations had gotten out to the world. The "transcripts" really weren't, they were notes the private investigator had taken on the sly after being stiffed by the Vice boys. When Russ Mason was confronted, he tried the equivalent of a first grader's "the-dog-ate-my-homework" — he said a mysterious fire had destroyed his backyard shed with all his records. The private eye clung to that story for about fifteen minutes before he confessed. The lesson was: Never trust an outsider to do your dirty work.

That's why the Gangster Squad had its own bug man.

"They say Native Californians all come from Iowa," observes the doomed main character in 1944's *Double Indemnity*, and Con Keeler was the embodiment of that, the closest thing the squad had to a purebred Angeleno. His American Gothic grandparents had come from Iowa in a Conestoga wagon in the 1800s and helped established alfalfa and long-staple cotton farming in California's Palo Verde Valley until Colorado River flooding washed out the ranches — the Hoover Dam had not yet been built to help control the darn river. The family moved in toward Los Angeles and Con's father became a cabinet maker and carpenter, being good with his hands. The red-haired Con was too, even as a child, building shortwave radios in his room and tinkering with any piece of machinery he could find.

He was a rawboned six-foot-one-inch by the time he joined the LAPD shortly before the war. When they gave the physical tests at the Academy the instructor couldn't believe his score on the hand-gripper and made him squeeze a second time. "What have you done for a living?" the instructor asked. "Well, I've been a mechanic," Con said, and the guy nodded, "That explains it." He paired the strength of the Iowa farm boy with a touch of the Freemason's moralizing, not hiding his disdain for the old-timers who had been taking gratuities for years. To Keeler, the highest compliment you could pay a man, or a cop, was to say, "He's down the line," and those old-timers weren't. Earning $170 a month as a rookie, he was assigned to traffic investigations to start, even as word spread of his other skills. But his country called and Keeler enlisted in the Army Air Corps with no ambition of being a hotshot pilot — all he wanted was to get his hands on the engines of the B-24 bombers being developed. He was about to head overseas, to Europe, when he got a near fatal lesson in the politics of bureaucracies.

We were shipping out and standing for the train for New York, and I got called out,

138

to report to medics. They told me I had hemorrhoids which I didn't have. But someone had marked it down in a page when they checked you over. The doctor checks you and a sleepy soldier marks it down and he put the check in the wrong place. So I knew a captain and went to see him. He said, "Don't you have an infected toe or something they can work on? You know officers don't make mistakes." And so anyway they rolled me into this operating room, fiddling around, give me a spinal and everything else. And they had to chase the two carpenters out, they were sanding the floors. It looked like a fog in there and of course it was an operating room so there were all kinds of germs and infection set in — they had to burn me with silver nitrates four or five times — and I became a casualty.

Con Keeler spent months in the hospital and once, after his fever spiked, they wheeled him into the Dark Room, where hopeless cases were left overnight to die. "I fooled 'em," he said, but the tragedy of medical errors left him hobbled, needing the iron brace on his leg. He didn't complain — he was a company man to the core — but it was one miracle he made it through the war and a second that the LAPD took him back, on limited duty, once again on the boring TI unit — traffic investigation — until Willie Burns phoned one night.

Keeler couldn't run like O'Mara and the others but he could cobble together crude bugs using telephone and hearing aid parts. He also knew a select circle of sound and electrical engineers working on new eavesdropping technology, including guys in Naval Intelligence and the Office of Strategic Services (OSS), the predecessor of the CIA. They were developing systems for overseas spying that did not use long, telltale wires. That was crucial, given that Mickey Cohen and his crew would be looking for suspicious wires.

The Gangster Squad was going to bug him again, whatever the Vice screw-up.

In the new system, a small microphone was connected to a transmitter that sent a signal over the air, which a receiver could pick up a couple of blocks away, like a radio broadcast. The major downside was that you had to hide a six-pack of batteries with the transmitter to power it, and those batteries died out — you had to keep replacing them. But the first challenge was planting the gear.

By the time they tried it, Mickey's home had become a fortress with round-the-clock guards, swinging searchlights and an armored front door with a porthole window. Their solution? Stage a diversion. The squad waited for a night when both Mickey and Lavonne went out, and then had Jumbo and rotund Archie Case start digging in a vacant lot nearby, as noisily as possible. As expected, Mickey's guards moved their way to check out the commotion. That was Keeler's opening to sneak through the lawn of the home behind Mickey's, climb a chain-link fence and creep through a backyard orange grove. He had burlap over his shoes for silence and ammonia sprinkled on his clothes to drive off the dogs. Mickey had two now, the pampered Tuffy and Mike, a boxer.

There was a crawl space under the house but wood splinters were everywhere. Keeler carefully avoided those, brushed aside the cobwebs and made his way around the huge hot water tank that enabled Mickey to wash his hands a zillion times a day. While Mickey's guards watched the diggers, shining flashlights at the pair over the shrubbery, Keeler worked on the padlocked vent under Mickey's personal wing of the house. The lock was surprisingly simple to pick — Keeler was in, near where Mickey could sleep away from his wife or hold meetings not appropriate for Lavonne's flowery living room. Keeler hid his microphone inside the cedar-lined closet where Mickey kept dozens of pairs of shoes and used a cabinet in it to conceal the two feet of wire leading down to the transmitter and batteries affixed beneath the house. The batteries would last only ten days, at most, when Keeler would have to sneak back under the house to replace them. But that was next week's problem.

He crept back out amid the cobwebs and splinters and back through the dark orchard, finally reaching the safety of the adjoining block. The squad had discovered that one resident was a doctor who had been a major in British intelligence during the war. After a little vet-to-vet sweet talk, the Englishman agreed to let them use his garage as a listening post, and even put a small antenna on the roof.

Hunched around a headset, Keeler and several others soon were hearing the yapping of Tuffy and Mike, the dogs. Then they heard friendly banter among Mickey's dinner crowd, back from the night out. A half dozen companions came home with the Cohens, including Florabel Muir, the *Mirror* columnist who had gotten so quickly to Bugsy's death scene and since then had been giving his successor a lot of ink. She kept telling Lavonne how nice her house looked. It was meaningless suck-up jibber-jabber, but their primitive radio bug worked perfectly, at least until something new arrived at Mickey's home, putting the entire operation in peril.

At a time when barely 10 million Americans owned televisions, Mickey had to have the fanciest, sold by the W & J Sloane department store. Set in a mahogany cabinet, it had forty-five tubes to guarantee clear reception. Only Mickey's reception wasn't clear. The bug overheard him ranting about the screwy lines on Channel 2. Listening from the English doctor's garage, the squad guessed what was up — their transmission was too close to the lowest frequency picked up by a TV: Channel 2. Mickey was sure to figure it out too. The first thing in the morning, he raised hell with W & J. Sloane, "Take this god-damn thing out of here or come out and have somebody fix it!" The store said it would send a repairman over.

O'Mara took it from there. Fortunately, the batteries on their shoe-closet bug were about to run down, deactivating that troublemaker. Why not intercept the TV repairman's truck on the way to Mickey's house and try something else?

> Followed him five or six blocks, pulled him over, talked to him. And I convinced him he should contribute something. He was scared shitless, but he agreed. "I'd like you to take a man," I said.

The repairman would take a member of the Gangster Squad, to be exact, but wearing a repairman's uniform. Mickey wanted service? He'd get two men fiddling in back of his beautiful mahogany TV cabinet. While there, they installed another bug, "right in the damn TV," using a frequency that (they prayed) would not put annoying oscillations on Channel 2.

"It's fine now, thank you guys," a delighted Mickey said, giving the pair a $50 tip to split.

"Mr. Cohen, you're so kind," the pretend repairman said. "Look-it, I'll be back in here once a week and take care of it, check it personally. There's a lot of bugs in televisions and stuff you have to work out."

Mickey had to think his lavish tips were why the repairman was that eager to get back into his TV every week. He couldn't have known that was the timetable for replacing certain batteries. OK, so the bug couldn't hear much when the TV was on, and it was on all the time. Mickey and his wife invited all their friends over to see their marvelous set with forty-five tubes.

But O'Mara sensed that their mission might be measured by small victories. And it was a small victory, for sure, to be able to tell a tale, a half century later, that ended, ". . . *and that's how Mickey Cohen wound up paying for his own bugging.*"

CHAPTER 10
L.A.'s YEAR IN THE GUTTER

The Gangster Squad's own fiasco involved
the Black Dahlia murder and set the stage
for the year when Los Angeles and its police
department were dragged down, down, down
into the muck, all but obliterating the opti-
mism and positive images of the post-war
years. Mickey Cohen was in the middle of
most everything then, driving the descent
even as he began dodging bullets, not always
successfully. But first came the disastrous
Dahlia sideshow, for which he bore no blame.

"I've got to go," O'Mara announced to his
wife on December 28, 1948, three days after
Christmas and two days before her birthday.

"When will you be back?" Connie asked.

"I don't know."

O'Mara did not want to tell her the case on
which he was going undercover — the slaughter of Elizabeth Short, the twenty-two-year-
old whose nude body had been found in a
vacant lot, surgically cut in half, drained of

blood, and mutilated. Though the body had been discovered on January 15, 1947, nearly two years before, the unsolved crime remained a preoccupation of the city. The Dahlia often was described as a wannabe actress who fell into the party scene in L.A. but she had spent much of her time in California around military bases, looking for a boyfriend or husband. She was a high school dropout from a small city outside Boston who plugged her decayed teeth with wax — another wandering soul denied a happy ending in the City of Angels and denied justice, as well.

Now the Los Angeles Police psychiatrist thought he had a hot lead — he just didn't want to give it to the Homicide detectives who had been flailing on the case from the start and still were monitoring the crazies it attracted, fifty of whom had confessed to killing the dark-haired woman with the alluring nickname. Dr. J. Paul de River thought his suspect was not a crazy. The doctor had been exchanging letters with a Florida man who had read about the crime in the detective magazines and was fascinated by sexual "psychopathia." The man knew a lot about the dismemberment, too much, the doctor thought. Plus he had lived in California at the time, working as a motel bellhop. Chief C. B. Horrall was sold. His deputy, Joe Reed, suggested using the squad and one sergeant in particular. O'Mara could forget about Mickey Cohen for a moment.

His mission was to pose as the psychiatrist's chauffeur after they lured twenty-seven-year-old Leslie Dillon from Miami with promises that he might serve as the doc's assistant. O'Mara drove the pair to a remote tourist camp then stayed in the next room, listening with the door cracked, his gun at the ready, as they discussed sex with the dead and how you bleed a corpse. Meanwhile other squad members worked up hundreds of pages of background on the man Chief Horrall agreed was "the best suspect we have ever had." O'Mara welcomed 1949 still at the lodge, the psychiatrist encouraging Leslie Dillon to explain how a painting of the Madonna reminded him of the Dahlia.

The doctor was questioning him on New Year's Eve and I was in the next adjoining room in the dark. I know this sounds kind of silly, but he had an awful look on his face just like he was going to pounce on the doctor.

But the former bellhop never did pounce. So they drove him to a vacant lot in Leimert Park. "Do you recall now this was where the body was found?" de River asked.

"What body do you mean?"

"You know what body I mean."

147

After a week of that, they dropped the ruse and officially seized this Dillon. The law required them to book him right then, but they didn't — they held him in the Strand Hotel downtown where Lieutenant Willie Burns took over the questioning and threatened to send the man to the gas chamber for what he'd done.

The squad members were never sure how Dillon slipped his HELP ME note out the window while being guarded by two of the bruisers, but he did. He used a picture postcard of their first bucolic tourist camp to scrawl a message pleading for a lawyer to rescue him from the crazed Dahlia investigators. It was discovered in the gutter near the hotel by a deliveryman for the *Los Angeles Herald-Express*. The bizarre card carrying a one-cent stamp wound up in the hands of Agness Underwood, the paper's city editor, who promptly called police headquarters to find out what in God's name this was about before she unleashed the headlines.

O'Mara and the others huddled in a panic when called before a grand jury to explain what had transpired with the sex nut from Florida. "Jeez, we kidnapped him!" exclaimed Giacopuzzi, who helped guard Dillon at the hotel. Now the man was free and heading back east, already plotting his lawsuit seeking $100,000 from each officer responsible for him being "nationally degraded by said incompetent agents of the city."

"They had me about convinced that I was crazy," Dillon said before he reunited with his wife and young daughter. "That maybe I did kill the Dahlia and just forgot."

They could handle his lawsuit, but were they the crazy ones for still thinking he might have done it? O'Mara was in that trance when he told the grand jury,

This man was inhuman . . . To my observation he's an individual that I have never seen the likes of before, and probably will never see again, if I may say so. He was — his facial expression would change and his temperaments would change very quickly and suddenly . . . There was something about the man, what you might call raises a man's animal instincts that there is something there, in other words makes the hair on the back of your neck bristle up.

One of the grand jurors asked, "Wasn't the man a frail, weakly, sloop-shouldered man, wearing glasses?"

It was another mind game they would never win. O'Mara said back, "These recollections can play awfully funny tricks with you."

Some called this period of bullets and blackmail the "Sunset Strip Wars" but a war normally has bullets going both ways — you don't have one side doing all the shooting (or garroting) while the other is merely ducking, disappearing, and dying.

The bloodshed was previewed the summer before, on August 18, 1948, when a man in a cream-colored Panama hat fired a shotgun into the new store Mickey was opening right on the Sunset Strip, moving up from the one where the Gangster Squad had staged its fake drive-by. This gunman was not faking. The double-barrel blast killed Hooky Rothman, Mickey's henchman, who had bashed a chair atop one of the Shaman brothers back in '45. Many suspected at first that Mickey had set up his man because of how he retreated into the bathroom moments before the shooting — not everyone understood Mickey's compulsion to wash his hands after taking a call, what with the germs you get from touching a phone. His large curving desk had three phones, a lot for a humble shopkeeper, beneath a portrait of the late President Franklin Delano Roosevelt.

Mickey's new place, "Michael's Exclusive Haberdashery," was in a two-story building on a slope at 8804 Sunset. The upper level abutted the busy boulevard so customers could wander in to peruse imported gabardine suits and camel-haired coats displayed in vault-like closets with sliding doors and walnut walls. The lower level was the office where Mickey's men gathered to conduct their real business late into the night, coming and going through a separate entrance on the side street, Palm Avenue, the route used by the killer and two associates. The carnage would have been worse if not for Jimmy Rist. Many of Mickey's crew were not much bigger than he was, swaggering little men, but Rist was a heavyweight, 295 pounds. He managed to grab the barrel of one shotgun and wrest it away, despite being wounded in his right ear. The assailants fled before they realized that the corpse on the sidewalk was not Mickey — he was on the bathroom floor with his foot braced against the door. "It sounded like the war broke out," Mickey said, so to that extent the "Sunset Strip Wars" descriptor made sense. But Mickey himself had it as, "The Battle of Sunset Strip."

His flight to the lavatory was enough for police to hold him, at least briefly, on suspicion. Little notice was given to the man who left the haberdashery moments before the shooting. Aladena "Jimmy the Weasel" Fratianno had come by with his wife, Jewel, and their daughter to pick up tickets for the hit show imported from Broadway, *Annie Get Your Gun*, which was running at Philharmonic Auditorium. Mickey had boasted, "I can get all the free tickets I want," and Jimmy the Weasel took him up on it. That was his cover story for coming over — he was eager to see the musical that had the great Mary Martin as Annie Oakley singing "You Can't Get a Man with a Gun."

Jimmy Fratianno had been born in Italy but moved as an infant to Cleveland, where he picked up his nickname by running away from a neighborhood kid after squashing a tomato in his face. He was not long out of prison for armed robbery when he headed west, he later explained, because, "They didn't have nobody to kill people."

While The Weasel dutifully attended Mickey's Sunday bagel brunches, he had a different sort of bond with Johnny Rosselli, for ages the main emissary between Chicago and Jack Dragna. Within weeks of the Gangster Squad's limo roust on Wilshire Boulevard, which rounded him up and five others, Fratianno had been beckoned by Rosselli to a winery south of downtown where a revolver and dagger were waiting on a long wooden table. Amid the pungent smell of fermented grapes, Jack Dragna personally presided over the ceremony where they pricked his finger to draw blood, said a few words in Sicilian, and everyone kissed his cheek. It was an induction they did not announce to the society pages . . . and of which the public still had not a clue, just as Mickey and his men had not a clue that Fratianno had given his other friends a signal as he left the haberdashery. If Mickey's crew recognized the man in the cream-colored Panama who blew Hooky's face off, they weren't saying. "He had a hat and a gun, that's all I know," one testified at the inquest.

But Mickey had a strong suspicion that the shooting stemmed from how he had stepped up after Bugsy got knocked in. "People like Jack Dragna kept feeling that their prestige was badly shaken," he figured later. To him, that's what it was about, recognition, even if the old-school Dragna had no interest in the public variety. They couldn't have been more opposite in that regard. Two decades had passed since the émigré from Corleone to Los Angeles had lent his name to the city's Italian-American banquet and he had learned the wisdom of staying as far in the background as possible. Dragna's office was a concrete-walled room behind a small grocery, not a haberdashery that sold gift suspenders and smoking jackets on the famous Sunset Strip, a place where the nightclubs and restaurants shot searchlight beams towards the heavens each evening. Mickey flew toward those lights.

That was not the sole appeal of the Strip to someone in the rackets. That stretch of the affluent Westside was like an island in the middle of Los Angeles, for it was in the heart of the city yet unincorporated county land, making it the domain of sheriff's officials more tolerant (for a cut) of gambling and other pleasures-for-a-price. On paper, the

Strip was not subject to the jurisdiction of the Los Angeles police. On paper, not in practice.

A month after the shooting at the haberdashery, a Gangster Squad car just happened to be driving by a club on Sunset as the manager of Mickey's store, Mike Howard, was walking out. The usual roust was from a car — get out, empty your pockets, hands on the hood, spread 'em — but you could do it on a sidewalk too. When the squad's imposing Giacopuzzi-Greeley duo patted down the store manager they found a snub-nosed .38 he had no license to carry. The former Meyer Horowitz was the oldest of Mickey's crew, at fifty-four, and a veteran of the actual clothing business, a real rag man. Mickey didn't want him rotting in a cell for thirty days.

"They should be looking for Hooky's killers instead of harassing us," Mickey griped. "They're setting us up as clay pigeons. We got no way to protect ourselves. And he's no ex-convict — he went through bankruptcy just like any other high-class citizen."

The next month, Lieutenant Willie Burns showed up at the haberdashery and gave Mickey himself the treatment, the grounds being his role in the beating of a card player. Mickey had $3,011.20 in his pockets when Burns made him empty them, holding true to a childhood resolution to keep an impressive roll. Mickey said his mother beat the crap out of him when he was twelve after he hung his pants on a chair and $300 to $400 fell out — she figured he'd robbed a bank. He still favored a roll with the largest dominations on the outside but now insisted on crisp, clean ones. He swore that waiters deliberately gave him change using the dirtiest bills they could find, knowing he'd leave them all as a tip rather than put that filth back in his pocket. Such were the mind games played on the famous Sunset Strip.

The best way to avoid blackmail is to not give ammunition to those who would blackmail you. The columnist Florabel Muir saw it as the most dangerous growth industry around town now that new methods of tapping phones and bugging rooms were available to private eyes of dubious ethics. They would feed dirt about the rich and celebrated to the scandal sheets, which then would offer to withhold the titillating expose for a fee. "Should a man of importance make the mistake of talking too freely to his light o' love over the phone," Florabel noted, "he's liable to find a gent at the back door with a recording and demands for a payoff." But the blackmail game could be played at a high level too, with a whole police department or a city, if they foolishly handed the ammunition to the wrong enemy. In Los Angeles, that appeared to be the personal mission of some of the Vice detectives who accounted for 150 of the LAPD's 4,300 sworn officers.

Sergeant Elmer V. Jackson had been lauded for bravery when a young man with a machine gun approached the driver-side window of his parked car and said, "This is a holdup, give it to me." Jackson pretended to reach for his wallet but got his revolver instead and shot dead Roy "Peewee" Lewis, twenty-three, whose machine gun turned out to have been stolen from the San Francisco armory. It was classic heroism, except for the minor wrinkle of the redhead seated beside Sergeant Jackson in the parked car. She was not an Administrative Vice clerical worker, as he listed her on the incident report. She was Hollywood's leading madam. A scarlet lie like that might be kept secret for months, or a year but not forever — the relationship between the Vice sergeant and madam Brenda Allen would have one of those Sunset Strip spotlights shined on it when Mickey went on his crusade against the Los Angeles Police Department in 1949.

What set him off first was an incident not much different than the Gangster Squad's rousts. That January 15, a group of LAPD Vice cops including the heroic Sergeant Jackson followed a pair of Cadillacs leaving Mickey's store and stopped them on the sheriff's turf, then arrested one of the drivers, charging Harold "Happy" Meltzer with having an unlicensed gun by the car's front seat. A New Jersey native with 26 entries on his rap sheet, Happy ran the jewelry shop adjoining Mickey's haberdashery, he was part of the crew. From his cell at the police lockup, he complained that the gun was a plant but didn't make a fuss, joking that in addition to peddling watches he was "sort of a professional gambler, but not a very successful one." Mickey was in no joking mood, however, not with one man dead, gun charges against two of his earners and the city coming down on him even when he tried to do good, for once, by helping a poor widow.

That was in the case of Alfred Pearson, operator of the Sky Pilot Radio Shop. Person had become a reviled figure about town due to his attempt to foreclose on the home of sixty-three-year-old Elsie Phillips over an unpaid bill for $8.95. An enraged LAPD captain assigned to the city's Police Commission got into a running feud with the greedy (and litigious) repairman and lined up a lawyer to plead the widow's case. The next day, Mickey's heavyweight henchman Jimmy Rist and several others paid the radio shop a visit posing as magazine reporters eager to hear the repairman's side of the story. "When Pearson invited the four men behind a partition . . . without any warning, they beat him about the head and body with a gun, clubs, iron rods, and other heavy objects," a subsequent court ruling summarized the action, failing to mention only the riding crop the crew used. "Pearson's arm was broken and his head cut in five places. They tore telephones from the wall and . . . made their escape in an automobile, which was double-parked in front of the store."

The vigilante justice might have worked had the escapees not made an illegal U-turn. A patrol car with two rookie officers witnessed the traffic violation and gave chase, then called for backup as a pair of vehicles sped away while the passengers tossed tire irons and other incriminating weapons out the windows. Though a police captain may have initiated the campaign on behalf of the widow Phillips, the ferocity of the beating forced authorities to bring assault and conspiracy charges against Mickey and his men, quickly dubbed "Snow White and the Seven Dwarfs," Mickey being the symbol of purity. It cost him serious dough, though — $50,000 bond for some of his crew, $25,000 for others, $100,000 for himself. Mickey may not have finished grade school but he asked a very smart question after that, "Why didn't somebody just pay the goddamn radio bill?"

He was boiling angry by the time his jewelry man "Happy" Meltzer came to trial on May 5, 1949, for violating the state's deadly weapons act in the Cadillac. Mickey arrived at the Hall of Justice with a secret weapon, J. Arthur Vaus, the 304-pound electronics expert who had helped him find the Vice bug in his wood box. On this day, Vaus carried a machine to play back wire recordings and ceremoniously placed it on the defense table before taking a seat next to Mickey in the front row of the courtroom.

Their attack was launched right in opening statements by the defense lawyer Mickey had lined up for Happy, Sam Rummel. He alleged that the gun-in-the-Caddy case was part of an eighteen-month effort by the LAPD's central Administrative Vice unit to shake down the esteemed Mr. Cohen. Why did its leaders arrest his flunky, not Mickey? Rummel answered, "They did not want to kill the goose they hoped was going to lay the golden egg."

In the days following, the lawyer and Mickey himself accused Sergeant E. V. Jackson and his boss Lieutenant Rudy Wellpott of trying to squeeze up to $20,000 in bribes from Mickey in return for a halt to the constant harassment. But why stop with them? Mickey said some of the payments they solicited were touted to him as political contributions — to Mayor Fletcher Bowron! It was quite a leap to accuse the gray-suited former jurist who used his radio speeches to promote the image of a booming and clean Los Angeles. Bowron at the moment was running for reelection, still warning about the insidious influence of "Eastern gangsters, big-time racketeers." But the sixty-one-year-old reform mayor was just another phony by Mickey's account, a crook like all the rest. He was going to bring everyone down to his level. They were freeloaders too, those cops — Mickey recounted how he often picked up their checks at places like the Brown Derby and Slapsy Maxie's, the Wilshire Boulevard nightspot fronted by Maxie Rosenbloom, the hulking former prizefighter who often played punch-drunk types in the movies.

That still was merely an appetizer for Mickey's main course, the explosive ammunition he had kept warming in the oven — details of how the red-haired madam had been paying off the same crooked cops. Mickey claimed to have recordings to prove it, made at her *hilltop house of joy* above the Sunset Strip, where else? That's why his man had brought the playback machine. "When the jury hears these," Mickey said, "it will blow this case right out of court."

The judge finally said, stop, *no more.* "Happy" Meltzer was on trial for having a gun he claimed was planted. That was the issue for the jury, not whether bribes (or mayor contributions) were solicited or whether the madam and the sergeant engaged in after-hours hanky-panky. But so much mud had been thrown some had to stick. Indeed, some

160

deserved to stick — when the Vice sergeant was questioned on the stand, he admitted allowing Mickey to pay for eats and drinks for him and his lieutenant.

Did you ever dine with Mickey Cohen?

Oh no, I have never eaten at the same table with him.

When you and Wellpott ate at Dave's Blue Room with your friends, did you pay the check?

I didn't pay the check. I don't know who did.

Ever eat at the Piccadilly?

Yes, I have eaten there with others.

Did you pick up the check?

No, I don't know who did.

Now how about the House of Murphy?

Well, uh — yes. I was there with another officer and a lady friend. Cohen and a party were at another table . . . When I asked for the bill, I was told Cohen had paid it.

After all that, the hung jury was inevitable. In the spirit of the times, the twelve men and women couldn't decide who was telling the truth, if anyone, in the city going down, down, down.

The grand jury investigation was a natural, particularly into whether the Vice cops' relationship with the madam had been adequately investigated by police higher-ups after she was in the sergeant's car the night he'd shot the robber named Peewee. It hadn't been. Chief Horrall could offer only a lame excuse for not getting to the bottom of the matter — he was too busy with his ceremonial duties, meeting with civic organizations. It was true that the bulbous-nosed chief napped more than ever on the cot in his office while his assistant, Joe Reed, largely ran the LAPD. But it was a sad scene when a haggard Chief Horrall came out of the grand jury room and pulled back the lapel on his coat to show his badge, trying to signal that he was still in charge. Mayor Bowron looked more chipper when he was called before the grand jury, fresh off re-election to another term — voters for some reason were not swayed by Mickey Cohen's assertion that he was a crook.

One star witness, predictably, was the madam Brenda Allen, born Marie Mitchell. Wearing heavy makeup on her face, the thirty-six-year-old redhead spoke in a slight Southern accent as she told the grand jurors that, yes, she was paying off Sergeant Elmer V. Jackson, $50 per week, per girl — but she began paying *more* to a Hollywood Vice cop after she discovered him parked outside her place in his car, wearing headphones. Then there was her complaint about other cops she let in free to the parties in her parlor where her real customers cavorted with her girls.

Her gripe with them? Those freeloading cops ate the nuts off the top of her pecan pie.

She instantly became another Los Angeles celebrity, the Hollywood Madam. Convicted on morals charges twenty-one times over the years, she said any talk of her having 114 girls was wildly inflated. But when Municipal Judge Joseph Call got a look at the black box with cards listing her clients he didn't buy that she was small-time. "In this box are the names of dignitaries of the stage and screen and executives of responsible positions in many great industries," the judge said while putting the box under lock and seal. Of course, that provided great fodder for the madam's lawyer, Max Solomon, who from then on would playfully threaten prosecutors, judges, and fellow attorneys that he had kept a copy of her version of the little black book. "I see you're in there," he would tell them, "as a 'bad lay.' "

Not that many years had passed since Mayor Bowron had gone on the radio to speechify, "There is no widespread commercialized gambling or vice in Los Angeles, no payoff. It is the cleanest large city in America."

The gangster squad was not immune from the mud throwing that sordid year. Their accuser was the second Vice cop the Madam herself had accused of taking bribes. At that time based in Hollywood but now drummed off the force, Sergeant Charles Stoker went wild unleashing his own allegations before the grand jury, to the *Los Angeles Daily News* (BIG EXPOSÉ TELLS VICE, POLICE LINK) and finally in a book filled with astonishing accounts of *mobster coppers* within the LAPD, a breathless tale of conspiracies around every corner. Did the public know the real reason Mayor Bowron tried to put the lid on gambling in L.A.? Not honest reform — the mayor was being bribed $250,000 by Nevada interests so Los Angeles gamblers would have to travel there! And Mickey? Los Angeles police needed a whipping boy. "Mickey Cohen is it," Stoker said.

As for the Gangster Squad, "I defy anyone to go back over the record and show me a single instance in which Lt. Willie Burns arrested one important gangster in which the gangster in question was convicted," he said. "It is well known that police officers under Lt. Burns were frequenters of Mickey Cohen's cocktail bar on Santa Monica Boulevard, where they sat hour after hour in a room drinking Mickey Cohen's whiskey . . . Why does Mayor Fletcher E. Bowron continuously bleat about the threatened invasion of eastern gangsters? . . . If the eastern gangsters came here, there wouldn't be room for the crooked cops — they'd have to go east!!"

The Gangster Squad knew this Stoker all too well. Once when a couple of the men were seeking out Hollywood bookies to determine if they might become informants, Stoker got wind of what they were doing and fed them a hot tip about dangerous hoodlums holed up in the Valley. Willie Burns instructed Con Keeler and his partner to go out there with their Tommy gun, to Keeler's eventual frustration:

Winter, real cold, supposed to be a big gambling deal going on. And we got to this address and watched the place and finally a lady came on the back porch and hung out some diapers. No cars, no activity. So we finally go back to the Hollywood station and Burns is there too. So Burns says to Stoker, "What was the address?" Stoker couldn't remember the address he'd given. He was trying to keep us busy and keep us out of Hollywood. Burns wanted to punch him out but I said, "Listen fella, if you ever send us out on a wild goose chase like that again I'm gonna go up on Hollywood Boulevard and book the ass of several of your bookmakers and tell 'em you sent me. Get it?"

By the standards by which Con Keeler measured his world, Sergeant Charles Stoker was not a down-the-line cop. But by the chaotic standards of 1949 Los Angeles, his ranting, like Mickey's, was the stuff of headlines.

Amid the snowballing scandals, Keeler got the job of visiting Big Jim Vaus, the private bug man now living on Mickey's dime. Vaus never did play his recordings for the grand jury, either — just as he was scheduled to bring them in he announced that six spools of wire recordings had been stolen from the trunk of his car. Then he said they were buried in his yard. If 1949 was the year a gigantic circus tent enveloped the city, the blubbery bug man was poised for his moment in center ring. The son of a minister, Vaus was having second thoughts about selling his soul to . . . well, one person's whipping boy was another's devil. The epiphany came to Vaus during a visit to a real tent, part of the canvas cathedral crusade of the sensational young evangelist Billy Graham. Big Jim Vaus found his way back to Jesus there and dedicated his life to repent — and perhaps someday save the soul of the man the Chicago mob boys called "the Little Jew." First, Mickey's private bug man admitted he had lied about what was on his recordings and went to jail for perjury.

But the bug man's repentance came too late for Chief C. B. Horrall. In Florabel Muir's words, "The county grand jury handed out spades and shovels and went to digging up dirt on a lot of badge wearers from the chief on down." Largely a figurehead now, the chief said screw it and on June 28, 1949, retired to the pigs and cows on his five acres in the Valley. Mickey Cohen could gloat that he'd taken down the city's top cop and gloat he did, when he wasn't dodging bullets again. The year was only half done.

The shooting up of Mickey's car likely would have become public knowledge eventually, but O'Mara credited the Secret Service Fund with bringing the incident to light almost right away. From the squad's first days, the fund was among its most important tools, up there with the Tommies. They had $25,000 at their disposal to pay informants — it often took more than Irish charm to get people to tell you things. Soon after the farcical Happy Meltzer trial, Jack O'Mara got a tip from one of the characters on his dole.

One of those funny deals, a guy was playing baseball out in the Valley and he knew somebody who knew somebody, a guy who worked in a body shop, who said a Cadillac had come in with a windshield blown out. So I got checking into it and found out it was Mickey's. At that time his guy Neddie Herbert was living in an apartment out there and Mickey parked his car and took Neddie

Herbert's Cadillac. Then they switched the plates. But Mickey's Caddy was in the garage, all shot up, his windshield and side window. He'd never reported it and when we got to him he denied the whole deal, you know?

Later in life, Mickey didn't deny it — he was rightly proud of his coolness under fire when his car was blasted. Just as he pulled it into his Brentwood driveway, gunmen started shooting from across the street. He ducked below window-level and floored the accelerator, going backwards out the driveway, and sped off virtually blind up the street. "The minute I sensed what was happening I fell to the floor and drove that goddamned car . . . all the way down to Wilshire with one hand. That's about a mile . . . With all the shooting, I only got hit with the flying glass." When Mickey finally returned home, bleeding and disheveled, he greeted his evening's startled guests, including actor George Raft, Bugsy's childhood friend. Mickey said he told 'em, "Don't worry what happened. Let's sit down and have dinner," so they did, including an apple pie made special for the movie tough guy Mr. Raft.

But guns fired continually in your direction are not likely to miss forever. Any doubt that Mickey was a target evaporated that July 20, when he was shot in the shoulder outside

Sherry's cafe on Sunset. The 3:45 A.M. shotgun blasts from across the street fatally wounded Neddie Herbert, the crew member who had been overheard by the wood pile bug worrying about living to be a grandpa — he wouldn't. Neddie fell under the front awning of the Sunset Strip hotspot, just feet from his Caddy waiting at the curb. The shooting also sent two women to the hospital. Dalonne "Dee" David was described in one of the papers merely as "a blonde," but was amplified in others as a "screen extra." She also could have been billed as "clothespin heiress," for her daddy had a factory that made them in Burbank. Someone commented that it was tragic when a girl aimed to get into the movies and wound up in the newsreels instead. The other woman shot was Florabel Muir, who took a pellet in her hindquarter. The intrepid columnist said she had been hanging by Mickey merely to get a story, "waiting for someone to try to kill him."

The final entry on the list of wounded was the oddest, an enormous special agent from the state Attorney General's Office named Harry Cooper who called out "I'm hit" when shot twice in the abdomen. He was an ex-wrestler and looked the part, towering a foot over Mickey. The state's agent was wearing a light double-breasted suit and two-tone shoes just like The Mick — they'd made for a comical sight earlier in the evening when they walked side-by-side out of the Continental Café, a pair matched in clothing and nothing else. California Attorney General Fred Howser scrambled to explain that he had assigned the giant agent to shadow Mickey because any citizen deserved protection when endangered — and also to encourage local police to stop harassing Mickey. Nonetheless, sheriff's deputies were all around the Strip, as usual, and the crowd at Sherry's included an LAPD sergeant as well, from the Detective Bureau headed by Thad Brown. He was still furious that the Gangster Squad had been brought in to work his Homicide crew's Black Dahlia case and he retaliated by anointing a few of his men as his personal gangster squad, a little up-yours to Willie Burns. There was a lot of competition to get in on the Mickey Cohen business.

Mickey had started the deadly night by having dinner with Artie Samish, a bald, cigar-chomping lobbyist with a seventh-grade education who had become the prime fixer for the state's railroad, racetrack, and liquor interests. Boasting that he could sense whether a legislator needed a baked potato, a girl, or money, the 300-pound Samish controlled a $153,000 slush fund provided by the California Brewers Institute, prompting the state's governor to concede, "On matters that concern his clients, Artie unquestionably has more power." After their dinner with the well-funded power broker, Mickey led his entourage to the Continental, of which he owned a piece, and then to Sherry's. That place was run by a former New York City policeman, Barney Ruditsky, who personally cased the parking lot and street whenever Mickey was coming, which meant nearly every night. On this night Mickey bantered with several reporters about the scent of the gardenias in his yard and about *Annie Get Your Gun*, which had just opened in a new location, the outdoor Greek Theater. Asked by the *Los Angeles Times'* Ed Meagher if he was reluctant to be out in public, Mickey said, "Not as long as you people are around." But the *Times'* man left with his photographer before the 3:30 A.M. closing time, leaving Florabel as Mickey's only media shield as the party walked out the door.

The club owner, Ruditsky, heard seven shotgun blasts from across the street, from next to a building owned by singer Bing Crosby. "I think it was a 12-gauge shotgun," Ruditsky said, "and they plugged them pretty good."

Jack O'Mara was among the swarm of investigators soon looking for discarded weapons and other evidence. He concluded that the gunmen indeed had waited across Sunset, by Bing's building, at cement steps leading down to a vacant lot. Coffee and pastries were left at the spot from which the gunmen had a perfect view of anyone exiting from Sherry's into its floodlit entrance area. The shotgun blast got Mickey solidly in the right shoulder, but he never went down. "I didn't want to get my suit dirty," he said.

For O'Mara and the others, it was not a fun moment to be a cop. They had botched the Dahlia thing and now shotguns were blasting up Sunset. They were pretty sure who was behind this shooting, the low-profile Mr. Dragna, but what were the odds of the Sicilian's crew, like the man they called "The Weasel," ever cracking? Meanwhile the disgraced former Hollywood Vice sergeant was running around calling them crooks — and worse. Sergeant Charles Stoker had his own theory of who carried out the ambush at Sherry's, "members of the Los Angeles Police Department, whose motive was to seal Cohen's lips."

Mickey knew better. "It's local punks," he said when he was able to hold court in his blue pajamas and slippers at Queen of Angels Hospital. "I talked to New York, Chicago, and Cleveland regular and I got no rumble of trouble there. I am a pretty well informed guy."

There was no doubting it then, he was L.A.'s GANGSTER. He posed at home for the national magazines showing off his closet full of suits and his miniature bed for Tuffy, so what if one piece in *Life* was headlined

TROUBLE IN LOS ANGELES. He had begun his hustling by selling newspapers as a six-year-old and he was selling them still. One of California's leading intellectuals, Carey McWilliams, did Mickey the honor of an analysis, albeit comparing him to Fitzgerald's Great Gatsby. "He has tried to acquire the airs and manners of a gentleman in an effort to erase the memory of those sordid days before he had acquired his present eminence," McWilliams wrote. "In fact if there were any evidence Cohen could read, one might suspect that he had consciously modeled his career after Gatsby's."

One paper's approach was not as high-brow or wry, though it did enlist a Ph.D. to interpret Mickey's handprint. Dr. Josef Ranald pointed to Mickey's short stubby fingers and said, "the type of hand is predominantly elementary and belongs to the simplest and least cultivated persons."

On July 29, 1949, Mayor Bowron again went on the radio to address the city. The day before, the grand jury had indicted the Ad Vice pair, Jackson and Wellpott, and three of the top figures in the LAPD, including the already retired Chief Horrall and Assistant Chief Reed, accusing the administrators of perjury — the grand jurors simply did not believe their accounts of what they knew about the Hollywood madam and their Vice

173

Squad. Almost as soon as the indictments were handed up, Mickey rubbed it in, "I bet the police are sorry they ever stepped out of city territory."

"That has the familiar ring of the underworld, one who thinks of retaliation," Mayor Bowron replied in his address to the city. "Well, Mickey, I have never met you. You have never picked up a check for me and I have never received a suit or other present from your so-called haberdashery. And you never will — and I never will."

Bowron could argue that the indictments covered five men out of thousands on the LAPD, and he could (correctly) predict that the cases against them would collapse, depending as they did on the testimony of a madam, a raving ex-Vice cop and a bug man who'd just found the Lord. But that sounded like weaseling to a public that could not be blamed if it now viewed L.A.'s cops as no better that the Sheriff's brazen grafters or than the LAPD of the tainted '30s. A decade of image building had been for naught.

Look magazine told its national audience,

Cohen's escapades provide overwhelming evidence that all too many of California's sworn law-enforcement officers have crossed the line and become partners in the lush profits of bookmaking, the shakedown racket, the narcotics trade, the slot-machine business, and that of the madams, the muggers and the murders who follow . . . The ugly glaring fact remains that California's law-enforcement agencies, from top to bottom, have proved worse than helpless in protecting the state against its great post-war wave of hoodlumism. By their internal squabbles, by peddling protection, by playing footsie with open and acknowledged criminals, they have encouraged and participated in the growth of the greatest little racket empire west of the Mississippi.

Dragna and his men may have been firing the weapons, but Mickey Cohen was doing far more damage to the city. Mayor Bowron allowed himself to use a little Wild West rhetoric in addressing the man directly over the radio.

"I give you full warning," the mayor said. "You have not intimidated me or the Los Angeles Police Department. We are coming after you."

CHAPTER 11
THE FUNERAL WREATH

Five hundred people attended Neddie Herbert's funeral in New York that had a casket adorned with a horseshoe-shaped arrangement of gardenias from someone in Los Angeles.

Lieutenant Willie Burns lived in Gardena, a small city in southern Los Angeles County built atop what once were strawberry fields. When his wife received a funeral wreath at home, the squad knew that the same someone had sent them, Mickey Cohen.

After two decades on the police force, Burns had been proud to be able to buy the small house (963-square-feet) on little more than a tenth of an acre. It had three bedrooms and one bath for him and his wife, their son, Richard, who dreamed of becoming a fireman, and their daughter, Patty, the teenager with polio and rheumatoid arthritis. The diseases cost her the use of one hand and most of a leg, but she liked to draw and paint and showed talent at both. Her parents had resolved to raise her as a normal child and they were.

Willie's wife saw the delivery truck and they were able to track down the florist. He said a kid had come in off the street with cash and asked that the funeral flowers be sent to the Gardena address. They guessed the kid had been paid $10 to place the order by someone he'd never met.

Burns phoned Mickey and told him to get his ass, pronto, to the Hollywood Plaza Hotel, near Hollywood and Vine. Burns grabbed O'Mara, Keeler, Jumbo, and another of the bruisers and said, "I'm gonna knock his balls through his fucking nose." They took their Tommy guns and left in one car, packed together like the early days.

The squad had carried the Tommies from day one but never fired them at anybody. Keeler had come the closest, the time Al Capone's youngest brother Matty showed up at the Biltmore, the same hotel where Al was given the heave-ho two decades earlier by Rough-house Brown. While O'Mara and another sergeant monitored the lobby, Keeler picked the lock on the 11th floor suite with Archie Case at his side. Keeler recalled their close call:

Anyway, I went up there to the room to check for weapons and everything else. We searched the whole place and then Arch and I stayed upstairs, waiting for them to come back. I had my Tommy gun, so I stood in this little kitchenette facing the doorway, there was semi-darkness. One of us heard a key, Archie's standing in the living room with his .38 and this guy walks in and Arch says, "Come in brother, come in boys, we're police officers." The first guy, his hands are clear. The second guy walks in, and he's got his hand in his coat pocket. Well, shoot. So I tell him to get his hands out of his pocket and he jerks his hand out and boy, for a minute there that looked like a .38, believe me. I squeezed down that Tommy gun and it was a full automatic and I never did figure out why it didn't go off. I just stopped it before it went, I guess. Man alive, I tell ya. I never did figure out how I didn't kill that guy. Boy, he steps back and says, "I was just reaching for a cigar!" Archie tells him to go ahead. He points at me, but when you have a Tommy gun you don't say anything. He reaches in his fingertips and pulls out a cigar, holds it up to show it to me, and backs off. They really respect those Tommy guns, believe me.

Jack O'Mara had to move his Tommy when he and Connie finally had their daughter. When he first got back from the service, they had rented the garden apartment in Leimert

Park, near Connie's sister and across from the church. But that was a trying time for reasons beyond the job, Connie's miscarriages. The fun-loving bobby-soxer bride often cried herself to sleep while suffering through one lost pregnancy after another. She was a good Catholic girl — why was God punishing her? It took seven wrenching years before a pregnancy did not end in miscarriage, and when God blessed them with little Maureen they followed the trodden path toward the American Dream. They could have been one of the hordes of start-up families shown in *Life* magazine heading outward from the urban centers to brand new cookie-cutter homes with postage-stamp lawns in suburbia — their three-bedroom ranch model on Pedley Drive in Alhambra was among 500 built atop a onetime country club and polo field. Streets nearby were named Pine Valley and Siwanoy after posh golf clubs back east that no one moving in had heard of. As soon as the houses went up, a Catholic church did too, and Jack again was anointed head usher, being a natural to entrust with the collections every Sunday.

Connie was in bliss as a housewife and mother, delighted to iron the boxer shorts of her policeman husband while the black cat, Spooky, kept her company. She made homemade jam from peaches, apricots, and plums grown there in the San Gabriel Valley where you could see snow atop the mountains when it was 80 degrees on the flats. When Christmas approached, she made candied kumquats and German-style fruitcakes and cookies, too, tons of gumdrop ones, fig bars, and sugar Santas. She gave boxes of those to the priests and nuns and set aside others for members of Jack's old high school fraternity, who each year came to visit. She did fret the holiday season when Jack had to go undercover on the Dahlia case, unable to call for days. But that homecoming was gloriously tearful as Connie hoisted their baby girl into the air and cooed "My Heart Belongs to Daddy," the Cole Porter song that was finally hers to sing.

The problem was the big gun in the violin case. Once little Maureen was old enough to crawl they could turn around for a moment and she'd be gone, scurrying to their room — a couple of times she made her way under their bed and began playing with the case. "Get it out of there," Connie said, and Jack said, "Yes, boss," and up it went onto a shelf in the closet.

Like the others, O'Mara sometimes practiced shooting the Tommy at the Police Academy range in Elysian Park. The public assumed the sprawling Academy complex was run by the LAPD administration but it wasn't. It had been built by the rank-and-file's Los Angeles Police and Athletic Revolver

Club after the shooting events of the 1932 Olympics were held in the hilly 575-acre park on the edge of downtown. Volunteer officers moved and reassembled part of the Olympic Village to serve as a clubhouse and added an ornate rock garden and waterfall and eventually a swimming pool, so you could drop your kids off and meet your buddies at the café or the pistol range. Even experts with other weapons found the Thompson submachine gun hard to master. One newer squad member, John Olsen, was an avid hunter who boasted, "I could hit a rabbit on the run with a shotgun and take the head off so I wouldn't ruin the meat." But he gripped the Tommy too tightly and it jerked up on him. "We learned that if you left 'em lying loose you could fire 'em more accurately. If you tightened up on the suckers, they'd ride right up over your head."

It was a coup when the squad got another new member who could really teach them how to use those things, Dick Williams. He was the son of Benny Williams, their leather helmet footballer who in the '30s had helped build the Academy on his days off. Benny was getting up in years and he lost it one shift when he heard through a callbox that his boy, then new to the force, was being shot at during a foot pursuit. Benny rushed to the scene and helped handcuff the gunman on the ground. Then he yelled "LET'S KILL THIS

181

SON OF A BITCH!" and he might have if commanders had not driven up. The good news was that they had a readymade replacement when Benny retired. His son had joined the LAPD fresh from service as an elite Army Ranger in the Pacific — Dick Williams and his fellow Rangers snuck ashore behind enemy lines in the Philippines before the mass landings by General MacArthur's troops. The six-foot-three Williams later provided jungle warfare training to Marine snipers, including a lanky actor-to-be, Lee Marvin. So Benny Williams' son was an expert with a Tommy gun and more. "He didn't talk about it much but he was in a part of the service where he had to go around killing people," big Lindo Giacopuzzi said. "Oh, yeah, he knew how to take care of himself. He could break your neck in a minute, Williams could."

Dick Williams was the fourth man Willie Burns asked to drive with him to the Hollywood Plaza Hotel to talk with Mickey Cohen about those flowers. You did not mess with a policeman's family.

Usually they kept the Tommies in their trunks when they drove. This time O'Mara carried his under his gray overcoat as they headed to Hollywood. Mickey was waiting on the sidewalk, giving a "Who me?" look, his blue Cadillac with whitewall tires at the curb, his men watching by the other Caddies.

Burns stepped up to Mickey, face-to-face and said, "Have I ever lied to you?"

"No, lieutenant."

"Well, I am going to tell you something. I know what all of you look like. I know what your cars look like. If I ever see or hear of one of them driving by any of our officers' homes, I'm gonna come pick you up . . ."

"Jeez, I don't know where my boys go."

". . . and we're gonna have the damndest accident."

With that, O'Mara and Keeler pushed up the bottom of their overcoats using the Tommy guns underneath, so the tips poked out. The two towering squad members, Jumbo Kennard and Dick William, flanked them.

"That'd be murder," Mickey said.

"No, no. Just like you, self-defense."

Mickey got the message. The public would never understand how different he was when alone with them, out of the spotlight.

After they got back to their office, O'Mara rushed home and pretended he'd left something there. He wanted to see if Connie had gotten flowers, or seen any Cadillacs on their street. O'Mara didn't know about the others, but that was the moment the job changed for him, the moment Mickey became his obsession. It was like his old boxing matches behind the frat house or his footraces at the

Academy — it was you and the other guy finding out who was the better man. There was just a bit more at stake now. He resolved to prove that Mickey Cohen, that strutting little showboat, was a killer.

Willie Burns would not be by his side. To start the recovery from the Vice scandal and the resignation of Chief Horrall, the mayor persuaded a spit-and-polish former Marine Corps general, William A. Worton, to come up from his retirement home down the California coast and serve as interim chief. General Worton's mandate was to make changes in the LAPD, and quickly.

A decade earlier it was notable when the city got a police chief who had graduated from any college. This new guy, Worton, had diplomas from both Harvard and Boston University Law School, and those were his least impressive credentials. He had joined the Marines a week before America's entry into World War I and fought on the Western Front in France, where he was wounded and gassed. In the mid-'30s, while Los Angeles authorities were masterminding their embarrassing Bum Blockade of California's borders, Worton was risking his life again, going undercover in Shanghai and pretending to be a disgruntled former Marine looking to start a new life as a businessman. In reality, he was trying to recruit spies against Japan, his secret mission for the Office of Naval Intelligence. Worton carried three passports and met many of his contacts in bars. In an oral history of the Shanghai operation, he was not idealistic about why people helped him — it often was money. "He was a man looking for a dollar," Worton said of one prime espionage recruit. He laughed at Hollywood's image of spying, offering an assessment that could apply as easily to certain law enforcement assignments, "This type of duty is not glorious. It is a lonesome, frustrating, and hazardous occupation."

During World War II, as a Marine Corps general, Worton merely helped command the III Amphibious Corps in the Battle of Okinawa, then assisted with the occupation of northern China. The case could be made that he was slumming by taking the interim chief's job in Los Angeles. After a little time in town he said, "I can't trust a soul in the whole department."

But there was one crew he wanted close by. Perhaps it was because Worton had worked in a thankless covert operation himself, or perhaps he thought that any group considered enemy by Mickey Cohen must be OK — he decided that the Gangster Squad should be at his side. The catch was that he wanted someone more like himself, more executive, to lead them. Captain Lynn White had been a lieutenant commander in the Navy and was a prodigy in the LAPD, already directing narcotics units on his way to becoming a deputy chief before he was forty. Worton reasoned that the squad, like a military operation, needed to get more serious about the intelligence portion of its mission — it was time for an administrator who was not so eager to be the front man of a flying squadron that left troublemakers strewn on a hillside. Effective October 7, 1949, Lieutenant Willie Burns was reassigned to uniform duty as a watch commander in the University Division.

General Worton put Captain Lynn White and the men in the office right next to his, in his suite on the first floor of City Hall. The Marine general did insist on a new name, one not so crude. The original members could still call themselves the Gangster Squad, sure, and they would. But on paper, for the moment, they would be Administrative Intelligence.

They had begun three years earlier working out of two rusted cars and then out of a cubbyhole in a station house with a turnaround for horse wagons. Now they were at the seat of power with windows over a patio. It was perfect. At night they could step out the windows and across a stretch of concrete right down to Spring Street — they could come and go from City Hall without anyone seeing them, as if they were invisible. O'Mara said:

We loved ole Lynn White, he was a helluva of a policeman, you know, so we behaved ourselves. But about our third meeting with him and the new chief we figure "What the hell?" What we do, someone gets ole Lynn's overcoat and the secretary does a little sewing, takes about two minutes. Then at the meeting someone picks up the coat and shows the General the label under the collar and he says, "What's this?" Lynn White, he takes back his coat and he says, "What the . . . ?" You see, we put a little label in there that said, MICHAEL'S, from Mickey Cohen's store, you know?

Someone had to spoil it by laughing after about ten seconds, but we sure had 'em going there awhile.

CHAPTER 12
FLORABEL TO THE RESCUE

Now they had to do something about the troublemaking woman who dared to ask, "What does a Gangster Squad do?"

Florabel Muir was a child of the Wild West, born in 1889 in a Wyoming mining town, Rock Springs, where she witnessed a shoot-out while clinging to her mother's skirt. "I had gunpowder with my porridge," was how she put it. After she conned her way into her first newspaper job in Salt Lake City she petitioned to attend an execution despite a law that counted only male witnesses. "She's no lady, she's a reporter" the Utah attorney general ruled. As a crime reporter in New York her claim to fame was speeding from Sing Sing to the *Daily News* in 1928 with the film that a colleague had used in a camera strapped to his leg to snap a shot of murderess Ruth Snyder in the electric chair. The "Spider Woman" housewife had enlisted a weak-willed lover to kill her husband for the insurance money, a scenario that inspired the

1944 movie *Double Indemnity*, in which Barbara Stanwyck seduces Fred MacMurray into doing the deed. The real-life Ruth Snyder became the first woman sent to any prison's hot seat, lending instant fame to the photograph Florabel helped sneak from Sing Sing.

By the time she switched coasts, she was the epitome of the hard-boiled newspaper dame, serving up a mixture of Hollywood scandal and gangster gossip while mocking, all too often, the LAPD. When her daily columns weren't calling them *Cops à la Keystone*, a favorite topic of ridicule was their pursuit of the undersized hoodlum who spawned oversized headlines.

If Mickey Cohen is breaking the laws, why not arrest him and charge him with such violations instead of handing out all this hot air?

Los Angeles is the third largest city in the country and it's high time the police department was growing up with it. The public loses confidence in the boys with badges when arrest after arrest flivvers.

Seems to me they're casting Mickey as a red herring to drag across the scene. He could pull a dirty trick by just disappearing. That would leave them with nobody to blame anything on.

189

Blah, blah, blah. Florabel Muir, at sixty-one, wasn't about to commit a crime or help Mickey heist anyone, they knew that. And a little ribbing was fair play, they dished out plenty themselves. But Los Angeles was embroiled in more than a war fought with shotgun pellets. Mickey attacked with words and Florabel, in their eyes, was his ally. That was far outside the concerns of a street cop like O'Mara, who just wanted to get his man. But image mattered to city fathers. Someone above their heads was always saying, "This doesn't look good."

So it was after their ill-fated attempt to prove that the sex-obsessed nobody from Miami had killed the Black Dahlia.

One guy came out of the recent Black Dahlia debacle with a reward of some kind. Willie Burns of the L.A. Police Gangster Squad took a trip to Florida to interview the wife of Leslie Dillon who was sprung as a suspect before Burns arrived in Miami. Probably Willie's trip to the Atlantic coast won't be entirely a waste of money for the taxpayers. He might turn up some gangsters who are contemplating a trip to California.

In posing that question, "What does a Gangster Squad do?" Florabel answered on her daily soapbox:

Looks like they devote part of their time to trailing Mickey around. But they don't seem to be stopping Mickey from doing whatever it is he is doing that they don't like. He keeps on doing it and they keep on rousting him . . .

Gangster Squads running around playing cops and robbers is not the way to cope with organized crime.

The capper for the brass came after the ambush at Sherry's, when the *Mirror* columnist saw fit to repeat the theory that even Mickey had discredited, that Los Angeles cops might be behind it. The LAPD. Them.

The most unfortunate aspect of this whole thing is the fixed idea that a lot of people have that it was police who were shooting at Mickey. Many people have remarked that to me.

It should be inconceivable to any right-minded person that police officers could bring themselves to shoot into a crowd of people just to get a man they didn't like.

That was Florabel. Blah, blah, blah. She'd never let up.

No one could have guessed that she would help save the squad when the LAPD got its permanent new chief in the summer of 1950, yet another child of the Wild West and the man who would help revolutionize police work in the United States.

No police chief ever had a more appropriately named birthplace than William H. Parker. He was born in Lead City, South Dakota, and raised in Deadwood in a family rooted in frontier law enforcement and a stern moral code. His grandfather was a Civil War colonel (on the Union side) who moved out to the Black Hills where he headed a mining camp militia, battled to close brothels, and became a district attorney and U.S. Congressman before dying of cirrhosis of the liver, the drinking man's disease. The grandson Bill Parker won a public speaking award in high school but started his working life humbly as a teenage bellhop and part-time detective at a Deadwood hotel before his mother announced that they were moving, without his father, to Los Angeles. The Parkers arrived in 1922 — the same year the Whalens came west from St. Louis and the O'Maras south from Portland — and settled near Westlake Park. While Fred and Lillian Whalen were stocking their store in that neighborhood with lingerie pilfered from rivals, young Bill Parker took jobs as a movie usher and taxi driver and enrolled in a local law school, at a time they didn't require a college degree. He still needed a paycheck, so before graduating he applied to the LAPD and entered in 1927, a timing that let him witness the department's worst years up close. He learned the need for policemen of good moral fiber to resist the temptations they faced — and for structures that punished those who didn't, at least until God passed final judgment. "Police history is not a pretty thing," he acknowledged. "It does not inspire confidence."

Parker's career was interrupted only by twenty-six months overseas in World War II, during which he was wounded at Normandy and developed the plan for prisons to handle Germans captured in the Allies' invasion. He also helped establish post-war police departments in Munich and Frankfort and was awarded a *Croix de Guerre* by the French government for his work in the liberation of Paris. An organization man in every sense, Parker held leadership posts back home in the Fire and Police Protective League, the American Legion and later the Boy Scouts. If he seemed too perfect, he wasn't — he inherited his granddad's propensity for drinking and with it a nickname, "Whiskey Bill." He was in his second marriage by the time he became chief at forty-five, and childless. Like Mickey Cohen and his wife, the Parkers made do with the company of dogs.

With his elevation to chief, Parker went on the radio on August 9, 1950 and spoke bluntly about the moral challenge in the community and within his own department:

"There are wicked men with evil hearts who sustain themselves by preying upon society. There are men who lack control over their strong passions . . . to control and repress these evil forces, police forces have been established . . . Sometimes wicked men elude the detection devices of the selection process and find their way into police service. Their evil acts, when discovered, cast disrepute upon the entire force."

Chief William H. Parker thus was the great exponent of Internal Affairs, of policing your own tougher than you policed the city. No more beat officers helping themselves to apples from the local grocery, no more free dinners on Sunset, no more Vice cops helping themselves to the local madam. And perhaps no more Gangster Squad.

Jack O'Mara was smoking his pipe, perusing the teletype, when the new boss stopped by. A few others were writing up reports noting which hoodlums they had seen having drinks where, and with whom, the night before. It looked to an outsider like they collected paychecks for sitting on their rears. Con Keeler had worked under Parker before the war and he warned the crew, "He's a very abrupt man. Believe me, you get out of line, you'll get clobbered." Now O'Mara saw Parker looking at them like: What are these idiots doing in my suite? What are they doing with Tommy guns? O'Mara heard the new chief mutter, "What the hell?" and soon after a commander warned him, "He doesn't know what the hell you do. He's going to derail you guys."

Just like that, Parker put the unit under the command of his most trusted aide, tall, stolid Captain James Hamilton, and had him prepare transfer orders for the men, pegging several for traffic duty, AI, Accident Investigation. The prospect was crushing to O'Mara, who had joined the LAPD as a scrappy kid with dreams of rising to chief himself. He'd taken hoods up into the hills, abandoned his wife at Christmas to pose as a crazy shrink's chauffeur and done other dirty work of the Gangster Squad. Now they were going to reward him by having him investigate fender benders. At least he had a little time before his career went in the toilet. He figured he might as well use it to make one last run at Mickey.

O'Mara had sensed an opening when he learned that a guard at Mickey's home had a warrant hanging over him. O'Mara *encouraged* the guard to quit and to suggest that Mickey hire "a buddy" as his replacement. The "buddy" was Neal Hawkins, who had a profile likely to appeal to Brentwood's most notorious citizen. Hawkins was a wiry Brooklyn boy who had come to Los Angeles when the Army assigned him to searchlight duty at the UCLA campus, defending against a Japanese air attack on the U.S. mainland. After that he was trained in munitions and demolition and sent to North Africa and Italy with a platoon assigned to disrupt the enemy by blowing up things like bridges. After the war, Hawkins came back to California as a civilian and went to work as a clerk and gun-toting protector of a liquor store in Santa Monica that did other business on the side — a lot about Hawkins would appeal to Mickey. But he also was a certain cop's paid informant. The Secret Service Fund won you a lot of friends.

Mickey's new guard earned part of his keep the summer of 1950 by patrolling Mickey's property every hour, investigating any noises, and answering the front door so a visitor with bad intentions would get him, not Mickey. Hawkins earned his other pay by alerting Sergeant Jack O'Mara to comings and goings at the house. So he dutifully reported in when he overheard Mickey planning a trip to Texas with, of all people, Florabel Muir's husband, Denny Morrison, a former newspaper copy editor and film publicist. Mickey later insisted that he had hired Morrison merely as a tutor to polish up his dese-dems-dose vocabulary, to *evolve* him some more by teaching him a new word a day, or a new phrase. Mickey once showed off his new knowledge by letting his bodyguard Johnny Stompanato win a game of gin and proudly calling it, "*Noblesse oblige.*" When Johnny offered the straight line, "What's that?" Mickey said, "Something a peasant like you wouldn't understand."

To Jack O'Mara, the fact that Mickey had hired Florabel's husband was confirmation that she was more than his ally. She was his paid mouthpiece. Yet while the LAPD often felt Florabel's bite, Mickey was not immune from a nip, either. The day after both of them were shot outside Sherry's, she wrote, "I would like to say to Mickey, 'Give it all up, my boy. Let those who want your unrealistic little kingdom have it. Pick up your marbles and get lost along the common and ordinary byways.' " But the fact that Florabel might occasionally question Mickey's wisdom hardly explained why her hubby was going to Texas with him, much less another detail about the trip — when O'Mara tailed them to the airport he discovered that they had registered for their flight as "Denny Morrison" and "Denny Morrison Jr."

O'Mara rushed back to their City Hall office and left a note asking the squad's morning lieutenant to cable the Texas Rangers that Mickey was headed their way under that alias. Then O'Mara headed home to bed, not knowing whether the Rangers would do what he'd hoped. They did — the Texas lawmen treated Mickey's arrival as akin to Bonnie and Clyde coming back from the dead. Rangers led by Captain Manuel "Lone Wolf" Gonzaullas just missed Mickey in Odessa, where he was hosted by a prominent Texas gambler. But they caught up with Mickey after the gambler's chauffeur took him to Wichita Falls, near the Red River border with Oklahoma. When the Rangers rousted him at 3 A.M. in a suite at the Kemp Hotel, Mickey protested that he was there on legitimate business, meeting with an oilman about leases on three wells. The Rangers told him to forget it. He needed to pack his bags — and his traveling companion was ordered to do the same. Mickey said the man was his publicity agent.

In Los Angeles, the publisher of the *Mirror*, Virgil Pinkley, was awakened by phone calls asking him why the spouse of his star columnist was consorting out-of-state with Mickey Cohen. But when the publisher called Florabel she denied that her hubby was in Texas. She said, "He's asleep right here — you want me to get him?" That's when Jack O'Mara had his own sleep interrupted by a ringing phone, along with a warning from a lieutenant, "Your ass is in a sling."

They were ready to hang me out to dry. All this is going on deep in the heart of Texas and the publisher Pinkley asks Florabel Muir, "Well, where is your husband?"

He's here.

I guess Pinkley said, "I'll take your word for it," you know? In the meantime, Pinkley got a hold of Chief Parker, "What the hell are you doing to my people?" So they call me up and get me out of bed.

I said, "What the hell you talking about?"

The lieutenant said, "Don't you know? The shit's hitting the fan. Pinkley's on Parker's ass."

I said, "Listen, I know those bastards and I watched 'em get on the plane. You tell Parker that's exactly what happened."

No one could doubt O'Mara's account after the Texas Rangers escorted Mickey and his small entourage onto a flight home and then invited the newshounds in during a stopover in El Paso, where Mickey was fingerprinted, photographed, and all but posed in a corral. The state's governor got into the act, saying, "If you're thinking of coming to Texas, stay out. If you are in Texas, get out."

Florabel tried to be nonchalant about why her husband had gone to Texas with Mickey — she said it was a secret mission to look for one of Mickey's henchmen who had vanished amid the violence on Sunset. The five-foot-four David Ogul and another of the "Seven Dwarfs" had disappeared a month apart and there had been not a trace of them since, other than car keys found in a storm drain. The disappearances were expensive to Mickey — he faced forfeiture of the $50,000 bond he had posted for one and $25,000 for the other — but he didn't pretend that he was searching for either man in the North Texas oil fields. "Dey is dead," Mickey said.

A throng was waiting at the airport in Los Angeles when the American Airlines flight from El Paso touched down on August 31, 1950. Mickey was the last one off the plane, in a gray suit and snap-brim hat but tieless and in need of a shave. "Why all the reception?" he quipped before offering one observation about life in Texas, "Well, the food was good." But the *Los Angeles Times* noticed someone else coming off the plane. He was one of the first passengers out the hatch and disappeared quickly into the crowd. "Denny Morrison, Mickey's traveling companion on the gambler's latest flight into the limelight, gave no evidence of being in the same party."

All that counted to Sergeant Jack O'Mara was the experience of Chief Bill Parker, who was less than one month on the job: First the chief received an effusive call offering thanks from the head of the Texas Rangers. Then came the apology from the publisher of the newspaper that had been clobbering the LAPD for sport. Parker had to attend a policeman's funeral the next morning, but another squad member saw him pull aside his favored aide, Captain Hamilton, for a conference right at the cemetery, in the chief's car.

They would not be disbanding the squad, after all, the one begun in 1946 with eight men who met on street corners. Chief William Parker and Captain James Hamilton did give it yet another name, the Intelligence Division. They ordered those Tommy guns locked in a closet. They moved the crew again — just across the hall.

But under their watch the squad would grow to have 50 investigators determined, like Jack O'Mara, to take down Mickey Cohen.

CHAPTER 13
FIFTY-EIGHT RUBOUTS
AND A WEDDING

Headline writers found an easy nickname for the lowlifes from Kansas City slaughtered the evening of August 6, 1951, "The Two Tonys." Anthony Brancato and Anthony Trombino were shot in the back of their heads and left slumped in their car on a Hollywood street. It made for a grim photo worthy of Chicago of the '20s, the two dead men in the front seat of the sedan with their heads leaning back, blood dripping down their faces, and bullet holes in the windshield.

In the wake of the double hit, the LAPD higher-ups decided to create a list of every local mob rubout of the twentieth century. Titled "Gangland Killings, Los Angeles Area, 1900–1951," the subsequent report went back to when the fruit peddlers fought over downtown turf and the Black Hand shook them down for a cut of the action. Joe Ardizzone predictably was the star of the early years as the gunman identified in the first murder, in 1906, only to be acquitted ("insufficient evidence, no witnesses that would talk") so he could make the list in a different capacity, as a victim, when he vanished after leaving his Sunland vineyard in 1931. No one knew how many people The Iron Man had killed during his quarter-century run.

The LAPD survey concluded that the first murders were tied to "the Italian element . . . Either for intimidation, extortion, revenge or jealousy," while the second phase, during Prohibition, was more purely profit oriented. "The opportunity to 'bootleg' liquor illegally gave this type of person a chance to make fast money in large amounts." The third phase of killings had an obvious theme, the end of Prohibition and rise of illegal gambling. But the study identified another trend at that point — the bid by a certain group to seize a large piece of the action from the established racketeers such as Guy McAfee, the former Vice captain. The report couldn't resist a little hyperventilated narrative in describing the new force muscling in on L.A.'s old guard: "McAfee refused and was reported to ask, 'Who the hell is Jack Dragna?' He found out! Stickup men raided the books; runners were roughed up . . . Soon the Italians were cut in!" More significantly, the report spoke openly of these new powers as "Mafia leaders."

Decades later, thanks to a few key turncoats

and scores of movies, the American public would think nothing of such a reference. But the Mafia was a controversial concept in 1951. As far back as 1928 two dozen Sicilian crime figures had been discovered meeting in Cleveland — New York's Joe Profaci insisted he was there in connection with the olive oil business, never mind that Cleveland did not have an olive oil business. Yet the nation's most prominent law enforcement official remained skeptical of any talk of a Mafia or of organized crime in general. There were plenty of desperadoes and local criminal rings, of course, and his agents helped fight those Public Enemies. But the FBI's J. Edgar Hoover dismissed the notion of a national crime syndicate as *baloney*.

The Los Angeles Police Department did not agree and when U.S. Senator Estes Kefauver decided to investigate organized crime in America he relied heavily on its files — Con Keeler's small notebook by then had grown into elaborate flow charts with tangles of lines connecting each suspected organized crime figure to a dozen or more others. The Tennessee senator's committee did identify one group of witnesses who embraced Hoover's skepticism about the Mafia. The suspected leaders and soldiers of the shadowy crime organization were 100 percent behind the FBI's director. "They were virtually unanimous in their complete ignorance of such a group."

The LAPD's internal "Gangland Killings" study had its own olive oil connection — the body of one bootlegger was found resting on six large cans of it in 1927. "Shot on public street" was the most common circumstance over the five decades of underworld bloodshed, with only one corpse having been "found in reservoir." As for weapons, handguns were favored over "shotgun," "blunt instrument," and garrotes ("strangled"). Among motives, revenge was more common than "strong-arm ('muscle')." One victim drove a Willys-Knight touring car and another a purple Cadillac — that fellow was presumed dead after he vanished and his distinctive Caddy turned up with traces of dirt from the Riverside County oil field. The oil field was being called the "Ganglands Cemetery" to complement "Shotgun Alley" downtown.

But there was one disturbing constant over the first half of the twentieth century — how easy it was to get away with murder in Los Angeles. The study listed 58 gangland slayings over that time. And one conviction. One.

There were a few instances of street justice in which suspects in the killings were felled themselves in the shootouts. But the only conviction in court was for the 1937 murder of George "Les" Bruneman, who fancied himself the rightful czar of Southern California gambling, not Bugsy Siegel or Jack

Dragna. Bruneman had been wounded earlier in a botched ambush and was recovering at Queen of Angels Hospital when he invited his nurse to lunch at The Roost café. Two gunmen came in and finished the job, firing fourteen times at him and also killing a waiter who ran out after them. Two years later, an informant told authorities that one of the killers was Pete Pianezzi, who had done time for bank robbery. Pianezzi expressed astonishment at his arrest and nine of the eleven witnesses to the killing could not identify him. But the wife of the café's owner said she had a perfect view of the two assassins. "They had big guns in each hand. One of them held me hypnotized with his cold, steely eyes — I'll never forget them." The prosecutor asked, "Do you see those eyes in court here today?" She said, "Yes, that's the man," and that was enough for authorities to obtain their lone conviction in fifty-one years.

So what if Pianezzi was the wrong man, bound to be exonerated, a classic victim of unreliable eyewitness identification? That wrinkle would take years to unfold. He was still behind bars when the LAPD surveyed the half-century of killings, enabling it to list that one success among the pages of case studies that reported "no clues" or "two unknown men" or "arrested but later released." It went on that way for pages, one gangland killing after another ending in "No prosecution" or the more optimistic "No prosecution to date." The 1907 New Year's Eve barbershop murder of Giovannino Bentivegna, whose body was found with a crude drawing of a clown and a policeman — the Black Hand's mark of a stool pigeon — was still listed, forty-four years later, as "No prosecution to date."

From the Black Hand days on, there was no overcoming the underworld's intimidating code of silence or the frequent lack of any witnesses at all. That was the case in the survey's first entry of Chief Parker's tenure, the rubout of Mickey Cohen's lawyer Sam Rummel, who had helped rev up the scandals of 1949. He was ambushed while walking from his car to his Laurel Canyon home at 1:00 A.M. on December 11, 1950. The only clue was the sawed-off Remington shotgun left in the "V" of a tree, a weapon that been reported stolen in 1913, making for one more *no prosecution to date.*

It was not hard to identify a motive or a suspect in the 1951 massacre of the Two Tonys. The veteran gunmen from Kansas City had recently raised the ire of the underworld chiefs by robbing the cash room at Bugsy's old Las Vegas palace, the Flamingo. They also sometimes pretended to be collectors for Mickey or Dragna — when they weren't — a practice that placed them "in disfavor of certain persons," a police report noted. They had it coming, in other words.

Hours before they took their last breaths they had been seen meeting with Jimmy Fratianno at the apartment of an actor who made book, on the side, at the studios. That night, Trombino was about to light a cigar in the front of their Oldsmobile, with Brancato beside him, when two gunmen in the back-seat fired seven or eight shots, blowing their brains out. A phone book found in the car had a Biblical message written on the cover, "Jesus is coming so are you ready to meet him . . . ?" The murder scene again was all-too-public, on North Ogden Drive, just off Hollywood Boulevard.

No one had to tell Los Angeles police whom to pick up first. Death followed closely behind Jimmy the Weasel. It wasn't only how he'd left Mickey's haberdashery moments before Hooky Rothman was shot-gunned. Fratianno also had been scheduled to have dinner with one of Mickey's henchman the evening he vanished. That was Frank Niccoli. When Jimmy the Weasel began talking about such matters much, much later in life, he said they'd used the old rope trick on Frankie — one rope twisted about the neck, with two men pulling it tight from the sides — and that the scene was not pretty, "The son-of-a-bitch pissed on my new carpet." But it was hard to make your living only as a killer, so

208

Fratianno traveled down to San Diego and got into the business of selling orange juice to bars — you know, pay me for a lot of juice, or else. The odd thing was, he did act like a weasel whenever the squad rousted him. The squad's Texas shit-kicker, Jumbo Kennard, often got the Fratianno duty and he'd do his bit where he clamped his giant hand atop someone's head to lift them up. Fratianno would go, "Don't hit me! Don't hit me! I got ping-pong balls in my lungs!" That was true, too — doctors had put these little balls in there to keep his lung inflated after a dangerous infection.

Fratianno naturally had an alibi for the night the Two Tonys were blasted — he'd had dinner at the Smoke House in Burbank with Nicola "Nick" Licata then spent the rest of the evening at a party at Nick's own joint in that city, the Five O'Clock Club. Licata was a grandfatherly looking former Detroit bootlegger who answered only to Jack Dragna in the L.A. mob. He dutifully backed Fratianno's account, as did eleven others rounded up in the wake of the killings. Everyone backed The Weasel's alibi. The cops tried to get a clerk at Schwab's drugstore to say that a stogie found at the murder scene was a brand Fratianno favored, but she said, no, that was too cheap, a three-for-a-dollar smoke. Jimmy the Weasel was an 80-cent cigar man. A waitress at the Five O'Clock

Club complained that two LAPD detectives burned her with a cigarette to get her to admit that Fratianno had snuck out of the festivities there. But she didn't budge and backed his alibi too. The double murder of the Two Tonys was destined to become yet another "No prosecution to date."

What you had to do, in Jack O'Mara's job, was settle for whatever victories you could manufacture. That's why he volunteered to help with the Licata end of the Two Tonys investigation. He didn't expect a miracle — a mob boss would never finger a loyal trigger-man. But you tried anyway, you moved your feet. "I said, 'I know Nick. I'll go out.' "

O'Mara had gotten to know the local Mafia's number two man by schmoozing at his club, even once accepting a fifth a whiskey from the proper Sicilian who kept a handkerchief carefully folded in his breast pocket. Accepting the booze was against O'Mara nature, but he felt he couldn't refuse the gift. The whole idea that night was to make like they were pals and keep Licata hanging around — long enough for Keeler to plant a couple of bugs at his home on Overland Avenue in the Palms neighborhood, towards the airport.

When O'Mara showed up at the house after the Two Tonys bought it, Nick Licata offered a "How are ya?" in his heavily accented

English before their pro forma Q&A.

You have any guns?

Yeah, O'Mara, I got guns.

You have any shotguns?

Yeah I got shotguns?

You keep 'em for your protection, huh?

Yeah, I keep 'em for my protection . . .

O'Mara and his partner loaded the weapons into their trunk and waited for Licata to get his coat, keeping it nice and friendly.

After the Two Tonys hit, all the suspects and alibi witnesses were taken to a secret interrogation center the LAPD set up on the third floor of the Ambassador Hotel, away from police stations where the press would be swarming. The questioning was handled above O'Mara's rank, with Captain Hamilton earning the privilege of interrogating Jimmy the Weasel. But the next day O'Mara got a call from Licata's twenty-year-old son, Carlo, complaining that the family had been unable to find his father. "Can I go see my papa?" he asked, and O'Mara arranged it, still being their best buddy, because *down the line* . . .

Down the line came the next time he showed up at the Licata home as part of another roundup of suspects for a crime that would never be solved. By then he was like family, the kindly cop, so the elder Licata asked one more favor in his heavily accented English, "Look, Mr. O'Mara, my wife she's a-fixin' me a nice chicken dinner. Before I go downtown . . ."

O'Mara said, "Hey, Nick, go ahead and eat. I'm in no hurry. You mind if I use your phone?"

The phone had a long cord, 50 feet or more, so Licata could carry it into his private office. O'Mara carted it instead into the kitchen. Then he began to rummage, "looking for anything I could steal." That's how he stumbled upon paperwork from the wedding. Licata's son had married the daughter of Black Bill Tocco, a Detroit Mafia boss who lived among the swells in Grosse Pointe, Michigan, in a mansion with an eighty-foot pool. The year earlier, Tocco's son had wed the daughter of New York's Joe Profaci — he was going coast-to-coast with these family unions. Under normal etiquette, the bride's side sent out the invites, but the Licatas had sent out a batch too, personally alerting their circle of friends to the glorious occasion. All the RSVPs and congratulations and flower cards had come back to the home on Overland Avenue where Jack O'Mara gave Nick

212

Licata plenty of time to enjoy his wife's chicken dinner.

So anyhow, I got the phone and I'm watching him from the kitchen and I'm pulling out drawers, you know, taking the wedding invitations, and I shove them in my trench coat, you know. I'm bulging with all these RSVPs, all the goddamn Mafia in the country, see. Actually, I committed a burglary, right, technically? After all, I'm not allowed to steal a guy's property out of his house. But I figured I was housekeeping . . .

Call it theft, call it housekeeping. O'Mara wouldn't argue. Other law enforcement agencies had to settle for camping outside the big wedding in Detroit with cameras and binoculars, trying to identify the hundreds of guests coming and going from limos. In Los Angeles, the Gangster Squad didn't have to rely on fuzzy photos to add names to files that now filled ten cabinets along a wall in City Hall.

Small victories, that was their reality. Like how they finally got to Dragna, by bugging his mistress's bed.

Chapter 14
The Bedbug

Dealing with Jack Ignatius Dragna from the start was the flip side of dealing with Mickey. Dragna once complained to Jimmy the Weasel that it was so hard to kill Mickey because of all the cops and reporters around him. Dragna desired the company of neither. Icy distance was the rule when the Gangster Squad camped outside his banana warehouse or the Victory Market, where he held meetings in a concrete-walled back room.

There was a shabby boarding house across from his warehouse on the south edge of downtown, just off Central Avenue, so the squad rented a second floor room there and pointed an 8mm movie camera out the window. It showed who was coming and going from Dragna's Latin Import & Export Co., and that was worth something — they spotted the Sica brothers and some other Italians who long had been with Mickey but now had "gone over to the other side," they concluded. But the pictures were of little use without sound and they couldn't hear much, even after Keeler bugged a telephone pole outside the warehouse. He put a microphone in a hole gouged in the pole, near where Dragna and his crew emerged for walk-and-talks. Any conversations were drowned out, however, by the noise of passing traffic. About the only incriminating evidence they got from their silent movies were shots of policemen arriving empty-handed and then leaving with arms full of the bananas Dragna hauled to Los Angeles. The cops helping themselves to free fruit were surprised with stern lectures only after the surreptitious moviemaking ended.

They fared little better at the market where Dragna had his fortified office. A security guard patrolled there all night, providing little opportunity to break in and plant a bug, much less to conceal it. But why not try? Con Keeler was the man to go in, as usual, while Dick Williams headed a backup team that watched for the guard from their darkened cars. Whenever Keeler was on a black-bag job he wanted the six-foot-three former Army Ranger around, the one who could break someone's neck if he had to.

Dick Williams, he was always my right-hand man when I went on something like that. I had the stakeout crew out front, as much coverage as I could get. Jack

215

Dragna's place, we had to go through Victory Market, through two locks there, and they had a night watchman that came by every twenty minutes and checked the place. We had to put a tail on him and go in between the times he checked the front door — we had to get in and open the lock on this concrete room back there, that's where they had a meeting place. They had a great big safe back there but I wasn't a safe man, there was nothing I could do about that. If I'd known what was in that safe, I'd of figured out some way to steal it.

Nothing's ever perfect, but we got in there and I did get the microphone in, hidden, best I could. Had it there a couple of weeks until they found it. Joe Sica, he comes outside holding the microphone hanging from a wire and he looks up and down the street, he takes that microphone and he bangs it against the curb. I don't know — he kept looking up at me, we had a stakeout on, and he's banging that thing against the curb.

They got us on that one. But after that we tried a little psychology. We had a team following Dragna around — Unland and Roberson, they were a good follow team — and he was going crazy, because he'd meet somebody on the corner or the sidewalk and our car would be across the street, those two officers sitting in it. So to add to his misery, I gave them a set of earphones. We had no bug working, but I said, "Next time you see him in the street talking to somebody, put these on. And when he looks over toward you duck down like you're trying to hide." They did it one day and, damn, Dragna came over shouting and screaming — whoever he was meeting was sure we were listening to them if these cops are wired with headphones.

The two squad members following Dragna had never heard of him when they recruited themselves into the unit from the Central Division. William R. "Billy Dick" Unland and H. E. "Robbie" Roberson were the hottest radio car team in a territory that included Pershing Square and its Biltmore Hotel when their lieutenant was transferred to the squad. "Take us with you," Unland said, and he did. But when told their assignment was the Dragnas, all they could think of was *Dragnet*, the radio show that had come on the air in 1949 with little known actor Jack Webb playing a by-the-book LAPD detective named Joe Friday who spoke clipped lines with a deadpan delivery and lived with his mother. Then Unland realized their assignment had nothing to do with the radio show. "We're working the dagos."

Unland had served with the Navy in the Pacific, set ashore on the Philippines from one of the Landing Craft Tanks, or LCTs, vessels like the one Dragna converted to haul his bananas. When Bill Parker became chief in 1949, he calculated that 3,000 of the LAPD's 4,493 sworn officers had joined since the war, and Unland was among them. He lived in the same suburban housing development as Jack O'Mara and when he joined the Intelligence Division he was asked to drive the sergeant to the office. "Well, I went over and picked him up. I was young at the time and Jack came out, he had a topcoat on and a hat and I think he was sucking on a pipe. I remember he looked so old to me." O'Mara was thirty-two.

The newcomer had a lot to learn. Early on, he and his partner were sent to question Dragna at his home in Leimert Park, near where the Black Dahlia's body was found. The local Mafia boss shooed them away, saying "Get off my porch." When they returned to the office and reported what had happened to Lieutenant Grover "Army" Armstrong, he said "If you guys want to take that shit from that wop, OK," and they got the message. After that, they rousted Dragna like other guys did Mickey, making him empty his pockets five times a day. They also followed him into his favorite barber shop in the Beverly Wilshire hotel and sat waiting while he had his hair trimmed and his nails manicured. When the barber said, "You're next," they replied, "We're not here for a haircut. We're following that asshole."

A few times the squad had its first-generation Italian, Lindo "Jaco" Giacopuzzi, go to Dragna's home in hopes that he or his men might say something revealing in their native language, unaware that Jaco spoke it too. The ploy never worked and Jaco's most vivid memory of the visits was seeing Dragna's wife in the bedroom, patiently ironing his beautiful shirts and arranging them, perfectly folded, on the bed. Frances Dragna was a nice, quiet lady and Jaco wondered, "If she knew he had that girlfriend would she still be ironing his shirts?"

Life magazine would never be invited into Jack Dragna's house to take pictures of his shirts or of his doggie bed, if he had one. Other than with women, Dragna remained cautious to a fault, reflected in his innocuous rap sheet since his short stint in prison thirty-five years earlier — seven arrests, no convictions. He was winning both wars, against Mickey and the squad, until the explosive first weeks of 1950.

Luckily for Mickey, he was on his wife's side of their Brentwood house in the early morning of February 6 when his outside alarm was triggered. He got out of bed and went to a front window, where he detected an acrid odor of something burning, then returned to Lavonne's bedroom near her mirrored boudoir and the walk-in vault that held her fur coats. The bomb went off about 4:15 A.M., blasting a ten-foot hole in the front bedroom where Mickey normally slept, destroying forty of his suits and catapulting one of his bedroom slippers into the yard. The damage would have been far worse but for a thick concrete floor safe, which deflected much of the blast, likely saving the Cohens and their live-in maid. Mickey soon was holding court amid the wreckage in his monogrammed silk pajamas, telling Florabel Muir and others who rushed to the scene how relieved he was to see Tuffy prance out from his little bed. Mickey quipped, "You know, I don't think I'm going to be able to rent this room now."

Yet the bombing could not have been a total surprise to him. Months earlier Mickey had discovered wrapped sticks of dynamite under his home, with a fuse that had been lighted but fizzled. He tried to erect a fence in front of the exposed house, but was told zoning codes limited its height to a puny three-and-a-half feet. He ordered a Cadillac with bulletproof fiberglass panels inside the doors, and windshields three inches thick, but authorities questioned the legality of that too, his custom-made $16,000 armor-plated car. Now the headline read, MICKEY COHEN'S/ HOME BLASTED, one more episode helping to explain his classic exchange when Senator

Estes Kefauver's organized crime committee subpoenaed him to testify.

Question: And you have been surrounded by violence, is that right?

Cohen: What do you mean that I am surrounded by violence? What do you mean that I am surrounded by violence? I have not murdered anybody. All the shooting has been done at me. What do you mean, I am surrounded by violence, because people are shooting at me, that is the way it is? What do you want me to do about it?

The Chairman: Just a minute, Mr. Cohen. Let me put it another way. . . .

Cohen: People are shooting at me, and he is asking me if I am surrounded by violence.

His neighbors didn't really care who was shooting at whom, or who was doing the bombing. The throat of a girl sleeping across the street had nearly been slashed by flying glass. One nearby parent said, "Our children can't ride their bicycles or skate in the streets. Bombs today — it might be machine guns tomorrow." When Mickey heard that some Brentwood residents were petitioning for him to move, he wrote them an open letter, composed with the help of (or entirely by) a writer friend. It said:

On Monday morning, my home was bombed. Though this outrage constituted a great threat to my wife and my neighbors and has deprived me of the sense of security and sanctuary that every man feels when he steps across his home doorstep, it didn't make me nearly as unhappy as the action, today, of some of my neighbors . . . trying to push me out of the community. . . . I took it for granted that if I could expect no breaks from the mad beast who bombed me I would certainly have no reason to fear hurt from my neighbors, whom I have never molested in any way. . . . In the words of some of the wide-eyed characters who have written about me for the public, you have been "bum-steered" and I have been "bum-rapped." Let's both stop being victimized. I am a gambler and a betting commissioner; no more, no less. I am not a mobster, a gunman, or a thug. I leave such antics to Mr. George Raft and Mr. Humphrey Bogart, who make money at it, or to certain other local actors — bad actors — who make the penitentiary at it. . . .

Very sincerely,
Your neighbor,
Mickey Cohen

A week after the fireworks on Moreno Avenue, members of the squad fanned out to pick up Jack Dragna's inner circle. The family patriarch was nowhere to be found, but they corralled six others, including his son, brother, and two nephews, and held them on suspicion of conspiracy to commit murder, for allegedly arranging the bombing. It wasn't the roust, however, that exploded Dragna's decades-long effort to keep out of view — that same day, February 13, a commission appointed by Governor Earl Warren issued its long-awaited report on organized crime in California. That headline read, COHEN-DRAGNA GANG WAR/CHARGED BY CRIME BOARD, and the Sunset Strip showboat, Mickey Cohen, was not the one branded "The Capone of Los Angeles." The commission, headed by a retired admiral, William H. Standley, said that description of Dragna had come from the late James Ragan, who headed the dominant Continental horse racing wire until he was gunned down in Chicago — then poisoned in the hospital — by the real Capone mob. Punctuating the point, authorities in Los Angeles revealed that a search of Dragna's home had uncovered checks showing he was receiving $500 a week from a racing news service in Chicago. Until this most Angelenos had never heard of Dragna. Now they were told he had an address book that "reads like a Who's Who in the Mafia."

One person did come quickly to his defense — the man who was bombed. "He's one of my best friends," Mickey said. "He might have mixed up in gambling once but he's fifty-five or sixty, an old man, and he's retired. He's in the produce business now and he don't bother nobody."

But when Dragna finally surfaced, he was furious. Though he did not fear prosecution for the bombing — the code of silence again could be counted on — he'd had enough of the LAPD's harassment. Dragna even spoke publicly, that's how mad he was. He had a simple explanation for his weekly checks from the racing wire — he wrote articles for it. "What do the cops want from me? They follow me everywhere I go. . . . I'm just minding my own business. Why don't they mind theirs?"

Then he had his son sue the squad. Frank Paul Dragna was twenty-six and a decorated veteran of World War II, in which he lost an eye serving his country. He was a college boy too, having attended the University of Southern California. He was the farthest thing from a Moustache Pete and thus the perfect plaintiff in the suit stemming from detention of six Dragnas for almost three days while under investigation for the bombing of Mickey's home. The younger Dragna's suit complained of unlawful arrest and of an attempt to "humiliate and embarrass the plaintiff" by holding him in a tank cell until 3:00 A.M. while reporters and photographers were ferried in to portray him nationwide as a mobster tied to an arsenal of shotguns, rifles, and pistols. Frank Dragna also complained that the cops did not let him communicate with his attorney — or his mother. His suit sought $350,000 damages each from Captain Lynn White and ten John Doe officers, two of whom were quickly identified as Unland and Roberson, the pair hounding his father.

It was a perfectly understandable counteroffensive against the cops and the Dragnas could be excused if they did not anticipate how the squad would respond by going after their patriarch, the Al Capone of Los Angeles, for how he enjoyed himself with a woman.

They normally ignored sexual peccadilloes, leaving those to the scandal sheets. Surveillance teams at Mickey's Brentwood house sometimes noticed his prim wife leaving twenty minutes after one of his men, Sam Farkas. They said nothing about that to Mickey, just as they said nothing to Lavonne about the women he dined with. It was the same with Jack Dragna. O'Mara once got a tip that he had an assignation with an employee of the *Los Angeles Times* and it was true — Dragna picked the woman up outside the newspaper and they drove to a motel. Some colleagues said O'Mara should have called Vice and had the pair arrested, but why, "just to embarrass them?" Men will be men, they played a little grab-ass. But Dragna had another girlfriend who did clerical work for the dry cleaners union, in which the mob had its hooks. If a cleaning shop didn't sign up, Dragna's men would send over suits with dye sewn inside so all the clothes in its vats turned purple or red. Extortion like that was the cops' normal concern, not hanky-panky with a red-haired secretary. But the man was trying to ding them for $350,000, and not total, each. Screw 'em.

The twenty-three-year-old clerical worker had an apartment off Wilshire Boulevard, near the Ambassador Hotel and Perino's, Dragna's favorite restaurant. That's where he took her for dinner the night the squad planted the bug. The elegant eatery had a marble entry leading to an oval dining room where waiters wore white gloves and the napkins were of Irish linen so the guests wouldn't get lint on their clothing. It figured to be a long dinner, giving Keeler enough time at the young mistress' apartment. Billy Dick Unland came with him — Dragna was his assignment — but an operation like this required a crowd of men. Two more watched the restaurant, including Jerry "The Professor" Thomas, and two sat in an unmarked car outside the apartment. If Dragna and the woman came back early, giant Jumbo Ken-

226

nard would clumsily get out of the car, making sure the crime boss saw him — Dragna was sure to drive off then, buying more time for the cops upstairs.

Even before Keeler finished picking the lock to the apartment he could see sweat seeping through the new felt hat of the younger Officer Unland. It reminded Keeler why he preferred to do such jobs alone. He had trained himself to sniff for any scent of a person before he stepped into a dark room. He didn't wear cologne or anything that might give the resident a clue that he'd been there. He looked for drawers or doors intentionally left open a crack so he could put them back the same way, exactly, when he was done. Keeler was a pro at this, but other guys poured sweat if you took them under a house where dogs might come barking or into an apartment where a Sicilian might come home with a gun.

The secretary's bed had a large padded headboard with a sunburst pattern. Keeler drilled a hole in the back so he could put his tiny microphone directly in the center of the sun. He ran its thin wire into the wall behind the bed, and fed that down with the phone lines into the basement. That's where they maintained their listening station for two months, in a little room that became home for Unland and others, crouched over a log book while listening through headphones.

They did overhear occasional talk of mob activity, including plans for a new casino in Vegas. But that wasn't what they used against the sixty-year-old Dragna. Their ammunition came from other goings-on in the bedroom. If they couldn't get him for ordering hits on Mickey and his men, why not for "lewd/vag," lewd conduct and vagrancy? Proving that wasn't a snap, however, because Dragna's close associate Simone Scozzari often visited with his own young girlfriend, having fun that was far too clean. Billy Dick Unland finally had to do something to end their wholesome activity of choice.

So we go in and they had a padded headboard and Con put the mike in there and wired it over and down to the basement where we set up our listening post where we could tape it and listen to it. In these days we didn't have tape recorders, we had wire recorders. Anyway we sat down there in the basement. And we used to spit polish our shoes while we were listening, really shine 'em up, the Marine and Navy way, like we were getting ready for inspection. My partner and I were listening one night to Dragna and Simone Scozzari and they used to sit in there with these girls and play canasta all night. All night. Drove us crazy. The card game was, oh, hell — we're sitting down listening on the bug and we finally just turned off the power from the basement, turned off the god-damned lights so they'd stop playing and go to bed. Sexual stuff. That's why we wanted them to stop playing canasta.

There was some sex play with a Coke bottle but what they mostly wanted to document was the sex beyond the missionary position, what they called "French love." In later years, the public would see it simulated routinely on movie screens, but it was a 288a under the California Penal Code, oral copulation, and enough to make a jury blush in 1951, as Keeler recalled it.

She says, "The farther down my throat it goes the better it feels." Then a few minutes later, he's calling out from somewhere in the bathroom and he says, "Where's the mouthwash, honey?" And she says, "Oh, there isn't any." Then she comes back, "It's alright, it won't hurt you."

Dragna was arrested that April 10 on his return from a trip to Vegas. His lawyers could argue all they wanted that the cops didn't have a warrant for their break-in and bugging — when did they ever? That June 2, Dragna was found guilty of three misdemeanor morals charges, a conviction that earned him all of thirty days in the county jail at sentencing by Municipal Judge Vernon Hunt. But that wasn't the point. How and where he was bugged stood to cost him respect in the mob — the case might *diminish* L.A.'s most powerful gangster, if not its best known. More significantly, a crime of moral turpitude could help get him sent back to Italy.

Dragna still was fighting a bid to deport him when he died of a heart attack a few years later. A maid discovered his body in a Sunset Boulevard motel where he had been registered under an assumed name. They found him in pink pajamas, with $986.71 and two sets of false teeth nearby and, in his luggage, a small statue of Jesus. There also was a news clip on how his son's lawsuit had finally been dismissed, one more small victory for the cops amid fifty-eight killings that went unsolved.

CHAPTER 15
MICKEY'S TURN

For years, Los Angeles' Mayor Fletcher Bowron had been lobbying the federal authorities
up to President Harry Truman to use the
same legal strategy that put away Al Capone
on the L.A. hoodlum who similarly flaunted
his high living while reporting meager income. Everyone on both sides of the law
knew what had sent Capone to federal prison
in 1932. One of the memorable moments of
the year long organized crime hearings
spearheaded by Tennessee's Senator Kefauver came when the nation's most powerful
Mafia figure, Frank Costello, was asked,
"What have you done for your country?"
With a raspy voice from the streets of New
York, Costello spit back, "Paid my tax!"

Mickey Cohen was well aware that the IRS
had a microscope over his finances by the
time the Special Committee to Investigate
Organized Crime in Interstate Commerce
brought its fourteen-city road show to Los
Angeles in November of 1950. He had the

231

right to take the Fifth and refuse to answer questions, or could have followed the lead of some of the committee's targets in Las Vegas and skipped town. But the ground rules of the subpoenaed testimony provided limited immunity — what he said there could not be used against him later — so Mickey went ahead and faced the committee's questions, and the television cameras, and pleaded poverty. He explained how he depended on the kindness of friends, and their generous loans, to survive. He even emptied his pockets to prove it to the committee's chief counsel, Rudolph Halley.

Cohen: For the last four years I have been constantly in courts and under harassment by the Los Angeles Police Department that is making it their business to see that I get broke. . . .

Halley: Now, you borrowed at least $60,000 this year? . . . You say you spent $25,000 for the bond on the man who disappeared? . . . How did you spend the other $35,000?

On my living, and I had a colored maid.

How else?

Lawyers' expenses, troubles.

Is it all gone by now?

All excepting what I have in my pocket.

You have nothing in the world except what you have in your pocket?

That is right.

What do you have in your pocket?

$200 or $300, $285 or so. Yes. $285.

That is all the money you have left in the world?

$286, I mean.

How do you expect to live from now on?

I can get money.

You borrow it?

Yes.

Mickey indeed had taken a hit when his two men vanished while out on a combined $75,000 bail for the beating of the greedy radio shop operator. Though Mickey was certain they were in lime-pit graves, not skipping bail, he was responsible — that was the explanation he gave for shutting his haberdashery on Sunset, he needed quick cash. His auctioneer-liquidator, J. W. Fetterman, announced the going-out-of-business sale in fitting style, "Mickey Cohen erstwhile entrepreneur herewith notifies the citizens of Los Angeles and environs of his intention of assuming the role of the good Saint Nicholas — alias Santa Claus."

Then they put up signs that blared MICKEY COHEN QUITS and SELLING OUT TO THE BARE WALLS, and trucked in a searchlight for the big event. Mickey personally greeted the mix of lookiloos and genuine customers checking out the promised 50- to 75-percent discounts on $200 men's robes, $15 belts, and $50 cuff links. One man of limited intelligence ran off with a $50 hat during the closing sale but was nabbed by a clerk when he came back to shoplift again.

The store was shut by the time the state crime commission issued its report spotlighting the Dragna-Cohen gang war and estimating that 500 bookmakers paid Mickey a cut at one time. Mickey had helped bring down the leadership of the LAPD and had goaded the mayor into going on the radio to deliver a "We are coming after you" speech. Just a year later, Senator Kefauver offered a very different appraisal than the state panel, which had made Mickey out to be this monster racketeer. While the Tennessee senator expressed

234

shock at what he discovered in the state ("Crime and corruption in California had a special flavor, exotic, overripe, and a little sickening") he sided with those who termed Mickey "a pipsqueak" or "a horsefly on the rump of human decency," as if the unkindest cut you could deliver to him was to his image.

Kefauver's Mickey was a "contemptible little punk" who inhabited a "dim and dirty world" and looked comical, as well. He wrote, "Cohen, a simian-like figure with thinning hair and spreading paunch, appeared before us in a suit coat of exaggerated length, excessively shoulder-padded and a hat with a ludicrously broad brim." The knock at the hat may have been unfair, though, coming from a politician who often hit the campaign trail in a Davy Crockett coonskin cap. Mickey did not testify with his hat on, anyway — he wore a dark suit, white shirt, and an elegant "MC" tie clip while seated before the microphone in the Los Angeles federal building. And Kefauver at least should have given Mickey credit for his own self-deprecation on one point, his boxing career.

Like much with him, it was hard to determine the truth about his performance in the ring. His record got mixed up with that of another Mickey Cohen fighting at the same time in the lighter weight classes, but out of Denver. Mickey may have hyped a tad when he suggested that his Cleveland-based pugilism often put him in the limelight, "That's right," he told the committee, "32 main events." The Bible of the sport, *The Ring* magazine, listed him as having only eighteen professional fights: six wins, eleven losses, and one draw. But the magazine did not tally nonsanctioned bouts, so the government could not get Mickey for perjury on that count. And when asked before the TV cameras, "Were you pretty good?" he told the absolute truth.

"Not too good," he said.

He was indicted for tax evasion within days of Jack Dragna's arrest was on the morals charges. A federal grand jury had assembled evidence that Mickey paid $49,329 for renovations and furnishing at his Brentwood house, spent $800 a year on shoes (at $50 a pair), and handed out $600 in tips at one lavish affair alone. They'd let him try to explain how he lived like he did thanks to $300,000 in "loans," not income, from bookies and others. "If it's against the law to borrow dough," Mickey jived, "I'm guilty."

The prosecution was based on what the IRS called the *expenditure method*, which calculates a taxpayer's net worth at the beginning of a time period and his spending during it. If his reported income doesn't cover the total, he'd better have a good explanation. Mickey had listed his net worth at only $3,110.82 shortly before January 1, 1946 and reported $72,777.52 in income over the next three years. But the government was able to document $345,933.53 in expenses through the end of 1948, leaving quite a gap. While some of the tallying of expenses came from obvious paperwork — for his home purchase, for instance — the Gangster Squad helped out by recording Mickey's cash on hand every time it rousted him and by going into restaurants after he left to find out what his habitual check-grabbing cost him each night.

Between them, the IRS investigators and the snooping of the Ad Vice Squad that Mickey had attacked (and fed for free), the government could show that he paid $150 to a dog training school and $111 to his pets' vet, $549 in one year for laundry service and $85 each month to the gardener Sam Miyotta, not counting the plants. Lavonne Cohen had been right to complain about the phone bills — one year alone Mickey placed 411 long distance calls to Boston and 318 to West Palm Beach to lay off (and take) bets. Prosecutors could show he paid $3,964 for a new Cadillac five days before Christmas in 1947 and $5,220 for another, a convertible, two days after the holiday. Mickey and his wife spent $280 on pedicures, $3,551 on bedding and table linens, $7,472 on a Beverly Hills tailor, $4,300 on monogrammed shirts and pajamas, and $7,076 one year on ties and socks. Mickey was addicted to wearing new socks — he was a man who never let his bare feet touch the ground and his buffer between his flesh and the dirty world had to be pristine.

Mickey never learned how the government got some of the evidence against him. He was careful not to receive sensitive mail at home — if his contacts didn't send their messages by a trusted courier, such as Neddie Herbert, they would address their letters and packages to him under assumed names at scattered restaurants and bars, where he could pick them up. At his house, Mickey had a backyard furnace to burn sensitive documents and letters after he looked at them, going outside to feed the paperwork into the fire himself. But when he went back inside, one of his security guards would stamp out the flames . . . and salvage what he could . . . and sneak the charred remnants to the other man paying him . . . who passed the charred paperwork to his bosses . . . who passed it along to the feds. That security guard was worth scores more than the $25 a week Jack O'Mara paid him. "My boy, Neal Hawkins," O'Mara said.

Yet even as they tricked him, O'Mara never underestimated Mickey, as he saw others do — Mickey invited that, of course, all those times he played the buffoon. But one day

O'Mara followed him on a whim after spending a boring hour on surveillance outside his lawyer's office. After a meeting there, Mickey didn't head home for his normal 90-minute hot shower before a night out. He headed south toward the airport, driving himself in his blue Caddy but stopping short of LAX, at the Athens oil field.

OK now, I'm figuring what the hell's this son of a bitch going out there for? He pulls into the oil field, parks. Pretty soon another car comes in and joins him. I've got a pair of field glasses and I'm watching from a distance and I see an exchange, a banter, maybe it lasted 10, 15 minutes. What the hell's going on? So I tailed the other car and he broke loose and went down Figueroa and I pulled alongside and got his license number and I look at him. I don't recognize him, he's a stranger, you know. So I go in and run a DMV on him. And it comes back as so-and-so. OK, it still doesn't ring a bell because I knew most of the hoods and all his business acquaintances. So I go down to the register of voters. I look up Joe Dokes. "Internal Revenue." It lists your occupation. I said "Jesus Christ, what the hell's going on?" Mickey's surreptitiously meeting an Internal Revenue guy out on the oil field like that. So I go into Hamilton and I say, "Hey, I don't know, here's what happened, Cap." He says, "Jesus Christ!" so he called the chief over there, Internal Revenue, and he said this guy's the chief investigator on fraud cases and he's due to retire in about a week.

Well, I wanted no part of it 'cause I didn't want to get on any IRS shit list. The guy was ready to retire and he was doin' business, you know, he was doin' business with Mickey. I didn't want any part of it, you know. It's none of my business, let the Cap take it from there with the IRS, let them handle it. They know what the hell they're doing. I don't want to stick my nose any further into it. Just another lead, another piece of police work.

Captain Hamilton never told him what happened and O'Mara guessed nothing, they let the agent disappear with his pension. But when Senator Estes Kefauver brought his hearings to Los Angeles, one of the subpoenaed witnesses was an IRS man who had worked on investigations of Bugsy Siegel and Tony Cornero, the king of the gambling ships, and had recently retired to enter a brief partnership with . . . Mickey's accountant. Former IRS agent Donald O. Bircher testified that he was acting as a private tax consultant when "Mr. Cohen" requested a meeting at the oil field to see about buying vacant property nearby. "So we walked down there, walked around for about five minutes . . . and then he said, 'Do you know if anything is available in this area?' And I said, 'No, I don't.' And that was the end of it," a perfectly innocuous conversation on a pleasant afternoon, you know?

O'Mara was not present to hear that Kefauver Committee testimony but he was not going to miss another session in the federal building seven months later. On June 18, 1951, he joined several other squad members for the one-minute walk up Spring Street from City Hall to the seventeen-story courthouse where Mickey Cohen would be testifying in his own defense, trying to talk his way out of going to prison for underpaying his taxes by $156,123. Mickey wore a dark blue gabardine suit, a white shirt, and a dark blue tie fixed in place by his initialed gold MC clasp. His shoes were two-toned black-and-white, the footwear style favored by gangsters and golfers. He carried a brown paper bag with life's essentials. "The restroom here ain't got soap and towels, I brought my own," he explained. Then he botched the first question out of the gate, when his own lawyer, Leo Silverstein, asked him his name.

Meyer Michael Cohen.

Isn't it Meyer Harris Cohen?

Oh, yes, Meyer Harris Cohen.

The record corrected, Mickey briefed the jury on how he'd been born in Brooklyn but grew up fatherless right here, with chronic truancy and scrapes precipitating his departure from school in the third grade before he devoted himself to hustling papers at 7th and Spring, blocks from the courthouse. The important part was explaining that while he once had been "engaged in the gambling business," in his lawyer's words, he was not a bookie but maintained a *betting office*, at the executive level. "My last gambling transactions were about three years ago," he added, with one winking semi-confession thrown in. "Oh, I made a couple of bets since then."

Mickey also entertained the jurors with an inside anecdote about his stint in the rag trade, describing a side deal he worked with his own $250 suits. "I had an arrangement with some people who liked them but couldn't afford them. They paid $100 for a suit after I wore it four, five, or six times," Mickey said, "but I wear them longer now," the laugh line buying him a little more time before the daunting task of detailing where he got $300,000 in loans, without paperwork, that he never paid back.

One loan appeared to be real, a no-interest $35,000 advance from the president of Hollywood State Bank, a man who ceased being the bank's president once the transaction was disclosed. "I guess he liked me," Mickey said. After that, Mickey cited a couple of dead men who couldn't testify to the contrary — the late Bugsy Siegel and Hooky Rothman loaned him $25,000 and $15,000, he said. But he was doomed by another supposed source of $25,000, Arthur Seltzer, a New York manufacturer of leather handbags who happened to be the son-in-law of his bookkeeper, Mike Howard. Seltzer evidently saw no harm in helping his father-in-law's boss until prosecutors reminded him of the consequences of perjury. U.S. Attorney Ernest Tolin instructed the New Yorker to share for the jury a conversation he'd had with Mickey.

He asked me if I could enter in my records the fact that I had loaned him $25,000 . . . I thought nothing of it and I said, "Yes."

Well, had you loaned him $25,000?

I had not.

Had you loaned him any money at all?

I hadn't loaned him any money at all.

During closing statements, Mickey's lawyer suggested that Mickey's earlier life might explain his confusion about his finances, "Those fights may have affected him in later life, who knows?" They called that the "Punch Drunk Defense."

Shortly before the verdict one of the Hollywood trade papers carried a for-sale advertisement for Mickey's house. The Brentwood home with the doggie bed and mirrored boudoir had been showcased in both *Life* and *Look* magazines and described in the state crime commission report as worth $200,000. The real-world asking price was $47,500. The contents, meanwhile, were the featured attraction of THE YEAR'S MOST INTERESTING AUCTION EVENT, so termed by the flyer from Marvin H. Newman Auctioneers. Ten thousand people showed up at its Wilshire Boulevard showrooms for the preview viewing of "the complete and luxurious furnishings from the Brentwood home [of] Mr. and Mrs. Mickey Cohen — nationally prominent personality." The offered items ranged from Mickey's collection of antique firearms to Tuffy's bed that matched his own. One remnant of the Sunset Strip haberdashery also was up for bid, the bulletproof doors reinforced with 300 pounds of steel. Mickey's similarly armored Cadillac, which the state of California never let him use, already had been sold for $12,000 to the Texas Stock Car Racing Association, which planned to put it on display.

"Sir, you are the proud owner of Mickey Cohen's bedspread!" auctioneer Newman declared on one of the seven nights it took to sell the household items. The entertainment console that Mickey had bought for $2,700 went for $1,150 while his bed and nightstand brought in $600. Someone paid $1,100 for the Steinway piano, while the French Provincial dining set, made of fruitwood, sold for $900. The doggie bed? Thirty-five dollars. "You should have seen Tuffy when they took his bed. He didn't like it," Mickey said. "Why, the linen on that bed was changed every day, same as mine."

The seven women and five men on the jury had to digest the testimony of more than 100 witnesses but deliberated only four hours before returning June 20 to declare Mickey guilty of three counts of tax evasion and one count of filing a false financial statement.

Sentencing was set for July 9 and Jack O'Mara was not going to miss that, either. The way their world worked was that the police chief, captains, and lieutenants got written letters of appreciation from the city while the anonymous foot soldiers got to go out and get drunk to celebrate what finally was more than a minor victory. A bunch of them first went to court to see Mickey be sentenced to five years in federal prison and a $10,000 fine. What they didn't expect was the lecture by U.S. District Judge Benjamin Harrison, directed at them — they were among the causes, you see, of Mickey's misfortune.

"This community has to take its share of the responsibility for his present predicament," the judge said. "There was no serious effort on the part of local law enforcement officers to stop you. If they had performed their duty you wouldn't be here now — you would be in some other line of business. . . ."

And Mickey? Where Senator Kefauver saw a contemptible little punk, the federal judge saw a "hard luck problem child" of "the Los Angeles melting pot . . . a very personable individual, at least a good salesman who has been able to sell himself very well. I think you have a good side. You're not as bad as you have been pictured. Perhaps more of us would be gamblers if we'd been as lucky at it as you."

Before they led him off to exchange his suit for prison blues, Mickey handed his wife his pearl gray fedora, his pinky ring, and his meager roll of fresh bills, only $50 not counting the lucky $2 note stashed in his wallet, which he hoped they'd let him keep while incarcerated. With interest and penalties, he was half-a-million dollars in hock to the government, worse off than when he was selling 2-cent newspapers on the corner down the street. He hugged Lavonne and said, "Take it easy" — no worry, they'd get 'em on appeal.

"Right now, though," Mickey said, "I'm hungry."

Chapter 16
The Trap

In the spring of 1949, as the Vice scandals and violence enveloped the Sunset Strip, the California Congress of Parents and Teachers met in Los Angeles to discuss the social responsibility — or lack of it — of gangster films. On the surface, the concern was nothing new. Gangster stories had been a staple of the screen from the silent era on and grumbling about them was one reason Hollywood in 1930 adopted the Hays Code, which mandated, among other things, that films "shall never . . . throw sympathy with the crime as against law and justice." The code meant that James Cagney and Edward G. Robinson had to get it at the end of the shoot-'em-ups that continued to proliferate through the '30s. One critic who adored the genre gushed that "the story of man against society, the villain pursued and punished — the 'gangster,' as a generalization — remains basic, A–No. 1 cinema stuff. . . . When it's done well you can't beat it for suspense, vicarious thrills and, at the end, the smug satisfaction ('There but for the grace of God, go I!') of watching justice vindicated."

But the 1945 film *Dillinger* had set off outraged protests and a boycott by religious and women's groups even though the title character was done in much like the real Depression-era bank robber — ambushed by federal agents waiting outside a Chicago movie theater where he had just seen *Manhattan Melodrama*. The protesters worried that impressionable adolescents would to be entranced by such rags-to-riches, authority-defying characters, however brutal their demise. The intense actor playing Dillinger didn't help — Lawrence Tierney was a real-life Hollywood bad boy known for boozing and brawling along the Strip. Columnist Louella Parsons declared that the country had enough of gangster films. "We have outgrown them," she wrote, and one of Hollywood's leading moguls agreed. Samuel Goldwyn's studio had produced similar movies in the past but he thought such fare perpetuated an unfortunate image of the nation that had just won World War II. "Any returning G.I. will tell you that many of our allies across the seas still believe that the gangster is a familiar figure in any American street," he said. In 1947, Goldwyn joined with other producers and distributors in voting to cease showing 25 titles including

Dillinger; Me, Gangster; They Made Me a Killer and *Ladies of the Mob.* As for the PTA, it was forever calling for more stories about *decent people* and did so again in 1949.

But by the organization's last statewide meeting of the 1940s something more disturbing was unfolding on the screen. In some new movies it wasn't a given that virtue would win out, if any virtue could be found. Even some Westerns no longer were simple good guy–bad guy morality plays. They too were going for *gangster angles*, the PTA lamented. A French critic had named this new genre "Film Noir" in 1946 — the year the squad was born — when a backlog of American movies finally reached post-war Paris. Part of it was style, the black-and-white, the dark interiors, the rainy streets with lonely lampposts and characters casting long shadows that seemed to represent a dark, second self. These films had a worldview, too, and it was hardly black and white. Paranoia reigned. And everyone lied, even women. They no longer were soothing innocents but schemers, *femmes fatales.* What's more, the official arms of society — police and prosecutors — were as crooked as the crooks, or irrelevant. If the bad guys got it, it wasn't because of anyone with a badge but through the work of a weary private eye, often a fallen cop. And where the early gangster films had been set in New York or Chicago, the backdrop for these dark tales more often was Los Angeles, the sun-washed city of palm trees and self-invention, the city that pretended that evil came from afar. In this world, truth was found not in the sunshine but in the shadows. Justice was obtained not in a marble courthouse but in the streets and alleys.

Jack O'Mara never bought into the noir worldview. Time and again his work as a cop played out at the edges, in episodes that ended in murk, not clarity. But into old age he thought that good and evil, and right and wrong, were obvious enough. He'd been raised to believe in heaven and hell and he knew where he was headed. He didn't expect to find Mickey Cohen in the same community.

When it came to movies, O'Mara's idea of a good one was *Oklahoma*, the musical with songs that begged to be sung in the shower. Rodgers and Hammerstein had a new musical out, *South Pacific*, and it had great tunes too, especially "Some Enchanted Evening," where you meet a stranger across a crowded room, the way he met Connie. You better believe he sang that in the shower. And if your wife and daughter started crooning another hit of the day, "(How Much Is) That Doggy in the Window?" somebody damn well better get them a doggy. The O'Maras' named their new Scottish terrier "Trouble."

■ ■ ■ ■

A lot of what was written about Los Angeles wasn't much better than the Film Noir bleakness. For decades, writers had competed to show how clever they could be in telling the city how phony and empty it was. "Los Angeles, it should be understood, is not a mere city," Morrow Mayo wrote. "On the contrary, it is, and has been since 1888, a *commodity*, something to be advertised and sold to the people of the United States like automobiles, cigarettes and mouthwash." A Kentucky native, Mayo decided after six years in Los Angeles, "Here is an artificial city which has been pumped up under forced draught, inflated like a balloon, stuffed with rural humanity like a goose with corn . . . the sunshine metropolis heaves and strains, sweats and becomes pop-eyed, like a young boa constrictor trying to swallow a goat."

Others told you that Los Angeles was built on a giant crime, the theft of water from the Owens Valley, and that evil things went on inside the city's pink stucco houses. "There is a bright side to Los Angeles," the Slovenian immigrant Louis Adamic wrote, "only to see it, one must have good eyesight . . . In spite of all the healthful sunshine and ocean breezes, it is a *bad* place — full of old, dying people, who were born of old, tired pioneer parents, victims of America." His buddy Carey McWilliams, who had come out from Colorado during the surge of 1922, had a unique take on the twinkling city you saw at night from Mulholland Drive, where Jack O'Mara took unwelcome visitors — the miles of lights below were "jewels on the breast of the harlot."

Raymond Chandler created a great detective, Marlowe, but he might be describing the desert winds that blew through the San Gabriel Valley and next thing you knew he was putting evil thoughts in the head of a man's good woman, "It was one of those hot dry Santa Anas that come down through the mountain passes and curl your hair and make your nerves jump and your skin itch. On nights like that every booze party ends in a fight. Meek little wives feel the edge of the carving knife and study their husbands' necks. . . ." Then Nathaniel West came out with *The Day of the Locust*, about the dreamers on the fringe of Hollywood who relieved their boredom with trash newspapers and movies that "fed them on lynchings, murder, sex crimes, explosions, wrecks, love nests, fires, miracles, revolutions, war. This daily diet made sophisticates of them. The sun is a joke. Oranges can't titillate their jaded palates. Nothing can ever be violent enough to make taut their slack minds and bodies. They have been cheated and betrayed. They have slaved and saved for nothing."

Jack O'Mara understood that men like those were deep thinkers. But he had two questions for them: "What does any of that bleakness have to do with how you live your own life?" And, "Do you ever go fishing?"

Everyone on the squad fished. Sometimes several of the men went together without the wives for the deep sea variety down off Mexico. But more often they traveled up into the Sierra Nevada seeking the smaller fish, usually rainbow trout. Con Keeler went so often they made him a fish and game warden. Archie Case made tackle boxes on the side. O'Mara led his extended family on excursions to June Lake or Lake Sabrina, at 9,000-feet, where they would sleep on cots in tent shelters and he would tease his young nieces and nephews with stories about the monsters lurking in the outhouses. O'Mara fished there in the cold months too, when common wisdom said the only way to catch trout was to go before sun-up and break a hole in the ice. He experimented and found *no*, you could catch 'em at all hours — he even sent an outdoors magazine an article he wrote called "Nine O'Clock Trout," to debunk the pre-dawn ice fishing myth. *That* was something worth racking your brain about, not figuring out the soul of Los Angeles.

The bottom line was that no egghead had to tell him or others on the Gangster Squad that bad shit happened behind pink stucco walls, or that young girls sometimes came to Hollywood with one thing in mind and wound up doing another. But here's what they did when they stumbled onto a pimp who was preying on underage runaways — they took him up into the hills to see those fucking jewels on the breast of the harlot. O'Mara was going to stick his gun in the guy's ear and do his usual sneeze routine until Jumbo insisted, "Let me." No one played the crazed I'm-gonna-kill-you cop better than Jumbo, no one. As with the pickpockets victimizing the World War II servicemen, it didn't take much to get him worked up about the pimp — the little sister he cared for at home, Betty, was the same age as the girls that scum made work the streets. So Jumbo started waving his six-inch and screaming motherfucker-this and motherfucker-that and finally charged at the pimp atop Runyon Canyon. The only way the terrified man could flee was down. But after a few steps, he fell and slid and tumbled, and it was like that all the way down the slope. He tumbled over rocks and through thorny brush that ripped his ace pimp clothes to shreds and tore at his skin, too. By the time he reached Hollywood Boulevard he was a bloody half-naked mess ready to call one of his buddies and plead, "Get me a couple hundred bucks — I'm getting out of this crazy town." Talk of that night spread within the LAPD until it became one of those legends no one knew for sure was based on a real episode, but it was. Eventually someone put a version of it in a movie, having no idea that a real cop named Jumbo had driven a real pimp down the mountain just like that.

Jumbo was the first of them to die. At the end of work on March 1, 1952, the big Texan did what he did most nights, had a few drinks with his partner Dick Williams, the ex-Army Ranger. Jumbo dropped Williams off at home in Westchester and headed in a driving rain toward his own house. A mile from it, on Western Avenue, his unmarked squad car skidded head-on into a bus. They naturally wondered whether another car might have forced his to swerve but Jumbo never was able to speak during the two days he lingered in the hospital as everyone gathered around. James Douglas Kennard was thirty-nine and left a wife, mother, seven-year-old son, and two sisters.

Next of the originals to go was Jerry Thomas, the quiet one with the memory, who had gotten their files started by perfectly recalling all the names and addresses mentioned in barroom conversations. "The Professor" was married to a nurse and both had a hard time handling the pressure of a job that sent you on fifteen-hour stakeouts.

"When will you be back?" "I don't know." Every marriage felt the strain. The squad's first secretary, Sally Scott, once had to deliver documents to Con Keeler's home in the Valley. Con's wife asked her, "Can you tell me what he does?" and Sally said, "You really don't want to know." One squad member, Jerry Greeley, had already gotten divorced in order to marry an LAPD secretary, so the wives weren't crazy if they worried what the men were up to. Jerry Thomas got ulcers from dealing with the life, then started showing up for work wearing one black shoe and one brown shoe. Finally they had him answering the phone, that's all, and one day he went home, sat on the Davenport sofa and shot himself in the head with his service revolver.

Tough little Willie Burns, who once took a bullet for the LAPD, did not appreciate being bumped off the squad he had commanded and sent back to uniformed duty. When the tiny city of Maywood had an opening for a police chief he applied and got the job. Burns lasted three weeks presiding over eighteen officers who patrolled barely one square mile. "I just sat around and suddenly I realized I was bored," he said, so he went back to being a lieutenant and watch commander for the LAPD. Then heaven called — he was offered the chief's job in one of the glorious old California mission cities up the coast, San Luis Obispo. Never mind the pay,

$495 a month, he didn't know life could be so good. But he barely had time to make his mark there before they diagnosed his inoperable cancer. "Go home," doctors advised and that's where he died, at the small house in Gardena where his wife once had received a funeral wreath. Willie Burns was only fifty-four.

On February 13, 1952, Mickey Cohen finally was flown to Tacoma, Washington, and taken to the ancient McNeil Island federal penitentiary. He was ready for the pen after growing tired of staying in Los Angeles jails while pursuing his appeal. He had a fine time in the Sheriff's custody but suddenly was moved to the Lincoln Heights Jail controlled by the LAPD, where he was miserable, he said through his lawyer: "I was afraid for my life. There were cops all around me and police are my deadly enemies. I'm shaggy as a beaver. They didn't let me shave for four days, gave me no exercise, and cut up the newspapers. My wife, Lavonne, was only allowed a four-minute visit. We had to converse through speaking tubes. They gave me no clean clothes. . . . The food was terrible. They wouldn't let me take a bath." The cops had figured that would be the worst part of confinement for Mickey, denial of his bubble baths.

More than five years had passed since the

Gangster Squad was formed with the streets as its office. It had a sanitized new name, digs at the heart of city government, and many more men. One Sunday when they had a squad picnic at Lincoln Park, Con Keeler had everyone present sit on a bench or stand behind it, by a chain link fence, for the only photo they ever took as a group. That was back in '48 or '49 and they had sixteen men even by then, the fifteen in the photo and Keeler, who snapped it. The picture showed O'Mara holding his pipe in his right hand and wearing a light suit and a wide tie that didn't reach down to his belt — most everyone wore a tie, even at a picnic. They ate franks and beans and afterward O'Mara goaded a bunch of the guys into taking off their jackets for a game of football, *touch* football, so he could dart by the giants and they couldn't pound him, at least those were the rules. The next day, Monday, half couldn't make their shifts. Now some were dead.

There were no guarantees in police work, or in life, but O'Mara hoped he was still around, and on the squad, when Mickey got out of prison. He wanted to see if another of his small victories might pay off. This too involved Neal Hawkins, his well-placed mole at Mickey's house.

I knew he had guns there and Neal was an Army man, what you might call a gunsmith specialist in the Army. I said, "See if you can get those guns from him, I'd like to check 'em out." Oh, hell, Neal Hawkins conned Mickey — he said he'd take 'em home and out to the desert, check 'em out on a shooting range, oil 'em up, grease 'em, make sure everything was working. Well, there were seven guns Mickey had, none of 'em registered to him. The numbers on those weren't worth a shit, they didn't check to anything, those guns were taken off the street.

So we got the guns and we went up to the West L.A. firing range and we had Ray Pinker, a famous ballistics man on the police department, and Russell Camp of the police lab. So we were up test firing and took test bullets out of each gun. Then I took the butt plates off and I scratched initials under them, inconspicuous that nobody would notice even if they took the plates off again. Then I wrote a special report for Hamilton and the Cap locked it up in the so-called safe — we used to have a safe there for all our top secret stuff and the Cap put it there with the bullets.

See, I figured they might be recovered from a body someday. I said, "He's got those guns. Somebody's gonna use 'em."

At the LAPD, only Chief Parker, Captain Hamilton, and a couple of others were let in on the trap that Jack O'Mara had set for Mickey Cohen. While Mickey was in prison, one of his flunkies would keep his weapons. But when he got out, he'd no doubt get back all those guns that now could be traced to him. Perhaps the judge was right and Mickey was merely a hard-luck problem child of the Los Angeles melting pot, a personable salesman whose main misfortune was that he'd sold himself too well as the city's signature gangster. "You're not as bad as you have been pictured," the judge said.

Or maybe he was a killer. It was true he'd mostly been shot at of late. But before that he'd gunned down one rival bookie in L.A. and perhaps been behind the deaths of three others, and who knew how he'd earned his stripes in his younger days, in Cleveland and Chicago. It was yet another mind game and O'Mara's trap was a long shot. But if Mickey got out, and got those guns back, and one was used to kill, Los Angeles police might actually solve a gangland murder after a century of failure — and put Mickey away for good. It was a long shot indeed, depending on many what-ifs. But some long shots pay off.

Sergeant Jack O'Mara merely had to wait a decade.

■ ■ ■ ■

Part III
Sergeant Jerry Wooters and the Deadly Night at Rondelli's

■ ■ ■ ■

CHAPTER 17
JERRY MEETS JACK

Sergeant Jerry Wooters first encountered Jack Whalen at the Mark Twain Hotel in Hollywood, where the big man was demanding that two members of the Gangster Squad show him their badges.

Sizing Jack Whalen up was a lot like family lore or explaining a shooting — the tales tended to wander. Depending on who you spoke to, he went from six-foot-one to six-foot-four and from 225 to 250 pounds. But everyone who shook his hands agreed they were the thickest they'd ever seen, or felt. An off-duty LAPD sergeant, not long before, had made the mistake of taunting him at a bar and Whalen did what he did to a lot of men in bars and elsewhere, knocked 'em cold. It was not like later on, where if you laid a finger on a cop they hauled you off — no questions asked or answered. A policeman back then was expected to handle himself — if he couldn't, shame on him. This was an older sergeant on uniformed patrol who was having drinks at a bar on 7th Street, where he got to jawing with Whalen and they took it out into the parking lot. The sergeant could not remember much when questioned at the hospital, and he retired soon after. There was little his colleagues could do, but word of the incident spread through the department and on April 14, 1952, nine months after Mickey Cohen was sentenced to prison, the Intelligence Division put Jack Whalen on its watch list for "muscle activities."

A few months later, a slender dance instructor named Jon Anton was leaving the Hollywood Post Office when three men confronted him to collect all of $15 he owed a bookie. Anton apparently had placed three $5 bets on a horse to win, place, and show. The horse had done none of those but Anton still hadn't paid Roger Matthews. The bookie was among the trio who approached him to collect and he brought along Jack Whalen to do the negotiating, such as it was. First thing, the big man pushed Anton up against the windows of the post office and reached into his pocket to see what cash he had. Anton tried to get to a pay phone to call police but Whalen gently advised him not to. "I will kill you," he said. "I will catch you in an alley with no witnesses." Anton was advised, equally gently, to deliver the money to the lobby of the nearby Mark Twain Hotel, which served as Whalen's office of sorts, the switchboard dutifully taking his calls. There Anton made the mistake of arguing that he didn't owe that much — he'd only bet $2 — and that ended the conversation. The first fist struck him between the eyes, a police report said, and after ten more rights and lefts he had enough internal injuries to keep him spitting blood for a month, plus "a chipped front tooth, a bruise on the left shin, lumps on the right side of the head, a swollen nose and his face was 'badly beaten up.' " It seemed like overkill to collect $15 but in some businesses, the report noted, you need to "send a message to a larger clientele."

Now Sergeant Jerry Wooters and his partner got a radio call to come to the Mark Twain Hotel, someone there was messing with two other members of the squad, making them prove they were cops.

Let me tell you how I first met Jack. Met these officers in this hotel, two guys from Intelligence, two guys from our office. They're sittin' there in the lobby and he's in the corner. Good lookin', well-dressed. Didn't look like a hoodlum, an asshole.

So Whalen's sitting in the corner of the lobby and these two policemen are there, both of them pretty good size. I got a little partner with me. So I said, "What the hell's the problem?" They said "Jack Whalen — we tried to place him under arrest and he wouldn't come." These were policeman, and I was a sergeant. That's why they called me. But I couldn't believe these fuckers let him sit there. I woulda got my nightstick and beat the shit out of him or something.

So I said, "Why wouldn't he come?"

"We didn't have the badge with us."

Well, we didn't carry a badge, just an ID card. It was too heavy. I guess we were copying the FBI or something. These badges wore out your pockets. So Whalen had stopped there to pick up a collection or pay somebody or something and they grabbed him. And they said "We're police officers, come with us." And he says "Get fucked, where's your badge?" They didn't have a badge.

They didn't know what to do. So I didn't care who the fuck Whalen was. He was just another bookie. I said, "Oh shit," so I went over to him, all my 163 pounds, and I said, "Whalen I understand you're a tough guy, really good fighter. Really good shape. Husky and big."

He said, "Where's your badge?"

I said, "I have a badge. I'm not going to show it to you, asshole." Of course, I didn't have one. So I said, "I heard about your reputation and I'll tell you one thing: you're going to go out of this lobby. You might take two of us out, but you ain't gonna take four because we're all comin' after you at one time. Now do you want to go easy or want to go hard?"

He says, "Dick, what's your name?"

So I tell him my name.

"Oh, hiya, Jerry, I heard about you."

Jerry Wooters figured that was pure bull, Jack Whalen shining him on with a grin more befitting a movie star than a hoodlum. But that's how the renegade cop met the renegade gangster and how they became friends for life, or however long life could last, in Los Angeles of the '50s, for someone named Jack "The Enforcer."

CHAPTER 18
HOW JACK WHALEN BECAME "THE ENFORCER"

The temptation is to say he saw an opening when Mickey Cohen was sent to prison and went for it. But Jack Whalen had been moving toward a life of crime well before then, spoiling the plan of his father, the notorious "Freddie the Thief," that he rise above the family trade. The Whalen patriarch held himself partly to blame, for he was why Jack didn't last as a cadet at Black-Foxe Military Institute, the elite private academy that was going to mold him into a pillar of respectable Los Angeles.

Fred Whalen, no surprise, had never been a conventional father. From the earliest age, the pool hustler-turned-bootlegger tutored his children in how to survive in this world — the Whalen way. At suppertime, many parents lecture their kids, "Eat your vegetables." Not in that household. Fred made a game of hovering over his children's plates with his fork and snatching their favorite foods — their potatoes, pie, and the like. That was his way of teaching them that the other guy wanted your goodies and you'd better protect 'em, or go after his first. If the kids refused to drink their milk, he'd drop a quarter in the bottom of the glass, a lesson in how the lure of money can get people to do what they wouldn't otherwise. He also played card games with the children . . . and cheated. He tried to make it obvious when he dealt himself extra aces from the bottom of the deck. He wanted them to squeal, "I saw that!" His daughter, at least, usually did.

Bobie was blonde in her early years, Jack dark-haired. The Whalen daughter was a daddy's girl — she'd jump into Fred's arms to be carried about, while Momma hoisted little Jack. His bond was with one of the Wunderlichs, the stocky ones without the same guile. "Each took a child and that was it," their daughter said in old age.

When Jack turned eleven, his father sent him off to Black-Foxe, a school founded by a wealthy developer and two former World War I majors, Earle Foxe and Harry Black. Tall and blond, looking every bit the officer, Major Earle Foxe had been a successful actor in silent movies before the war and continued appearing in the talkies. He was one reason show biz luminaries felt comfortable turning their children over to the military academy, and the cadets included the sons of the silent film giants Charlie Chaplin and Buster

Keaton, and later of Edward G. Robinson, who'd just made a splash as the rags-to-riches hoodlum in Warner Bros.' *Little Caesar*, dying with the last words, "Mother of mercy, is this the end of Rico?" The singing-dancing child star Shirley Temple also came to visit while Jack Whalen was at the school — her brother was a cadet too. So was the grandson of the fellow who owned Seabiscuit, the horse.

Black-Foxe was designed to be an island of moral rectitude amid a city that remained outrageously crooked through the '30s. That was the era of Mayor Frank Shaw and the 2,600 bookies, brothels, and gambling parlors — some of that sin and graft flourishing blocks from where the sons of the fortunate learned to march in uniform with straight backs and practiced their public speaking, a skill Major Earl Foxe believed essential for society's future leaders, like the Whalen boy. The school's main campus was in the shadows of the Hollywood studios, but it had a second in the Valley for its sports and stables. Coached by a former captain in the Royal Canadian Mounted Police, the polo team took on college squads from Berkeley, Stanford, and the like. Though hardly raised in horse country, Jack Whalen scored a goal his first season, remarkable for a baby-faced cadet not yet a teenager. The son of Freddie the Thief was a natural at *polo*. He was a physical marvel in every sense, becoming captain of the junior gymnastics team and a standout in the pentathlon, which included the high jump, shot put, and 50-yard dash.

On the academic front, Black-Foxe offered a full college-prep curriculum plus military training in everything from cavalry tactics to aviation, using a leftover World War II plane. The Whalen boy had a head start on the flying front, for few of the cadets, even there, had daddies with a biplane. Jack did get homesick, like other new cadets, so he kept handwritten letters from his mom under his pillow — he liked the familiar scent of her perfume sprinkled on them. He wrote letters back in beautiful slanted penmanship, drawing little circles over every "i" instead of dotting thcm.

Veterans of the school said it was unheard of for a cadet to become commander of his class his rookie year. A photo commemorating the 1933 appointment showed Jack posed in white dress uniform with a leather belt and chest sash, three medals over his heart, and a ceremonial sword on his left hip. A stickler might quibble at how his officer's cap was askew, tilted to the right, and how his hands were not exactly in the classic position for standing at attention. Or maybe it's only after we know what he would become that our eye is drawn to young Jack Whalen's hands, and how they were balled into fists.

■ ■ ■ ■

Black-Foxe old-timers say it would have been grounds to force the boy to leave once the school discovered how his father really could afford the tuition — it wasn't through dry cleaning. Fred Whalen's role as a rum-runner came into public view only after the lifting of Prohibition, in a *Los Angeles Times* feature on the daredevil smugglers who had brought whiskey to a supposed dry California. There he was, dubbed the "Wild Irishman," alongside the likes of Tony "The Hat" Cornero. Fred was one of the few never to land in prison for *that*, but when authorities did get him — well, that was one more reason Black-Foxe couldn't let his boy stay.

In later life, Freddie boasted that authorities never really caught on to his scams, at least not after the early misunderstanding over the swiped lingerie in the store, which he dismissed as ancient history. But the truth is they nailed him after Prohibition, too, when he began reselling the cheap drugstore liquor in Johnny Walker bottles. The concept was inspired: You bought up gallons of the least expensive stuff you could find — Brunswick Drug Scotch, say, or the Sontag Drug Company's Royal Clan — and poured it into glassware available from C&O Bottle and Cork Supply. By the time Freddie was done, it looked exactly like premium Black Label and he could sell it by the case to doctors down in Long Beach, the film crowd in Hollywood, or even to priests. But to make the enterprise really pay he needed a network — why not cover Watts? So he enlisted six others to operate franchises, in effect, out of rented garages, the helpers including Leo Chapman, James Woods . . . and George Wunderlich.

The Whalen clan was convinced that the youngest of the brothers-in-law was the one who eventually rolled over and tattled to authorities, under pressure when he faced unrelated legal troubles, something to do with a young lady. Whatever the reason, the feds got wind of the whiskey scheme that Freddie the Thief had milked brilliantly for two years. Freddie made the best of it by copping to one count of "buying, selling and transporting intoxicating liquor in unstamped paid tax containers." The plea bargain called for him to spend less than six months in the nearby Terminal Island prison where his wife and kids could visit for picnics on the grounds while he enjoyed the first real vacation of his life. "He had a ball," his daughter said. "He played pool, you know?" When Freddie completed his sentence, he convinced the relevant officials to waive any probation given how he had totally reformed and entered a promising new field, selling imported china.

Chief Probation Officer Thaddeus Davis was either a true believer, or a little richer. He wrote of Freddie, "due to the fact that his present employment will probably carry him into the countries of South America, and the fact that his family ties are extremely strong, we feel that further supervision in this case would serve no useful purpose."

Freddie could shrug off the conviction, but his son landed in public schools, among the common kids. The football part, at least, came easy. Jack had filled out quickly as a teenager, to a point where he couldn't wear regular pajamas. "He would just bend his arm and they would split right open," his sister said. "Bend his leg, same thing, split right open." But when Jack was sixteen he and several friends took a '36 Chevy from a used car lot and didn't bring it back for five days, "driven nearly 1,000 miles and returned in deplorable condition," a police file reported.

Fred Whalen gave his son a hard slap when they released him after the long joyride. That could have been a show for the cops but Jack's sister said the friction between the father and son was real — Freddie was furious that his boy had screwed up like that. Or perhaps he was disappointed that his son had been caught so easily. Another time Jack was riding in a convertible with his sister, who kept her hair platinum and did some modeling — she looked OK. When a man in a passing car called out his appreciation, Jack swerved in front of the other car to block it. "Well, see, my brother just yanked him out of the car and just worked him over. He said, 'Nobody should talk to women that way.' "

When Freddie saw that his son enjoyed fighting, he decided to cure the habit ("it's a dirty business") with the help of a locally based boxer who in 1939 was training for the biggest shot in that game, a title bout with Joe Louis, the heavyweight champion. Jack Roper was old for a pro, at thirty-six, and worked a regular job as an electrician at the studios, where he also picked up bit parts acting in character, playing the "club bouncer," "restaurant gangster," "barfly" and the like. Roper later would be cast as the boxer whom John Wayne kills with his fists in *The Quiet Man*, sending a despairing Wayne fleeing to Ireland, vowing never to fight again. But in real life Roper had survived more than 100 bouts, and while he lost quite a few, thirty-nine, he had a solid left hook that had enabled him to score nine first-round knockouts, enough to earn a supporting role in L.A.'s first heavyweight championship fight in three decades. After Roper set up a training camp at a ranch north of the city to prepare, Fred Whalen volunteered his son as an impromptu sparring partner, meaning cannon fodder. Using his persuasive talents, Fred told the heavyweight's trainer, "just have your guy go three rounds with him and have him cold-cock my son. I don't want him doing this."

For one round, the real-life contender and the muscular teen did the usual in sparring, they danced and pawed. But in the second round the 194-pound Roper performed as requested and unloaded, knocking down the youngster. Jack Whalen got up, shook off the daze and got angry, as they say, with his right hand. "One punch," his sister recalled, "one punch," and the professional heavyweight title contender didn't get up — so went the Whalen family legend.

That April 17 a crowd of 30,000 including a "Who's Who" of the film colony crowded into Wrigley Field, L.A.'s minor league ballpark. Some spectators tried to watch for free by climbing high up on a wall at the back of the stadium so security guards sprayed them with fire hoses. But the night did not provide much of a show in the canopy-covered ring — Jack Roper landed one good left on Joe Louis before the champ unleashed a combination in a corner and put him away at 2 minutes, 20 seconds of the first round, the sixth successful title defense for "The Brown Bomber" and his third straight opening-round knockout. Other than his paycheck, the only consolation for the local fighter was that he had lasted longer than Germany's Max Schmeling, who the year before had been felled by Louis in 2 minutes and 4 seconds in the bout cheered as a triumph for America against Hitler's surging menace.

The war and a wedding gave Jack Whalen a fresh start in life. Despite his youthful brush with the law, he was accepted for pilot training, commissioned a lieutenant, and sent to the College of Idaho for a crash course by its professors — in mathematics, physics, history, geography, English, medical aid, and civil air regulation — as a prelude to taking to the air as a flyboy. But before leaving he scored a coup that on paper trumped any scheme his father ever dreamed up. Jack married into one of Los Angeles' oldest families, the Sabichis, with roots in L.A. dating back to Spanish land grant days. It was a clan that embodied the mythic merger of Anglo and Spanish cultures (and bloodlines) that gave birth to a fledgling city long before the arrival of the railroads and the unpleasant hordes of the twentieth century.

Much as the Old South was given a rewriting by *Gone with the Wind*, Southern California had its rancho-and-pueblo era romanticized by popular fiction such as *Ramona* and *Zorro*. But to the degree such a world existed, it had a real Adam and Eve. William Wolfskill was born in Boonesborough, Kentucky, in the time of Daniel Boone, so he naturally caught the pioneer spirit. Wolfskill joined a party of mountain men heading west into the wilderness to collect beaver skins, and by 1831 he had gone as far as possible, settling just inland from the Pacific, where he planted grapevines and orchards — lemons and oranges — in "the little Spanish village which nestled in the hills." He also met Dona Magdalena Lugo, who was part of a Spanish family (from Lugo, Spain) that owned considerable property up the coast, in Santa Barbara. They married/merged in 1841, seven years before the Mexican-American War won California for the United States, setting the stage for statehood in 1850.

But the development of Los Angeles took one more human merger, of the couple's daughter, Magdalena, with an English-educated merchant (and lawyer) Francisco Sabichi. Frank Sabichi served for years on the City Council, including a stint as president, helped bring water to the arid city, and was counsel for the Southern Pacific while donating the thirteen acres that became the railroad's central station. He also was a fixture in the West Coast versions of the Mayflower Society, helping found the "Pioneer Society of Southern California" and serving as grand trustee of "Sons of the Golden West" at the time of his death in 1900. To the degree that Los Angeles had a high society, Frank Sabichi embodied it. He would have rolled over in the family vault in

Calvary Cemetery at the thought of his granddaughter marrying a big lunk from the Whalen clan.

Katherine "Kay" Sabichi spent her first years in the family's twenty-seven-room Victorian mansion on South Figueroa, which had eight bedrooms and an elevator to its third-floor ballroom housing Los Angeles' second oldest piano — an instrument manufactured in New York, shipped by boat around Cape Horn, and carted inland on the backs of eighteen Indians. Grandma Magdalena Sabichi spun tales of the gracious life on the hacienda back when you took in wandering travelers and attended exhibitions of horsemanship by riders atop elaborately carved saddles. "Modern turmoil has swept away forever the wondrous beauty and tranquility of the past," her grandma said. "I often long to escape from the roar and artificiality of modern life but it is not possible, for the golden sands of the past have run once and for all."

When she was old enough, Kay went to finishing school where "they teach you only to be a lady," she explained, "and fine manners." But this Sabichi girl was not exactly the demur society lass. Sporting cascading dark hair and an exotic look that reflected her Spanish heritage, she hung with the movie crowd and took small parts in two films, one with Marlene Dietrich and the other *Madame X*, in which an adulterous wife is cautioned, "Life isn't a storybook." The gossip columns linked her to the early movie cowboy Hoot Gibson, who was twice her age and thrice married. Jack Whalen was not quite as talented a horseman as the Western star but he was swaggeringly confident and much better looking than the old prune Hoot Gibson. Jack proposed to Kay Sabichi with a diamond engagement ring he swiped from his older sister's cedar chest.

Both the bride and groom lied about their age on the marriage certificate. Kay listed herself as twenty-six when she really was past twenty-eight. Jack gave his age as twenty-four, when he was only twenty-one — he was at least seven years younger than the blue-blooded bride he married on January 27, 1943, with a reception at the Aces Officers Club in the Hollywood Roosevelt Hotel. The age difference was only part of the reason the bride's wealthy daddy was wary of his dashing new son-in-law with the pool-playing father. The father-in-law, Louis Sabichi, had just one arm after a streetcar accident but drove a Pierce-Arrow touring car and enjoyed being a privileged heir within the small world of true Angelenos. He refused to meet the ex-bootlegger Fred Whalen. "He has a feeling that we are trying," the groom later said, "to use him."

■ ■ ■ ■

Jack Whalen made it through military service with, as best as can be determined, one fight. Sent to Waco Army Air Field in Texas, he got into it with a superior officer he suspected was flirting, or more, with his society wife. Though finished with his training too late for combat, he piloted both B-25s and B-29s and at war's end commandeered one of those to fly his wife and new baby daughter, along with their furniture, home to L.A. He began offering his services as a charter pilot for film crews, and as a trainer of horses for the movies, that on a small ranch in Encino, in the Valley. He also enlisted an up-and-coming Hollywood photographer who specialized in glamour shots, pinups, to create a portfolio that might get him jobs as an actor.

One photo showed him posed in cowboy gear leaning against a shiny '47 Cadillac convertible, a pinky ring on his right hand and a slender cigar between his fingers, but with a smile on his face and white hat on his head — he had good guy roles in mind with that. Another spotlighted his sex appeal by posing him leaning against the peeling bark of a shady sycamore tree, the Caddy behind. The would-be leading man also adopted a stage name, *Jack O'Hara*. At least that's what he told police it was, a stage name, when they found two sets of identification in his wallet.

His Hollywood dream was real, who didn't have that? But for all his flirtation with the other straight-and-narrow stuff, and ventures that never quite made it — there always was an excuse — Jack Whalen was possessed by the same addiction that drove his father, for the criminal's elemental thrill of getting over on the other guy, the suckers (in his father's case) and weaklings (in his). Where the father was the bullfighter's red cape — now you see it, now you don't — the son was the charging bull. Don't give me b.s., give me the money.

His first arrests were for trivial crimes such as breaking-and-entering then (quickly) for assault and extortion, the *muscle activities* cited by the Intelligence Division in adding him to its watch list. The trademark of Jack the Enforcer was that he was so tough he never needed a gun. He liked it when people gave him the (slightest) excuse to knock them out. For some jobs he had backups and he kept clerks on his payroll when bookmaking himself, not merely collecting. But mostly it was just him and his fists, as the racetrack scammer Michael Rizzo discovered.

Rizzo was no Freddie the Thief, but he had a good con running for years. A former horse trainer, he'd tell gullible gamblers he could fix a race if they came up with the cash to take care of the jockeys. Then he'd introduce his mark to a real jock or to an associate posing as one — one pretend rider used a lighted match to burn a blister on his thumb to make the ruse look authentic, part of a sting that took a retired oilman for $4,000. So one day Jack Whalen, aka Jack O'Hara, showed up at the apartment of Mike Rizzo.

He come in real friendly and shook my hand, sat down on an end table. I was sitting on the couch. . . . He says, "How you been doing?" . . . and the conversation was friendly. So a few minutes later he said, "You're going to be with me."
I said, "With you doing what?"
"Whatever you do — it don't make any difference what you do, you're with me now."
I laughed. . . . I thought he was kidding. The first thing I know . . . he hit me here in the eye — I have a big scar on my eye here — and my nose and my eyes and my lips, and I was covering up and I was still on the couch. I couldn't get up and he was hitting me and cursing me, "You dirty motherfucker . . . let this be a lesson to you."
I says, "Alright."
"Give me some money."
"I don't have any money."
Then he told me to get $300 and he's coming back. Meantime he went through all my drawers and all through the apartment looking for money . . . "I'll be back for the $300."

Like most everyone in his position, the racetrack scammer Mike Rizzo did not dare call police to report what Jack Whalen/O'Hara had done — he didn't want to get clobbered again, or worse. What's remarkable is that the slender dance instructor Jon Anton, enforced over three $5 horse bets and beaten to a pulp at the Mark Twain Hotel, did go to the cops. Despite the threat to take him into a dark alley, Anton cooperated in every way with authorities and signed any documents they needed.

After the $15 horse bettor agreed to testify, Captain Hamilton assigned Con Keeler and Dick Williams, the six-foot-three former Ranger, to bring in "Jack the Enforcer." All they had to do was stop by the District Attorney's Office to get the paperwork. They spoke to a young deputy D.A., who told them it was routine, no problem, Keeler recalled. They just hadn't counted on a father's influence.

Everything was fine. Good case. Good witness. So he took it down to the senior deputy for his approval. He comes back in a few minutes and says, "Well there's a stop order on this. The chief deputy won't sign it."

"What's a stop order?"

"Well, I don't know."

So Williams and I went down the hall, all

286

these locked doors in the D.A.'s office. There was a conference going on in there and Williams and I busted in and the Chief Deputy D.A. looked up, "Who are you?"

I told him who I was. "I want to know where in the penal code it says anything about a stop order." I guess I wasn't exactly a gentleman. He excused everyone out of the room. Got up and came around. He says, "I read the case," and we start going down the hallway.

So I told him, "In the underworld, Freddie Whalen is supposed to have a stop order on the D.A.'s office. This kind of verifies it, doesn't it?"

Well he blew his top, threw the papers up in the air and stomped down the hallway. So we picked up our papers and went on over to our office. I told the captain, "Well, I kind of spoke out of turn over there." About ten minutes later he called me in, "I have a call from the D.A.'s office — your warrants are waiting for you over there," and he kind of grins. Williams and I went over to pick up the warrants then went over to pick up Jack Whalen and of course he was long gone. We found later he was in Palm Springs for three weeks.

When Jack Whalen returned from his convenient getaway in the desert he surrendered at the courthouse to deal with the piddling case stemming from the $15 collection. His wife, Kay, submitted a handwritten letter pleading for him to receive probation, at the worst, so he could support a family that now included a second child, a boy. "I have no vocation whatsoever," the former debutante wrote, "you see, I only attended girls' schools when I was younger . . . and fine manners, that I have, but that doesn't enable me to make money." She went on about her husband, "I wish you could see him through my eyes — his love of children, dogs, horses, sunshine, picnics with all his relatives on Sunday at Griffith Park . . . so many normal things that make the right kind of man."

In his own letter pleading his cause, Jack Whalen provided a peek into the dynamics between the Whalens and Sabichis, which hadn't worked out the way he'd hoped. "My wife's father has quite a substantial amount of financing behind him," The Enforcer explained, but "he has never helped my wife and I since our marriage." What's more, the suspicious Louis Sabichi still had never spoken to Jack's father until an encounter that week — Freddie the Thief made it look like a chance meeting with their rich relative who was not acting family-like. "My father informs me that on the evening right before last . . . he had an occasion to meet my father-in-law at a restaurant they both frequent. . . . I am told that the meeting on that evening and the conversation that followed was not exactly on a friendly basis."

The deft Fred Whalen would never stop trying to help his son — to bail him out, somehow, if he couldn't talk the boy out of his foolishness.

But Jack Whalen still couldn't understand why the cops were giving him the treatment once reserved for a Mickey Cohen or Jack Dragna. "In my own mind . . . this case is one of persecution," he wrote. "I know over twenty-five officers of the Intelligence Department personally whom I have met on different occasions, namely, 'pick-ups' for questioning." When they got to court, he elaborated, "All of these officers have told me at one time or another that they needed someone to pick on and that I was as good a prospect as anyone." He did not mention that one of those cops, at least, was now a friend.

CHAPTER 19
THE $1 CAREER

It's possible that Jack Whalen wasn't puffing when he said he'd heard of Jerry Wooters, for the Gangster Squad sergeant had a way of earning mentions in the papers. In his first months on the LAPD, a botched gambling raid won him the headline, FAITHFUL FIDO MUTILATES SEAT OF RAIDING OFFICER'S PANTS, and from then on stuff always was happening around the cop who exuded the same screw-you edge to crooks and his bosses alike.

Like most everyone but the Sabichis and their crowd, he was not a native Angeleno. Gerard Wooters was born in Philadelphia in 1917 to parents with a biblical pairing of names, Mary and Joseph. His mother died soon after, however, and his father carted Jerry and the two other children west in 1922 — that year again — with dreams of finding gold in Mexico. Joe Wooters settled his family in Los Angeles and set off to pursue the perilous gamble later depicted in the Humphrey

Bogart film, *The Treasure of the Sierra Madre*, trekking south and into the hills looking for a strike. Jerry was the baby of the family, so his brother and sister (nine and eleven years older) looked after him while their dad was consumed with that boom-or-bust life. Jerry might come home from school and see a gleaming new car outside, or discover all their possessions on the street and his roller skates gone — he sobbed when he couldn't find them. When his brother and sister grew old enough to be off on their own, he landed for a time in an orphanage in Woodland Hills, at the end of the Valley. He was a lonely kid who learned to be cynical about the world from the youngest age — and who vowed, like Scarlett O'Hara, to never be hungry again.

While his dad did operate a mine in Baja, he once asked his sons to drive the payroll down in an ancient Model T. Jerry rear-ended a pickup full of Mexicans and, at twelve, had to bribe his way out of a local lockup, an encounter not likely to inspire an exalted image of law enforcement. A couple of years later, he was picked up in Hollywood for peddling dollar-a-bag oranges out of a truck and taken to the city's Lincoln Heights lockup, where an old sergeant lectured the arresting officer, "We can't have any kids in this goddamned jail." Jerry insisted that the same old sergeant who sprung him still was on duty there when he became a cop and hauled someone in. "Well, you're back, huh?" the old sergeant said.

Where Jack O'Mara always dreamed of a career in law enforcement, Jerry stumbled into it. After high school he hustled work driving a taxi, gave tourists quick tours by movie stars' homes, and occasionally hauled lights at Twentieth Century Fox and Paramount studios, where his older brother was an electrician. By 1941, he also was taking a few English and pre-law classes.

I was going to L.A. City College, kind of fooling around, and there was a kid in the class by the name of Elliot. We had jobs part-time. Just before that Mayor Shaw had been thrown out and there were a lot of policemen fired or took retirement. They had like 250 vacancies they were filling. He said, "The police are giving an exam. Let's go down and take it. It cost a buck." Turns out he didn't take it. So I took it. Did quite well.

On April 10, 1941, for the price of a bag of oranges, Jerry Wooters, too, became part of the generation that was supposed to change the LAPD, except he was recruited into a unit that hadn't entirely left the scandalous '30s behind.

I had a terrible time in the Academy. Guns scared me to death. There was some sergeant who would stand behind me to make sure I passed. Then the night after gradua- tion we had a big party and a sergeant came up, I didn't know who he was, he said, "Have you got an assignment yet?" I said, "No." So that's how I got on the Vice Squad. I guess I didn't look much like a policeman.

Central Vice was looking for new faces that wouldn't be recognized to go undercover on the sex beat, "B-girls, homos . . . degeneracy work," as he described it. One form of the last was interracial coupling, spelled out by the disgruntled Vice cop Charles Stoker, who joined the LAPD a year after Wooters. "In the confines of Los Angeles are innumerable places known in police parlance as 'Black and Tan' joints where whites and blacks inter- mingle sexually, for the purpose of enjoying homosexual relations, smoking marihuana, or for reasons of general debauchery . . . Their proprietors, generally Negroes, engage or lease large houses frequently located in exclusive residential sections, where well- to-do white women engage in sinful liaisons with colored males." Candles provided the only lighting in one such establishment cater- ing to the rich "silver fox and mink coat trade," and the help dressed like characters from the Arabian Nights, with baggy silk pants, embroidered blouses, and turbans on their heads.

But before Jerry Wooters was set loose on such bastions of sin, they gave him a trial run at a plain old massage parlor, with a catch — this one was owned by a policeman who had been tipped that a rookie undercover officer would be coming in to ask for extra service. "I went in there with the masseuse and she slapped the hell out of me. I later heard this policeman had six to eight massage parlors." Jerry did not fare any better in the "Faithful Fido . . ." raid on a house where twenty people were gambling on the French card game Piquet at a party in honor of one Ruth Beyer, according to the newspaper account: "The fidelity of Fido, a white fox terrier, gave Detective Jerry Wooters an embarrassing moment early yesterday and also enabled several persons to escape a Vice-Squad raid . . . as Wooters started toward Miss Beyer, her dog Fido went into action and took a healthy mouthful of material out of the seat of the officer's trousers. During the excitement, most of the people escaped."

Jerry could take the inevitable ribbing, for he quickly realized how to handle the Vice gig. All you had to do was make a few meaningless arrests of hookers or bookies' phone clerks, or preferably a lot of arrests, each evening shift. "You go to work at four and hit the street and you'd have everybody booked and your work done in four hours," he said. "It was a great job."

For half a century, colleagues would cap stories about him by saying "That's Jerry," usually after an account of some finagling gone wrong. So it was when he plotted how to avoid getting his butt singed if America got drawn into the war ongoing in Europe and the Far East. On September 4, 1941, five months after he'd joined the LAPD, he listed his occupation as *photographer* on an application to enlist in a Naval Reserve photo unit based at the Fox studio. If the country did go to war, he'd be making training films, at worst, on the green, green grass of home. That was the scenario Jerry Wooters envisioned in joining the Reserves.

Then Vice sent him undercover to a hotel above a gay bar on Hill Street, where he would sit having a drink until a man made a pass at him. Jerry and the suspect would go upstairs to a room where backup officers had drilled a peephole so they could rush in as soon as the fellow made a move — between pinches they'd plug the hole with chewing gum. As luck had it, one of the first suspects Jerry nabbed was the great-nephew of an appellate judge.

After the arrest, suddenly a couple of detectives are wanting to speak to me in the parking lot, "Hey you think we can do anything for the kid?" I was approached two times by two teams of detectives. "Can you

295

do anything?" I said, "I don't think so." Then suddenly I get called to active duty. Goddamned war hadn't even started but suddenly — bang — I got orders to report, "Report Monday!"

He was long gone by the time the peephole case came to trial but he heard how the jury found all sorts of deficiencies in his arrest report. The hotel room wallpaper he described as rose-colored now was green and the door was solid as could be, there was no hole of any sort in it. "It was my first exposure to clout," said Navy P.3c Jerry Wooters, who would not be spending the war making training films on the green grass of home.

"Gee sis I feel like a lost soul up here. . . . Sitting out on this bay front is a bit lonesome," he wrote in November, 1941 from the U.S. Naval Air Station in Alameda, outside San Francisco. "There are a few books on photography here. Maybe I had better look a few of them over." The head of his small section quickly saw that he had lied about having experience as a photographer — the first pictures he took came out overexposed and he forgot to put film in the camera another time. Jerry wrote his older sister, Margaret, that his stomach ached like hell after every meal. "I think it's from being nervous. The strain of trying to pretend you know something you don't. . . . The Navy has a beautiful lab here, everything a person could want as far as photographic equipment goes. What a boon this would be if a person were interested in the damn stuff."

He spoke differently with his sister than with anyone else — he idolized her. With the war brewing, Margaret Wooters took a job in Washington, D.C., where she met and married a brilliant Macedonian émigré, Stoyan Christowe, who was working in U.S. military intelligence but already had written a book chronicling his experience as an immigrant, "This is My Country," which had become a favorite of President Roosevelt. His sister was entering a whole different strata and it left Jerry concerned, but also more aware of what he didn't have. "How is it for you . . . with money and health? Are you happy?" he asked. "Are things easy for you, I mean more so than they were before you were married?" As for himself, he confided that even going out with the guys for a drunken good time couldn't lift his mood since he'd been yanked into active duty, at a third of is police pay. "I realize that I've never in all my life been satisfied so why it should be any different now I don't know," he wrote. "If in eighteen months I'm still here I'm going to feel pretty bad. . . . God, I'd love to see you."

The good news was that the ladies liked how he looked in uniform. Jerry took pictures with a slew of women through his time in the service, one showing five crowded around him as a brunette slung an arm around his neck. Another was taken through a window, framing him and a dirty blonde, his head tilted down to gaze into her eyes. Another showed a full blonde with her head back, seemingly laughing at something he'd said as they sat along a long table crammed with uniformed sailors, a hundred empty beer bottles lined up behind them. Another shot was on the dance floor, cheek-to-cheek. He was just under six feet and lanky — everything about him was lean, including his hawk-like face, which narrowed sharply to his chin. He was not particularly handsome but his rubbery mouth formed a wry, casual smile, as if he didn't care much about anything, he was just kicking back. Maybe that attitude is what got to them.

They wrote him letters too, one drawing a caricature of him exaggerating the cute little moustache he'd grown. One woman called herself "Your sweet faithful thing" and spoke of "All my wasted love." One letter suggested they train pigeons or doves to carry messages back and forth, and worried what he was up to, "Put down that nurse! I'll have you know she's a nice girl!" "Do you still smoke stinking cigars?" "Do you still have baggy pants? Do you still have freckles on your back?" That woman also asked, "Who reminds you of

298

your sister these days? (If my memory's still clicking, you once told me I did — a stinking line but some guys WILL use it.)"

His own letters to his sister changed after Pearl Harbor instantly brought the nation into combat. He reassured her, "As far as armed forces go, my work is as safe as any I can think of. I want to get out of this war in one piece and feel as though I will. My desire is certainly to do all I can for America but . . . there are a few old-timers here who say damn few of us will come through." The scary part to him was how war was so different from police work, which pitted one man against another. In war, it might be you against a 1,000-pound bomb. "Take it easy," he told his sister.

In later life he exaggerated a bit the time he spent floating in the raft after his plane was shot down over Guadalcanal — he sometimes stretched it to five days. In reality, according to his military records, the crew of the B-17 was left adrift in the ocean for two days, or thirty-eight hours, to be precise. Speedy Japanese fighter planes had caught up to them while Jerry was taking reconnaissance shots of the enemy's positions below, pointing his big Brownie-like box camera out the bomber's open side bay. Then again, he never mentioned that his planes were "knocked down" *twice*, as the records indicate, during his 270 hours of combat flying for the first Navy combat photographic unit. In the ditching episode that left them in the raft, one of the crew had a broken back and kept moaning while they waited to see if a Japanese ship would find them first and finish them off. Jerry had the only pistol and when the pilot asked for it, he said, "Over my dead body." He was uninjured, though — his Purple Heart stemmed from a flight a month earlier during which an enemy shell killed the side-gunner next to him in the plane and slashed him under the chin. "I got the shit beat out of me," he summarized his time overseas. His Air Medal citation said "in numerous flights over enemy held territory, Wooters was successful in obtaining aerial reconnaissance photographs, many times carrying out his task while under fire from enemy planes and antiaircraft guns."

After the close calls he began vomiting at the end of each flight and reporting pain again in his stomach. He was told that might be an outgrowth of the yellow jaundice and malaria he caught on the islands. It didn't help that he'd be sleeping in a tent and feel sudden pressure on his chest — from the land crabs that crawled in and jumped on him. The damn crabs scared him almost as much as the Japanese Zero fighter planes. When he kept complaining about his stomach, the medics worried he might be a psycho case until further tests produced a simpler diagnosis, ulcers.

He turned it all into a joke when he got sick leave to come home and stopped by the LAPD's Central Station. The visit generated the headline WOUNDED MEDAL WINNER BACK FROM PACIFIC WAR with an account of Jerry having given another member of the crew of the downed plane 2:1 odds that they would be picked up by friendly forces. "A few hours after I made the bet one of our destroyers pulled up to our life raft. They uncovered their guns thinking we might be Japanese but we shouted at them and identified ourselves and were taken aboard," he said. "I won $30."

When he returned to the department for real, he asked, "What's open?" and was told, "Anything you want." He picked the Vice unit with citywide scope, sixteen-member Administrative Vice, run by the man who had recruited him out of the Academy, now Lieutenant Rudy Wellpott. Promoted to sergeant himself, Wooters was assigned to a largely black area of the Newton Division, to work the big-time bookies there. But he also led occasional raids on gambling clubs where he'd bring the largest backup officers he could find and his largest overcoat. He once jumped up onto a card table with all the cash on it and asked the gamblers, "Does anyone want to claim this money?" No one did, naturally — that would admit their guilt — so he scooped it all up, using his coat like a sack. He left the impression that he treated all the Vice boys to several long nights of drinking that way. On another raid, he kicked in what he thought was a wooden door but it was glass, painted black, and he severed his Achilles tendon. While in a cast, he was assigned to man the listening post set up in a motel for the bug that Ad Vice had planted in Mickey Cohen's house in Brentwood, by the wood box. Jerry had the headphones on the night Bugsy Siegel was hit across town. No matter what others thought, "Mickey had nothing to do with that," he said. "There was no turmoil in his house, nothing that wasn't routine."

Jerry's two mentors in Ad Vice here the ones at the heart of the scandal that enveloped the city in 1949, accused of being cozy with the Hollywood madam. But as in the war, he was a survivor. "They indicted the commander and they indicted the day watch sergeant. And I was the night watch sergeant," he summed it up. "I didn't get indicted. I got transferred."

Effective July 11, 1949, he was busted back to uniform duty, on foot patrol along Wilshire. That's what he was doing, pounding a fucking beat, when he crashed the Christmas party of the Gangster Squad.

The main purpose of the Christmas party
was to thank the civilians who secretly helped
the squad during the year. One guest was the
chief investigator for the phone company,
who helped them get a phone truck so it
wouldn't look so suspicious if they were
messing around telephone poles. They also
invited the people who helped them set up a
fake music company as a front for leasing
phone lines to carry signals from their bugs
planted about town. But no one had invited
Sergeant Jerry Wooters, a busted-down refugee from the infamous Ad Vice unit about
whom there were all sorts of rumors. Sergeant
Con Keeler, the squad's stern Mr. "Down
the Line," heard that his older brother was a
bookie and that's why he was so plugged into
the betting scene. Keeler was the one who
discovered Jerry in a backroom at their affair,
separating some of their guests from their
money.

We had the party over on Figueroa Street,
in a hotel, all invitational, and I went back
into one of the rooms in this big suite and
there was a craps game going. Well that's
illegal. So I just looked in, OK? Well, OK, so
some of our guests are playing craps on
the floor. But also playing with them was a

303

uniformed sergeant, in uniform, with his cap on and everything, down on the floor playing craps. Well, I just closed the door, walked off. It was Jerry Wooters.

We had guests there, like from Water and Power, from various places that were cooperating. Our Christmas party, it wasn't for us. It was for our contacts, not our hoodlum contacts. And goddamn, here's Wooters in full uniform, sergeant's bars, playing craps with the guys. Well, you know, god dang, to have a man in uniform, especially a supervisor, a sergeant playin' craps, which was illegal . . .

Imagine his surprise when Jerry joined their ranks.

That was the doing of their boss, Captain Hamilton. He sat on an LAPD disciplinary board that decided cases against wayward cops, including — sometime after their party — a Vice officer accused of enjoying the company of prostitutes he met on the beat. The accused officer brought Wooters with him as his defense lawyer of sorts, and Jerry spun an elaborate argument on his behalf, all pure bullshit, with a straight face. The panel didn't buy it, but afterward Jerry approached Hamilton. "I asked if he needed a good sergeant."

In fact, the squad did. With Mickey Cohen in prison and Jack Dragna then on the ropes, the brass saw an opening to finally crush bookmaking in Los Angeles. Hamilton needed a man who knew the ins-and-outs of gambling and could think on his feet — dealing with informants required a touch of bull. Hamilton said he'd see what he could do. Then Jerry waited and heard nothing so he went to see Richard Simon, the LAPD's deputy chief in charge of administration.

I was trying to get out of that god-damned uniform. He said, "What's your problem, sergeant?"

"I have an offer to work Intelligence, requested by the captain, but somebody up here is putting the kybosh on it."

He said, "I don't know that word."

I said, "Redline. I'm being redlined."

He said, "That's true. That's me. It's my understanding that you've been playing footsie with the bookies."

"Have you investigated it?"

"Yes."

"What have you found?"

"Nothing."

He got on the phone to Hamilton. He said. "You still want this Wooters?"

That's how the squad took on the cop who headed the investigation that changed the ground rules for policing in California.

Chapter 20
A Lecture from the Court

As a newcomer Jerry Wooters felt the wariness of the veteran squad members. They would cluster in a corner talking in low voices and cover their papers when he walked by their desks. They hardly socialized with him, either, given that they were married and raising children while he was a bachelor, known for inviting flight attendants to parties in his Elysian Park duplex — police wives would not always cotton to their husbands mingling with young stewardesses. Those other guys were godfathers to each others' kids, passed down their baby clothes and went on fishing trips together. Jerry had spent enough time atop the water.

From where he sat, it was hard to understand the mystique that surrounded the men who launched the Gangster Squad. He heard talk of what Jack O'Mara used to do with hoods up in the hills but found it difficult to believe — with his tweed coats and pipe the guy looked more like a scholar than a head-knocker. In fact, O'Mara was one of several squad members using the G.I. Bill to go to college in their spare time. The University of Southern California had a program tailor-made for cops and other civil servants, offering classes in downtown offices after the day shift and before night duty. Many of the family men also hustled outside jobs in their off-hours to help pay for their suburban ranch houses. O'Mara and a couple of colleagues who lived in the San Gabriel Valley had started doing part-time security work at Santa Anita Park, the horse track that helped keep all the bookies in business. Wooters wondered whether O'Mara and those others were more interested in getting their degrees and padding their savings accounts, with an eye to the future, than getting all the wannabe gangsters looking for a piece of Mickey Cohen's old action.

But if older squad members such as O'Mara seemed cool and incommunicative, the younger breed, the ones who joined the department after the war, couldn't resist Jerry. It was as if he said, "Hop in and come along for the ride," and they did. He'd invite them to see films late at night at the Academy — leftover evidence from Vice, not for children. Then the next day he'd offer to take warm and fuzzy photos of their families. He was a pro with the camera, right? One taker was his first partner on the squad, Jack Horrall, the son of the old chief, C. B. Horrall. Jack had grown up witnessing hush-hush meetings in his house when his father gathered his right-hand man, Joe Reed, and others he trusted safely away from office eyes. The younger Horrall entered the force in 1947 after serving as a Navy gunner's mate at Okinawa, then became eager to join the mob-fighting squad when Mickey Cohen revved up the scandal that forced his father to retire. The old man was all for it — "he handed me two black loose-leaf notebooks with nothing but pictures of organized crime figures in them." Now the younger Horrall was paired with a fellow Navy vet offering him baby pictures.

Jerry was good at that — he came out to my house in the Valley and took some pictures of my first boy, and my wife cooked a meatloaf dinner. And if you know Jerry he'd say, "Gee, I don't want to eat this," or he'd say to me, "Do you eat this garbage?" My wife was in the kitchen but she heard. She said, "Just don't eat it, then." He backed off and ate it. I loved Jerry. Jerry was one of a kind.

Of course, when Jerry got serious about a sweet young TWA flight attendant, Jean Louise Jettie, and they spoke of marriage, Horrall did pull her aside. "I said, 'Jeanie, are you sure you know what you're doing?' "

While he was courting her, Jerry would invite the other guys to drop by the house she shared with a group of stewardesses on a winding street in the Hollywood Hills, an idyllic spot surrounded by blooming bougain-villea. Jerry's own rented duplex was near the Police Academy and he'd invite the fellows there too, especially on paydays, when he'd say, "C'mon, c'mon over," so they could play poker for their checks — so what if he peeked at their cards? Billy Dick Unland, who worked on the Dragnas and the other Italians, grew uneasy at such shindigs when Jerry would offer him and his partner bottles of booze or a spare watch — no one knew how he got them — as if he was setting them up to ask a favor. Unland couldn't fathom what Jerry was doing in Intelligence where you had to have the patience to tail people day after day and tap sources to get background information that could help in the long run. Jerry came in with the mentality of a Vice Squad player, working games you couldn't understand while seeming far too eager to book someone. Jerry admitted it, "That's all observation," he said of what Billy Dick and others did. "I like to put people in jail. I don't like to just follow them and get nothing."

His first assignment was Charles Cahan, a husky life-of-the-party sort who, with his brother Joe, had come from nowhere to become a major player in the gambling scene just as Los Angeles officials thought they had the bookies cornered. Local authorities had been trying various tactics since the heyday of the racing wires, which had provided the main means — in addition to muscle — for Bugsy, Mickey, and Dragna to gain a stranglehold over a large number of bookmakers. The racing wires became as essential to the bookies as a ticker was to stockbrokers and the California Commission on Organized Crime saw them elevating a petty local nuisance into a national racket driven by "bloodshed, violence, intimidation, bribery, corruption." Authorities moved to ban the wires in the state in 1948 and the following February the Ninth Circuit Court of Appeals affirmed that Western Union would have to cease providing leased lines to the dominant Continental Press. Even then, the LAPD suspected that a local offshoot, the Los Angeles Journalists Publishing Company, still was offering bookies $2,500-a-month packages that included bail bonds, legal help, and an array of racing information provided from a nerve center with twenty-five phones.

The next legal maneuver was national, snuck into federal tax legislation that most notably raised the levy on packs of cigarettes to 8 cents, up a penny. Effective November 1, 1951, the federal government required that all bookmakers purchase $50 occupational tax stamps, post them at their place of business and pay the Treasury 10 percent of their gross handle, meaning all their profit, if not more. Someone living in fantasyland estimated that the measure might bring in $407 million nationwide. In reality, it was unworkable on many counts, and of dubious legality, but in Los Angeles six bookies actually registered for the $50 stamps and the policy caused momentary confusion in the ranks. That's when the cops detected the emergence of a group of rugged-but-engaging up-and-comers who were undeterred by the government's ploy, including Jack "The Enforcer," Lloyd "Sailor Jack" Woods — an accomplished golf hustler on the side — and Chuck Cahan, who became the target of the newest member of the Intelligence Division, Sergeant Jerry Wooters.

The feds had just passed a law that a bookmaker had to buy a stamp and I don't think they knew what the hell they were doing. But it frightened all the bookies because they didn't know whether to take a stamp out or not. Because if he took a stamp out, the feds were going to come after him for his net worth, you know? So there was turmoil in the city and everybody stopped booking horses. Cahan was just a kid in a gas station, big tough kid who' d been a runner or something for a bookmaker. All these other people stopped taking book and he opened up like a bomb. He had about six joints, and probably would have been good if he'd just laid under but he was suddenly the big gangster, had the Cadillac convertible, had the two-level penthouse, all the fancy broads, and he got the reputation. Chief Parker said "I want this son of a bitch in jail, I don't care what it costs." That was my first assignment. Walked in the door and I worked twenty hours a day for six months.

To be fair to his reputation, Jerry did try to save himself all that effort — he tried a shortcut first, an extreme one right out of the early playbook of the Gangster Squad. His young partner, Jack Horrall, listened in amazement as Jerry phoned the rising bookie and pretended to be an angry hoodlum much higher up on the food chain. "You fuckin' greaseball motherfucker, if you don't leave our thing alone, I'm gonna kill you," Jerry yelled into the phone and the voice on the other end responded, "Who's this? Who's this?" and Jerry said, "If you want to fucking find out, come meet me." So Chuck Cahan said, "OK, I'll meet you," which was not what Jerry expected to hear. He apparently had tried this act in his Vice years and either gotten a hang-up or the reaction he wanted — the asshole got out of town. No one had ever accepted his offer.

Never had one want to meet me before. So I said, "Fine," and I borrow the chief's car, he's got a big black Oldsmobile. Put new plates on there. And I get two big dago kids out of my office, give 'em hats and overcoats. We park up off Sunset Boulevard, behind a restaurant there. Told them meet me at nine. Took the two dago kids, sit them on the fender on this big black sedan. So they come. They stop in the street, look in the parking lot half a minute and they're gone.

In short, the Wooters' shortcut didn't work. Cahan went nowhere and the real investigation began. They gave him a team to help with the grunt work, which started with following the bookie. But someone in Cahan's position rarely visited his bet-taking sites — the clerks often did not even know their real boss. They had two types of phones, some only for incoming calls from bettors, runners, or field outlets such as barbershops. Another phone was set aside solely for use by the bookie's back office, which would call in regularly to get a rundown of the bets, at which point the clerk could destroy the evidence, whether a slip of paper or a scribbling on a slate board, easily erased. But every location needed to have the morning line before the tracks opened, the preliminary odds on the horses still running. As an old Vice hand, Wooters had sources who could point him to the publisher's overnight printing site, which he would watch to see who picked up the paperwork, and then follow them to learn where they delivered it. He discovered that the Cahans were operating out of a series of rented houses maintained like normal residences, especially on the lower levels, but with extra phones upstairs. It was time for the bug men.

Con Keeler had recruited another "electronics expert" to their ranks, Beauford "Bert" Phelps, who had an unusual LAPD pedigree: his father was the department's first pilot, except he never flew. Phelps' dad was a Minnesota native who served as a lieutenant in World War I and homesteaded a ranch in Oregon before coming down to Los Angeles and taking a job with the May Company department store, as a piano polisher. The elder Beauford Phelps also knew how to fly, and the LAPD wanted someone with that skill in the event of an emergency up in the Owens Valley or elsewhere along the 223-mile aqueduct providing the city's lifeline of water. The problem was, the department didn't have an airplane so Phelps' dad was a given a motorcycle instead and gained renown not for flying, but deadeye shooting. "As a little kid, I used to see him with a gun and notches on the the side," the junior Phelps said. "What's that for, Dad?" "Well . . ." Well, Daddy had killed suspects in '32, '34, and '35, once in a shootout with robbers who had used an underground tunnel to get into a Bank of America branch, and he had four slashes carved into his revolver to prove it. The elder Phelps served as a reminder of how the progression of generations worked on a police force — each new one could look back at those before and ask, "How did they get away with that?"

The younger Phelps wanted to become a pilot too, in World War II, but the military had enough at the tail end of the war so he was made a radio operator instead, on a B-25 converted into a general's flying command center. Phelps was six-foot-two and 220 pounds but was baby-faced and less than physically scary — he was no Jumbo Kennard. He was clever as they come, though, and brought a new generation of skills. Where Keeler tinkered with simple hearing aid parts, Phelps took a big old street corner fire alarm box and turned it into a device that could detect every phone number dialed from a bookie's telephones. Phelps also proved in the Cahan case that he could think on his feet, in the breakfast cereal episode.

It was in one of the back offices, one of

the offices nobody knew about. It's funny because we had to get through — we couldn't open the door, kick the doors open. We went around the side of the yard, I always had a bag of goodies with me and I pulled out my shims and shimmed up one of the windows. It was the old-style glass window, and as we got it shimmed something popped out and it was going to crash — this was 2 o'clock in the morning and I just barely caught it, it would have made a sound heard a mile away if it crashed. We went in, went upstairs. Of course, Jerry was obtaining some evidence, which there was a lot of. We wanted to put in a permanent mike because we didn't know whether or not we were going to get back in, so we looked around and the other investigator with me said, "Can we get behind the wallpaper?" The wallpaper had flowers on it.

So I took a razor and I cut around a flower, and I gradually peeled it away and cut out the plaster in back of it, put a hole through the wall, planted the mike in there along with the wire that went to the outside. Then I scraped the wallpaper with the razor blade so the air would be able to get in to hear what was going on. I was going to put the wallpaper back on, the flower, and reached in my bag for the glue — and no glue, no stick-um, no nothing. So we got the bright

317

idea and went down to the kitchen and looked in all the cabinets. There were some Wheaties. We got a bowl, mixed it up with water and made a paste, brought it upstairs again, got it real nice and pasty, put on just a thin coat of it around the edge there, put the wallpaper back on again, smoothed it out real nice. We were able to get back in several weeks later and it was still there doing a great job.

No one would spot the wire they fed along the home's phone lines to the nearest pole, then off to their listening station. They had phone company uniforms in addition to the look-alike truck so they could work around the poles without drawing suspicion, even during the day, though that was not wise with well-armed targets on the lookout for surveillance — then the work had to be done under the cover of night. Keeler had red tags to hang on their connections on the poles, signaling that only a supervisor could mess with that line. They had sharp cleats to climb the poles and both Keeler and Phelps did it. But Keeler had grown weary of battling the splinters and Phelps was a bit burly to set speed records on a pole. Luckily, the squad also had enlisted Roger Otis, who once worked as a phone company lineman and could scamper up those things like a monkey.

But posing as phone workers was almost

too predictable — their termite ruse was far more inventive. They used it on a home rented by the horse-betting operation's accountant in West Los Angeles, as Phelps recalled it.

We found out who owned the house through the legal records. The person lived in San Diego. A couple of investigators went down there and talked to the person. Before they went down they ran his records to be sure he was clean. He was, a regular upstanding citizen. They talked to him about the situation on condition that he be quiet about what we were going to do and also under the advisement, I should say, that if he didn't he might become involved with the conspiracy that was going on. So anyway Sergeant Keeler and myself went out to the termite company that Keeler knew. We went for a day and learned how to do termite inspections, how to write the charts up and all this stuff, a 9 by 11 chart. They showed us a couple of uniforms we could take. Then we borrowed a truck and knocked on the door. Some hoodlum came to the front door. We told him, "We're here to make a termite check." We showed him the clipboard and all this stuff and he could see our uniforms with the termite sign on it and also the termite truck we had. He made a phone call and came back and said "OK," so we went

319

under the house and we're banging and everything like we were inspecting it, and while we're banging we're drilling holes and putting microphones in.

I don't know how Keeler found out where the office was located. He drilled a hole up through the bottom and came to the carpet and slit the carpet and placed a microphone in there. In the meantime I was pounding and making charts of where the termites might be. We finished there, went over to the front door and told the man that we found termites, showed him the chart where they were located and we'd give him an estimate of how much it would be and he could send it on to the owner. We backed out and said, "Thank you very much," and we left. I think it was $700 or $800. It wasn't very much. We wanted to keep it low. We wanted to give the guy a break.

Charles Cahan and fifteen others were rounded up in raids on nine locations in April 1953. Jerry Wooters signed the criminal complaint but in the tradition of the squad others got to make most of the collars, a task force of thirty-five Vice cops. Cahan and his brother Joe both beamed for the cameras when the press was let in to document the cracking of what was billed as a $20,000-a-day bookmaking ring. "I am innocent of any wrongdoing!" Chuck Cahan announced.

Later, at the trial, the cops were matter-of-fact about never bothering with search warrants during their long investigation. When did they ever have them? They also were matter-of-fact about how they got into various homes. "I forced entry through the front door," one testified under cross-examination. "I kicked it open with my foot." At another location, the door wouldn't budge.

We tried to knock it down, yes sir.

With what . . . a shoe, a foot?

Tried to kick it in, yes.

And then you moved over and broke the window to gain entrance, is that right?

We did.

What was the big deal? Sure, there was a crime called *breaking and entering*, but when did it ever apply to them?

As far as the bugs were concerned, they thought they had legal cover under a 1941 state law inspired by then-new "dictograph" technology, the systems that essentially captured and amplified the natural sound in a room — that was just a notch up from listening in through an air vent, wasn't it? The penal code made it a misdemeanor for any civilian to install such an eavesdropping device, without consent of the owner, in "any house, room, apartment, tenement, office, shop, warehouse, store, mill, barn, stable, or other building, tent, vessel, railroad car, vehicle, mine or any underground portion thereof," pretty much covering all bases. But there was an exception for a law enforcement officer operating in the line of duty — a cop could use such bugging equipment when "expressly authorized thereto by the head of his office or department or by a district attorney."

So what if Keeler and his mates didn't always have such authorization? If they planted a bug at night, they could have the boss sign off on it the next day or week, with a little backdating, if necessary. "Nobody paid too much attention to it," Keeler said. "There were a lot of things that were sneaked in."

Phone tapping was more problematic — that was a felony in California, even when done by police. Law enforcement lobbied for the right to listen in on calls but the word was that a powerful politician had become enraged when his wife wired their phone, suspicious of his relationship with his secretary. The influential pol insisted that remain a felony for anyone, so Keeler and the others had to be careful when messing with phones. While the phone company's chief investigator was a secret ally, one of his underlings, a fellow nicknamed "Red," was forever trying to catch them in the act. They once almost shot the fool when he burst in on them in the basement of an apartment where they had clips hooked onto the phone box, merely a ground, Keeler swore, "but he was a pain in the side." Attorneys for Jack Dragna tried to show that they had tapped a phone in the case that nailed the local Mafia boss on morals charges — defense lawyers alleged that Keeler and Billy Dick Unland had done more than plant a mike in the mistress's headboard. Dragna's lady friend once noticed a thin wire going to her phone and summoned her landlord up to see it. But later on, when they came back, the wire was gone. Imagine that.

The truth of what the squad did was in an 8-by-10-inch Operations Book carefully locked away in their safe in City Hall. The gray logbook contained the basics on scores of surveillances: address, type of device, where it was hidden, where the listening post was. "It had everything," Phelps said. Only Chief Parker, Captain Hamilton and a few others — and the bug men — had the combination to the safe that protected their secrets.

The *realpolitik* of their time was underscored when Mayor Fletcher Bowron's long tenure in office finally ended. He was defeated by Congressman C. Norris Poulson, an Oregon native who'd come to Los Angeles in 1923, gone to night law school and three decades later ran for mayor as an arch anti-Communist. When Poulson took office on July 1, 1953, he asked Chief Parker if his bug men could sweep his suite in City Hall. Con Keeler and Bert Phelps got the job.

Phelps: We did a lot of work for the City Council. Every time they heard a noise on the phone, "OK, call Intelligence." They were scared that somebody was listening. I didn't find one tap, except one time — when Bowron went out and Poulson came in. Connie and I were detailed to check out the mayor's office, so we went in and tore the place apart and sure enough we found a bug on Bowron's telephone, in the mayor's desk, hidden in the woodwork. There was a mike, there was a connecting device and apparently it had been placed on there for some time. It looked like it was quite old. So we took that off.

Keeler: There were two layers of walls in the mayor's office, the regular walls and then another for decorative purposes. And in between were these wires. When they were put in there who knows? Supposedly somewhere along the line way back, under Shaw, he supposedly had it wired to a room across the hall and had someone record conversations in his office when everything was graft. But nobody wanted to talk about

324

it. It doesn't pay to talk about things like that in city government. The bug in the mayor's office, someone may have wired Bowron, you never could put your finger on it. But yeah, we worked in a gray area, a lot of gray area.

Jerry Wooters warned prosecutors to protest when lawyers for Chuck Cahan began harping during his trial on a particular bug stashed under a dresser. It was in a two-story structure attached to one of the bookmaking ring's rented homes, with its own entrance off the driveway. The room in question had the clothes dresser but also a couple of phones and paperwork strewn about that had nothing to do with getting a good night's sleep. At the trial, Jerry kept telling the D.A., "You've got to bring out that this is not a bedroom, you can't violate a man's bedroom." The prosecutor snapped back, "Jesus Christ, who's prosecuting this case?" It was no different than what they'd done for years, after all.

They also had an ace card under the rules that long had guided criminal prosecutions in California — even if police had acted illegally, the evidence they gathered was not excluded from court. The federal system already had a so-called exclusionary rule. But in state court, if you got the goods, no matter how, you could use 'em. In the Cahan case, there were plenty of goods. Jack Horrall, the chief's son, prepared elaborate charts showing the damning evidence gathered at each site. Facing all that, six of the defendants pleaded guilty. When the others were tried by a judge, without a jury, all but one was convicted, including Chuck Cahan, of conspiring to engage in horse-race bookmaking. It still was just a gambling case, no more, and Cahan was sentenced to only ninety days in county jail, a $2,000 fine and five years' probation. He appealed nonetheless, alleging that the cops had trampled on his basic Fourth Amendment protections against illegal search and seizure — and the state's top court could not have agreed more.

Appeals moved slowly so it took the California Supreme Court until April 27, 1955, to decry the "flagrant violation of the United States Constitution (4th and 14th Amendments), the California Constitution and state and federal statutes." The court named names too, starting with Sergeant Gerard Wooters, though it got his first name wrong — and got Bert Phelps' last name wrong — as it lashed out on what had been standard operating procedure in the LAPD.

Gerald Wooters, an officer attached to the intelligence unit of that department testified that after securing the permission of the chief of police to make microphone installations at two places occupied by defendants, he, Sergeant Keeler, and Officer Phillips . . . entered one "house through the side window of the first floor," and that he "directed the officers to place a listening device under a chest of drawers." Another officer made recordings and transcriptions of the conversations that came over wires from the listening device to receiving equipment installed in a nearby garage. . . . Such methods of getting evidence have been caustically censured by the United States Supreme Court: "That officers of the law would break and enter a home, secrete such a device, even in a bedroom, and listen to the conversations of the occupants for over a month would be almost incredible if it were not admitted. Few police measures have come to our attention that more flagrantly, deliberately and persistently violate the fundamental principle declared by the Fourth Amendment. . . ."

The evidence obtained from the microphones was not the only unconstitutionally obtained evidence introduced at the trial over defendants' objection. In addition there was a mass of evidence obtained by numerous forcible entries and seizures without search warrants. Thus, without fear of criminal punishment or other discipline, law enforcement officers, sworn to support the Constitution of the United States and the

327

Constitution of California, frankly admit their deliberate, flagrant acts in violation of both Constitutions and the laws enacted thereunder. It is clearly apparent from their testimony that they casually regard such acts as nothing more than the performance of their ordinary duties for which the city employs and pays them.

So the squad got a tongue-lashing from on-high and California got the Exclusionary Rule, mandating that illegally obtained evidence could no longer be used in court. The message was clear, recalled Bert Phelps, one of the chastened crew facing a changing world no longer so tolerant of the practices of the past.

"From then on we couldn't do it," he said, "supposedly."

Fred Whalen and family, including son, Jack, circa 1927, on the road with their prized Sterns-Knight Touring Car. (Courtesy of John F. von Hurst)

Jack Whalen, left, commander of his class at the elite Black-Foxe Military Institute, where he played polo and was groomed to be a leader of men. (*The Black-Foxe Adjutant*)

Fred Whalen hoped his growing boy, Jack, would avoid his own criminal path. (Courtesy of John F. von Hurst)

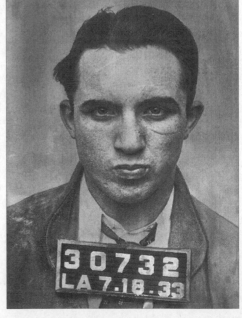

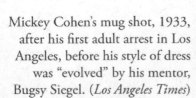

Mickey Cohen's mug shot, 1933, after his first adult arrest in Los Angeles, before his style of dress was "evolved" by his mentor, Bugsy Siegel. (*Los Angeles Times*)

Jerry Wooters bet his Navy raft mates that they would be rescued after their plane had to ditch at sea while flying over Japanese positions in the Pacific. (Courtesy of the Wooters family)

Jerry Wooters at 23, about the time he joined the LAPD as a Vice officer sent undercover to massage parlors and other houses of sin. (Courtesy of the Wooters family)

Jack and Connie O'Mara at their 1940 wedding for which Connie made her own dress by copying one she saw at the I. Magnin and Company department store. (Courtesy of Felix Paegel and the O'Mara family)

Jack O'Mara had to stuff himself with ice cream and bananas to make the minimum weight for the Los Angeles Police Department in 1940. (Courtesy of the O'Mara family)

Sergeant Jack O'Mara, center, after a big burglary bust in 1946, shortly before he was recruited onto the Gangster Squad. (Courtesy of the O'Mara family)

Sergeant Conwell Keeler preached the need to be "down the line" but he walked a fine line as the Gangster Squad's bug man. (Courtesy of Kathleen Irvine and Mary Jean Hardin)

A page from one of Sergeant Con Keeler's early notebooks, listing Gangster Squad colleagues (top) and addresses for Mickey Cohen and others (bottom)—the notebooks were their files until they got an office. (Courtesy of Kathleen Irvine and Mary Jean Hardin)

Mickey and wife, Lavonne Cohen, in their Brentwood home with Mike, one of their two dogs overheard barking when the Gangster Squad hid a bug in their TV. (*Los Angeles Times*)

Jack "The Enforcer" Whalen wanted to be an actor in Westerns. (Courtesy of John F. von Hurst)

Mickey Cohen feared that germs, and not bullets, would do him in. (*Los Angeles Times*)

Jack Whalen, shortly before the fatal night at Rondelli's. (Courtesy of John F. von Hurst)

The Gangster Squad, circa 1948, with Sergeant Jack O'Mara sitting on the far left in the bottom row, holding his pipe. Doug "Jumbo" Kennard stands directly behind O'Mara; Lieutenant Willie Burns stands in the center, hat down over his eyes; broad-shouldered Lindo "Jaco" Giacopuzzi stands just to the right of Burns; Big Archie Case, the "Mayor of Watts," sits below Giacopuzzi; Jerry "The Professor" Thomas, stands above Burns' right shoulder. Bug man Conwell Keeler is not in the photo because he took it. (Courtesy of Kathleen Irvine and Mary Jane Hardin)

Mickey Cohen was not pleased after being rousted by the Gangster Squad's Lieutenant Willie Burns in 1949. (*Los Angeles Times*)

The gunmen fired from across Sunset Boulevard as Mickey and his crew left Sherry's restaurant in July 1949, at the peak of the Sunset Wars. (*Los Angeles Times*)

Columnist Florabel Muir mocked the LAPD as "Cops a la Keystone" and dared to ask, "What does a Gangster Squad do?" (*Los Angeles Times*)

The first person Chief William H. Parker met with each morning was Captain James Hamilton (standing), head of the Intelligence Division, aka the Gangster Squad. (*Los Angeles Times*)

Sergeant Jerry Wooters, in 1950, after being busted back to uniformed duty amid Vice Squad scandals. Shortly afterward he talked his way onto the secret Gangster Squad. (Courtesy of the Wooters family)

Mickey Cohen, flanked by U.S. Marshals, after authorities finally used the same tactic that had gotten Al Capone—a tax case—to land Cohen in federal court in July 1951. (*Los Angeles Times*)

Detectives and newsmen surround the car of the Two Tonys, after the August 1951 double murder that became another "no prosecution to date." (*Los Angeles Times*)

Mickey Cohen signs autographs for high school students on his way to court in April 1958. "I can spit on the sidewalk and it will be in the headlines," he said. (*Los Angeles Times*)

Mickey Cohen had survived three shootings before the dynamiting of his Brentwood home in February 1959, all orchestrated by his rival Jack Dragna. (*Los Angeles Times*)

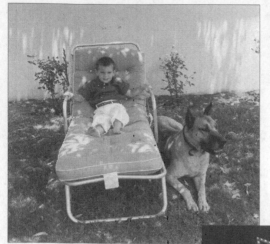

The watchdog Thor, a gift from Jack "The Enforcer" Whalen, with Jerry Wooters' son Gerard Jr. in the LAPD sergeant's backyard. (Courtesy of the Wooters family)

Rondelli's restaurant on Ventura Boulevard in the Valley, where "The Enforcer" confronted Mickey Cohen and his armed crew on December 2, 1959. (*Los Angeles Times*)

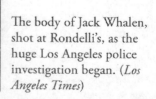

The body of Jack Whalen, shot at Rondelli's, as the huge Los Angeles police investigation began. (*Los Angeles Times*)

Frank LoCigno (center) turned himself in to Chief William Parker and announced, "Well, I'm the man that shot Jack O'Hara in self-defense." (*Los Angeles Times*)

Fred Whalen, demonstrating his trick shots for servicemen at the USO in Hollywood, perfected his hustling along the Mississippi near his hometown of Alton, Illinois. (Courtesy of John F. von Hurst)

"Freddie the Thief" was a born salesman and never stopped selling, a product or himself, until the day he died. (Courtesy of John F. von Hurst)

Mickey Cohen with aspiring model Sandy Hagen and talent manager Joe DeCarlo attending the March 1960, murder trial of Sam LoCigno. (*Los Angeles Times*)

Mickey Cohen gets a kiss from girlfriend Sandy Hagen in February 1962, after being released on bail from Alcatraz, pending an appeal of his second tax conviction. (*Los Angeles Times*)

CHAPTER 21
A FAVOR FOR MR. DRAGNET

Police chief William H. Parker went nuts over the *Cahan* decision, absolutely nuts. His passion seemed surprising given that it was not entirely unexpected that the courts might want the police to get a judge's OK — a search warrant — before they broke into someone's house. As a lawyer, Parker knew that the U.S. Supreme Court was pushing the states inexorably in that direction, that it was just a matter of time before all of them enforced the Exclusionary Rule. What's more, Parker was the first to argue that there needed to be checks against wayward cops, those wicked men who cast disrepute upon all their colleagues — he just didn't think that setting suspects free was the best way to discourage police misconduct. "The almost positive implication to be drawn from the *Cahan* case is that the activities of the police are a greater social menace than the activities of the criminal," Parker said in one of many rants in the wake of the ruling. "This, even as

329

a suggestion, is terrifying."

Parker saw America as imperiled on several fronts at once — by godless Communism, organized crime and degeneracy in society at large, the general lapse of values. It was one gigantic battle with the future of the nation on the line. The Cold War was revving up when he took office and within a year Los Angeles authorities prepared the city for nuclear bombardment. Two thousand firemen fanned out to L.A.'s households in 325 vehicles to deliver 600,000 copies of a booklet entitled *Survival Under Atomic Attack*. Parker warned a subcommittee of the state legislature that the *Cahan* decision signaled a setback even in that international war:

> One of the basic aims of the Communist Party, as you gentlemen may know, is to drive the police of America into a state of fear. And if the police are driven into a shell of fear, then God help the people of this country! . . . This is the action long sought by the masters in the Kremlin. The bloody revolution, long the dream of the Comintern, cannot be accomplished in the face of a resolute police.

From the moment of the California Supreme Court ruling, the chief also predicted that crime would rise, and within months he was wielding a pointer before huge graphs streaking upward to show a 31.7 percent increase in robberies and 30.9 percent in auto thefts. "Unfortunately, my prophecy of a crime increase has come true," he told the city's most prominent women's club. The ruling was not only a gift to the Communists but to "members of the underworld who prey upon law-abiding citizens," and there were plenty of those. In a law review article, Parker estimated that six million Americans made their livings through crime.

> This is obviously not a game in which police play "cops and robbers" for the amusement of society . . . This is a case of a lawless criminal army warring against society itself . . . The most dangerous criminals are professionals — people who refuse to work productively or legitimately, people who sneer at those who do and refer to them as "suckers" and "chumps."

Parker blamed judges far removed from the streets for hampering the police, who had to confront the criminal element there. "It is often a dirty business — a very dirty business — because of the warped nature of the criminals with whom police must often deal . . . They can discharge that responsibility only to the extent that society supports them . . . The effect of this decision has been catastrophic as far as efficient law enforcement is concerned."

Yes, indeed, Chief William Parker was furious at what the courts had done. And he had a prominent ally on the outrage front, Mr. Dragnet.

Jack Webb was a native, born in Santa Monica and raised in a struggling household after his father split, his mother forced to take in boarders at a rooming house through the Depression. Webb briefly attended L.A. City College about the same time as Jerry Wooters before enlisting in the military in hopes, like many, of becoming a flyboy. But he washed out of pilot training, obtained a hardship discharge — on grounds he had to support both his mother and grandmother — and moved to San Francisco to pursue a career as a radio performer, writer, and producer. Webb became the deep voice of the title characters in two detective shows, *Pat Novak for Hire* and *Johnny Madero, Pier 23*. Both radio dramas featured hard-boiled pulp dialogue and corny noirish metaphors *("The street was as deserted as a warm bottle of beer." "I felt about as safe as an alligator walking through a handbag factory.")*, and private gumshoes who worked their cases over the wishes of hapless police Homicide detectives.

Webb began seeing law enforcement in a different light when he was cast in a secondary role in a 1948 film, *He Walked by Night*, about an electronics expert who steals equipment and kills an off-duty policeman to keep his scheme going. The film was based on a real LAPD case, used real officers as advisors, and even used the names of real cops for some characters. It also resisted the usual extremes in depiction of policemen — as either one-man crime-fighting wonders or clueless flatfoots — in favor of an account of the painstaking procedures used by under-appreciated professionals Webb came to see as "a group of men trying to upgrade their life against all odds."

The next year, 1949, he approached the LAPD hierarchy — then Chief Horrall and Joe Reed — with a proposal for a radio show based on the department's cases. Webb must have made a resonant pitch because Horrall told him, "You're on the right track reflecting the day-to-day drudgery of police work." More on point, J. Edgar Hoover's FBI already had demonstrated the public relations potential of radio by lending the bureau's closed cases to such shows as *Gang Busters* and *This Is Your FBI*, though they were more melodramatic than what Webb had in mind, featuring lots of shoot-outs. Webb was not yet thirty when *Dragnet* hit the radio airwaves in 1949 with its trademark lines, "The story you're about to hear is true. Only the names have been changed to protect the innocent."

Listeners were told the show was created "in cooperation with the Los Angeles Police Department," and it developed a devoted Friday evening following.

By the time Webb decided to take his show to the still-young medium of television, he had a more impressive film credit on his résumé, a mid-sized role in Billy Wilder's acclaimed *Sunset Boulevard*, playing Artie Green, a nice-guy second-unit film director who loses the girl to his ethically challenged pal, the doomed William Holden. But Webb was not going to be second-banana to any corrupt glamour boy in TV's *Dragnet*. The LAPD had a new brain trust by 1951 — Chief Parker and Captain Hamilton — and he reassured them that they would be able to review every script to make sure his Sergeant Joe Friday remained a dedicated robbery detective who knows the rules and obeys them. His character's head wouldn't be turned by a pretty skirt, either. The upright sergeant was still living at home with Mom — he was married to his job and his partner. The show would provide tangible benefits to the department too, $25 a week to officers who served as technical advisors and contributions to build classrooms at the Police Academy and to the Widows and Orphans Fund. *Dragnet* debuted on the small screen on December 16, 1951, with Webb announcing, "This is the city, forty-five square miles of it . . . two million people. In my job I get to meet 'em all. I'm a cop."

Any doubts Chief Parker had should have eased after he read the review by one New York critic who confided that before *Dragnet* all he knew about the LAPD was "it didn't do very well with the Black Dahlia murder." Now, week after week, thirty million households tuned into a thirty-minute love affair with the department, promoted as "the documented drama of an actual crime, investigated and solved by the men who relentlessly stand watch on the security of your home, your family, and your life." Webb did not ignore the possibility of a wayward officer — a landmark episode featured one who steals a fur coat for a dame he has stashed in an apartment. But Sergeant Friday gives him a reaming out that echoed themes voiced earlier in Mayor Bowron's angry radio speech of 1949 and in Chief Parker's own inaugural address.

You get this through your head, Mister: you're a bad cop. You wanna know what that means? . . . You'll be all over the front pages tonight. . . . Everybody's gonna read about you. A bad cop. It makes great news. They're not gonna read about 4,500 other cops. The guys who walked their beats last night . . . The traffic boys on the motorcycles, the men in R. and I. or the Crime Lab crew, or the guy in Robbery who stopped two slugs last night . . . We could've piled up a hundred years of great policemen and great detectives, men with honor and brains and guts, and you tore down every best part of them. The people who read it in the papers, they're gonna overlook the fact that we got you, that we washed our own laundry and we cleared this thing up. They're gonna overlook all the good. They'll overlook every last good cop in the country. But they'll remember you, because you're a bad cop.

When *TV Guide* debuted as a national publication in 1953, its first cover featured Lucille Ball. Its second had Jack Webb, whose "Just the facts, ma'am" cops were one of the two ways America was sold a glistening new image of the LAPD throughout the 1950s, the other being Chief Parker himself with his paramilitary style and calls for a spiritual rebirth of the nation. Before long, Parker had only one rival as a symbol of honest, square-jawed law enforcement in America, the FBI's J. Edgar Hoover.

It was inevitable, then, that the chief and his biggest fan would be eager to see *Dragnet* elevated to the big screen, as a feature film. When that finally happened, in 1954, Jack Webb set the story in the Intelligence Division, a.k.a. The Gangster Squad, and turned it into a lecture not on bad cops but on the danger of giving criminals all those rights.

Con Keeler was amazed at how the movie's technical crew swarmed over their office.

> Webb was a very nice guy, a funny guy. But like everybody else, he was a Hollywood person who had friends and so forth, some of whom we wouldn't have approved of. So we went out a couple of times to talk to him and just advise him. But he was a perfectionist, I mean a perfectionist. He sent men in our office, six or eight guys came in one day and they photographed our office, guys with tape measures measuring the floor space, measuring the walls, measuring the glass, and it was like a bunch of ants. And other guys were drawing out the thing, OK? When they made up the set at the studios out there I was called as a technical advisor on a thing. Webb says, "Well, how does this look?" Well, I looked in there, walked in, they even had our transmitting radio in there. It was all props but it was just as if I'd walked in our office.

They even got the spittoon down right for the film version of *Dragnet*.

The main (paid) technical advisor on the film was Captain James Hamilton, the boss of the unit in real life and a major character in the movie, played by the gruff-voiced actor

Richard Boone. Three years later Boone would become a TV star as the cultured gunslinger Paladin in the Western series *Have Gun, Will Travel*, on which he spoke lines often written by a former LAPD sergeant. That unusually creative cop, Gene Roddenberry, would go on to create the series *Star Trek* and base its stoic Mr. Spock on none other than Chief William Parker. But in 1954, Boone was the perfect choice to play the chief's best buddy, for he had a tall, commanding presence, rugged face, and a real-life pioneer heritage. The actor traced his roots back to Daniel Boone while Captain Hamilton's people came from the very territory Boone settled, Kentucky. Like Con Keeler's clan, Hamilton's came west in a covered wagon — his family lore suggested that his father may have been born right in the wagon, in 1865, en route to California's fertile San Joaquin Valley. Almost a century later, the settler-stock Captain Hamilton was an imposing figure in public while living through daily trials in private, excruciating migraines that left him paralyzed at times in his office next to Parker's. Yet he always was there to huddle privately with the chief first thing each morning. They had the sort of rapport people are lucky to find once in a lifetime, trusting each other with their lives, careers, and the combination to the safe that kept the secrets of the LAPD. They also shared the belief that the nation did not grasp the threat of organized crime.

Hamilton spent months helping Webb find the right mob story from the squad's files. They later suggested that the real crime was from the mid-'40s but the plot borrowed suspiciously from a 1951 case that was still quite live, the Two Tonys murders, in which the underworld's code of silence enabled Jimmy Fratianno to remain free. Jimmy The Weasel later insisted that he actually saw his name on the cover of a script on Hamilton's desk when the squad dragged him in for questioning another time. Fratianno asked, "You going to make a movie?" and the captain replied, "Maybe." The Weasel said he told Hamilton they'd never get him back in prison for that crime, or any other, "The only way you're going to send me back is by framing me. . . . Frame me and both you and Parker will die miserable deaths." The cops' account was a bit different: they said Fratianno was docile whenever they honored him with the same harassment as Mickey, Dragna, and a few others. Their heat helped foil his bid to set up a business selling orange juice to bars down in San Diego — buy it, or else — and they finally caught him threatening the president of an oil company in a bid to extract 2 percent of the take. Fratianno said that indeed *was* a frame — his third cousin had called the man, imitating his voice — but he was back behind bars, for extortion, by the time the movie version of *Dragnet* hit theaters in September 1954.

The plot had Sergeant Friday trying to solve the killing of a mob underling with the help of an informant or two, a bug or two, and lectures about the unfair justice system. Only one low-level ex-con is gunned down at the start, but his fatal sin is failing to give his underworld higher-ups a share of his collections of gambling debts — he's a greedy renegade, like the Two Tonys. The hoodlum we see directing the rubout, a character named Max Troy, has to eat baby food because of a bad stomach, a parallel to Fratianno's diseased lung with Ping-Pong balls in it.

The fictional Max Troy does not think much of cops. "I pay your salary," he reminds Sergeant Friday when they try to question him. "What do they pay you to carry that badge around, 40 cents an hour?"

"That badge pays $464 a month . . . worth $1.82 an hour," Friday says. "So Mister, better settle back in that chair because I'm gonna blow about twenty bucks of it right now."

But the tough-talking hero is frustrated when four gangsters show up before a grand jury with their Fifth Amendment rights ("I refuse to testify . . .") written on slips of paper. Webb's sergeant has phone records showing a suspicious pattern of calls among them, but admits he can't be sure what was said because the law (unfortunately) won't let police wiretap.

"You mean cut in on private telephone conversations?" asks a shocked female grand juror, obviously an ACLU liberal. "Why, that's an invasion of privacy. How do we know that all you policemen wouldn't be running around listening to all our conversations?"

"We would if you talked murder," Friday deadpans.

The prosecutor has to tell him they don't have enough evidence against the hoods. "Release 'em."

"Why does the law always work for the guilty?" Friday asks.

"Because the innocent don't need it," the D.A. says.

Red-meat preaching aside, the film did provide audiences with realistic glimpses of rousts ("put your hands up on the car . . .") and of bumper-to-bumper tailing after Captain Hamilton instructs his men, "Put 'em to bed at night and get 'em up in the morning." But the big-screen *Dragnet* suffered from stylistic schizophrenia, mixing the dark look of film noir and its sardonic asides with Webb's poker-faced earnestness and his insistence that this mob rubout be solved in the end by the good guys paid, however little, to solve crimes. After one of their bugs overhears top mobsters plotting to kill their own triggerman, Sergeant Friday uses the recording to persuade the killer's wife to lead them to a piece of smoking-gun evidence: the barrel of the sawed-off his shotgun he used in the murder. When Friday presents the new evidence to the D.A., he says, "You got 'em!" and a miraculous clap of thunder punctuates the point. But when they head out in their raincoats to arrest the main mobster, Max Troy, they have to go to the hospital ("All Saints") because his illness was real — he's just died of gastric cancer.

"I'm sorry, was Mr. Troy a friend of yours?" a young intern asks.

"No sir, we hardly knew him."

Standing in the rain, on the street, Friday drops a slip of paper onto the wet pavement — the crib sheet from the grand jury room on which the mobster had written his rights. As the cops walk off, buttoning their overcoats, the rain washes over the paper, obliterating the hood's name.

The entire squad was invited to the Warner Bros. premiere and most attended. Con Keeler, Mr. Down the Line, drew a few glances by bringing one of his informants who looked suspiciously like a lady of the night — he was merely rewarding her for some good leads, he explained later, that's all. Like a number of the cops in the audience, Keeler was a minor character in Webb's film. "Keeler, you and Stevens want to cover the back?" Sergeant Joe Friday asks in one scene. "Right, Joe," says the actor playing Keeler. Big Jerry Greeley got a mention too, as did Billy Dick Unland.

Their newest bug man also got a plug, in the critical scene where Sergeant Friday wants to play a wire recording for the killer's wife. He asks, "Can Phelps meet us out there with playback equipment?" The real Bert Phelps got a charge out of that, as anyone would. But it also left him uneasy, for he knew the backstory, why Jack Webb was rewarding him.

To Webb's credit, he married gorgeous Julie London before he was a TV star. They were wed in Las Vegas in 1947, when he was still making his mark in radio and she was a twenty-one-year-old pinup girl and start-up actress, not yet discovered as a sultry singing talent who would score a million-selling hit with "Cry Me a River." That was her future, but in 1953 she was mostly a glamorous mommy, taking care of their two children at their Encino home. The marriage was on shaky ground, though, according to London's subsequent testimony in divorce court, where her lawyer actually said, "Give us the facts, ma'am." She then described how Webb would turn on the TV at the house and tune her out. She also complained that he talked down to her as if she were a three-year-old. "He'd tell me something ten times when I'd already understood it," she said. The star of *Dragnet* finally just split.

"Last April, my husband left for work and said he'd be home for dinner. Then he called later in the day and said he would not . . . then I did not see him for six weeks," London testified, wearing a pink chiffon scarf at the court hearing in November 1953. Webb did return home after the weeks away but "said he wasn't sure about continuing our marriage, and he wanted to think it over," she continued. "He stayed two months then asked me for a divorce. . . . He said his career gave him no time for marriage." Webb's career did give him time for actress Dorothy Towne, however, who had played a bit part on one *Dragnet* episode — he forgot to mention that detail to his wife.

So Jack Webb was caught like many in Hollywood, facing a nasty divorce and worried how his estranged spouse might go after his wealth. He thus called his friend and technical advisor, Captain James Hamilton, and asked if he could get a different sort of technical advice. Julie London and the kids still were living in the Encino house and Webb wanted a private eye to wire it up — he wondered whether Hamilton could come over with one of his bugging experts to lend some expertise. Bert Phelps got the nod.

I was asked by the captain to go with him out to Jack Webb's place, his home. It was just off of Ventura Boulevard in Encino. He and his wife, they were having all kinds of battles, they were going through a bitter divorce and when we got out there a private detective was out there and he wanted to bug the rooms for Jack Webb. Now, why the captain brought me out there for a civil situation, I felt very uncomfortable out there. Anyway, they asked me for my opinion and what should be done and so on and I told them. I said, "Whatever the captain wants me to do, OK," so thereafter it did happen, he got evidence he wanted to get. Jack Webb and the captain were very close. I think it was, "Scratch my back and I'll scratch yours."

Amid the scope of all they did, the help they gave Jack Webb was minimal — and apparently not of much benefit. The sultry Julie London was awarded $150,000 cash, $150,000 in Dragnet Productions securities, and $21,000 a year in support payments, guaranteed by a $150,000 insurance policy on Webb's life. But the episode still left Phelps feeling uncomfortable. Though the lines were always fuzzy in their world, this was a leap away from eavesdropping on a major bookmaking ring, the LAPD's public voices of morality secretly helping a Hollywood big shot bug his wife. Then again, maybe they knew what they were doing.

Webb came through for them again after the top court used the *Cahan* case to proclaim that law enforcement could no longer use illegally obtained evidence. First, he produced an episode of *Dragnet* titled "The Big Ruling," in which Sergeant Friday and his partner get a tip that a heroin shipment is coming and search a pusher in the area. They find the damning drugs — and stolen sweaters — but have no warrant and can't use the evidence, so they have to set the pusher free. Jack Webb's character gives America a lecture in answer to the question "Who's better off?" It's not society.

Webb also joined Chief Parker in appearing before the State Assembly's Judiciary Subcommittee to plead that legislators untie the hands of police. The actor's tool of persuasion? His film pointing out the foolishness of giving criminals all those rights.

CHAPTER 22
MICKEY GETS OUT

Sergeant Jerry Wooters was in one of the three LAPD cars waiting at the airport on October 10, 1955 when Mickey Cohen flew home from prison. Thanks to 480 days off for good behavior, Mickey had completed his tax term in far less than the maximum time at McNeil Island federal penitentiary in Washington. He was met in Los Angeles by his wife, Lavonne, and by Mike, their boxer. The other dog, Tuffy, the trick-performing terrier heard barking on the Vice bug, had died. But Mike was still wagging his little tail to greet his master. There was lots of speculation over what Mickey might do with his new start in life, but no one anticipated that he'd pick the nursery business. He would sell and rent out plants, real and fake — plastic greenery — and later manage an ice cream parlor. A state commission once estimated that he had five hundred bookies under him. But beauty and sweets, that was the new Mickey, so he swore.

347

■ ■ ■ ■

Mickey Cohen told of the bleakness and sick violence of life in prison, where a guard might beat a Mexican inmate with his flashlight through the bars for failing to understand his English. Another time, Mickey said, he found a con in agony on the blood-covered floor of a cell — the guy had stuck a lightbulb up his ass and it broke. Most of Mickey's prison stories emphasized how he had played the system: scoring a job in the clothing commissary that enabled him to win guards' favor by giving them new uniforms every month, rather than every year; growing fat from the steak sandwiches made for him by the Chinese chef in the officers' dining room because of favors he'd done, years before, in L.A.'s Chinatown; getting the choice assignment of examining crates shipped in from the Pacific with war surplus items, from playing cards to cologne, waiting to be plucked; wrangling up to a dozen towels for his cell, along with a large hope chest he stored under his bed; and, most important, gaining access to a shower near the clothing dispensary so he wouldn't be limited to the normal two cleansings a week. "Otherwise I probably would have flipped out," Mickey said. He might have had Gus Wunderlich to thank, too, for the hot water that saved his psyche at McNeil Island

— that's where Gus had been sent years earlier for pirating the gambling ship, and used his mechanical wizardry to fix the ancient boilers.

Mickey had hoped to slip out of the Washington prison unnoticed. Fat chance. The plan was for prison officials to escort him onto the boat off the island at 4 A.M. so he would reach the mainland town of Steilacoom well before sunup. There he would be met by his brother, Harry, who would come in from Chicago for the big day while Lavonne waited in L.A. But the first hitch stemmed from Lavonne's method of getting him suitable new clothes. The city editor of the *Los Angeles Examiner*, Jim Richardson, talked her into letting a reporter haul the clothing up there, so more than kin were waiting for Mickey to step off the prison launch amid a pouring rain. When Mickey did walk up the gangplank, his expected welcoming committee was nowhere to be seen — his brother, Harry Cohen, and two men with him were off staying dry in a coffee shop. With only reporters to greet him in the downpour, Mickey took off running, in a raincoat but hatless, toward his brother's blue '54 Cadillac. Realizing that he had missed the boat, literally, Harry finally came scampering after him and the mob of newsmen. "Where in hell have you guys been?" Mickey asked.

They had arranged for him to get a haircut and manicure at a Seattle hotel, to blow off the prison stink, but authorities discouraged any local stop. Mickey suggested they go to Portland instead — he knew a slot machine guy there. On the way, the drenched quartet stopped for breakfast at a restaurant where he celebrated his freedom by ordering double portions of orange juice and pancakes and three eggs, then left a $20 tip. He still owed half a million in back taxes and penalties, but some habits were hard to break, and not only for him. Portland police rousted Mickey and his entourage shortly after they checked into a hotel there. It was off to the airport and a Western Air Lines flight that landed at 11:07 P.M. in Los Angeles, where another media throng waited along with the three police cars, Lavonne, and Mike the boxer.

Mickey had floated the idea that he might open a restaurant along Wilshire's Miracle Mile or in Beverly Hills, forgetting that his federal parole prohibited him from being anywhere liquor was served. The eatery thus was a nonstarter, but Los Angeles city councilman Gordon Hahn was taking no chances — he introduced a motion to ask the state to deny Mickey a liquor license if he applied for one. "If he wants to sell ice cream cones, that's ducky," Hahn said. With the restaurant nixed, rumors had Mickey getting back into the haberdashery business, but in Vegas, going to Texas to give oil another try, or heading to Alaska to prospect for gold.

The chief federal probation officer in Los Angeles, Cal Meador, appealed to the LAPD to leave Mickey alone, to give him a chance — he thought Mickey might be an ideal person to speak to delinquent boys and other down-and-outers. But Chief Parker was not about to share his strategy for dealing with the newly released Mickey, noting "the German army didn't come over and tell their plans to the allies." It's a fair guess that he didn't buy into the positive role model theory, though, especially after Mickey was picked up in Palm Springs on February 11, 1956, for failure to register as an ex-con. That was a minor infraction that cost Mickey only $75 to resolve but authorities were curious as to why he was in the desert resort with veteran Chicago lawyer George Bieber, who had once represented Bugs Moran. Four days later, Mickey opened Michael's Tropical Plants in L.A., out of a greenhouse on South Vermont Avenue, just north of downtown. Mickey revealed that a brother-and-sister pair had written him in prison suggesting he join them in the business. He was good for publicity, at minimum — the Associated Press took his picture posing in a green smock and holding clippers as he explained how he was a 9-to-6 working stiff now, turning over a new leaf, so to speak, from his profligate past.

It used to cost me two, three hundred bucks to walk out on the street with all the bites put on me. Dinner, every night a couple of hundred bucks.

Show you how crazy I was. I was going over my clothes after I got back and I found 600 pairs of socks, five bucks and seven-fifty a pair, all with the labels still on. . . .

Just the other day I get a call from a fella high up in gambling circles, "How's the flower business?" he asks.

I tell him it's not flowers, it's plants, but he don't know the difference.

"Look," he says. "What you fooling around with that stuff for?"

Then he lays his proposition in front of me, but I'm not interested.

"Look," he says. "What's the score? You just doing this 'til your parole is up?"

That's what everybody thinks.

That wasn't what Sergeant Jerry Wooters thought.

By 1956, Wooters no longer was partnered with Jack Horrall, the old chief's son. They gave him Bert Phelps, the electronics whiz whose cop father had four notches in his gun. Bert was a blessing from on high. Assigned to watch one bookie they suspected might realign with Mickey, they rented an apartment above a pizza parlor across the street.

The book opened for business at 6 A.M. and worked eight or more phones, providing a lot of chatter to overhear. Bert said one Friday, "I got an idea," and over the weekend he invented a device to capture every number dialed to and from each phone — and *perhaps* what was said — "so we didn't have to do much work for the next six months," Jerry boasted. He may have puffed up the time-saving a touch, but there was a reason the CIA was constantly trying to hire away Bert Phelps.

After the opening of Michael's Tropical Plants, Jerry and his brainy partner planted themselves in their car across the street from the greenhouse that instantly became Mickey's office, playing the same role as his paint store and haberdashery in years past. Jerry quickly figured out Mickey's scam — he and his men were "renting out" plastic philodendrons in about the same manner as Jimmy The Weasel peddled orange juice to bars.

It was a phony nursery — he'd come in and tell you you needed artificial plants, cost you 1,000 bucks a month, or else, you know? So you could almost walk in and tell every place that's paying Mickey Cohen. The joint would have all the plants around it. Some guys did it with linen, some guys had soft drinks. He had plants. But he had one soft spot at the nursery, the half an hour

353

between when the office help left and his bodyguards arrived. Well, anytime he turned around and farted we'd be there. I hadn't said a word to him. I just was there. The captain, Hamilton, he says, "The chief says, stay away from Cohen. Anything happens to the son of a bitch, you're going to get the beef."

Sometimes the bosses knew what they were talking about.

Lavonne Cohen filed for divorce a month after the plant business opened. She said, "We've both changed since he's been gone. . . . I'm sure there can't be a woman in a million who has had a marriage like mine. I've lived in a dream house furnished with every luxury a woman could desire. I've had mink coats and racks of wonderful clothes. I've been smothered in jewels and bought a new Cadillac every year. . . . Now they are all gone — the money, the jewels, the clothes, the cars . . ."

Mickey said, "Lavonne married a dashing, colorful rough-tough hoodlum and when I came out she found me quite a bit different." He also said, "Who'd want to marry a guy like me? Always washing his hands and stinking up the place with cologne? Nobody would ever put up with it, except Lavonne."

So that's why they split — that, and the

actress he was seeing.

The bullshit amused the cops who for years had watched Mickey flit about with one wannabe glamour girl or another. But they also had noticed how Lavonne had started leaving their old home twenty minutes after one of his men, Sam Farkas. When she eventually remarried after the divorce, Sam became husband number two. For the moment, though, Lavonne was living in an apartment in West L.A. — their old house had long ago been sold for the taxes and their possessions put up at auction.

As for Mickey, screenwriter Ben Hecht tracked him down to an apartment that was tiny but with enough room for his essentials. A new Caddy was parked outside, and inside "thirty pressed and spotless suits crowded in the closet, all in tan shades. Twenty-five Chinese, Japanese, and Persian robes of silk hang there and thirty-five pairs of glistening shoes stand on the floor neatly." The essentials.

Hecht — who won the very first Academy Award for Original Screenplay, for the appropriately titled *Underworld*, and also wrote *Scarface*, the movie in which Paul Muni, a Jew, played a fictionalized Al Capone — had met Mickey a decade before, in his prime strutting days. The co-author of *The Front Page* was roped in back then to give a short speech at a fundraiser Mickey was staging at

Slapsy Maxie's for the Irgun, the underground Jewish group fighting to establish a state of Israel. In his memoir, *A Child of the Century*, Hecht recounted showing up and seeing all these battered faces, "some in society rig," and asking Mickey's man, Mike Howard, who they were.

Mr. Howard, tempestuously in charge of everything, answered. "You don't have to worry. Each and everybody here has been told exactly how much to give to the cause of the Jewish heroes. And you can rest assured there won't be no welshers." . . . I addressed a thousand bookies, ex-prize fighters, gamblers, jockeys, touts, and all sorts of lawless and semi-lawless characters . . .

Now Hecht found the post-prison Mickey in his small apartment, fresh from the hot shower, dusting himself with talcum powder. He was nude except for green socks, held up by maroon garters. Mickey assured him, "I'm a different man than the wild hot Jew kid who started sticking up joints in Cleveland, who lived from heist to heist in Chicago and Los Angeles."

"What changed you?" Hecht asked.

"I lost the crazy heat in my head."

The first Jerry Wooters–Mickey Cohen confrontation came behind the giant Ambassador

Hotel on Wilshire. Jerry had followed a strong-arm character to that spot and was giving him the usual roust when the guy suddenly peered up. Everything escalated up the ladder from there, or into the sewer.

I was behind the Ambassador and talking to a collector from Vegas, just shakin' him, but he didn't have anything. I was standing on the fender and I noticed him look behind me. And it was Mickey and a little guy, Ruffy Goldberg, they were together, naturally in a Cadillac. Mickey had just gotten out of the joint. When I turned around, he stopped and backed up.

He said, "Come over and shake my hand."

I said, "I don't shake hands with no fucking pimps."

He said, "You fuckin' whore, I saw your picture in the paper when I was in the joint. That gal, she used to suck my dick."

I said, "I understand you got the sweetest ass in the joint, everybody got a piece of you."

So he comes charging out of the car. I came out with a .38. Unfortunately, he didn't try anything.

I got pissed, I just hated him. I hated him. He's a guy that's always pulling a gun on somebody and always belting somebody. You know, all you have to do is catch him once and kill him and your problems are solved.

They were not strangers, those two, hardly. As a sergeant of Administrative Vice during the postwar years, Jerry had orchestrated the busts of bookies backed by Mickey during his rise to power. Mickey in turn had fueled the scandal that broke up the Vice unit and got Jerry busted back into uniform. So there was blood between them, plenty of fuck-yous held in reserve. And, yes, it was possible that Mickey had seen Jerry Wooters's picture in the paper with a gal while he was in the joint, assuming Mickey was keeping up with the news from back home. When the bachelor Wooters finally got married, it did make the papers, with a colorful account of how he'd met his TWA stewardess bride on a flight while escorting a prisoner from the east. His colleagues at headquarters laughed at that tale and at how Jerry trimmed a couple of years off his age so he was only a decade older than sweet, beaming twenty-four-year-old Jean Jettie, bless her soul.

But if anyone thought Jerry was puffing up the encounter with Mickey behind the Ambassador, forget it — Mickey filed a complaint with federal authorities, asking them to investigate the cop who pulled a .38 on him and seemed poised to blow him away. Jerry Wooters found himself having to explain why he was accused of violating the civil rights of Los Angeles's best-known hoodlum.

I got the perfect wife. Absolutely never offered any advice. Never. But sometimes you get involved in that shit, my wife got a little edgy. I came home one day from work and we had her relatives for dinner. Jesus Christ, two of the nephews are ministers. And on the back porch is some goddamned newspaper. It's got an article, "Killer Cop Stalks Mickey Cohen." That was me, the killer cop.

Chapter 23
"It's Hard"

Sergeant Jack O'Mara had kept busy while Mickey was in prison. One of the first of the state crime commission reports had used the term "Invasion of Undesirables" and the big-time undesirables had not stopped trying to gain a foothold in Southern California. Or maybe they were just tourists with $12,000 in tip money.

Colleagues decided that O'Mara had a sixth sense for spotting them but it mostly was luck, he said, and good (paid) informants. He gained his reputation, oddly, in the wake of the ill-fated Dahlia investigation, when he posed as the shrink's chauffeur. During his days undercover on that case he had almost been arrested himself one night at a motel up north off Interstate 5. Local police were searching for three hoods who had robbed an unemployment office in San Francisco and they thought O'Mara was acting suspiciously. He sure was — he was sneaking off to call Connie.

A couple of weeks later, safely back in L.A., he was smoking his pipe, studying the teletype, when he got a call from a hotel detective downtown, a guy he greased for information, reporting *three suspicious men*. O'Mara drove there with Keeler and Archie Case and shouted "That's one!" when he spotted a man leaving the hotel. O'Mara slammed on the brakes and ran after the fellow, who quickly disappeared into a bar. Inside, the cops found a row of men having drinks, but only one with a full glass, freshly poured. Keeler held up three fingers and big Archie cuffed the third man down the bar — yes, one of the robbers of the unemployment office. They got the other two in the hotel. Amazing. It almost madc up for botching the Dahlia thing.

A year and a half after Mickey was locked up, O'Mara got lucky (or good) again, when one of his old high school fraternity mates virtually handed him Leo "Lips" Moceri, the fugitive hit man sought for two decades by authorities in Toledo, Ohio. A member of Detroit's old Purple Gang, Moceri was on the FBI's most wanted list as well when he was discovered in Los Angeles putting slugs into a pay phone. Two phone company investigators were watching a booth at a farmers market off Vine a week before Thanksgiving when they spotted a middle-aged man plunk-

361

ing in four quarter-sized washers and two fake dimes to make a long distance call.

The caller saving himself $1.20 had an I.D. giving his name as "John Baker" and listing an address that was an abandoned chicken ranch. He also had $1,800 in his wallet along with a $10,000 bank deposit slip. When the phone company investigators confronted him he waved a couple of hundred-dollar bills and asked, "If I give each of you a single can you forget about this?" They refused the bribe, so he ran — and was tackled by Robert Skibel, who said, "If you make another move, I'll tear your head off."

Skibel years before had been the fleet end on the semi-pro football team formed by working class boys from Manual Arts High School. O'Mara was the pledge master when he joined, the one who swatted his fanny with the paddle. "Tremendous coincidence," said Skibel, who made two calls that night: the first to the LAPD's nearest station, the Hollywood Division, to get a squad car right over; and the second to his old fraternity brother, who then followed "John Baker" after Hollywood detectives released him with a citation for petty theft. The man didn't look like a "John Baker" to Jack O'Mara.

I said, "That guy's a god-damned Sicilian. He's giving us bullshit. We're gonna print him, let's check that SOB." This buddy of

362

mine comes in, "Bingo, O'Mara." He comes up a Mafia hit man wanted for seven murders. So I call Hamilton's home. I said, "Hey, Cap, I got an old friend in your office waiting to see you. Guy named Leo Moceri."

You know, guys like this, they're petty thieves at heart. We had another, this big boxing promoter, stealing magazines out at the international airport, taking magazines without paying for them. They work their way up and wear $200, $300 suits but they're still just thieves.

How O'Mara got on the trail of the mob boss of Gary, Indiana, was more of a fluke. When Connie's father became ill they moved for several months in with her folks in Sicrra Madre, a quaint town right against the foothills of the San Gabriels. Across the street was a big property where the shrubbery had been cleared within five feet of the house and a wall erected around the front, with an iron-gate entrance. Large cars with out-of-state plates came and went and the men who got out wore dark suits and ties, not the usual dress in the foothills. Neighbors said the owner had paid cash for the house. "Oh, he's a great guy, you know."

O'Mara began peering through binoculars out his in-laws' window to get the license numbers of visiting cars — what else did he have to do? It turned out the visitors were coming to see Anthony Pinelli, who ran the gambling and other rackets in Gary for the old Capone crew — he just did it at a distance now, having invested his profits in eight properties around Southern California, including a motel near the Hollywood Bowl, which his son managed. The motel served as a temporary home for the elder Pinelli's associates coming in from the Midwest. But one day he went to the airport to personally greet a distinguished trio led by Tony Accardo, one of the figures on the first page of the slender notebook Con Keeler began keeping in the first days of the Gangster Squad.

Mob lore had it that "Accardo, Anthony a.k.a. Batters, Joe" may have been one of the machine gunners in Chicago's infamous 1929 St. Valentine's Day Massacre, which solidified Al Capone's rule over the underworld there. After Capone's jailing and death, Accardo rose up the ranks with the opposite style — he diligently avoided scandal and publicity while becoming the nation's second most powerful mobster, after Frank Costello. On this occasion, Accardo had flown into Los Angeles with his personal physician, Dr. E. J. Chesrow, said to be an administrator of Cook County General Hospital, and with a bodyguard traveling under the name Michael Mancuso. That man listed himself as a car dealer but he looked remarkably like Sam Giancana, who within a decade would take over the outfit upon Accardo's retirement and, like Capone, display an affinity for both scandal and publicity until the day he was shot down in his Chicago home.

Accardo's arrival was not quite the equivalent of Capone's coming to Los Angeles a quarter century before, but it was close enough — O'Mara helped form a large LAPD task force to watch the Chicagoan and his entourage to see where they went. The answer: Perino's, the same fancy Italian restaurant on Wilshire where Jack Dragna had taken his mistress. Police officials higher up the ladder later gave the impression that the cops promptly treated the Chicago trio to the bum's rush onto the first plane out. In reality, Accardo and his buddies took the flight on which they already had tickets, leaving at 1:30 A.M. for Las Vegas. But Chief Parker's LAPD again got the sort of publicity it craved (EX-CAPONE CHIEF GETS COLD SHOULDER IN L.A.) and O'Mara got another of his small victories, along with the opportunity to demonstrate the squad's standard operating procedure for the amiable Tony Accardo before his plane took off. The boss had $7,000 on him, Sam Giancana $5,000, and the good doctor $250.

That's when I shook him down and found all that money in his pocket. Accardo, I'll never forget, "Hey, kid, help yourself. That's just tip money." And it was hundred-dollar bills. He had no other bills in there, about 12 grand or something, just a tremendous amount of money. He says, "Hey, that's tip money."

Well, we found out they were going to Vegas. We let them go, we turned 'em loose and of course the press came in, they got all their pictures and knocked off Pinelli's hat. He was very irate, he thought that he had blown the deal for Tony Accardo and the mob would be unhappy with him. We had nothing on them — hell, all we wanted to do was heat 'em up so bad and give 'em publicity. It made good copy, you know, the hoods coming in.

Sam Giancana, oh yeah, he looked at me when I was shaking down Tony, you know, giving him kind of a heavy frisk, I wasn't being too gentle with him. And Sam, he stared at me. Those snake eyes glittered. Boy, I'm telling you he had blue eyes. They were icy blue. I'll never forget that. I never had a guy look at me like that. If anybody could kill, that was him.

When O'Mara's wife, Connie, heard him go on about Sam Giancana's killer blue eyes, she shook her head and said, "Like *your* eyes."

After Connie O'Mara's niece announced that she was engaged to a policeman, Connie didn't try to talk her out of it, but she said, "They're gone and you never know what they're doing. It's hard."

The last few years had been hard for her not only because Jack spent his nights rousting the likes of Tony Accardo and his days either moonlighting at Santa Anita or going to school, still using the G.I. Bill in pursuit of his degree at USC. Connie's nighttime tears again had been over a series of miscarriages. She had waited seven years for their first child and assumed a second would come quickly. But after the birth of Maureen another seven years came and went and she and Jack still didn't have a second child. At Christmas she gave her daughter baby dolls and baby cribs and baby high chairs — being a mommy meant everything. She still baked cookies for the priests and nuns. Jack was head usher at the church. They cared for her ailing parents. Jack battled evil in Los Angeles. It just wasn't fair.

Connie played the bouncy homebody most of the time and family members called her "Lucy," after TV's antic comedienne, but she never fully adjusted to the strains of being a cop's wife. When they had parties or barbecues with couples from the squad she sometimes drank as much as the men, which was a lot. Jack had grown closest to Jerry Greeley, the burly Navy vet who divorced his first wife and married an LAPD secretary. Greeley wasn't a good drinker — he became loud and belligerent. His new wife put up with it until she became pregnant, then stormed out of one of their parties after another alcohol-fueled scene. "I can't do it," she said, "if this is how it's gonna be." Greeley stopped drinking after the ultimatum and stayed sober for years. But Connie O'Mara liked her martinis and vodkas on the rocks and she could get loud too. Jack once prodded her, "Let's go, boss," and put his hand on her elbow. She brushed his hand off.

A specialist who examined her said that corrective surgery might help her get pregnant, but it was a long shot.

Jack O'Mara caught himself wondering whether it made sense for the squad to be devoting all these resources to getting Mickey now. He'd seen a picture of the man posing with his pruning shears and telling jokes like a comedian. He didn't buy the buffoonery, but still . . . All these other characters continued to come knocking on the city's door — the Moceris, Pinellis, Accardos. Real hit men and old-school hoods with organizations . . .

Captain Hamilton had asked if he wanted to go to the airport and meet Mickey returning from prison and O'Mara said, "I'd love to, Cap." Then something came up and he had to be at home. O'Mara called the captain back and said, "I'm sure you can get one of the other guys."

Connie got pregnant almost immediately after the corrective surgery that was supposed to have little chance of success. They hoped for a boy, to balance the family, and had a name ready, Michael. But when God blessed them with another girl they named her after the niece who carried the flower basket at their wedding, Martha Ann — "Marti," for short. Connie wrote in her Baby Book:

> Our littlest angel made her debut on February 23, 1955, approximately 8:20 P.M., weighing 6 pounds, 10 ounces. Her first day at home was quite an education for us. After six hours had passed and she hadn't awakened to eat I was sure something was wrong. I called the hospital and they assured me everything was all right and let her sleep. . . . She awoke and was hungry about ten hours later.

The O'Maras had moved by then to El Monte, a bit farther out in the San Gabriel Valley. Their new home had only two bedrooms — the girls had to share the pink one — but there was a cottage out back for Connie's parents, who were getting on. They had a large yard with plenty of fruit trees, peach, apricot, lemon, tangerine, kumquat, and

Santa Rosa plum. Connie could go wild making jam. She also planted lilac bushes like the ones she remembered from her childhood in Minnesota, though their gardener warned her that Southern California was too hot for those. Their gardener had been interned during the war for being Japanese and tended the fruit trees wearing a pith helmet, a comic counterpoint to Jack's gray fedora. Life was good again. Peggy Lee had even come out with a new version of one of Connie's favorite songs, so she started singing it once more, now with two little girls in tow.

But my heart belongs to Daddy,
Yes, my heart belongs to Daddy.

CHAPTER 24
BAD %$#@ WORDS

The second Wooters–Cohen confrontation was in a waiting room outside the D.A.'s office but it stemmed from an incident at Schwab's, the drug store where starlets were said to be discovered. On December 18, 1956, Mickey strode into the pharmacy on Sunset Boulevard and worked over one of the managers to collect a $500 debt — onlookers said he spit at Harry Maltin, punched him about the face, and kicked him in the groin. Mickey started to walk out but returned to tell the manager to go screw himself. It did not sound like a discussion about renting fake tropical plants.

Jerry Wooters and his partner were in their unmarked car around the corner when they got the radio call but arrived too late to catch Mickey at the scene. They did line up several witnesses, including the woman who sat up in the cashier's perch and a waitress at the drug store's famous soda fountain. But the witness who counted — the battered Harry

Maltin — wanted nothing to do with them. Even after Wooters pleaded with him to sign a complaint, he refused. Then Maltin went home to recover and his phone rang with a mystery call, from an angry, anonymous voice claiming to be speaking for Mickey. Within an hour, guess who showed up at his house? Sergeant Wooters and his baby-faced partner, Officer Phelps, asking if he had gotten a threatening call from Mickey that might have changed his mind about pressing charges. "What call?" the guy responded. Hey, you win some and you lose some in any game.

The district attorney subpoenaed everyone involved to come downtown and appear before a grand jury nine days later. The panel was being asked to consider an indictment for felonious assault in the Schwab's incident and also conspiracy charges in another matter involving Mickey — an attempt to fix a prizefight. On the same day as the Schwab's encounter, welterweight Dick Goldstein had been scheduled to fight L.A.'s reigning Mexican-American boxing hero, Art "Golden Boy" Aragon, in San Antonio, Texas. The planned bout was upended, however, when Goldstein told authorities of a bizarre attempt to get him to take a dive.

According to the welterweight's account, Aragon had approached him directly with an orchestrated scenario for their fight that seemed more suited to professional wrestling:

372

The Golden Boy (gold trunks, gold robe) proposed that Goldstein go down in the second round but rise heroically after an eight count, then stage a furious comeback in the next round, and finally drop his hands in the fourth so he could be tagged for good, lights out. Plus, "Aragon asked me to hit him only around the body because it was almost Christmas and he didn't want to wear eye patches." Goldstein said he was offered $500 to take the dive at first, then a more generous $800, plus his hotel expenses. Police and prosecutors in Los Angeles suspected the plot to fix the fight was hatched in L.A. because Mickey and Aragon were buddies there. The Golden Boy was a charismatic figure in and out of the ring, regularly filling Grand Olympic Auditorium for his bouts while providing fodder for the gossip columns by squiring the most va-va-voom of actresses, including Mamie Van Doren and Jayne Mansfield.

Two days after Christmas, the lot of them were gathering to tell their stories to the grand jury. Aragon had already scoffed at how absurd it was to suggest that he would have to pay Dick Goldstein to tank a fight. "Any good boy can beat him any night of the week," the Golden Boy said. Sitting outside the D.A.'s office, Mick echoed the sentiment, "Nobody would risk a nickel on Goldstein's chances." As for his encounter with the manager of Schwab's, Mickey played the in-

373

nocent. "I just went in and asked the man for my money, that's all." But his wisecracking ceased the instant he saw Sergeant Jerry Wooters come into the waiting room. Mickey's face tensed.

"You're the son of a bitch that's trying to kill me!" he called out. "I'll come down to the Intelligence squad's office and you can shoot me there."

"Aw, you fight like a woman," Wooters said. "With your mouth."

Mickey threw him a few more expletives and readjusted his pants as if to tuck in his shirt, or maybe drop his trousers. A tiny fellow with him, Ellis "Itchy" Mandel, no taller than Mick, but his current bodyguard and constant companion ("I'm just around alla time"), started toward Wooters's partner, Bert Phelps, who suggested that someone might soon go flying out the window. It was one more pleasant afternoon among friends.

The positive note for Mickey was that the Schwab's manager still would not tattle. Without the victim's damning testimony the grand jury declined to indict him for the beating. The downside was that the encounter in the courthouse gave Wooters a brainstorm: If they couldn't yet get Mickey for assault, or for extortion with his plant rentals, or for returning to bookmaking — they suspected that, too — why not for cursing? Cursing before women, to be specific, the district attorney's secretaries who were seated within earshot of the waiting room. And why not throw in a second count for cursing earlier before the nice ladies working in Schwab's? The LAPD actually had tried a similar tactic on Mickey years before when he cursed out a couple of cops at his Brentwood home. But the bystanders then had been several reporters, a lower breed known to spout dirty words with their morning coffee. This time Mickey had exposed respectable womenfolk to his tirades. The cases were entirely different, right?

On December 28, the day after the grand jury session, Captain Hamilton announced that Mickey had been arrested at his nursery on two counts of disturbing the peace based on a complaint signed by Sergeant Wooters. But when Mickey returned to the courthouse in February 1957, to stand trial for cursing, his lawyer promptly turned it into the trial of someone else. "This is not a case of the *People v. Cohen*," he said, "but of *Wooters v. Cohen*."

A jury heard three days of testimony about a few epithets, mostly the phrase suggesting that someone has canine ancestry. One of the D.A.'s secretaries insisted that she lost sleep after being exposed to the foul words, but Mickey's lawyer, Rexford Eagan, established that all had heard (or used) such language before. Then he went on the offensive, spotlighting the LAPD's "crusade" against Mickey since his release from prison. The defense's main witness in that regard was Jerry Wooters. Called to the stand on the trial's last day, he acknowledged drawing his .38 on Mickey behind the Ambassador.

If Mickey was doing something suspicious that day, why hadn't he searched Mickey's car? "I had on a new sport coat and I didn't want to get it messed up."

Was he aware that the chief federal probation officer had implored police to lay off Mickey? "He seems to think that Mr. Cohen is a wonderful man."

In closing statements, Mickey's lawyer told the jury that the cop pushing the case had a very thin skin and a very thick head. "If Mr. Cohen is found guilty," Rexford Eagan said, "it will give Wooters a license to hunt, to harass."

The jurors took only two hours to decide that this was not the case to send the city's celebrity hoodlum back behind bars. Not guilty on both counts.

Mickey pumped the hand of the jury's foreman and said, "I'll try to live up to your verdict."

Then he went on television to rub it in.

CHAPTER 25
EXPENSIVE %$#@ WORDS

Mickey periodically insisted that he didn't like all the attention. "I feel happier when I'm anonymous," he told Florabel Muir during the tumultuous year of 1949. "Where does a guy like me get off sharing headlines with the mayor of this great city? It doesn't make sense, does it?" Mickey made a similar case to the Kefauver Committee, explaining to the senators that others thrust the perverse celebrity on him, especially a police department eager to divert attention from its own dirty laundry.

Halley: What are they trying to cover up?

Cohen: I don't know what they are trying to cover up. Every time that something comes up where they want to get it in the papers, I am the best medium for them. All they have to do is throw something at me.

Halley: I don't think you should be vague.

377

I think as a citizen, if you think something is being covered up, you should say so.

Cohen: I am the greatest newspaper copy in this city and they have used me for any kind of a purpose. Ninety percent of the people in the city will tell you that.

Senator Tobey: In a Senate committee hearing on interstate commerce, we had another gentleman of the same profession come before us. His name was Frank Costello. I began to question him and in all pomposity he beat his breast and said, "I am front-page stuff. Every time I speak, the papers carry it on the front page." That is called egotism.

Cohen: That happens to be my case and not egotism. I can spit on the sidewalk and it will be in the headlines.

Tobey: I won't say any more at this time.

Cohen: These are actual facts.

Some smart people agreed with Mickey that he was not wholly to blame, given that he did not exactly issue press releases when he began his climb up the ranks of organized crime, such as it was, in Los Angeles. Enterprising city editors (and Florabels) sought him out, recognizing that the novelty of *real gangsters* in L.A. made for great copy that fed the paranoid fears of the City of Angels. That was the Frankenstein theory — that Mickey was a creation, a monster brought to life from semi-nothingness who then became nearly impossible to kill once he escaped the castle. It was a provocative theory, up there with Mickey-as-Gatsby, well worth pondering.

But it's likely that the exponents of the Frankenstein theory never saw a blurb that ran in *Ring* magazine back in 1931. In addition to covering the major news of prizefighting, the Bible of Boxing ran monthly columns from the hotbeds of the sport. The "Cleveland Chatter" column was put together by "Parson" Tom McGinty, who in January of that year included this tidbit several items down on his page:

> Mickey Cohen, local flyweight, called me on the telephone, thanking me for writing him up in the RING. This youngster looks like a real find. He is ready for any of the high-class flyweights. . . . He is certainly a classy little fighter.

Mickey Cohen, at seventeen, was on the phone pushing the ink! A quarter century later, he couldn't help himself — he was as addicted to the attention as he was to his scalding ninety-minute showers. Maybe the explanation wasn't in literature or horror films but child development, him being the youngest of six kids, waving to be noticed. What difference did it make? Chicago's Tony Accardo could come and go from L.A. with a smile and a shrug and resist any temptation to taunt the cops who harried him. A prudent commitment to avoiding the limelight worked well for The Big Tuna — later in life he returned to California with little resistance, wintering during his twilight years in a golf community in Palm Springs, having spent one night in jail his entire career as a mobster. But that wasn't Mickey — not back when he was holding court on the Strip as he was being shot at, and not in 1957, when he signed on to be the fourth guest on a national talk show launched that April 28 by the ABC television network.

The host was Mike Wallace, a cigarette-puffing former quiz show front man who had made a splash doing blunt interviews for a local New York TV station. His new *The Mike Wallace Interview* was live, meaning viewers heard whatever came out of Mickey's mouth unfiltered, a recipe for disaster if ever there was one.

Mike Wallace's resonant voice made him a natural as an announcer in any medium and he took whatever paying work he could get to start. After serving in the Navy in World War II, he lent his voice to a series of radio dramas before making his leap to TV, where he did commercials and hosted quiz shows, the rage of the day. His included *The Big Surprise*, in which contestants could win up to $100,000 by answering questions in their area of expertise. That was NBC's attempt to one-up CBS's *The $64,000 Question*, on which the pretty psychologist Dr. Joyce Brothers had become a national celebrity by showing off her knowledge of boxing. On *The Big Surprise*, a twelve-year-old hit the jackpot by answering questions about the stock market. Take that, Dr. Joyce.

Wallace fortunately escaped the quiz show carnival before it was exposed as being (sometimes) as fixed as the Golden Boy's fight. He found his niche when he began hosting newscasts in New York and then *Night Beat*, for which he conducted interviews from 11 P.M. to midnight four nights a week. Wallace had done some acting over the years (playing a lieutenant in an early TV series *Stand By for Crime*) and he brought that skill to the interview show, even using his cigarette as an effective prop, holding it between his middle and index fingers and puffing and exhaling for dramatic effect. But his genius was his avoidance of smiley-faced politeness — he was willing to ask his guests about more than their pets or their latest motion picture. He was like a coiled snake, poised to lunge forward and strike. Six months after he began the New York talk show he was invited to do the same thing on a national stage. *The Mike Wallace Interview* would have just him and one guest for a full half hour each Sunday night.

Given that the show was based in New York, Wallace's staff didn't have to look far for a gangster if they wanted to book one. The Kefauver committee had identified New York and Chicago as America's two centers of organized crime, both cities having large, concentrated Italian immigrant neighborhoods that served as early breeding grounds for the criminal networks that eventually controlled whole building trades, trucking, and the docks. One gambling overlord in the New York area might have sixty enforcers under him. He in turn answered to Frank Costello, whose influence was underscored by a wartime episode involving the Brooklyn prosecutor who had helped cripple Murder, Inc., Bugsy's old gang, and send Louis "Lepke" Buchalter to the Sing Sing chair — in New York, there had been convictions in mob murders.

But Kefauver's report described how William O'Dwyer, soon to be elected mayor, had to go hat-in-hand for help during the war when asked to combat the racketeering inflating the cost of aircraft parts purchased by the military. "According to Ambassador O'Dwyer, when he was an Army officer attached to the Air Force in 1942 with orders 'to keep Wright Field clean,' he found it necessary to obtain some information from Frank Costello. Despite the obvious disinclination which the former prosecutor of Murder, Inc., must have had to go into the home of Costello, O'Dwyer did not even think of calling Costello to the offices of the Army Air Corps; he went to Costello's home."

They called Costello the "prime minister of the U.S. underworld" and he would have been a marquee guest for a TV show, and one who it would cost nothing to get to the ABC studios — his apartment was blocks away, on Central Park West. Of course, absent a subpoena, a mob boss like him would have laughed off any invitation to sit down for half an hour with a camera in his face. Costello had other things on his mind, anyway, as ABC's new show was launched. On May 2, rival Vinny "The Chin" Gigante ambushed him in the lobby of his fancy apartment building and fired a .38 slug at his head, saying, "This is for you, Frank." The bullet bounced off, but the likes of Frank Costello was not about to face a TV host eager to ambush him in other ways.

Fresh off his triumph in his court case for cursing before women, the Los Angeles plant pruner Mickey Cohen asked ABC to send a limo out to meet him at the airport when he flew in for the May 19, 1957 show. Mike Wallace's young researcher-writer Al Ramrus got the job of meeting their guest and taking him to the Hampshire House hotel, understanding that it wasn't Frank Costello who'd be walking off the plane from the other coast, but expecting at least a facsimile of James Cagney.

I was twenty-seven and it was less than a year after I had been a crime reporter in Hamilton, Ontario. A big story for me there would be a stickup of a gas station. Here I am in New York and I'm told by Mike Wallace and our producer, Ted Yates, we're doing Mickey Cohen. He was colorful, sensational, controversial, an ideal guest for Mike Wallace. I was told that I was to meet Mickey Cohen at Idlewild Airport in a limousine because he wanted a limousine to take him into the city. And I was sitting in the back and sort of fantasizing what this would be all about. Was he in danger of getting rubbed out? Was I in danger of getting rubbed out? I also had been given word that he was traveling incognito and therefore I had to have a secret password to go up to him and identify myself. The password was "Mr. Dunn." So I rehearsed that, "Mr. Dunn, Mr. Dunn, Mr. Dunn," all the way down to

384

the airport. And I recognized Mickey from some news photos. I said "Mr. Dunn, I'm Al Ramrus." He said "What Dunn? I'm Cohen." He was not in on the secret password gimmick.

Mickey was short, sort of stocky, overweight, sallow-faced, and you got the feeling he was badly out of shape. In a street fight, unless he could kick a guy's balls or chew his nose off in the first minute, he'd be a limp noodle in a fight, despite his reputation. Mickey Cohen did not radiate the charisma of a Cagney or a Bogart. He was a rather nondescript, colorless-looking guy. It reminds me of Hannah Arendt's concept of "the banality of evil." He was a banal guy from everything I could see. He was accompanied by another guy, maybe an associate or a gofer. On the drive back to New York, I talked about the weather, I talked about New York. It was rather awkward. We reached the hotel on Central Park South and went up to the rooms we had reserved for him and his associate. It was two bedrooms and an adjoining bathroom. Mickey took one look at that adjoining bathroom and said, "No, I ain't gonna stay here." He wanted a private bathroom. I had to go down to the desk and find some other arrangements.

Mickey didn't want to talk then. He invited me to a party he was holding that night at his place, which I guess was a getting-together party with the mob from New York and New Jersey, maybe fifteen guys and a handful of hot-looking girls. But strangely enough the atmosphere was not very romantic or very sexual. It reminds me of something the writer Ben Hecht told me, that mobsters generally are not overly interested in sexual intercourse. They're obsessed with money, power, scheming, and survival.

I tried to do the preinterview, prepare the show, in the middle of this loud noisy party. And it was very, very difficult. How do you sit and talk about this man's life and his crimes and his conscience and whatever while he's surrounded by his pals from the mob? I didn't see any drugs and I didn't see very much drinking, either. Mostly it was a lot of pineapple cheesecake, cherry cheesecake from Lindy's. I was very happy with the cheesecake. Mickey made it very clear to me, however, that he wanted to publicly attack Chief Parker and Hamilton. There was no doubt in my mind that was what he wanted to do on the show. Mainly his motivation was to attack the cops. That should have set alarm bells off in my head. Maybe it was the excitement of being with a mobster or the controversy and the headlines we would get, but it sounded OK to me. And when I went back it sounded OK to Ted and Mike. We were somewhat out of our minds. I can't give you a better explanation of why we didn't say, "We can't do this. We gotta stop him."

As soon as the studio lights went on, their guest turned on too. The banal schlub of the airport and hotel suite became Mickey Cohen, gangster — or ex-gangster, for he reiterated for the nation that he had gone straight with the greenhouse, even if Wallace hadn't invited him to give the lowdown on floral arrangements. "What we wanted from him were stories about the Bad Old Days," the host said. Mickey obliged by asserting that he once took up to $600,000 in bets daily, but never made a penny from prostitution or narcotics, providing an opening for his host to uncoil. Wallace said:

Wallace: You have made book, you have bootlegged. Most important of all, you've broken one of the commandments — you've killed, Mickey. How can you be proud of not dealing in prostitution and narcotics when you've killed at least one man, or how many more? How many more, Mickey?

Cohen: I have killed no man that in the

387

first place didn't deserve killing.

Wallace: By whose standards?

Cohen: By the standards of our way of life. And I actually, in all of these killings — in all of what you would call killings — I had no alternative. It was either my life or their life.

Had they left it at that, both parties would have gone home happy. Wallace had a guest talking about killing (!) and Mickey had come up with a signature quote worthy of his obituary: "I have killed no man that . . . didn't deserve killing." Though there was but one fatal shooting conclusively tied to him, he had been able to upgrade himself into a (possible) mass killer, while revealing nothing specific. A win-win, as they'd say later. But Wallace had to push him in another direction. "Now, Mick, without naming names, how far up in the brass do you have to bribe the cops to carry on a big-time bookmaking operation?"

Without naming names? Mickey had been handed a coast-to-coast megaphone to settle old scores. He said, "I have a police chief in Los Angeles who happens to be a sadistic degenerate." When Wallace linked the words "apparently respectable" to Chief Parker, Mickey could hold back no longer:

I'm going to give him much to bring a libel suit against me. He's nothing but a thief that has been — a reformed thief . . . This man here is as dishonest politically as the worst thief that accepts money for payoffs . . . He is a known alcoholic. He's been disgusting. He's an old degenerate. In other words, he's a sadistic degenerate of the worst type.

Parker was not the only target. After Mickey said, "He has a man underneath him that is on an equal basis," Wallace pressed him three times to say explicitly who that was, so Mickey obliged. "His name is Captain James Hamilton, and he's probably a lower degenerate than Parker." On a roll, he brought up two enemies from the past, the long-retired Chief Horrall and ex-Mayor Bowron, out of office since '53. It was the same strategy he had employed in 1949, dragging everyone down into the muck with him.

Mike Wallace was years away from being the grand old man of the interview game as the face of *60 Minutes*, but he knew the basics of slander. It was one thing to call the Intelligence Division "the Stupidity Squad" — that was a clever dig — and another to call people crooks and degenerates. Wallace's scrambling only got him in deeper when he returned to Chief Parker and said, "Well, Mickey, you're a reformed thief just as he's a reformed thief. Isn't it the pot calling the

389

kettle black?" By the interview's end, Wallace had to remind his audience that the views expressed by Mickey were Mickey's alone. After the crisis conferences following the show, Wallace and his producer hurried over to their guest's suite on Central Park South, where they found him coming out of the shower, wearing only a towel and with not a care in the world. Mickey reassured them not to fret about Bill Parker — he knew too much about the chief. "He'll never sue."

But they had invited "Mr. Dunn" to be their guest and they'd been dumb, dumb, dumb. While the show was broadcast live, that didn't cover the West Coast, where it was scheduled in the same time slot, meaning three hours later. They let the venomous dialogue be aired there anyway, while offering Parker and Hamilton time to respond. That wasn't what the two men wanted.

ABC issued a formal apology the next day and the following Sunday the network's boss went on the show to again retract Mickey's slams, all too late. The LAPD officials filed suit against Wallace and his guest, the network, and the show's sponsors. By the time the legal dust settled, they had too, with Chief Parker collecting $45,975.09, enough to have bought Mickey's Brentwood home, and Captain Hamilton getting $22,978.55 from the deep-pocket defendants. Mickey had no assets in his name to collect and was not a party to the deal. "Any retraction made by those spineless persons in regard to the television show," he said, "does not go for me."

The broadcast was costly in more ways than one for Wallace and his creative team — they lost some of the quality that had got them to the national stage, their swagger. It took several years to get that back, along with their reputations, according to the lowest man on the totem pole, the researcher-writer Al Ramrus.

For someone like myself, who grew up on James Cagney movies, Cohen was a big disappointment — aging, out of shape, drab, unattractive, colorless except when talking about crime. An unsavory specimen, nothing like Cagney. Of course, Hollywood doesn't make movies about "real" gangsters because there'd be no audience. When Cagney went to the chair in *Angels with Dirty Faces*, you felt empathy, even sympathy and admiration. Had Mickey Cohen gone to the chair, you'd have felt good riddance.

While Cohen was good show business, you still felt somewhat soiled and tainted about giving network television time to such an unsavory creature. He was kind of Damon Runyonesque in a way. He was an aging Jewish guy from New York — perhaps he was doing his best to be Cagney-like. Once the camera went on, he turned it on more. He was acting like Mickey Cohen the gangster, yeah, absolutely. "I didn't kill nobody who didn't deserve killing." It was colorful. It sounded like a good line from a movie, didn't it?

I think he was trying to be Mickey Cohen as best he could. Just to be a small-time petty gangster, that's no big deal. Whose gonna pay attention to that kind of guy? Why would Billy Graham, for instance, want him to convert to Christianity and appear at a rally, just a petty thug?

Two days after he wreaked havoc on Mike Wallace's show, Mickey was one of 17,500 people who filled New York's Madison Square Garden for the crusade of America's rising voice of evangelism. Billy Graham and his people had hoped that Mickey would do the full bit of coming down the aisle and accepting Jesus into his heart but they had to settle for him standing there for all to see, or take his picture, immaculate in his dark suit, white shirt, and light tie. Hands clasped in front of him, Mickey gave every appearance of listening intently as the charismatic Graham preached, "If you'll say you will, tomorrow morning when you wake up and face the same old life you'll find that you have the new power to say 'no' to the tempter. And you'll have a new power to live a new life in Christ." Billy Graham also warned that New York would be one of the first places wiped out in an atomic war.

Mickey had been playing the North Carolina–based preacher and his crowd for years. His entrée to Graham and his devotees had come through his 304-pound former bugging expert Jim Vaus, who had seen the light at a tent crusade and gone to prison after admitting his perjury on Mickey's behalf. Vaus came out offering his salvation as a testimonial at Graham's crusades and intent on saving Mickey's soul too, recognizing what a coup that would be for the cause. The Jewish gangster would be the ultimate celebrity convert, eclipsing the hillbilly radio star Stuart Hamblen, who gave up his life of sin and racehorses to join them on the sawdust trail.

As early as 1949, Vaus brought the then thirty-year-old Graham by Mickey's home for hot chocolate and cookies. In 1951, as Mickey was awaiting his tax trial, he was invited to join more than one hundred local luminaries for a Graham-led revival at a manufacturer's Los Angeles mansion, an event that was supposed to remain private but inevitably wasn't. "Can't the poor man find God without the newspapers hounding him?" asked actress Jane Russell, who had become famous after Howard Hughes suggested she wear a steel bra in *The Outlaw*. Another sexpot actress was there too, Virginia Mayo, along with the wholesome Dennis Morgan, Roy Rogers, and Dale Evans, to hear Dr. Graham talk about how to become a Christian. "Mickey Cohen just happened to be at the meeting," the evangelist said.

The two men seemed to have a perfect understanding, for mutual benefit. Mickey would say in public, "Billy wasn't trying to convert me." Or, "How can he convert me? I'm a good Jew." Or, "If I want any spiritual help, I'll go to my rabbi." Then Billy would say in public, "Thousands of people are praying all the time for Mickey Cohen to get religion." Or, "I am hoping — no, change that to praying — for Mr. Cohen's conversion to Christianity. My only concern is to get this man to turn to God. After all, Jesus visited Zacchaeus of Jericho, who was a tax gatherer of shady reputation."

Mickey was fine with all that — Billy Graham could say anything he wanted about him. It really started paying off after he got out of prison and needed the cash. The now Reverend Vaus personally gave Mickey a little on-your-feet money and introduced him to a Downey, California, businessman who wanted the former haberdasher to hear his testimony. The man had been orphaned when his father killed his mother, then himself.

"When I took Christ into my heart, it took away my tears," he told Mickey. "If you take these words, your troubles will cease."

Mickey cried at the sad story and said he would consider converting but that was difficult with all the financial pressure on him. When the businessman offered a $1,500 loan, Mickey said that wasn't enough. He eventually got $6,000 from the guy.

Mickey went a step further in working the printing company executive and evangelist W. C. "Bill" Jones, who spent $4,500 on him. Once a drinker and gambler who placed bets with the likes of Mickey, Jones said they met at a Sunset Boulevard restaurant, then went to Mickey's apartment where, "We prayed together for twenty minutes and we knelt together and he turned his life over to Christ in my presence."

After witnessing the conversion in private, Jones urged Mickey to announce it at Madison Square Garden — winning over a sinner like him would give sizzle to Graham's crusade in the nation's media center. Weeks before the New York extravaganza he paid Mickey's way out there to talk it over face-to-face with Graham and do some Bible readings together. Mickey this time stayed in a suite at the Waldorf, charging the $507 bill to his benefactor. Mickey later said he had them eager to pay $10,000 or more if he proclaimed his allegiance to the Lord at the

Garden.

So his time in New York may have been costly to the ABC television network and to Mike Wallace, but it was a profit-maker to Mickey Cohen, and helped get him more firmly on his feet. But that was all he did the night of the crusade at the Garden, stand on his feet. If that angered the suckers who expected more for their money — a conversion of the Little Jew — well, fuck 'em. He wore a gold mezuzah on the watch chain dangling about his waist.

Los Angeles police gave Mickey their own welcome back when he returned from doing the TV show in which he called their chief a degenerate: a patrol picked him up for an offense a few notches below murder. Mickey had stopped his Cadillac in the street through two green lights while he ran to a newsstand and got a paper, no doubt to read about himself. His crime? Blocking traffic.

CHAPTER 26
JACK WHALEN TRIES
"THE SCAMUS"

No one pretended to understand Jerry Wooters, but his partners got some perspective when they met his older brother. Jim Wooters was crazier — bat-shit crazy, in fact, literally crazy about bat shit. His brother was the studio technician rumored to have taken a few bets in his day. Jerry told one squad member that was nonsense, Jim absolutely was not a bookie, though "he might have been at one time, before the war." In later years his brother settled on a get-rich-quick scheme he insisted wasn't a gamble, to the amusement of Bert Phelps, the genius bug man.

His claim to fame was that he had the bat guano market locked up. He had tons and tons of bat guano stored in some warehouse. He was always going to sell it and make a million dollars. Yeah, fertilizer. That went on for years and years. Last time I saw Jim, "You still got the bat guano?" "Yeah, man, we're gonna make a lot of money."

A few colleagues thought Jerry Wooters had no business being in police work — what was the LAPD thinking? — much less in one of the most sensitive assignments on the force. It's only fair to note, however, that both of his partners from the 1950s called him the best street cop they ever saw. Even on an elite squad you could be paired with an old-timer whose idea of field work was stopping by a store with a TV in the window to watch professional wrestling. That's what happened to Billy Dick Unland when he joined the squad and was put in a car with Archie Case, the rabbit-punching onetime beat cop from Watts. Archie was a fan of Gorgeous George and the other wrestlers and would go cruising to find an electronics shop to catch their matches. Finally Unland went for advice to Jack O'Mara, his supervising sergeant, who said, "You've got to take the leadership."

That was the nature of police partnerships. One guy usually was a damper — if not an anchor — while the other was a pusher, the leader who occasionally needed pulling back. Jerry Wooters was the pusher, no matter his partner. He'd have you out all night on the Strip, shadowing Mickey club to club — OK, and enjoying a few drinks on the house. But getting Mickey's goat wasn't all he did. More than any squad member he set up arrests of bookies who gave any hint of aligning again with that phony. It was as if Jerry still had a

pipeline directly into L.A.'s underworld —
and he did, thanks to one particular source.
"God, for a few years, you know, they thought
I was the best detective in town," he said.
"As long as you had Jack, you had the world."

As Wooters saw it, there were three gangs
in the city: the Italians, of course, including a
couple of Dragnas, the Licatas, and Jimmy
The Weasel, when he was out of prison; the
Jews, meaning Mickey and a lot of bookies
and whatever new group of flunkies he assembled; and the homegrown one-man Irish
gang who took bets himself, collected debts,
and shook down anyone he could, whether a
racetrack scammer, abortion doctor, or fellow bookie. If they didn't pay off Jack Whalen,
they might see the law on their tail. "What he
didn't get a piece of, I got word of," was how
Wooters described their delicate arrangement. "I never discussed the Whalen thing
with too many people."

He certainly did not tell his bosses about
him and Whalen, nor how he was working
surreptitiously with a Vice cop — Captain
Hamilton and the others would never understand the age-old ways of Vice. Jerry's partner
on the sly was veteran detective Pete Stafford,
who lived within walking distance of him in
Arcadia, just north of Jack O'Mara's town.
Jerry and Jean Wooters had moved there after
their marriage, when his bachelor duplex by
the Police Academy did not seem like the

right place to raise a family. Their neighbor Stafford was a no-smoking, no-drinking bruiser who in his off time helped the downtown YMCA weed out perverts in exchange for use of its gym, where he worked out at 4 A.M., bench-pressing 400 pounds. Stafford had become an expert in the increasingly popular gambling on football and other sports, as opposed to horses, but his MO was not what they taught at the Academy. He was known to tell a bookie, "I want to learn about this a little better — let me work your phones." Then he would sit in as a betting clerk while praying that his Vice colleagues wouldn't burst in and discover his means of research.

Stafford also said straight-out of certain bookies, "When you get to know 'em well, you kind of do 'em favors." If their daughter got picked up for drunk driving, he steered the family to an attorney who could get the case knocked down to a straight drunk rather than a 502, driving under the influence. That was their understanding — you do him a good turn, he does one for you, and sometimes it was a tip leading you up the ladder. So when Jerry Wooters got a lead from Jack "The Enforcer" Whalen, he often called Pete Stafford, the weight lifter who played things fast and loose on the job.

He'd get me on the phone and say, "Meet

me at Intelligence but go in the back door and I'll be there and take you to a room, because I don't want those guys to see you up there." I'll tell you, policemen have this little jealousy. And some people were jealous of Jerry because he got more information. Anyhow, we all kind of knew the bookmakers. Jerry Wooters and I knew them better than the rest of the guys. You know what I mean.

He was very good at getting information from people and that's who he got it from, bookmakers. See, he'd give me information and sometimes he'd say, "Find out what kind of a deal, if it's takin' horses or sports," you know, so I could find that out. Sometimes he'd say, "Hey, make an arrest on this one." So I'd make the arrest. And then he would call me and he would say, "OK, Pete, where's the weakness on the case?" I'd say, "It's on the search and seizure, that's where it's weak . . ."

From there, Jerry could put the bookie away for a while, squeeze him for cooperation, or offer him a friendly way out. There were lots of ways it could go after Jack "The Enforcer" Whalen turned him on to bookies remaining too tight with the dagos or with Mickey, or simply refusing to do business with him. The Enforcer wasn't afraid to muscle in on any of them. As Stafford explained:

401

You see, Jerry used to tell me about Whalen. "That Irishman's got too much guts, Pete." I said, "That's the way we are." He said, "But you can't tone him down. You can't tell him not to be so cocky and tough." I didn't want to know him because he was too hot. I always tried to stay in the background. You never know who's following him.

Whalen was always pleading poverty when he got hauled to court. He'd claim that his wife and children would starve if he couldn't keep selling aluminum cookware or bartending in his sister's tavern or pumping gas at a service station. It was true that he had gotten rid of the private charter plane he once flew on a dare under the Oakland Bay Bridge, but he still lived mighty well for a self-described $277-a-month gas pump jockey. By the mid-'50s he had given up the ranch where he used to train horses in favor of an Encino home with a pool out back. There was a pool house, too, with enough room to show films at family gatherings. Sometimes they had sleepovers for the young kids in the extended Whalen-Wunderlich clan and Jack The Enforcer would pretend to be a monster, contorting his face and making grunting noises and threatening to lock the youngsters in a dungeon . . . before tucking them into bed. He arranged the ponies for their Sunday picnics in Griffith Park and treated everyone to trail rides into the hills from the rental stable below the Hollywood sign.

By surface appearances, one side of the clan had gone straight by then — the Wunderlich brothers gave every impression that they had learned from their time in court, or prison, that the fun (and profit) of crime wasn't worth it. Gus Wunderlich would never stop telling tales of their rum-running days and never stop tinkering to invent things, whether an electric hot dog cooker or the proverbial perpetual motion machine. But Gus now applied his mechanical wizardry to the irrigation business — he built a crane-like device in the back of his '51 Dodge pickup and made the rounds of area ranches and farms, helping fix the pumps that brought them water. His kid brother George, who had playfully listed himself as an aviator in the 1930 census, had become a florist — with real greenery, not plastic stuff. He had a retail outlet downtown and acreage in Torrance where he grew beautiful calla lilies and narcissus. Fred Whalen's side of the clan never stopped believing that George had told the feds about their post-Prohibition whiskey scheme, but that wound had healed — he, too, was invited to the gatherings around Jack Whalen's pool or at the real center of family activity.

The "Big White House" was perched on a

hill in the stately Los Feliz neighborhood below Griffith Park Observatory and resembled the White House in Washington, complete with a curved, columned portico. The house was owned by Jack's older sister Bobie, now Bobie von Hurst after a few trial runs at wedded bliss had led her into a successful (and unlikely) marriage with a former army colonel. The onetime platinum model in her early years had followed the Elizabeth Taylor philosophy of courtship whenever the lust got to her, which was often. "In my day you didn't fool around," she explained, "you got married. At least I gave 'em a year. When I first got married, if they couldn't get me pregnant in a year, I let 'em go and tried somebody else. That's all I wanted. I passed up some good things. Clark Gable . . ."

Well, there was a story about Mr. Gable and a nightclub and her in a fur coat without much under it. But after a half dozen try-'em-and-divorce-'em marriages, she stuck with the super-square Colonel Derek von Hurst who, after time in the service, became an aeronautical engineer and executive while still doing military-like inspections of the kids' beds in the Big White House.

Bobie's daddy, Freddie The Thief, still lived in an apartment on the flats of Hollywood but gave everyone the impression the house was his. Freddie kept a professional Brunswick pool table in the basement, with tall upholstered bar stools around it for onlookers. He also hosted lavish holiday parties at the house, with carved turkey and ham, to which he'd invite a straight crowd early, including his friends in law enforcement, then have the pool sharks and others come later. His boy, Jack, used the big house, too, keeping his reel-to-reel tape recorders in the basement. Like any substantial bookie, he had various bars and other sites taking wagers for him around town. They would call in their rundowns of bets using phone numbers he provided, but linked in his case to dead apartments where he kept no furniture, only phones. If the calls were traced, authorities would get those meaningless addresses while the calls were forwarded to his recorders in the Big White House.

His sister, Bobie, sometimes helped with Jack's bookmaking when it came time to pay off winners or collect from losers. Needless to say, Jack handled any collections from those who hesitated to pay. But how many cops would be suspicious of a middle-aged mom making the simpler pickups, and payoffs, while carting three children home from parochial school? Her son John was one of the passengers.

She'd pick us up from the nuns at three in the afternoon and we'd go out with a car full of — we used to take our lunch in those little brown bags and the payouts were all wrapped up in those bags with names on 'em and we'd drive around to various gas stations and bars and people would run out and hand my mother those same sort of bags wrapped up with the payoffs, or she had to pay them. There were times we didn't get home until after dark. We'd sit there and do our homework in the backseat.

John von Hurst was a Whalen without the name. As Bobie (Whalen) von Hurst's eldest son he was the nephew of Jack Whalen and grandson of Freddie The Thief. He also was the toddler being taken for a walk when Freddie was abducted off the street in Hollywood years before. By the mid-'50s he was living with his mom in the Big White House, still not yet a teenager, when a frantic long-distance call came in from Grandpa Fred. The Whalen patriarch was back east with old buddies pursuing his favorite scheme, posing as a hospital doctor eager to place bets on the ponies. But this time Freddie apparently had taken bookmakers who were really *connected*, and it must have gone badly — he was calling for help, and fast, from Jack, the son he'd come to frown on. As John explained:

He and a couple of the "honorary uncles" were busting bookies. So they'd take these guys for $3,000 to $4,000 at a crack and it usually took them three or four days to figure out that they were beaten bad. And Grandpa would leave and go to the next town and do it again. But this time in New York, I guess he had busted a number of the "family's" bookmaking operations and two thugs came to the hotel and threatened my grandfather. Well, my grandfather called the house in California and we went and put my Uncle Jack on one of those Constellation four-engine TWA flights to New York and off he went.

Jack Whalen managed to get to Freddie before the East Coast muscle returned and he greeted them with his own muscles, and threats, after which they returned with their boss, who suggested a compromise with Freddie The Thief and his very strong son.

He said, "Let's do it this way — you leave my bookmakers alone, I'll give you the name of my competition's, you bust them. And we'll take half the money." And my Uncle Jack said, "No, we'll take all the money but we'll bust these guys for you. They're out of your hair." And the man said, "Yeah, I'd rather have these guys out of business." So that's what they'd do.

According to Whalen family lore, that's how

407

Freddie The Thief began putting on his white coat and stethoscope on behalf of the New York mob and busting its uncooperative bookies. But there was a different outcome when his son Jack tried the same scheme, on his own, back home. The Whalen clan had by then adopted a name for Freddie's favorite con — the *scamus*.

Jerry Wooters stopped trying to figure out why Jack Whalen didn't go straight. You'd hear the stories of him beating on people, yet he could act with civility and polish anytime he wanted.

Jerry's wife assumed they were going out with another policeman when he told her they were having dinner with a friend. But their companion was Whalen, who brought along his society spouse, Kay. Jean Wooters assumed then that Whalen was an actor because he spoke of how TV westerns needed cowboys who really knew how to ride, who looked at home in the saddle. It was believable that he was an actor, too, with his dark, rugged looks and engaging manner. Whalen stood up when Jean and Kay excused themselves to go to the powder room. In the time they were gone, he tossed down two shots of whiskey. When they returned, he stood again to pull out Jean's chair.

Jerry had picked a steakhouse near where he and Jean lived — now with two little boys

— out in Arcadia, in the 'burbs. The town was far from The Strip or even the Valley, places where Whalen might be recognized and where other cops might be lurking. They took a table in a far corner, just in case. Jack told a great story of meeting the decorated World War II soldier Audie Murphy, who was now a movie actor and going to help him get parts. The former Katherine Sabichi shared a great tale about her family's ancient piano that had to be shipped around South America.

"Had a great old time," Jerry said of their night out, though he had some explaining to do when his wife saw a photograph in the paper.

She asked, "Is this the guy we had dinner with?"

Jack was sure he could pull off the *scamus*, the great con of his dad, and in L.A. As a police report spelled out the episode, "the supposed victim, Ted Hersk, had been told there was a doctor who worked at Queen of Angels Hospital [and] was looking to take bookmaking action for the employees. The victim was introduced to the defendant . . . dressed in a white jacket, stating that he was a doctor of the hospital. The victim became suspicious and notified Sergeant Gerard of the Bunco Detail, who advised the victim to play along."

The bookie let the unusually muscular physician pass him a bunch of wagers, a few of which proved to be astute, winning close to $1,000. The lucky doctor said he'd be waiting in his car at the corner of Bellevue and Waterloo — the bookie could pay him there. As the bookie, Hersk, climbed into the passenger's seat to complete the payoff, the plainclothes bunco cop approached the car window to make the arrest and Dr. Jack Whalen did what came naturally. "Defendant stepped out of the car and struck Sergeant Gerard on the right side of the face, knocking him to the sidewalk where his head struck the edge, knocking him out . . . Sergeant Gerard was conveyed to the Georgia Street Receiving Hospital."

That was just like cops, claiming that the sidewalk knocked their guy out, not the fist of Jack the Enforcer. In his own defense, Whalen said the man smelled of alcohol, was sloppily dressed, and had a gun — what was he supposed to do? His mother, Lillian, spoke up for him, too, telling a court officer, "He had a calm childhood and it looked to her as if somebody did not like him, as the plainclothes men from Intelligence are always taking him down for suspicion."

Fortunately for Whalen, it was much like his earlier KO of a policeman — they still expected a cop to be good with his fists so they didn't make it a federal case if you got the better of one. Jack Whalen by his own estimate had been arrested forty times but guessed he could plea bargain the hospital mess down to a few weeks in the cooler and probation. He may have crunched a cop unconscious but all they charged him with was "resisting public officers in discharge of their duties." The bad news was, he'd tried his father's con and failed.

CHAPTER 27
MORE MONEY FOR MICKEY

Bill Peterson was a fledgling big-band trumpeter and a student at UCLA when he read Raymond Chandler's *Farewell, My Lovely* and fell in love with the fictional Philip Marlowe, who mucked around the city's seamy underside and actually solved murders. Peterson admired the private eye's jadedness — no one impressed Marlowe — and he began looking at people through similar eyes when he started getting trumpeting gigs as a sideman in clubs along Central Avenue and on the Sunset Strip. The Hollywood glamour types who drew so many stares? They were "famous folks getting bombed," that's all. Then someone else came into the Crescendo, Gene Norman's jazz club that showcased the likes of Duke Ellington and Louis Armstrong and such edgy comics as Mort Sahl and Lenny Bruce. On this night, it had a torch singer on the bill.

Peterson first noticed two large men in wide-brimmed hats and dark suits get the big-time treatment from the maître d' and brush past the blond hat-check girl dressed in gold lamé. The pair kept their wide-brims on as they made their way to a front table for the show. Then the young singer was told to wait, to hold off her performance, and the piano player whispered, "I guess some big shot is late." Finally he arrived, the sort who peeled a hundred-dollar bill off a thick roll and asked that the drinks keep coming for his entourage, though he personally didn't imbibe — he went for ice cream and pastries. On stage, the singer's set began and finished and as soon as the applause died Peterson headed for the men's room, bursting to relieve himself. The big shot also got up, along with one of the men in the hats . . .

Oh Lord, now what? But I can't linger, I've got to go. I dash in past José, the little Mexican guy who is the attendant, and thank God all the urinals are vacant. I make it, and unzip just as the big wide-brim guy comes through the door. He glances at me, checks the rest of the room, then gestures with his thumb to José, and barks, "You! Outside!"

Jose manages a nervous smile, and scrams out the door. After Jose has exited, Mr. Widebrim nods to someone at the door. In comes Mickey Cohen! I've seen his picture in the paper, but he's bigger and stockier that I thought. He's got a real five-o'clock shadow, which is kind of covered up with powder. He's still got the hat on and to my complete terror he sidles up into the urinal compartment next to me. Now there are only three people in here: Mickey Cohen, his big bodyguard, Mr. Widebrim, and me. I can see the headlines in tomorrow's *Times* —

HOLLYWOOD MUSICIAN MURDERED IN NIGHTCLUB REST ROOM. GANGLAND SLAYING SUSPECTED!

And even worse is that fact that I can't even pee! I'm too scared to let go! Mickey has no problem. He finishes, and then he reaches inside his coat, not fast, just real relaxed. Oh God . . . I grit my teeth and glance frantically around. What would Philip Marlowe do? I turn back to watch with a feeling of horrified fascination as Mickey Cohen's hand comes out of his coat in a kind of slow motion. Now I know how Philip Marlowe feels when the heavy has the drop on him. But instead of a blue-steel automatic he is holding a little can of Johnson's Baby Powder! With his other hand, he pulls his pants out and sprinkles the powder into his pants, and a cloud sprays up. I can smell the scent. Then he proceeds to give the can to Mr. Widebrim, who shakes some more into Mickey's hands. Mickey then pats his face to cover his stubble. He turns, washes his hands like a surgeon, takes a towel from Widebrim, and dries his hands. He throws the towel down, glances at me, and says:

"Now you can say you took a leak with Mickey Cohen. Take it easy, kid."

Mickey had more to sell than his soul. His celebrity had to be worth something, right? He couldn't go out in L.A. without a bunch of people wanting his autograph and a few brave ones asking for it. While he was in the pen, Ben Hecht had written him about possibly doing a book — Ben Hecht, co-host of his wild Slapsy Maxie's fund-raiser for Israel but more important, a two-time Oscar-winning screenwriter and co-author of *The Front Page*. While Mickey was away, Hecht had given him a cameo in his own memoir, *A Child of the Century*, briefly playing him and their gala for comic relief, but so what? Hecht floated the possibility of doing a book and Mickey's mind swam with it. In the summer of 1957, he gave the old Chicago newsman his own suggestions for a manuscript about his life, in his trademark dese-dems-dose lingo. "He must have done it himself," Hecht said. "No one but Mickey uses words that way."

Hecht saw an opportunity to peer inside the mind of a gangster — "looking as deeply as I can into the disordered soul of a fellow human" — but also into the ethos of the underworld he had glimpsed as a reporter during the heyday of the Capones. It could be a fine shoot-'em-up, but with sociological overtones. Hecht wrote in his notes:

The underworld is not a geographic area. Its trail runs thru slums, fine hotels, swank residences and office buildings — cafés, theaters and the sanctums of government.

The stamp of the underworld citizen is his citizenlessness. He must be an enemy of society — and hold its laws and pretentions in contempt. Such a point of view cannot be faked any more than savagery can be faked.

Mickey was no more than a stick of a man till L.A. His social life consisted chiefly of proving he could lick any enemy. He had no greed, nor sense of organization.

The corruption of government — the bribing of its large and little factotums — is the perquisite of what Mickey calls "the higher echelon" of society . . . Railroad, oil, and manufacturing empires have been built in the Republic with the aid of canny bribery.

The yearning for respectable society, for the good opinion of his betters, is a confused wish for a magic change of self.

Exhibitionism is a rare matter. Invisibleness is the social norm.

Ben Hecht had a lot to say about the underworld and the world above too. Still, the project made him uneasy — he had concerns he didn't share with Mickey. On a purely practical level, Hecht couldn't see himself scurrying around behind the man with his notebook. As nostalgic as he was about his newspaper days he was sixty now, well past the cub reporter grind. But then Hecht would visit Mickey's new apartment and witness the talcum routine for himself, hearing Mickey bang a can of the stuff on the bathroom walls to loosen up the powder after his third therapeutic bathing of the day. It was impossible not to be intrigued by the sight of Mickey emerging naked except for the hat and gartered socks to *faire la toilette* and ready his sagging torso to be transformed by a covering of monogrammed linen and natty gabardine. Hecht was invited to watch Mickey's daily rendezvous with his new crew of hangers-on, including that tiny "Itchy" fellow and some of his old heist partners as well, like the Sica brothers, to relive the days when he "took over" Los Angeles. So Hecht would

417

be pumped up again and tempted to do The Mickey Cohen Story, even if this wasn't quite an invitation to witness Al Capone's private moments with Frank Nitti.

Hecht had other concerns more substantive than the demands of being a fly on the wall to that crowd. As much as he admired Mickey's innate skill as a corruptor, he did not want to be the mouthpiece of a criminal. He was wary of resembling the defense lawyer who cites extenuating circumstances to explain away his client's bloodthirstiness and thefts. He sensed that most people tended to admire crooks in fiction and despise them in real life. And while they thrilled at seeing the gangster in his prime, they were more exhilarated by his demise, especially if the fall was as dramatic as the young Cagney being wrapped like a mummy and toppling facedown into his old household in *The Public Enemy* or, better yet, Cagney in *White Heat*, perched atop the oil refinery about to blow shouting, "Made it, Ma, top of the world!" — that one filmed only a few years back by one of the oil fields that fueled modern Los Angeles.

In contrast to that the reform of the gangster was a bore, and that's what Ben Hecht feared he was witnessing in Mickey — the reform epilogue, the toothless tiger talking about his hunts of yore. True, great details about the underworld MO came out when

Mickey recounted pieces of muscle work he did back in Cleveland and Chicago, like mentioning how he "raised" people during heists at bookie joints — he'd explain then how that meant lining 'em against the wall, hands raised. But even as he offered up the gangster version of sausage-making, Mickey would point out how he wasn't the wild, hot Jew kid anymore, having become older and more sensible during his years on McNeil Island. "I didn't reform that I know of," he told Hecht, "but I began to think with a head that didn't belong to me at first."

Here was Hecht's problem, then — the new Mickey. Even the gangsters at the top often lost their zip once they escaped the streets for hotel suites. They became little different from any other honorable tycoon or dull factory owner counting his profits. He wrote, "The odds are three to one that Mickey Cohen, if not stopped by a bullet, will wind up a Rotarian."

None of those worries were shared with Mickey, whose own reasoning was more elemental: How could the thing not be a bestseller? A hundred thousand cops alone would want to know what he was thinking. Mickey also reasoned: Why wait to sell the mother and the real moneymaker too, the movie version of The Mickey Cohen Story? Mickey didn't bother to tell his Oscar-winning collaborator, Ben Hecht, that he was going to start doing that pronto, peddle shares in a movie that didn't exist to anyone who would bite — except he'd call them loans for the benefit of the IRS. Pure genius, no?

A guy in the appliance trade advanced him $25,000 and a retired manufacturer the same. He got $7,500 from a juke box dealer and an equal amount from an L.A. business-woman. Mickey actually signed a contract with vending machine manufacturer Aubrey Stemler, guaranteed his $15,000 back with 6 percent interest if no book or movie was produced within a year, good luck collecting. Mickey reassured them all that his film would gross $10 million and his smallest investor agreed — agent Lou Irwin thought it could rival movies about Capone and Baby Face Nelson. But Irwin was smart enough to hand Mickey only $1,000 from the pocket money he often doled out to needy actors to tide them over for the weekend. Not so frugal (or bright) was an L.A. psychiatrist who, like Hecht, was eager to get inside Mickey and his past, "the way he behaves, what motivates him." The shrink advanced him $25,000 and was promised a 10 percent interest in his life story. "I was very impressed with Mr. Cohen. He is a gentle and nice fellow," the doctor said. "In return for my efforts he said he'd commit himself for psychiatric study — but he is a very busy man, you know." Alas,

420

Mickey never did have the free time to sit on his couch. But he kept the cash.

The public relations woman Elinor Churchin thought she might write Mickey's biography herself, or help package his book and movie, and she came up with a novel way of gaining the inside track: she purchased the plant business for $17,000 from the brother and sister who originally brought Mickey into it but found, somehow, that the enterprise lost money. The PR woman never did get to write her bio and six months later signed over the nursery to Mickey's sister, Lillian Weiner.

Mickey may not have told Ben Hecht what he was up to but he did boldly inform the IRS. In March 1958, he met with agent Guy McGowen and proposed a deal. As the IRS man later detailed it, Uncle Sam would get the first $50,000 in profits from the book and movie based on Mickey's life, "Cohen would get the next $50,000, minus of course taxes on that, and all future monies would be turned over to the government." Mickey cautioned the federal agent not to be alarmed if it looked like he was leading a lavish life again — that was a necessary act that would benefit them all.

"I must keep up a front. My only asset is the motion picture," Mickey explained. "If I lowered my living standards it would take away my reputation. If I was to make myself unknown I'd be out of the picture.

"You can't expect Mickey Cohen to go around like a three-dollar-a-day-bum."

But if you are going to sell your life story the one thing you don't do is give it away. In the summer of 1958, Mickey agreed to let *Saturday Evening Post* writer Dean Jennings be his new fly on the wall and witness the same shower-and-powder routine as Ben Hecht, along with his nights with the regulars and a new addition to the crew, a bulldog dubbed Mickey Cohen Jr. The dog had his own set of pink-and-white plastic dishes, an extra-wide turquoise lounge chair, and a red leather leash. Fred Sica had dog-walking honors.

Running over four consecutive weeks, "Mickey Cohen: The Private Life of a Hood" was packed with trivia about Mickey's new apartment in West L.A.: the door with three locks and a peephole; the dozens of pairs of shoes stacked two-deep on a rack below the pants and jackets still tailored by Beverly Hills' Al Pignola; the red-velvet *MC*-monogrammed bedspread; the bar with a built-in fountain dispensing root beer, cola, club soda, and water, and on a shelf above, different wines and liquors for the drinking guests, each bottle illuminated by its own blue light at night; the white drapes that opened and closed at the touch of a button thanks to an electric motor; the three TVs, two black and white and one a color model, quite a novelty then; the (unused) fireplace decorated with satin-finished black bricks; the walnut bookcase with decorative hard-cover books he never read; the baby blue stationery imprinted FROM THE DESK OF MICKEY COHEN; the Italian-made red leather cigarette case with a silver plate engraved with his name, a gift from Mike Wallace for his slander-filled interview; and no less than six telephones in different shades, quite a communications setup for someone now in the sundae-and-banana-split business. The nursery had been sold to Japanese investors and the back office so essential to Mickey had moved across town to the Carousel ice cream parlor, purportedly owned by his sister.

One day Mickey got a call at the apartment from Helen Phillips, wife of his longtime bail bondsman. She asked, "What are you doing tonight?"

"Nothing."

"Nothing? Well, go out and kill me a couple of people."

That was the take on Mickey, the harmless ex-gangster who could only joke about the days when his wife, Lavonne, would complain that he wouldn't eat a Spanish omelet and he'd retort, "Hon, is that any way to talk to the number-one hoodlum in Los Angeles?" Or when he'd tell *Examiner* city editor Jim Richardson, "The people of Los Angeles ought to get down on their knees and thank God for Mickey Cohen, because if it wasn't for me the wops would have this town tied up."

The narrative agreed that Mickey's only real asset now was his life, and he was stunningly candid about his attempts to peddle it, matter-of-factly detailing the *loans* he'd lined up for shares of a promised book and movie, the $10,000 here and $25,000 there that kept high-test gas in his Cadillac with the reinforced steel roof, and funded the long nights out when he still wouldn't let anyone else pick up the check. The author, Jennings, summed it up: "He is doing the best he can to scrape together a few hundred thousand tax-free dollars."

Thus did Mickey simultaneously thumb his nose at the IRS and guarantee that the great Ben Hecht would write him off, not write an epic about him. Hecht hadn't a clue that Mickey was giving away the goods (his story) or lining up suckers to invest in a nonexistent property. He called Mickey to confront him. "I told Cohen what I had been told. He didn't admit it or deny it, but I understood what the silence meant." Hecht also contacted producers he knew to ask about the potential for a Mickey Cohen film. "None," he said, "was particularly interested."

The *Saturday Evening Post* series concluded that Mickey and Los Angeles now were like the two ends of a dumbbell, stuck to each other. In the magazine, the pieces were filled with photos of Mickey out on the town, dining with a nightclub dancer, in front of his Caddy, visiting entertainer Sammy Davis Jr., scowling under his fedora, washing his hands (of course), and in the barber's chair being pampered with a shoe shine and a manicure while the dog, Mickey Jr., was hoisted up to say hello. There also was an inevitable shot of his former bodyguard Johnny Stompanato with actress Lana Turner, in whose home Stompanato had been stabbed to death months earlier.

The four weeks of *Saturday Evening Post* articles used only one photo of policemen, a deadly dull shot showing Chief William Parker posed seated in his office with Captain James Hamilton peering over his shoulder while one of their foot soldiers stood at the far end of the chief's desk. The third man looked rail thin and angular in his dark suit and had his hair trimmed as short as his bosses' for the occasion. There were dozens of investigators in the Intelligence Division now and the one posing with the brass was never quoted in the pieces. But Sergeant Jerry Woote was described to America as having ulcers from the role he'd taken on as "Mickey's relentless Javert."

Jerry was amused by the effort Mickey was

putting into portraying himself as a pitiful and defanged ex-hood and how he had snowed his federal parole officer — that clown who arranged for Mickey to give how-I-turned-my-life-around talks on behalf of Volunteers of America, the service organization dedicated to reaching and uplifting those in need. He must not have seen the Mickey that Jerry saw in his confrontation with the lawyer Paul Caruso. That Mickey was rather like the old one.

Caruso was a newly minted attorney fresh out of the Marines and looking for clients like crazy when Mickey, just out of prison, hired him to handle several civil matters. Mickey would come to Caruso's home and have dinner and be the perfect gentleman with the wife and kids. When the rabid L.A. cops accused him of cursing, Caruso couldn't believe it — the Mickey he saw wouldn't tolerate a word of profanity, "he was a dream guest." But just as Mickey was about to go on TV with Mike Wallace, Caruso decided it was time to collect his overdue legal fees, up to $7,900 by then. Mickey said sorry, no — Caruso actually owed *him* $1,000, money left in trust in the lawyer's office. Caruso said he had a family and needed the fees he had earned.

He was telling people he didn't owe me money. I was stupid and young and an ex-

Marine. I said, "You were born a small-time hoodlum and you're going to die a small-time hoodlum."

He said, "If you're man enough, come down and get it."

His sister had that greenhouse then, Lillian Weiner. He'd go in and say, "You need plants around here." So I went down there and two of his men were sitting on each side of his desk and within thirty seconds he had a .38 pointed at me. Fortunately his sister walked in.

Caruso stunned Mickey by grabbing his sister and using her as a shield to back out of the nursery and escape to his car. But after the lawyer made it home, he got a phone call, one of the henchmen announcing, "The little guy's unhappy with you. He wants $1,000."

That's when Caruso called Captain Hamilton's squad and five of the men came over, right in the middle of the night. Keeler the bug man was among them and so was Dick Williams, the lethal jungle fighter. But the one who settled him down was Jerry Wooters. Jerry had been by his house before, with his partner, Phelps, feeling him out and trying to turn him against his hoodlum client. Caruso had a bar in his home and Jerry would crack a beer and say, "You know, you're being taken for a ride."

"They were telling me I was being played

427

for a sucker and they were right. They tried to get me to crack on Mickey. I was too dumb and too impressed with Mickey to know they were really looking out for my welfare."

After Mickey pulled the .38 on the lawyer, Jerry never lorded it over him how they were right. All Paul Caruso saw that night was a taciturn cop standing erect, like Gary Cooper, ready with his gun if Mickey or his men came by to follow up on their threats. The cops stayed there for most of a week, just in case, and Caruso decided "Jerry was the one who would have done something if Mickey just gave him an excuse."

CHAPTER 28
COINS AND A CUCUMBER

Jerry Wooters would argue at times that his dealings with The Enforcer — surreptitiously trading information and favors — were little different from any cop's with an informant. "There are no freebies in this world," he said. "You got to give to get." But that didn't stop the whispers in the ranks, especially after he and Bert Phelps noticed a car following them.

They had a healthy paranoia — watching one's back seemed prudent in the job — and they sensed that the sedan was staying a convenient distance behind them. Jerry made a couple of turns to see if it would follow and it did, until they reached a red light. When the light turned green, Jerry didn't go anywhere, he stayed put, forcing the suspicious sedan to drive ahead. At that point, they turned the tables and began following the other car, finally edging alongside and waving for the driver to pull over.

Instead, the son of a bitch tried to run off.

I could drive pretty good and I caught up and swerved in front of him to jam him against the curb. I got out and approached the driver's side and I see he's reaching under the dash. So I stuck my .38 in his ear. But he was just turning off his radio.

It was not the sort of radio that plays music.

He took out his ID card. I went to a phone and called the office. "We just grabbed an FBI guy." Hamilton checked it out and told me, "Hell, they've been tailing you for a week." This is where I came up as the bag man.

The bosses told him not to worry, they'd handle it. They almost laughed it off, in fact. They said the tail only showed how desperate J. Edgar Hoover was to embarrass the LAPD — it would make his year to embarrass the squad at the core of Chief William Parker's mission.

It was no secret that Hoover and Parker were bitter rivals as they competed to be the nation's paragon of law enforcement virtue. The enmity surfaced in petty ways. Jack Webb had continued to use the line "I'm a cop" in the introduction to the LAPD's great image booster, *Dragnet*, while the show held its own in the ratings against the '50s Westerns and Lucille Ball's antic comedy. But the line was axed after Hoover wrote in an FBI bulletin, "I abhor the word 'cop.' Especially deplorable is use of this term — a standard derisive invective of the underworld — in a careless or disdainful manner by . . . law abiding individuals." Meanwhile deputies from the L.A. County Sheriff's Department routinely were admitted to training programs at the FBI Academy while candidates from the LAPD were told they might have to wait a decade. "I guess we are an unfriendly foreign country," Chief Parker said.

There also was a substantive difference between the two men and their institutions, over organized crime. While Hoover built the FBI's reputation chasing down bank-robbing desperados such as Dillinger and Pretty Boy Floyd, he denied for decades that there was any nationwide crime network, much less a Mafia. "Baloney," he famously said, pooh-poohing any notion of a dominant "coalition of racketeers." Led by its Gangster Squad, since morphed into Intelligence, the LAPD had been working for a decade to document just such a criminal enterprise. In 1946, back when they wouldn't know a Mafioso if he rang their doorbell, Willie Burns and Con Keeler had been pioneers merely by creating crude charts on which they listed the undesirables found in the city and drew lines to their suspected associates around the country — just assembling files of news clips on the

431

hoods was novel then. Early in Parker's tenure atop the force, he delivered a speech in Chicago to the National Automatic Merchandising Association spelling out his philosophy of a three-segment "Invasion from Within" threatening America and listing the Mafia, by name, as "the most ominous of all criminal cartels," a menace to be taken as seriously as Communism. "It is difficult to believe the Mafia exists," Parker told the luminaries of the vending machine industry, who were not naive on the topic. "Yet it does exist, and its inner circle of members do control organized crime in America!"

In a thinly veiled swipe at you-know-who, Parker said, "It has repeatedly been stated that law enforcement is primarily a local responsibility and that, even though criminals may be organized on a nationwide basis, the majority of their criminal acts involve the violation of local laws." Fine, then — he'd do the job locally and get the credit. Parker proudly quoted a columnist who wrote, "I have found only one local setup that recognizes the peril of this situation. Los Angeles has the only police agency designed to combat the Mafia and its collateral mobster connections." Only a few years had passed since Los Angeles and its police department were enmeshed in scandal and made a farce of in the national magazines by a pint-sized tax cheat whose only virtue was his clean hands.

Yet Chief Parker was ready to revive a term taken from the early booster days of his city of sunshine, back when the hordes from the Midwest arrived by the carload with dreams of a new life. "Today, Los Angeles is referred to by authorities as the 'white spot' amid the black picture of nationally organized crime," Parker said, and no one was going to tarnish that white spot if he could prevent it — not J. Edgar Hoover, not any blowhard gangster, not any wayward cop.

Frustrated by the FBI's willful blindness, Parker and his trusted second, Captain Hamilton, in 1956 spearheaded creation of the Law Enforcement Intelligence Unit (LEIU), a coalition of twenty-six local and state agencies committed to sharing confidential data about the underworld, with federal agencies explicitly excluded. Hoover naturally saw the coalition as a slap at the FBI and a challenge to his power, and sought out participants to serve as his spies. A field agent in San Francisco subsequently wrote a memo discussing "tactful and discreet steps to 'clip the wings' of Hamilton and this group . . . his orders come from Chief Bill Parker, who could perhaps be described as the symbol of frustrated 'kingmakers' in law enforcement."

The snooping went the other way too. When veteran FBI agent Julian Blodgett was recruited to head an intelligence unit in the

Los Angeles County District Attorney's Office he received an icy reception from his counterpart in the LAPD and soon after spotted an unmarked car following him. Only when the report came back "he sings loudest in church choir" did Blodgett settle into a working relationship with Captain James Hamilton and his crew.

Though it was conceivable that Hoover simply was misguided in denying the scope of the mob, the squad's Billy Dick Unland was convinced the Mafia had to have some dirt on the head of the FBI. Why else would he take such a see-no-evil stance and leave local law enforcement on its own to penetrate the underworld's formidable wall of silence, omerta? Hoover had been openly disdainful of Senator Kefauver's televised 1950–51 hearings spotlighting organized crime, refusing even to protect its witnesses, all while the Tennessee senator touted the help he got from the LAPD and a couple of other police departments. The same dynamic was evident in 1957 when another Southern senator, John McClellan of Arkansas, launched hearings into labor racketeering with the assistance of an aggressive young staff attorney, Robert F. Kennedy. That committee's most explosive material focused on the Chicago-based Teamsters union but Kennedy also spent time on the West Coast, where Captain Hamilton made available his squad's voluminous files, including records of one case that left Kennedy's mouth agape, involving an organizer from the union that represented juke box repairmen.

The unfortunate Hal Sherry had traveled from Los Angeles down to San Diego and checked into the US Grant Hotel, where he was visited by three Italians who announced that they would be fifty-fifty partners in any labor deal in the area. Sherry said his union never made such agreements and promptly received a working over, nothing jaw-dropping about that. But one memorable detail left some wondering whether the episode might be a fable, like Jumbo Kennard's sending a pimp tumbling down the Hollywood Hills. This one, too, was 100 percent real, however, as Hamilton laid it out for a government panel in California.

There were certain things done to him in that beating. He went to his own doctor in Pasadena for a medical treatment and the more or less unusual things done to his body were verified . . .

Q: Didn't the doctor, on that occasion, remove a cucumber from this man's body?

A: He did. He removed a cucumber from the rectum.

Q: How big was the cucumber?

A: It was my recollection that it was a medium-sized cucumber.

That particular hearing in San Diego underscored that J. Edgar Hoover was not alone in finding denial convenient. Representatives of that city's police department and the county sheriff both testified that they knew of no large-scale bookmaking, prostitution, or any organized crime in the area, a viewpoint that won the enthusiastic endorsement of Jack Dragna's pal down there, Anthony "Papa Tony" Mirabile. Papa Tony seemed to have a piece of half the bars and clubs in San Diego, one of which employed the son of L.A.'s Nick Licata. But he was perturbed when not everyone listening bought his testimony that he had never heard of that M-word — it was like they wouldn't believe him if they said someone was dead or alive. "God almighty, what a man have to do to make you believe it?" he asked. "Bring you the dead people and they are dead?"

Papa Tony did recall hearing vaguely about a Black Hand as a kid ("All I know was dirty hands") but not this Mafia. He knew of the Ku Klux Klan. He knew of the Knights of Columbus. He knew of the American Legion and the VFW, too, Papa Tony Mirabile said. "Whenever they have a convention,

I see they wear that red cap with the long thing."

Such bull was harder to serve up after November 14, 1957, when local state troopers interrupted a barbecue at the ranch home of Joseph "Joe the Barber" Barbara in the upstate New York town of Apalachin, population 277. For a distributor of Canada Dry soft drinks, Barbara had a lot of friends with nice cars — Lincolns, Imperials, and Cadillacs — and with far-flung addresses, from Brooklyn to Cleveland and Havana to Los Angeles. The ragtag outfit on the coast accounted for two of the approximately sixty Sicilians who tried to flee when the local cops stumbled upon the gathering. Fifty had criminal records. Nine had been in the coin machine business.

One of the attendees from Los Angeles was lawyer Frank DeSimone, who had taken over the mantle of the late banana importer Jack Dragna. Ten days before the gathering at the remote New York town he had paid a courtesy call on Jimmy The Weasel, still serving his extortion sentence up at the Soledad prison. The other L.A. representative was Simone Scozzari, Dragna's old late-night canasta buddy who still was, on paper, merely the proprietor of a candy and tobacco counter at the Venetian Athletic Club on North Broadway, "a very important sounding title for a very small operation," in the words of Captain Hamilton, who was amused to hear that Scozzari had $10,000 cash on him when stopped at a roadblock outside Apalachin. "Well, $10,000 certainly never came out of that cigar stand. It would take a long, long time of accumulation and living on nothing but air to accumulate $10,000 from that business."

The coals in the barbecue pit at Apalachin were barely cool when the FBI of J. Edgar Hoover had an angry visitor at its Washington headquarters. Robert Kennedy, still with the Senate's McClellan Committee, wanted to see the bureau's records on the dozens of men detained up there in the middle of nowhere, a list including Paul Castellano, Carlo Gambino, Joe Profaci, and Vito Genovese. The FBI had nothing, or little more — mostly newspaper clips — on forty of them. A chastened J. Edgar Hoover promptly announced a new Top Hoodlums Program.

The next day, two of his agents from Los Angeles made their way to the offices of the LAPD's Intelligence Division asking for a look at the files. They entered the sanctum of the Gangster Squad with their fedoras in hand.

For the men who toiled there every day, some for more than a decade, this was not just another small victory. It was a big one. The victory was not in humbling the FBI, it was in the validation of one part of their mission. Chief Parker had almost disbanded the squad because he didn't understand why they were sitting on their asses writing reports about who was seen drinking whiskey with whom at 2 A.M. Now it was clear that it was important to know who was playing canasta with whom too — that was one more piece of evidence pointing to a problem that suddenly seemed bigger than anyone imagined. They were going to start working right away to help the feds deport the canasta-playing cigar-stand operator Simone Scozzari — he was history. But there was plenty more unfinished business at home, and others to take care of.

When Robert Kennedy came back to Los Angeles on another fact-finding mission, Captain Hamilton called in one of his investigators for a confidential offering of evidence. Con Keeler was past his fortieth birthday and a veteran of more black-bag jobs than he could count. He was excited about the evidence he had — a shoebox full of checks — sure it would interest the Senate team, which included three young lawyers working under Kennedy. Kennedy asked,

Sergeant, where did you get these?

Err, sir, can't you just say we found them

in the street?

We can't say we found them in the street.

Then, sir, I don't know where we found them.

Who are they from?

Who do you want?

Kennedy graciously omitted the shoe-box episode when he wrote up his experiences for the Senate investigation. But his account, "The Enemy Within," a variation on Parker's "Invasion from Within" speech of a few years earlier, did include another tidbit from his time on the coast, in addition to the cucumber episode. Kennedy reported: "A major vending machine company paid Mickey Cohen $10,000 simply to remain 'neutral' in a battle over locations for machines in Los Angeles."

"I wanted to keep Cohen and his crowd from in any way infiltrating our industry," explained George Seedman, who made the payment to Mickey and his dog walker, Fred Sica. The only detail in dispute was whether Mickey had been offered far more, $50,000, to "put out the lights" of a cigarette vendor.

To that Mickey said, "I got nuthin' to do with electricity."

CHAPTER 29
A RING FOR THE STRIPPER

Sergeant Jerry Wooters developed a theory about Mickey and all those women — nothing was going on there. Mickey's friends laughed at that, swearing that Mickey scored high on the carnality scale and there was a certain thing he liked done to him, like any man. But Jerry decided that Mickey's germ phobia had to get in the way. "I think he was a real closet case, always washing his hands. I spoke to these gals he was with, they said he was always looking out the window, never did lay 'em."

The bigger issue, of course, was whether Mickey was for real — as a womanizer or a gangster — or a fake; whether he was all an act, especially now, in his second go-around.

Liz Renay was the first of the three strippers who became fixtures beside him during those last years of the '50s and she was a good match, a certified exhibitionist. She also had a lot to show off — she had a thirty-nine-inch rack by age thirteen, when she already was entertaining the servicemen around Phoenix, doing her part for the war effort as a V-girl. She was twenty-four, with two marriages behind her, and two kids, when a film company came to the Arizona city and put out a call for extras to be in a crowd at a lynching. A photographer for *Life* was doing a feature on what happens when a city far from Hollywood gets a taste of the traveling circus and his eye became fixated on a particular $25 red-haired extra, birth name Pearl Dobbins. She gained a five-page spread in the magazine, *Pearl's Big Moment*, which did mention that she had been anointed Miss Stardust of Arizona by a bra manufacturer but left out the 39D specifics of why a bra maker might have embraced her. When Pearl's Big Moment turned out to be a crowd scene in which she appeared on screen for less than a second, *Life* celebrated it as her "first and only chance to appear in a movie." Little did they know.

Liz Renay's next stop was New York, where she put her attributes more overtly on display as an exotic dancer and was noticed by Tony "Cappy" Coppola, the pudgy driver/ bodyguard to Murder, Inc.'s Albert Anastasia. She became the classic gun moll, complete with mink and diamonds and a sugar daddy who wanted her dreams to come true. After she mentioned her ambitions, her mob boyfriend said, "Let's call The Mick."

Years later, when Liz got around to recounting her flamboyant career, seven marriages, and many more dalliances in her memoir *My First 2,000 Men*, she recalled coming to Los Angeles and strategically meeting Mickey in her hotel room, fresh from the shower and in a black sheath that needed zipping. He had never been matinee-idol material and by now was, in essence, bald and dumpy. But she noticed the perfect manicure on his soft hands and, of course, his clothes. Then he drove her somewhere in his Eldorado and she spotted a woman's high-heeled shoe perched atop the backseat. She wondered if it was a prop placed there for her benefit, to make an impression.

The ground rules were known to all — thou shall not trespass on another gangster's gal — but he asked, "What would your friends in New York think if you and I decided to play sweethearts?" That meant he'd call her "hon," but they'd say *we're just friends* until later in life, when she insisted that he didn't really keep off the grass.

The best part was, he did have connections — he could get her in to see people in the industry and, unlike most aspiring bombshells, she had the goods: copper-haired beauty and personality too. She quickly had a Screen Actors Guild card, a Warner Bros. contract, and a guest spot on Groucho

Marx's quiz show, *You Bet Your Life*. She spoke with Cecil B. DeMille about appearing in one of his biblical epics as Esther, the harem virgin who becomes a queen. She also was up to play the girlfriend in red in a picture on Dillinger, the bank robber, that part less of a stretch.

It probably would have happened for Liz Renay if not for the barber-shop assassination of Albert Anastasia back in New York. When authorities called her in for questioning about the fallen Murder, Inc. boss and his crowd, they found $5,500 in cancelled checks in her purse . . . written to Mickey Cohen. Liz said she'd simply done him a favor — someone would put money in her account and she'd make out the checks marked *for personal loan*. "I simply allowed him to use my bank," she explained. It took a while for her role in the funneling of money, and her flailing attempts to explain it, to land her in federal prison. Before then it landed both her and Mickey back in *Life* magazine, posed at 4 A.M. in his Carousel ice cream parlor enjoying enormous sundaes with whipped cream and a cherry on top.

Candy Barr came next. Singer Gary Crosby called Mickey about that stripper, real name Juanita Dale Slusher. The native Texan was the highest paid dancer at Chuck Landis's Largo club, with dimensions nearly equal to

Renay's. Mickey had seen Candy's act but had never met her or heard of her crisis: Police back in Dallas had found a small amount of marijuana in an Alka-Seltzer bottle stashed in her bra and on Valentine's Day, 1958, a judge had sentenced her to fifteen years. Crosby wondered if Mickey might help the stripper and urged him to call Candy's manager, Joe DeCarlo. Mickey was outraged, DeCarlo recalled.

He couldn't believe it was true that she was gonna get fifteen years for having less than an ounce of marijuana. So I told him the story and he wound up getting lawyers for her, getting Walter Winchell on it and everything else. Then I said, "You're doing all this stuff — aren't you going to meet her?" So I told Candy, "You ought to meet this guy." So from that day on they were a pair. He had never seen her at all.

Before they met the first time, Candy received an orchid in a champagne glass with a note, "Don't worry, little girl, you've got a friend." Mickey guaranteed her $15,000 bond in Texas, paid a private detective $75 a day to work her case, and hired three attorneys to pursue her appeal, including flamboyant Melvin Belli. The manager, DeCarlo, swore the relationship was real — he could tell by their childish spat when Mickey

445

began talking to one of the other dancers at the club to make Candy jealous, and she threw a fit in the (un)dressing room. "It was stupid, the games they played. I don't know about love. He said he loved her. Who knows?"

The day the U.S. Supreme Court refused to hear the appeal of Juanita Dale Slusher, a.k.a. Candy Barr, Mickey announced their engagement. He shared the happy news at a party promoting his new association with a marvelous Italian restaurant on Ventura Boulevard in Sherman Oaks. That was in the San Fernando Valley, the dense grid of bedroom communities over the hills from the epicenter of nightlife on the Westside. The thinking was that if Mickey moved his nightly feast, others would follow, in this case to his new haunt, Rondelli's.

He never wed the lovely Candy, however. The dancer got married in Las Vegas before leaving to serve her pot sentence in Texas, but not to him — her Beverly Hills hairdresser got the honor of her hand and everything attached. "When you follow your heart instead of your head," Mickey said, "you fall into a trap."

Now the business about him marrying "Miss Beverly Hills," that was pure farce, a total fake. "That was bullshit," said Joe DeCarlo, who managed that burlesque star too. She was another of the performers at the Largo and a legit beauty queen, gaining "Miss Marines" and other titles, though they made up the "Miss Beverly Hills" when she started exotic dancing at seventeen. Mickey called her a nice piece of real estate and liked how she was *statuesque*. But she also was married, and happily, to her childhood beau, Bill Powers, another hairdresser. That detail was not advertised when Mickey announced their engagement and slipped a 12-carat diamond on the finger of Miss Beverly Hills. "She's a real lady, her morals and concepts of life are real high," Mickey said, and all that was true of the real-life Beverly Powers, who stripped down only to a bathing suit and would go on to become a minister.

He had been engaged to be married to Candy Barr, who was a dancer too. However, when she went to prison it must have been Joe who approached me. "How would you like to be seen around town with Mickey Cohen? You know, nothing will happen." And we came up with this publicity stunt and it was just that. Candy Barr disappeared and I was asked to take her place, which was hysterical. I don't know where Mickey got this engagement ring but it was a massive ring, massive diamond ring. And that was the whole publicity thing with me wearing this humongous diamond, you know.

No less than Meyer Lansky once warned about the danger of glamour broads — they drew attention to you, like getting your name in the papers. Well, screw that. The cops were watching Mickey's every move anyway, now with Stripper No. 3 at his side during the nightly spectacle on the town.

I would meet him and his protégés, and a lot of starlets and all, all the people he hung out with around Beverly Hills and Hollywood. Generally there were fifteen, twenty at a table. Very rarely was there anything less, eight to ten people on each side of the table. He would always sit at the head, of course, because that was his party, and he generally had me sitting on his left. We never went out ever that people didn't approach us. People would come up and would be really in awe of meeting him and I didn't understand that. They wouldn't wait for dessert — they would come up while he was about to take a bite and you couldn't get a glimpse or a glimmer of annoyance on his face. He was always the gentleman. He stood up. He was gracious to the people. He had the disease where you wash your hands anytime you touch anything — during a meal he might leave four or five times to go to the restroom. But he would never not shake the person's hand. He would sit down graciously and wait till they left and

then he would get up, and that touched me.
  They even did it to me sometime. They'd
ask, "Are you somebody?" And I'd say, "Not
really."

Beverly Powers did not get to wear the humongous diamond long before Joe DeCarlo
said the time had come, Mickey needed it
back. But she kept it on her finger until then,
even when she went to the supermarket and
carried the groceries home to the apartment
she and her husband rented in Sherman
Oaks. She never saw the men watching from
the unmarked sedan across the street or hiding in the bushes. She never heard the clicking of their camera with the telephoto lens as
it kept taking shots of her finger sporting the
glistening 12-carat diamond bought by someone who had claimed to have made his living
from a plant nursery and ice cream parlor
since his release from prison.

CHAPTER 30
"BEND YOUR KNEES AND ROLL"

To Jerry Wooters's partner, those years were like being in a movie, and not a Jack Webb clunker. To Bert Phelps, Jerry was Humphrey Bogart incarnate, the defiant hero on the hard-boiled fringe. Phelps relished having a front-row seat as Jerry and Mickey went at it cursing — they once grew so foul trying to out-motherfucker each other that Mickey began laughing, never mind his federal complaint against the *killer cop*. Phelps got a kick out of being chased by the FBI, too, or whoever that was with the two-way radio in the car following them. He got a charge out of his partner taking him to street corners or bars to meet Jack Whalen, though he was skeptical at first when Jerry assured him the man was no donkey and had piloted bombers during the war. Then they sat down to lunch and Phelps learned that Whalen had been stationed at one of the same airfields as him and indeed knew the workings of the B-25s and B-29s. Whalen really had been a flyboy for his country and now was a strong-arm hood. Amazing.

One day they were in the courthouse as the veteran defense lawyer Max Solomon was pleading out several prostitutes. Old Max was full of stories about representing Bugsy Siegel and the "Syndicate" gambling czars in the days of the crooked Shaw Administration and then the Hollywood Madam with her box of cards telling who in town was a bad screw. Whenever he saw Wooters he dredged up a case from Jerry's Vice days in which the prosecution's crucial testimony came from a woman named Gaybreast. Old Max would ask, "How's your witness 'Happy Titty?' " Anyhow, on this day the counselor Max Solomon was pleading out hooker clients one after another. Bert Phelps said, "Gee, Max — hell, I could do that."

Max said, "Well, why don't you? Go to law school."

"Really?"

"Sure, you can do it."

That's how the genius bug man Bert Phelps got the genius idea of going to law school in his spare time — inspired not by Chief William Parker, who had done the same thing decades earlier, but by a mob lawyer.

Bert Phelps relished every moment of his wild ride with Jerry Wooters — right up to the night he fell off the telephone pole.

■ ■ ■ ■

It was nearly pitch-black and he was fifty feet up, in an alley outside a bookie's place off Vermont. Wooters, on the ground, thought he saw a shadowy figure peering at them. "Hey, Bert," he said, in the tones of a whisper but the urgency of a shout. Phelps turned to look, then reached back to grab the pole. They might have wondered later whether what happened that night was an omen of what was to come, but it was an accident, nothing more — the spikes on Phelps's climbing shoes slipped, that's it, and down he plunged. No omen, just an accident, said Bert Phelps.

Once upon a time, in a place far, far away, we had found this Italian, some guy working for Mickey. So I went up there, I had my little small device with me that would transmit the telephone calls, both sides of the conversation, plus give you the telephone numbers they dialed. It was a nice little device. So I went up there and I put it on, it worked great. But something happened to it, we didn't know what it was, maybe rain. Jerry and I decided we got to go back and take a look at it, bring it down, repair it. About two, three o'clock in the morning, I climbed the pole and went up to the top and was looking at it. Then suddenly I heard

Jerry, "Hey, Bert!"

I said, "What is it?" He pointed and you looked down there and you could just see in the background a figure. Some son of a bitch I think is going to shoot me. So I quickly turned around on the pole and I reached, and it wasn't there. I went, "Whoooa." Telephone pole height, a long ways down.

I remember going down, I'll never forget this, going down, my old parachute training in the Air Corps, "Bend your knees and roll. Bend your knees and roll." You know, so I did. I put my head out and rolled. And I hit the cement. God, it just knocked me unconscious.

Jerry said, "Get up! Let's go, Bert!"

I couldn't get up. Jerry says, "Get up, get up, let's go!" I couldn't. I finally heard him. I said, "I can't breathe."

Jerry says, "Get up."

I said, "Call the ambulance."

Jerry told him their car radio wouldn't work in the alley — he had to drive the unmarked Chevy out to the street. So off he went, leaving Bert sprawled unprotected on the pavement, praying no other vehicle would turn into the dark alley and run him over. But after Jerry drove off, he didn't use the car radio. He found a landline instead to call the office. Sergeant Jack O'Mara was acting as

453

night watch commander. He had a question.

"Wait a minute. He's in the alley?"
"Yeah, he's layin' here in the alley. I'll drag him out to the street."
"Don't touch him!"
"Well, I don't want to burn the thing."
"To hell with burning it — don't touch him!"

O'Mara called for the ambulance, telling the paramedics to rush down *now* but "kill the lights, kill the siren." By the time they got there, Jerry had eased the unmarked Chevy back into the alley and parked it crossways so no one would run over the fallen Phelps. Bert's arms, feet, and back had been broken. He needed to get to the hospital fast. But before the ambulance pulled away, one of the paramedics asked Jerry, "Why didn't you radio from your car?"

The Humphrey Bogart of the Intelligence Division just shrugged. He wasn't going to explain to that moron that he didn't want to use his police radio lest anyone overhear and ponder what they were doing, at that hour, in that alley, on that pole.

Jack Whalen was in trouble again, for trying another past-posting scam. He had a partner in this one, Lloyd "Sailor Jack" Woods, who was a tough character, too, but did tote a gun — he once fired five shots into the bookie

Charles Cahan in a dispute outside a bar on Santa Monica Boulevard. They supposedly were squabbling over a girl named Dixie, but who knew?

The target of their scam was a Hollywood gambler named Don Giovanni, like the opera, who wanted to be a bookie. The two tough guys — Jack Whalen and Sailor Jack — told him, sure, there was room for one more bookie in the Valley. They would even send a few bets his way, from employees at the General Motors plant, to get him started. And they did.

What the neophyte bookie did not realize was that some of their bets were on races that had just been completed. It was not quite as clever as Freddic the Thief's past-posting charade in hospitals, but it nearly worked. At the end of Don Giovanni's first day as a bookie, he was $4,000 in the hole. When he pleaded that he didn't have that much, Jack Whalen and Sailor Jack Woods took all he did have, $500.

Unfortunately, Don Giovanni had not been tutored in the etiquette of their realm — like the slender dance instructor years before he turned to authorities for help. The past-posting victim named for an opera swore out another complaint that no detective, however friendly, could derail. On July 31, 1959, Jack Whalen and his buddy Sailor Jack were sentenced to one to ten years in prison for grand theft by past-posting. Though Whalen would remain free while appealing, and probably could drag out the proceedings for a year, the immediate indignity was seeing himself described, at the time of the sentencing, as "a self-styled actor."

Bert Phelps was in that hospital room two and a half months, staring at the ceiling, counting the little holes in it. Then they put his body in a metal cage to help it heal. His peers on the squad paraded in to console him and Captain Hamilton did, too, but not Chief Parker, that mean-tempered (and damn intelligent) son of a bitch. "The chief probably thought 'You dumb shit, you got caught,' and wanted to give me a pension, pension me off. Bullshit, I wanted to work."

But Phelps was not ready to get back in the unmarked Chevy when his partner got a call from Jack Whalen asking for a favor. It was the sort of matter The Enforcer normally would have handled himself, and left a body laying there, but the legal heat was on him. So he called Jerry Wooters.

You know, Mickey had a gang. The other guys had a gang. Whalen was Whalen. So he had a bookmaker in the south end — he had some bookmakers down there paying him protection. So another guy got out of San Quentin, a great big Mexican I guess,

456

this guy stands six-foot-nine and he's strong from layin' bricks at Quentin. He was down there saying that he was Jack Whalen and he was gonna be collecting the money from this one bookie. So Jack called me. I said, "Where's the meeting?" He says, "Some restaurant, eight o'clock in the morning." Bert was in the hospital and I didn't want to expose Whalen to any of the other guys at the office. So I went down myself.

It wasn't complicated. You just go down and flash your police ID. Maybe the fool giant pretending to be Jack Whalen sees your shoulder holster. You leave him guessing whether you're there on official business or just a friend helping a friend. "Never had any problem," Jerry said.

He did wonder at times what the bosses knew, or suspected. He had been tempted to think that nothing could get to him after he survived being shot down over the Pacific. But the ulcers that flared up during the war never went away. "My hot gut," he called it, and it was flaring up again. But that wasn't an omen, either.

Sergeant Con Keeler learned what the bosses knew. The moralizing bug man was the greatest contradiction on the squad. He was always talking about the need to be "down the line" and yet his job so often put him over it. After Anthony Pinelli got his motel, Keeler picked the lock of a room and left a playing card by the pillow of a visiting hood — an ace of spades — just to mess with him. He used a small Minox spy camera to copy movie industry labor contracts he found in the home of Johnny Roselli, Dragna's *consigliere.*

He broke into Johnny Stompanato's place, too, to look for address books or guns, and wound up trapped in the bathroom — the squad's lookouts down the street hadn't realized that Johnny Stomp was returning because he was in a woman's car, not his convertible. When Keeler heard them at the door, he hurried into the bathtub and pulled the curtain . . . only to have the woman come in to use the pot. He imagined her finding him and screaming, then Johnny rushing in, armed. Keeler had it all played out in his head — he was going to step calmly from the tub and say, "Just passing through, Johnny . . ." But the woman flushed and left without discovering him and she soon drove off with the mob's great lothario. Keeler then found a revolver in a dresser, rushed it to the police range for test firing, and broke into the house again to place it back in the same drawer, beneath the same underwear.

One day Keeler went to check out a few lowlifes from San Francisco staying at a Hollywood Boulevard hotel, and followed his usual MO. When they left their suite at night, he went in, no warrant — screw the *Cahan* case, he was just fishing. But he found dozens of expensive new cameras, clearly the fruit of recent robberies at local shops. The problem was he had no grounds to be there. So the next night he watched from the lobby as the punks came out with bulging laundry bags and tossed them in the back of a white Cadillac. Keeler called the West L.A. station and was connected to a patrol car. The young patrol cops sounded naive when he described the Caddy. One asked, "Well, how are we going to stop it, legally stop it?"

Keeler had to spell it out. "You know, nobody stops at a boulevard stop sign — they roll up and go about one mile an hour through it. That's your grounds for stopping 'em. And since you're going up to the driver's side, turn your flashlight to the backseat and you'll see these sacks. They're probably gonna tell you it's laundry but you're going to be able to see the outline of what looks like tin cans. You've got your probable cause."

"OK, OK, great."

The young patrol cops did as told, making the bogus traffic stop and arresting the punks with the hot cameras. Then they called their tipster back. "When are you coming to the station?" They assumed he wanted credit for the collar. They still didn't get it. Con Keeler didn't exist.

"I'm not coming. Our officers aren't coming. *You fellas* just made a helluva good pinch. Congratulations."

"OK, great, thanks."

The next morning, Keeler drove to the office. The squad was gone from City Hall by then — the LAPD had finally gotten its own headquarters a block east, an eight-story, whitish-gray monolith everyone called the Glass House. Keeler pulled into the basement parking area, got on the elevator, and pushed the button for the seventh floor. But before the door closed, two other men stepped in, Chief Parker and Daryl F. Gates, his protégé and frequent driver. Keeler started sweating but managed to say, "Hi, Chief." The door closed and the elevator started up. Nothing more was said until the door opened on the sixth floor, home of the chief's office. As he was stepping out of the elevator, the formidable William H. Parker turned and said, "Nice job you did last night, Sergeant."

Chief Parker knew. He knew everything. Their bosses knew everything.

Out of the blue, Jack Whalen offered Jerry Wooters a gift. "I got a dog for you," he announced. That was one thing Whalen had in common with Mickey, dogs. Mickey went for boxers and bulls, the squat, powerful breeds. Whalen favored purebred German shepherds

460

and Great Danes, the big dogs. But Jerry Wooters wanted nothing to do with any pooch, and not only because one took a bite of his hind end back when he was a rookie. He told Whalen:

They die on you, then you're miserable.

No, no, you'll like this dog.

No, no, Jack, I don't want the fucking dog.

I'm telling ya', Jerry, take the dog — you're hurting the wrong people.

Who am I . . . ?

Trust me, the thing'll let you know if anyone's sniffing around your bushes or you car . . .

C'mon . . .

No, listen, I'm tellin' you, you're gonna open up that garage some night and you're gonna get your ass blasted off.

Where do I pick up the dog?

The Wooters' new pet was named Thor, after the Norse god of thunder.

CHAPTER 31
"DON'T FUCK WITH THAT LITTLE JEW"

Jack Whalen and Mickey Cohen had something else in common besides dogs. If you saw photographs of each at a packed table at a Sunset Strip club, surrounded by soused frivolity, they might be the only ones scowling. Jack usually could force a smile if he knew a camera was on him, but sometimes he forgot and the edges of his mouth sunk. Mickey almost always looked that way.

Whalen's older sister came up with a fable to explain the bad blood between the two men by the tail end of 1959, an enmity beyond the natural tension between competitors in the gambling rackets. From her perch in the Big White House, Bobie von Hurst decided that her (big) kid brother had enraged the deranged (little) showboat by coming to the rescue of street-corner newsboys. Mickey, of course, had been one himself in Boyle Heights by age six, having been instructed by his older brothers to sit on a stack of two-cent *Los Angeles Record*s. He was

462

eight, by his own calculation, when he started getting nickels from the local hustlers (including the pool-playing Dago Frank) to hold their betting slips. So it was hardly news that the kids hawking papers on the corners sometimes played a role in the re-creation of gambling. But it seemed a stretch to believe, as Bobie von Hurst did, that the grown-up Mickey was demanding a cut of the newsboy action even as he was raking in money from gullible evangelists and investors in a film based on his life. As Bobie explained:

The thing was, all the little newspaper guys on the corner, you know, on Hollywood Boulevard, they took bets, just small bets. Mickey Cohen came around and told them they had to give the bets to him. And my brother didn't like that. He didn't think Mickey Cohen should do it. And that's when he got into trouble with Mickey Cohen. A lot of things started with Mickey Cohen harassing the little news kids taking bets. He told Mickey that any of his collectors that came around, he'd beat the bejesus out of them. Jack was taking care of the newsboys, that's all. And Mickey was washing his hands every twenty minutes. I don't know what he was trying to wash off of them.

Jack Whalen's sister didn't much like that

Mickey Cohen, either.

Undercover Cop Quintin Villanueva heard a different story and he had a seat closer to the action. What he heard along The Strip was that Jack "The Enforcer" Whalen, in one encounter, had punctured the quality that Mickey had spent two decades building up for himself in Los Angeles. Not fear or wealth — those seemed more East Coast virtues — but his stature, how he looked.

Only six members of the force knew what Villanueva was doing for the Intelligence Division in 1959, or even that he was part of it. He was a Marine tank unit veteran of the Korean War who made the mistake of beginning his police career in his hometown of Newark, New Jersey. His reward for finishing atop the recruit class there was an assignment that included visiting twenty-three bars to collect envelopes full of cash to be shared up the line. When Villanueva had the bad manners to balk at being a bag man with a badge, they yanked him off the street and put him on a shelf. A friendly judge told him where he might find an honest big-city police department, so he flew across the country over a weekend, on his own dime, to take the entrance exam for the LAPD. The earnest live-with-momma image projected by *Dragnet* may have seemed hokey, and it was, even to cops, but the moralizing Chief William Parker really was redefining what professional policing meant in America. Villanueva joined up and was given a trial-run assignment that took advantage of his being a new face in town — they used him in an undercover narcotics sting. After he pulled that off, a supervisor in narcotics said, "You're going to this house at six o'clock, just be there," and gave him an address in West Covina. That was the home of Captain James Hamilton.

Hamilton was waiting with two of his sergeants and two lieutenants from Intelligence, an intimidating reception committee for a probationary officer. They laid out Villanueva's next mission, should he accept it, though in reality he couldn't refuse: he was to infiltrate a crew of out-of-towners who had moved into the Halifax Apartments in Hollywood and seemed to have a proclivity for staging holdups. They were not averse to taking over a restaurant at gunpoint and lining everyone against the wall, like in the movies, the sort of stickup Mickey had pulled in younger days to prove himself in Cleveland and Chicago. This crew included Michael Rizzitello, a reputed associate of the Gallos back in New York, enough of a profile to warrant a major charade. Officer Villanueva was given an identity as a young Jersey guy with a record and set up in his own apartment in Hollywood, so he could invite any new friends over for poker games (and free liquor) and then excuse himself to run errands ("See you later, guys") so they could talk freely among themselves . . . always within earshot of the microphones. The bugs had been hidden in the living room and bedroom by an LAPD veteran the rookie didn't really know, a man named Keeler. Villanueva would hang out at the gang's favorite watering holes and at the delis and coffee shops where they migrated after the bars closed to have breakfast and kibitz or play cards. Often Mickey and his own delegation would be at nearby tables at the Gaiety and Carolina Pines, capping off their own long nights on the town.

Once Villanueva began running with the "Halifax Gang," he was struck by how two-bit they were for bad-asses — they'd steal ice cream cones if they could. Another thing he noticed: "They were always kowtowing to Mickey. If they stole something that was really nice they wanted to give it to Mickey." Mickey had come out of prison playing the harmless ex-hood swooning over the floozies, but this crew treated him as the big man out here, worthy of paying tribute.

By those last months of 1959, Mickey was being treated very differently by another character on The Strip, someone who acted as if Mickey owed him money. Villanueva's best guess was that a bookie had laid off bets with Mickey and Mickey had not bothered to place them, he just kept the cash. When the accounting turned in the bookie's favor, Mickey told him to bug off. So the bookie enlisted a third party who was experienced in resolving such disputes without an excess of conversation, whether dealing with a nobody $15 horse bettor or the somebody spotlighted in a four-week spread in the *Saturday Evening Post*, and posed in an ice cream parlor in *Life*, sharing a table with a stripper while eating a vanilla-and-chocolate-sauce sundae, topped by a cherry.

The word on the street was that Mickey was into Whalen for quite a few bucks. Whalen confronted Mickey at the Crescendo one night and in front of Mickey's cohorts literally went through Mickey's pockets searching for money.

Villanueva's main cover sergeant from the squad, Gene James, added one detail about the encounter whispered about in certain circles along The Strip. Jack Whalen had lifted Mickey up by the lapels of his suit jacket and plopped him on the bar before going through his pockets, setting up a short repartee.

This time you've gone too far.

You're still into me . . .

Too far, too far.

■ ■ ■ ■

The Whalen family had a specific date for that confrontation, but provided a different setting and back story: October 18, 1959, the Formosa Café, right by Sam Goldwyn's studio. Jack was at the bar with a friend named Hickman who wanted to place a bet in the back room. It was a Sunday, with six NFL games in the schedule including the local Rams playing the Green Bay Packers. Hickman had $30 of his own and borrowed $20 from Jack so he could bet $50. Hickman went to the back room, where Mickey and two other men were taking the action. Another family acquaintance completed the account:

Hickman returned to the bar and told Jack Whalen about the bet and his choice of teams and said he had received six points. Whalen said, "Go get your money back, you have been robbed, you can get more points than that." Hickman was scared and hesitated. Whalen went to the back room, made Cohen take his money out of his pocket and place it on the table. Whalen took $50 from Cohen's money and told Cohen to put the balance back in his pocket and slapped Cohen, calling him a THIEF. Cohen said, "YOU HADN'T OUGHT TO HAVE DONE THAT."

Whalen returned to the bar and gave the $50 to Hickman.

Mickey dismissed all those tales as utter nonsense, street gibberish — how would anyone believe he'd let that nobody lay a hand on him, or on his money? It was his buddy Fred Sica, Mickey said later, who was abused by that "great big enforcing bullshit cocksucker." To elaborate, "He enforced himself around here with everybody in my outfit. He had no respect for nobody. Everyone knew what a vicious, bullying, rotten bastard Jack-this-so-called-Enforcer Whalen was."

Hadn't that cocksucker Whalen gotten the word?

"Don't fuck with that little Jew."

CHAPTER 32
A PHONE CALL AT THE JAIL

Jerry Wooters's two little sons were taking rides atop Thor the Great Dane in the family's backyard in Arcadia when Captain Hamilton summoned him into the office and told him he was out of the squad. He was being transferred to the 4 P.M. to midnight shift at the city jail in Lincoln Heights, back in uniform in an assignment a notch below working traffic.

Well, you know, I put in a lot of years. What the hell is going on?

The transfer's effective tomorrow.

I feel I deserve —

Tomorrow.

Wooters said he pumped everyone he knew for an explanation but never got one, not a word about his relationship with Whalen or

470

anything. "I was kind of on the shady list, I guess."

But another squad member knew what had been the clincher after the years of whispers. Sergeant "Down the Line" knew. Con Keeler knew. An officer relatively new to the unit suddenly had asked for another assignment after working on a bookie. He wouldn't say why he wanted to transfer out, following the code that applied to cops and as well as crooks. But his partner confided to Keeler that Jerry Wooters had unnerved the new squad member with a proposal — suggesting that they arrest the bookie then offer him a *way out*. It sure smelled like a shakedown to Keeler.

Well, it was a bookmaker out on Wilshire Boulevard, he had a store out there, a haberdashery, something to do with clothing. And one of our officers got next to him and he was an informant and a good one and we didn't bust him for bookmaking. Jerry Wooters had worked Vice so he had good knowledge of bookmakers and stuff and that was the reason he was in the division. And so he went to the officer who had this informant and tried to work a deal with him — if they could set him up for something, Wooters could make a bust on him then set him loose. In other words, get something on him, arrest him and shake

471

him down. I really don't know what the plan was. But the officer tells his partner about it and I don't know why — I was always father confessor or something — anyway, the partner comes to me and tells me. So I found the officer and took him back in my laboratory, and he wanted to transfer out. I said, "What do you mean?"

"Well, I don't want any part of it."

So we talked for a little while. I told him he owed it to the rest of the guys to blow the whistle. "Hey, your buddies here you've been working with, you going to leave them hanging?" Well, finally I convinced him to talk to the skipper.

So I went in to Hamilton. I told him, "Captain we've got a problem."

"Oh?"

So I told him that one of our men had propositioned another man. Well, my cap went right up in the air. He said, "Who's the guy?"

"Wooters."

Cap looked at me just kind of shook his head. He wasn't surprised when I told him. He just sat there and thought — nodded his head kind of. So Hamilton brought the officer in, the skipper talked to him. Wooters the next morning was working the jail and Bert the next morning . . .

That was the hard part for everyone in the

know, how they also transferred Bert Phelps, the son of the LAPD's first pilot who had proven to be a genius at bugging and could have been using his technical wizardry for the CIA at three times the pay. Bert had given his body for the cause, literally breaking his back, and had returned to work rather than take disability. But none of that could save him in Chief Parker's no-excuses LAPD, which held one partner responsible for the other, no matter what. "Bert should have known some of the things Wooters had done," Con Keeler reasoned. "I said, 'Bert, you're not stupid.' "

Phelps could argue all day that he didn't know and that Jerry might merely have wanted to squeeze the bookie to snarc a bigger fish, like Mickey. They didn't understand the crazy way old Vice guys worked. They didn't understand the whole, "That's Jerry." When Captain Hamilton called him in, Phelps said, "Captain, shit, I've been here for years, I've given it my all." No use. He, too, found himself working as a jailer — in his case in the lockup at LAPD headquarters, midnight to eight A.M., the graveyard shift. It all was done quietly without the formality of a disciplinary hearing, and both men kept their ranks as sergeants. There wouldn't be any blot on their records. The world outside didn't have to know a thing. Keeler even told Phelps the new assignment could be a blessing, with its regular hours. "Why don't you finish law school and get your degree?"

A blessing? The midnight-to-eight shift at the jail? Phelps would come home in the morning, have "dinner," take a brief nap, and then study before his law classes, which ran from 6:00 to 9:30 P.M. Then he'd drive over to the police station and try to nap two hours in his car before the next graveyard shift in purgatory. A blessing? It would take him a long time to get over his anger at the "sanctimonious assholes" who had never hesitated to tap his talents for *special assignments*. "Tonight, you're going to Yuma." "Yes, sir." "Tonight you're going to San Diego and bug this place." "Yes, sir." "Tonight go debug the chief's office." "Yes, sir." Tonight go help a cheating Hollywood bigwig eavesdrop on his wronged wife. "Yes, sir."

Now it was "Tonight sit in the fucking jail" and count your blessings. At least it was conceivable they might someday forgive and forget with Bert, whose only crime had been to be someone's partner. It was not the same with Jerry Wooters. Barely a year before, he'd been the only foot soldier pictured with the bosses in a national spread about Mickey Cohen in the *Saturday Evening Post*, described there as the little hoodlum's Javert. Now it was hard to imagine him ever escaping the Lincoln Heights jail, right back where he'd once been hauled as a kid for hawking dollar

474

bags of oranges. Jerry Wooters had gone nowhere and gotten there fast.

Wooters was just a month or two into his exile at the jail when he got a call from the familiar voice of Jack Whalen. The big man was still free on bail while appealing his grand theft conviction for scamming $500 from the Giovanni guy trying to be a bookie. It was Wednesday, December 2, 1959. Whalen did not sound overly agitated.

Ah, I got a real rough beef, can you give me a hand?'

What?

Well, I got a showdown with that god-damned Mickey.

Where?

Rondelli's, in the Valley.

Jack, I'm in uniform. I'm active duty. I can't just walk out and wind up in the Valley. You know I can do a lot of things, but I can't do that. But I'll see if I can get you some help.

Wooters phoned the old squad, where a couple of the guys still might listen if he had a tip.

I called a guy who I thought was a friend of mine — not a friend, an acquaintance, a guy down there who was a lieutenant. I called him and said, "Listen, if you guys go by Rondelli's tonight around eleven o'clock, I think you're gonna find Whalen and Mickey and some other bigs. And I'm pretty sure you'll find some firearms."

He said, "Oh, yeah, thanks a lot."

Then I called Whalen. I said — he never had a reputation for carrying a piece, with Whalen, it was always hands, he beat the shit out of them — so I called him and said, "Don't take any firearms down there."

The caution was something of an insult given Jack Whalen's pride at needing nothing more than his fists. But Jerry Wooters drove home the point, anyway — don't be packing. And Jack the Enforcer did not carry a gun on the last night of his life.

CHAPTER 33
THE DEADLY NIGHT
IN THE VALLEY

Jack Whalen's beef was not directly with Mickey, but with a couple of his crew and it revolved around familiar issues in their realm: Who was scamming whom? And who would back down first?

The dispute had its roots in November 21, 1959, raids by Vice Squads on five locations that took bets for Al Levitt, a Valley-based sports bookie suspected of handling $50,000 in wagers on a good day. Periodic raids were an expected cost of business in that trade and your clerks rarely got much jail time, if any. The real hassle came if the cops penetrated the back office and seized your betting slips. If word leaked out to the clientele, a few bold gamblers might call in to gush about how brilliant they'd been with their picks and, hey, where's our money. How could you prove otherwise?

So it was that a pair of bettors began clamoring for $390 they claimed they were due on their wagers on college football games after the LAPD raids on Levitt's bookmaking operation. The pair bet under the code name "George for Ram."

When asked in an official setting, like a courtroom, George Piscitelle, a.k.a. George Perry, and Sam LoCigno, a.k.a. Sam Lombardo, listed themselves as unemployed — as a laid-off drug store manager in Perry's case and as an unemployed bartender and asphalt salesman in LoCigno's. Both lived well, though, for people without paychecks, driving new Cadillacs. "I don't believe anyone can win on horses," LoCigno said, "but I was just lucky."

Sammy LoCigno had grown up in Cleveland while Mickey was still there making the leap from boxing to rooting, then come West himself in 1944 after being discharged from the Army because of a nervous condition he blamed on bad water from a well. He was picked up from time to time for running games of chance but after fifteen years in town had only one jail term on his sheet, five days for speeding. At thirty-nine, he seemed to be little more than "a smalltime bookie who was a flunky and errand boy for Mickey Cohen," as a probation officer described him.

Now the errand boy Sam LoCigno and his friend George Piscitelle were looking to finagle $390 from the just raided Al Levitt. The pair collected $140 of their supposed winnings before the bookie had second thoughts and — unfortunately for them — found evidence to back his suspicions.

Normally their gambit would have worked without a blink, but they hadn't counted on the ways of LAPD Vice. One of the sergeants leading the raids on Levitt's operation did not immediately take the seized betting slips downstairs to book into evidence. He stuck them in his locker — he said he wanted to study 'em before he wrote his report. Then who should call him but a veteran lawyer who represented lots of bookies. The lawyer said, "Listen, we're having trouble with some of these guys claiming they won big and Al doesn't think they did . . ." Most times, you tell a bookie's lawyer to screw himself, but this counselor was always cooperative, a go-along, get-along sort. What was the harm?

The sheets listed two college football wagers by the pair who called themselves "George for Ram" and both were losers. The two fools had put $220 on the school for smart boys, Northwestern, which had dreams of making the Rose Bowl if it beat Illinois, then lost 28–0. Al Levitt, out on bail and not in the best of moods, did his own calculations and decided that he didn't owe those scammers anything — they owed him $910. Levitt's chief clerk suggested that he forget the matter, given the players. But their way of life was all about thinning out the weakest of the herd and Al Levitt could not afford to look like the weakest of the herd. On the morning of December 2 he got the scamming bettor George Piscitelle on the phone and endured a frustrating barrage of indignant denials and demands for the phantom winnings. Levitt finally said, "Well, look, I am through with the thing. I am having J.O. call you."

George Piscitelle did not have to be told who "J.O." was. The man was turning the matter over to Jack O'Hara, a.k.a. Jack Whalen, a.k.a. The Enforcer.

Five minutes later the phone rang again in Piscitelle's apartment.

When Jack Whalen took over a marker it meant the debt was his and the fight was his and he didn't intend to waste time listening to waffling. George Piscitelle said the message from the "head-buster" was to the point: "You dago bastards better pay up."

This was an intimate society, this slice of Los Angeles in the waning days of the 1950s, and Piscitelle was familiar with The Enforcer's modus operandi. When Piscitelle worked at Turner's drug store on The Strip he had seen Whalen pound three men in the street, sending one eight feet back into a row of garbage cans. And sharing Piscitelle's North Hollywood apartment at the moment was someone who knew Whalen more personally, the young lounge singer Anthony Amereno, a.k.a. Tony Reno. Another fellow described Tony as "five-foot-nuthin' " and "120 pounds soaking wet with a hard-on," but he had found a niche in Los Angeles after using a $26 Greyhound bus ticket to flee New York and its shylocks. The crooner had become a mainstay at the joint next to Turner's drug store, the Melody Room, and had a gig upcoming in Glendale, which made the call from Whalen fortuitous. The big man was one of his biggest fans. "Every place I worked, singing that is, I called Jack and he used to come down, you know, spend money like — it's always good for a nightclub to have a little following, you know. Bosses like you to spend money and he used to come down and buy drinks, for anybody I was with."

What's more, when Tony was broke The Enforcer had given him a job for five months handling the phone in the back office of his horse book. The singer knew of Whalen's con man father too, enough to refer to him as Doc, as in Dr. Whalen. So when Tony Reno realized who was ringing up George Piscitelle about a gambling matter, he said, "Give me the phone, because I know Jack."

"Just stay out of it, you little punk," Whalen told his crooning former bookmaking clerk. "I want my $900 and I don't want no from nothing."

Whalen said the two scamming bettors had until noon to pay, but he gave them a break, making the deadline 12:30 P.M. He'd send an emissary to the Salem Manor on Sunset to pick up the cash. When the time came, LoCigno and Piscitelle were not there, only their volunteer middleman, Tony Reno, wanting to blab some more. Whalen's emissary got the big man on the phone with Reno again to explain the obvious. "Those two dago bastards, I am going to bust them all up. Who do they think they are fucking around with, some kid? They don't have the money down there right now?"

"No, I told them for you."

"They've both got to go."

Jack Whalen did not have to ask where he could find the two welshing cheats.

They were all social vampires, that crowd — they lived for the night — and they had a typically full evening ahead. The party was going to start with supper at what quickly had become their usual spot, Rondelli's, then continue back over the hill at the Cloister, on The Strip, where it was the closing night of comedian Joey Bishop's successful run at the club. Bishop might have kept going there but needed to get ready to shoot a heist caper film in Las Vegas, a little romp called *Ocean's 11* with pals Frank Sinatra, Dean Martin, and Sammy Davis Jr. Mickey Cohen had reserved a full table for Bishop's final show at the Cloister and the Bronx-born comic was going to meet them for the dinner beforehand — he liked the gnocchi made fresh at Rondelli's every Wednesday night. So did talent agent Joe DeCarlo, the manager of Mickey's favorite strippers, who was all set to drive Bishop to the restaurant until the comic decided to play an extra nine holes of golf and begged off. That was fine, though, for when DeCarlo called Mickey with the news the little fellow said, "OK, pick up Sandy for me."

Mickey's 12-carat charade of an engagement with Miss Beverly Hills was still ongoing but for the last ten days he had been seeing an eighteen-year-old with cascading blond hair, Claretta Hashagen. Originally from St. Paul, Minnesota, she went by Sandy Hagen in L.A., where she aspired to make it as a model. She kept a French poodle named Brigitte and a parakeet named Blue Boy in an apartment that had a bedroom done up in red and white satin, like a valentine. Police later said she had 290 names in several address books — the pretty young thing had gotten to know a lot of people in town. She'd been introduced to Mickey through a mutual friend at a restaurant on The Strip and then phoned him — she called him — and now they were an item. "He's a perfect gentleman," she said. "He never drinks. He never swears. He never smokes."

Tony Reno got his hair cut that afternoon

— all those men had marvelous hair: dark, wavy, and poofed up just a bit, then held in place, perfectly, with goop. Most got in a nap before they rendezvoused at Joe DeCarlo's apartment in Hollywood to head out for the long evening. Sammy LoCigno wasn't supposed to drive, his license had been suspended, so Joe took the wheel of his gray-silver '59 Caddy convertible with George Piscitelle beside him up front and Sammy relegated to the back of his own car. Tony followed, driving a nice car, too, one belonging to Piscitelle's girlfriend. George was a good looker, up there with the late Johnny Stomp, and the ladies threw themselves at him. This one had a '58 T-bird. The entourage took off at 9:40 P.M.

As requested by the Mick, they headed first to Sandy Hagen's place off the 101 Freeway, across from the Hollywood Bowl. But when they tooted the horn outside she came down in a housecoat and said she wasn't ready, they should go ahead, she'd take a cab to Rondelli's.

Sammy LoCigno figured he had eaten at Rondelli's fifteen or sixteen times over the past month alone. He liked the place because the waiters knew he preferred the pasta without any of the spicy tomato sauce that inflamed his nervous stomach — the chef, Nick, cooked it up special for him, as he wanted, bland.

LoCigno wore one of his perfectly tailored suits for their night out, with a side pocket just the right size for his .38. "It hung in there real nice," he said.

Tough as he was, Whalen wasn't about to go out on the job alone — he'd been smart enough to fly bombers, after all. Following his phone call with his old pal from Intelligence, stuck now in the jail, the big man arranged for a frequent helpmate, Rocky Lombardi, to meet him at 8:30 P.M. on The Strip. Whalen wasn't worried about anyone in front of him, anyone he could see. "He wanted me to watch his back." Rocky said. "If anything happened, to watch his back."

Whalen was in no rush — he downed half a dozen shots at their first meeting place, the Rondelet tavern on Sunset, while Rocky had just a beer. Sailor Jack Woods was there too and normally might have joined their road trip, packing as usual. But Sailor Jack also was appealing their conviction and one-to-ten-year sentence and he didn't need to give authorities any reason to revoke his bail. So he'd hoist a few beforehand with them, that's it.

Their next stop was the Melody Room, the place where Tony Reno often sang, and Whalen put away another half dozen shots, still in no rush. He was dressed business casual in gray slacks, an open white shirt, and sports coat. Finally, he said it was time to go. He made no secret of where — the scuttlebutt even reached the young under-cover cop from Jersey, Quintin Villanueva, who was out mixing with his Halifax Gang suspects on The Strip. "I was in one of the nightclubs," he said, "and the word among the rounders was that Whalen was hot and was heading for the Valley."

Whalen did not go directly to Rondelli's, though. He and Rocky Lombardi stopped first at a Mexican joint, Casa Vega, to meet a second backup. José Sanchez Herrera was known as Big Joe, with good reason — he was six-foot-three, 320, and sometimes got bit roles playing giant Polynesians in the mov-ies.

The Mexican restaurant was almost within crawling distance of Rondelli's but they took their cars, anyway. Rocky and Big Joe went in one, The Enforcer in his own. The two backups got there first, at 11:25 P.M., and walked right in the front door, entering under the canopy and the neon sign advertising NEAPOLITAN CUISINE. Inside, they veered right by the phone booth into the narrow, dimly lit bar area, where salesmen from the swimming pool business next door were laughing it up over the piped-in music while two young women chatted up the bartender. Rocky Lombardi and Big Joe Herrera took positions at opposite ends of the bar, ordered

486

drinks themselves, and waited. You might almost think they'd done this before.

Rocky had not yet touched his glass when Jack Whalen burst through the swinging doors of the kitchen at 11:28. He had pulled up a back alley, past the Anthony Pools building, and come in Rondelli's by the back way. He did not say a word to Rocky as he marched along the bar toward the phone booth at front of the restaurant. The tiny crooner Tony Reno, five-foot-nuthin' and 120 pounds with a hard-on, was visible inside the glass-sided booth, making a call. The bar itself was packed. All the stools were filled, as were the four small cocktail tables. Several patrons stood with their drinks. Whalen knew the two women chatting up the bartender, Ona Rae Rogers and Jo Wyatt — they both sometimes waitressed along The Strip — but he did not speak to them either. He brushed one aside as he headed toward Tony Reno in the phone booth. "I knew he wasn't there for pleasure," Jo Wyatt said later.

You couldn't see the dining room from the bar. The two areas were separated by a long planter filled with fake greenery, plastic philodendrons rising nearly to the ceiling, the sort of stuff that had been a staple of the nursery Mickey Cohen operated when he got out of prison.

Mickey had arrived between 8:30 and 9 P.M.

487

in his black and white '59 Caddy convertible, accompanied by his bulldog, Mickey Jr. The dog had his own checkered bib so he could eat in style, off a plate, at his master's feet. At a hearing just a week before on Rondelli's application for a license to offer live entertainment, Mickey had taken the Fifth more than fifty times when asked if he was a hidden owner. "I got no piece of that restaurant," he said. "I wouldn't take a piece of it on a silver platter." This night he came early to the restaurant he didn't have a piece of to meet with a man named Waders who was managing a black singing duo and wanted his help — Waders and his singers were waiting in the bar for him. Mickey also had a meeting with his old friend Roger Leonard, who used to be in the pest extermination business and sold ultraviolet equipment. Now Leonard fancied himself a writer-producer, like his brother, who was one of the principals behind the New York cop drama *Naked City* and was developing another TV series, *Route 66*, about two young guys who explore the famous highway in a Corvette. The former pest man Roger Leonard hoped, in turn, to become producer of The Mickey Cohen Story.

Table 15 was reserved for them, in the back of the restaurant, by the pastry cart. One of the Sica brothers, Fred, was there for a while but made it an early evening. He excused himself and left Rondelli's just as Mickey's main entourage for the night arrived.

Sammy LoCigno of the nervous stomach went first into the kitchen to pay his respects to Nick the cook, then took a seat on Mickey's left. The ex-drug store manager George Piscitelle sat on the other side of the round table, where he could see anyone entering the dining room. The faux Sinatra crooner Tony Reno was an anomaly — he was wearing an alpaca sweater, not a suit — but he was at table 15, too, as were Joe DeCarlo, the man with the strippers, and Roger Leonard, who wanted to make a movie. The seat on Mickey's right was kept empty awaiting the girl Sandy.

There was a lot of flitting about — someone always was getting up from the table or coming back. Mickey constantly was off to the restaurant's office to make calls or to the men's room for his hand washing. Sammy LoCigno kept going to the bar to schmooze with the women, Jo Wyatt and her roommate, Ona Rae Rogers. He knew Ona Rae especially well — they'd had a couple of dates — so he invited both to come into the dining room and join the party. "We already had dinner," Ona Rae said, but they accepted his offer to come later, to the Cloister, to catch Joey Bishop's last show. Meanwhile, Tony Reno kept going to the pay phone, just trying to find his manager, he said — he needed a cash advance to get his clothes out of the cleaners before his gig in Burbank.

Others in the restaurant were regulars too. Harry Diamond was dropped off by his son and planted himself at the bar to inhale shots of straight scotch — fifteen, eighteen, twenty shots. He was blind in one eye already and the second didn't work too well when he tried to read the fine print on that most important publication, the Racing Form. Diamond weaved from the bar to a table to join Joseph Friedman, a.k.a. Joe Mars, who had his own café on North Highland but came here to eat. They quickly began arguing over who owed what from another night's check.

Michael and Toni Ross came over after a traffic accident — they'd been hit by a drunk driver and needed sustenance to recover. Michael Ross was an actor who subsisted on small parts, one in the 1950 noir classic *DOA*, the film that began with Edmond O'Brien showing up at a police station to report a homicide and being asked, "Who was murdered?" "I was," he replies. Ross and his wife sat down to eat with Al Siegel, Hollywood Al, who was there with his mother. When Mrs. Ross got up to use the washroom, she encountered Mickey coming out and gave him a nodding hello.

The teenage Sandy Hagen had not yet arrived so Mickey asked George Piscitelle to drive him and Mickey Jr. to the nearest Western Union place, up on Van Nuys Boule-

490

vard, where $800 was being wired to him. Back when he was squiring the stripper Candy Barr, a Florida club owner had come to Los Angeles and asked about flying her to Miami to perform, and also asked where he might place a bet while in town. Mickey said Sammy LoCigno could help him out with that. Now the fellow was paying off his losses and Mickey, in all his kindness, was picking up the money order for Sammy.

The cab with the young blonde finally pulled up soon after Mickey and the bulldog returned to Rondelli's. Sandy Hagen ordered an orange juice and the veal scaloppini but was just starting to dig into it at 11:28 P.M. Sam LoCigno had finished his salad and was ready for his pasta with no tomato sauce. Mickey was back in his seat, not off at the soap and water. His dog's plate of linguini was below the table, licked clean. Tony Reno was gone once more to the glassed-in phone booth up front, on the other side of the fake philodendron. He was on that pay phone again when a familiar (large) figure pushed through the kitchen doors and strode along the bar in his direction, looking like he was not there for pleasure.

The unmarked police car had been sitting outside Rondelli's since 8 P.M. — the night lieutenant in Intelligence had asked the two men in it to watch the place. They parked on a side street where they would not be so obvious while keeping an eye on the front entrance, the velvet rope, and ATTENDANT PARKING sign. They could not see the back alley or back entrance at all.

One of the pair on surveillance was Jack Horrall, son of the police chief from the '40s and Jerry Wooters's old partner. "There was supposed to be a meeting in there," was about all he'd admit knowing. They did notice Mickey leave in LoCigno's Cadillac and dutifully followed him and his dog to the Western Union on Van Nuys Boulevard, recording the excursion in their log. But when Mickey returned to Rondelli's they merely repositioned their car on the side street to keep an eye again on the front of the restaurant.

The other cop watching was Jean Scherrer, who had been entrusted with sensitive assignments from the day he joined the LAPD. A naive rookie in 1949 when the scandals rocked the force, Scherrer was sent down toward the Coliseum, the huge stadium, for what he thought was routine traffic control. Instead, he was told by a sergeant, "We're taking over Administrative Vice." With that, Scherrer became part of the small task force that broke into the tainted unit's headquarters and found "stuff in lockers — money, stacks of it, things of that nature." The public quickly learned that everyone in Ad Vice had been fired or transferred but never was told about the cash. Some matters were best kept quiet, then and now. Scherrer also worked the famous *Cahan* bookmaking case led by Sergeant Jerry Wooters. "The best investigator I ever worked with," he said.

But on December 2, 1959, Scherrer had not been told whose tip prompted the bosses to send them to Rondelli's — he did not learn until years later where the lead came from. Had he known at the time, he might well have done more than sit in the car.

We weren't given that much information. We could only see the front door and there wasn't much going in and out. We were there quite a few hours and it was very inactive. Somewhere it was decided within the office that nothing was going to happen. We were told, "Forget it. Leave." We left just before the shooting.

Tony Reno was plunking another dime into the pay phone when a giant hand reached in and grabbed onto his collar, effortlessly lifting him off his feet and out of the booth. Jack Whalen said, "Where's them friends of yours, them two dagos?" Or maybe it was, "Hang the phone up and show me where those bastards are." Or maybe it was simply, "What you doing?" Tony Reno had to recount the moment many times later — could he be blamed if the dialogue varied?

"Tony, who you calling?"

"I'm calling my manager."

"Where's them two cocksuckers?"

"Jack, take it easy . . ."

"They're going to go. Are they in there?"

"Yes, in the back."

Whalen prodded little Tony ahead of him, around the planter with fake greenery and into the dining area. But the big man loosened his grip as soon as he saw who was in there. Whalen forged ahead and Tony scurried back to the safety of the bar, or so he said in the days following — he was up front by the phone booth, where he couldn't see what happened, he only heard the shots. One shot, a short pause, then another.

Tony Reno looked toward the other end of the bar, at Rocky Lombardi, the big man's backup. After the second shot, Tony gave a hands-up gesture, like "What can you do?"

Mickey's story that night was that the shots came from a nearby booth, along the wall, and he didn't see nuthin'. He held steady all night, didn't see nuthin'.

Later he changed it, of course. Then it became OK, the shots came from his table — but he still didn't see much. Mickey's eventual account had that rotten bastard Jack Whalen walking up and saying, "Good evening, Mr. Cohen," but not giving him time to respond because The Enforcer put his huge left hand on George Piscitelle's shoulder and asked, ' "Have you got something for me?' " George said, "I don't have anything to talk to you about, Jack" and George turned back to his food — "And Bingo! He hit George a shot," a powerful right, "and George went to the floor." Whalen grabbed hold of the empty chair at their table and turned toward Sammy LoCigno, the big man starting to lift the chair as he said, " 'You dago bastard, you're next' or something of that sort . . . The next thing, I heard the shooting, and that was it. I never seen any gun."

Mickey insisted that he had ducked from force of habit after the first shot and stayed under the table, down there with the dog, Mickey Jr., and when he finally looked up, the restaurant was all but empty. That eventually became Mickey Cohen's official story, to be believed or disbelieved, as with anything he said. But all that first night, it was "I didn't see nuthin'."

Of all the patrons in the restaurant that night, only Mickey and the two young women at the bar did not flee. Amid the screams and panic and cries of "Let's go!" the other regulars and the drunks and the swimming pool salesmen had gotten the hell out, most via the back way, through the kitchen and the alley. But the roommates Jo Wyatt and Ona Rae Rogers stayed. They knew the man sprawled on the floor from their time on The Strip — Jo Wyatt knew him very well. She hurried to the dining area and found Jack Whalen lying on his right side, next to the pastry table. The big man was breathing faintly, bleeding from his head, so she eased him onto his back, got napkins and towels, and asked her friend Ona to get ice. After Whalen was rolled onto his back, his feet pointed outward, unmoving, and his left hand lay on his stomach, as if he had reached there, thinking that's where he was shot.

Like most everyone else, the actor Michael Ross had rushed from the dining room, leading his wife though the kitchen. But the couple paused there a few minutes, as if paralyzed. Then they realized that Toni had left behind her purse, cigarettes, and lighter. The actor hurried back to their table to retrieve them and that's when he saw young Jo Wyatt over the body on the floor. It looked to him like she was kneeling in prayer over Jack Whalen.

Wyatt pleaded with Mickey Cohen, "Please call a doctor," and he did — he phoned his own physician, Dr. Max Igloe.

"Next thing," Mickey said, "I went and washed my hands."

Authorities weren't called until 12:04 A.M. and then not by anyone still in the restaurant. Rocky Lombardi made the call. After the second shot, and hands-up gesture from Tony Reno, he did briefly look into the dining room and saw his friend Jack sprawled there. "He didn't look too healthy. He wasn't moving none. I left. I went out the door with the rest of the people." But Rocky alone stopped at a pay phone and dialed the operator to ask her to send an ambulance to Rondelli's on Ventura Boulevard. "A man got hurt."

Patrol Officer James C. Newell got the *man down* radio call at 12:10 A.M. He worked out of the Van Nuys Division, in the heart of the Valley. He and his partner arrived at the restaurant just as the ambulance was pulling up.

Whalen was dead by then. The first bullet had missed him, whizzing through two leaves of the fake philodendrons before blasting through the ceiling toward the attic. The second bullet got him just over his right eyebrow, almost between the eyes, and lodged at the back of his skull.

Mickey Cohen was coming from the bathroom when the first policemen walked into the restaurant, the only diner still there. His table had been cleared. Everything on it was gone, the dishes, the napkins, and the glassware that might have fingerprints. Only the white tablecloth remained, still with the checkerboard pattern of creases from how it was folded overnight. The waiter said he'd cleared the table by habit, nobody told him to. He also cleared the drinks from the bar on the other side of the planter — he polished off the booze in every glass himself. He had started in on the cooking wine in the kitchen too. He was feeling no pain, that waiter.

Chief Parker and Captain Hamilton were there within an hour, part of the largest concentration of police brass at a crime scene since 1950, when Mickey's lawyer Sam Rummel was ambushed outside his Laurel Canyon home. Back then, the chief had said, "This case can, and will, be solved, if it takes every member of the police department." But that rubout had never been solved, like so many others in L.A. Now it seemed like the entire force was mobilized again — everyone available from Homicide and Intelligence was called in to round up anyone who had been in the restaurant that night. The owners of record, James and Hazel Rondelli, had hung around, along with the waiter and a couple of other employees, and they helped by naming some of their regulars. A few were just up the street, in a coffee shop. Others were surprised with knocks on their doors at home.

While those cops were fanning out around the city, the honor of questioning Mickey fell to Thad Brown, the cigar-chomping deputy chief and supervisor of detectives. Brown had clashed with the Gangster Squad when it was called in on the Black Dahlia investigation, an insult to his Homicide boys, but it was hard not to admire his old-school guts. Despite his rank, Brown was the furthest thing from a desk bureaucrat — he personally arrested two of the three women sent to the gas chamber at San Quentin, including Barbara Graham, whose case had been made into a film (*I Want to Live*) that won the best actress Oscar for Susan Hayward. In real life, when it came time to storm the converted store where the murderess was hiding out with two men, Brown snatched a shotgun and insisted on going through the back door first. The deputy chief knew about tough and he knew about the fellow on the floor of Rondelli's.

"He'd been flirting with the undertaker for a long time," Thad Brown said of Jack Whalen. "He was big, rough, and as mean as they come."

Brown asked a uniformed officer to clear out of the back room at Rondelli's so he could question Mickey alone. The only witness was the dog, Mickey Jr.

"So help me God, Chief, I didn't shoot him," Mickey said.

"Who did?"

"I don't know."

"Who else was seated with you at the table?"

"No one."

As others were rounded up that night, they slowly filled in the details. One salesman from the swimming pool company next door, Gerald Sumption, said he had told his companions, "Let's leave" only to be blocked by Mickey, who apparently had not remained under the table all that long.

"Where are you going?"

"Out."

Then Mickey cuffed the salesman on the right cheek, hard.

Sumption weighed 245 pounds and was fit — he knew judo — and Mickey apparently mistook him for one of Whalen's backups, for he said, "You were with them, you dirty . . ." and slapped him again. The burly salesman could have manhandled the pint-sized Mickey but thought better of it — two other men were standing behind him, not so small. The moment Mickey turned his attention to someone else with him, a girl with cascading blond hair, Sumption scrammed out the door.

The cops found Sandy Hagen at her apartment across the freeway from the Hollywood Bowl, along with her older sister and another young woman, a dancer visiting from Vegas.

Mickey's Caddy was parked outside — he'd flipped Sandy the keys when he told her to get lost from Rondelli's. At the apartment, her older sister fought with the officers who came to take her away, but teenage Sandy displayed aplomb worthy of her ten days at the side of the infamous Mickey Cohen. She said of the night, "I heard shots. It ruined my dinner — I dropped my fork."

Other witnesses were little more help. The wobbly scotch drinker Harry Diamond couldn't see much with his one good eye. The actor's wife, Toni Ross, had seen a flash from Mickey's table, not much else. "I didn't see any faces."

Tony Reno had fled in the spiffy Thunderbird with George Piscitelle over the hill to another of their haunts, the Carolina Pines, for cups of coffee. The cops later found him in the Melody Room — where else? — but he swore he hadn't seen the shooting, he'd been in the bar.

Only Sam LoCigno, of the nervous stomach, and Joe DeCarlo, the man with the strippers, were nowhere to be found. One of Joe's dancers, Miss Beverly Hills, had planned to meet the crew after her show at the Largo but arrived at Rondelli's at midnight, amid the mass exodus.

"Joe DeCarlo greeted me, 'Get outta here, get outta here, get outta here!' " And she did. So did he.

The police did not know much that night. Chief Parker nonetheless reassured the swarm of press at the scene that his department had not been entirely in the dark about the goings-on at the restaurant. He disclosed that Captain Hamilton's squad had been tipped earlier that Whalen might be heading there "for a showdown with the top gambling man in Los Angeles, to settle a beef."

Parker did not say where the tip came from.

Jerry Wooters was awakened by the phone ringing in his Arcadia home a couple of hours after his shift at the jail had ended. It was not a friendly call or conversation.

So now I'm home in bed, about two o'clock in the morning, and I get a call from Hamilton. And he says, "Where can we pick up —" See, now suddenly he knows I'm close to Whalen, he didn't know it before. He says, "Where can I pick up Mrs. Whalen, Whalen's wife?"

I said, "Captain, you're talking to a uniformed sergeant. I got thousands of prisoners. I don't know any of that shit. You got all those high-powered detectives down there. Let them find out where she is."

So he says, "Listen, I'm gonna tell you something. God damn, you think you're so

502

fucking smart." And Jesus he went on with stuff I never heard about.

And I said, "Listen, I assume you're recording this. And I have no desire to talk any further. I'm on overtime if you pull me down."

He said, "God damn it." Blah, blah, blah, blah.

So I didn't tell him anything.

Jerry Wooters was not told much in return, either. Only later did he learn that the unmarked car had been sent to Rondelli's following his earlier call but that the two cops in it had simply parked off Ventura Boulevard and never gone in. He learned that detail from a day-shift lieutenant. "You know, in that Rondelli's killing there was an Intelligence car sitting out in front of that god-damned place and they drove off?"

That's what his years as the secret buddy of Jack Whalen had come to, then — him stuck in the jail, Whalen sprawled dead on the floor with a bullet in his brain, and his own Los Angeles Police Department on the outside without a clue.

When the sun came up in the morning, one of the swarm of officers still at the scene searched through a trash can down the alley and found a plastic bag with three .38s in it. That was the moment an original member of the Gangster Squad had been anticipating for a decade.

Sergeant John J. O'Mara had gotten to Rondelli's while the body still lay there. After that, he was sent out to track down Joe Friedman, a.k.a. Joe Mars, the restaurateur who had been squabbling with the near-blind horse bettor Harry Diamond. The man was sitting five feet from Mickey's table but looking into Mickey's back, blocking his view of everything except the big body falling, or so he insisted that night. "I didn't want to get involved," Joe Friedman explained later. "I had a place of business." So that part of O'Mara's night had been frustrating.

All that changed in the morning's light, at 6:30 A.M., when the uniformed patrolman who had been the first one at the restaurant made his discovery. Officer James C. Newell used the first daylight to scour the roof of the pool business next to Rondelli's and the parking lot and a fifty-gallon drum sitting there in the open. Voila. Amid the trash was the plastic bag with the trio of .38s: a Colt, a Smith & Wesson, and a pearl-handled snub-nose, just a two-inch. All were loaded. Officer Newell ran inside the restaurant to tell the bosses.

When the word reached Jack O'Mara he ran off, too, to find Captain Hamilton.

"Cap, they could be the guns I took."

It seemed like a lifetime ago, but Hamilton remembered well. He was one of the few on the force who knew of O'Mara's great coup those many years ago — how O'Mara had convinced a snitch to sneak seven guns out from Mickey Cohen's house in Brentwood and then etched his initials under the butt plates in hopes of one day proving the man was a killer. The Gangster Squad had been trying to make that case, but failing, since 1946.

CHAPTER 34
"I'M THE MAN . . ."

December 3, 1959, the same day the guns were discovered, one Los Angeles paper ran a short article under Mickey Cohen's byline. Front pages naturally were filled with WAR BREAKS OUT headlines reporting the slaying at Rondelli's. Some monkey was being shot up in a rocket as part of the nation's fledgling space program, but it was hard to match MICKEY COHEN SEES L.A. CAFÉ GANG MURDER. So the *Herald-Express* carried a second page piece titled COHEN'S OWN STORY OF CAFÉ SHOOTING complete with BY MICKEY COHEN.

Mickey didn't actually write anything, needless to say; the piece was based on his blabbing that night. But whether written or spoken it was a comedy of lies, start to finish, with emphasis on the comedy. Near the top he said, "I'd sure like to know where my car is now," when he surely knew he'd given the keys to the Caddy to the gal whose bedroom looked like a valentine. Near the end he said,

"I wasn't with anyone," when he never went out in public without his personal audience. But such quibbling was pointless, for that string of paragraphs was all about the tone, the absolute embrace of the goof. All that had happened was one giant goof.

> I walked into the place with my dog, Mickey Jr. I think I'm going to have to get him an attorney too . . .
>
> I was seated at a table with my dog beside me eating linguini (That's a type of Italian spaghetti with clam sauce).
>
> Suddenly I heard shots . . . you can bet I ducked . . . I turned around to someone behind me and I asked, "Look to see if I'm bleeding."
>
> When I ducked the first thing I did was take off his [the dog's] bib — you gotta wear one when you eat linguini . . .
>
> It doesn't do any good to duck under the table. I ought to know. I've been in too many of these before . . .
>
> I only got one complaint. I didn't get to finish my linguini.

On December 8, 1959, six days after Mickey didn't get to finish his linguini, he announced to the world that the killer of Jack Whalen — a.k.a. Jack O'Hara, a.k.a. The Enforcer — would turn himself in. Mickey said he had convinced the gunman to come in and end the manhunt, "to save the taxpayers' money."

Thus did Sam LoCigno finally come out of hiding. Since the deadly night at Rondelli's he had holed up in the Tropicana Motel off the Sunset Strip, stopped by the Miramar by the beach in Santa Monica, and made his way 155 miles north to Santa Maria, where a friend of Mickey's, the operator of a card club, put him up. LoCigno's attorney arranged for him to return and surrender at LAPD headquarters, but only after they went on television to have their say. Then Sammy was ready to turn himself in to none other than William H. Parker. Los Angeles' chief of police had a tape recorder by him to take down the confession. It flicked on as Sammy said:

"I'm the man that shot Jack O'Hara in self-defense."

■ ■ ■ ■

PART IV
JUSTICE

■ ■ ■ ■

Chapter 35
Freddie Loses It

When the coroner put Jack Whalen's body on a slab it measured 72 inches, exactly six feet tall. He was smaller in death than in life. But he did weigh 230 pounds. He was thirty-eight years old.

For his death certificate, his family gave his occupation as "Actor" and his industry as "Motion Pictures." The death certificate listed his last employer as Revue Productions, which had been the force behind one of the prime weekly series embracing an idealized image of the American family, *Leave It To Beaver*, and a series of Westerns including *The Restless Gun*, which starred John Payne, the wholesome-looking actor best known for playing the lawyer who saves Santa from the loony bin in *Miracle on 34th Street*. In *The Restless Gun* he was a weary gunslinger who roams the West but survives all challengers. Each episode required a slew of cowboy actors and four times in the show's last year they included a muscular former schoolboy polo player. They were bit parts, but no one could call Jack Whalen a wannabe any longer — he died with a Screen Actors Guild card in his wallet thanks to writer-producer David Dortort, who had just launched yet another TV Western, the first ever filmed in color. Everyone said that was crazy, given that most televisions sets still presented the world in black and white. But it was conceivable that Jack Whalen might have gotten a bit part in that risky series done in brilliant colors, the one Dortort called *Bonanza.*

"We hired him through Revue Productions with a bunch of other cowboy actors," the writer-producer said. "I sure didn't know he was a mobster."

The last days of 1959 were filled with wild conjecture over the killing, including innuendo that police may have been behind it. A spokeswoman for the California Attorney General's Office disclosed that someone claiming to be speaking for Jack Whalen had sent feelers to the office months before indicating that the big man, facing up to ten years in prison for grand theft, wanted to meet. "He said Whalen had been pushed around and wanted to tell a story that would blow the lid off the Los Angeles Police Department."

The attorney general's spokeswoman, Connie Crawford, said the emissary later told them to forget the whole thing, it was a no-go. But state prosecutors hadn't forgotten the events of a decade earlier, when the LAPD had been among the cynics when the attorney general assigned a giant investigator to serve as Mickey's personal bodyguard along The Strip. The chief deputy in the office now sent Chief Parker a note suggesting that *his* cops may have been taking "juice" to protect Whalen's gambling interests.

The inference was ludicrous — the man had been shot dead at a table seating Mickey and his newest crew of suck-ups. All the nobodies had fled. Yet the cops killed Whalen to keep him quiet? It was nuts, but the LAPD brass did whisper an explanation to a reporter for the *Herald-Express* who foozled it into a single paragraph about an anonymous cop, easily lost among the drama of the shooting of The Enforcer. "It is known that he was on very intimate terms with at least one minor police official," the *Herald-Express* noted. "That official, reports have it, was transferred from a responsible position to a less important job when he was allegedly trapped by fellow officers into admitting that he had accepted payoffs."

Even Sergeant Con Keeler, Mr. Down the Line, was taken aback by the last tidbit. There had been no allegation of an actual payoff, much less any admission — it was just Jerry Wooters being Jerry Wooters, playing some

513

game outside the lines and perhaps hoping to collect juice in the end but nobody knew that.

Jerry himself was not fazed by the gossip. They didn't name him, thankfully, and he refused to believe that Whalen had been ready to roll over on him — maybe the old man, Freddie the Thief, had gone to the AG in hopes of saving his boy from prison. But all that was irrelevant now. He still was stuck in the fucking jail and Jack was planted in the fucking ground. Jerry went to the funeral, of course.

They had it at Forest Lawn Memorial Park, the burial ground started by a fellow from Missouri who decided that Los Angeles should have a cemetery of sunshine and not darkness. It was on a hillside near where Jack Whalen had taken his cousins' kids on pony rides and overlooked the backlot where they filmed several Westerns. The Episcopal preacher who presided admitted he didn't know the deceased but told the three hundred mourners, "There is no cause for bitterness. No place for hopelessness. We should ask God in his eternal power for forgiveness. We cannot ask why things are . . ." Someone thought they heard the dead man's society widow sob, "He didn't believe in God." But who knew? The former Kay Sabichi was not the only woman crying for the dead man. His body had been indentified at the morgue by a twenty-three-year-old blonde, said to be a good friend. A mysterious nineteen-year-old wearing all black and a veil was at the cemetery, too, near collapse, and had to be helped away.

There was inevitable speculation over one floral piece that had a card signed by "Nell, Fred and Mick," but it was from the actor Mickey Rooney, his mother, and stepfather. His mom, Nell, a former vaudevillian, had become good friends with the dead man's mother, Lillian Whalen. Lillian had to be helped from the chapel herself, her left arm supported by husband Freddie and her right arm held by her brother, Gus Wunderlich. The onetime gambling ship pirate looked like a patrician now, gray-haired in a light gray suit.

Sergeant Jack O'Mara was one of several plainclothes officers from Intelligence assigned to keep an eye on the services, just to see who might attend. There was not much to report other than that the bookie Al Levitt was one of the pallbearers and the backup from the fatal night, Rocky Lombardi, was among the mourners.

O'Mara saw their recently banished squadmate Jerry Wooters sitting there, as well. Jerry was never one to hide so he came up to say hello to his former colleagues. O'Mara might have thought of asking, "Which side are you on?" But he didn't. Jerry was the one to speak as they shook hands.

"Don't worry," he said, "we'll get 'em."

Freddie the thief had been out of town the night of the killing. The elder Whalen was back East with his suitcase with the white coat and stethoscope in it. After he rushed home to L.A. the salesman's smile was gone from his face. He started drinking too.

He made every official event — any grand jury hearing, every court session — and was remarkably candid about his son, except for embellishing his background a bit, elevating Jack to a graduate of Black-Foxe and a law student in Idaho, where he'd merely done his preflight training in the war. Freddie's audience of reporters and assorted onlookers had little idea who he was. Other than that he played pool — that everyone knew — he was any distraught dad rambling on, sometimes repeating himself and sometimes contradicting what he'd said the time before.

I tried to talk Jack into giving up the rackets many times. Maybe he wasn't the best apple in the world. He may have pushed some people around. But when he went into a place he went in with nothing but his fists. No guns, knives, or clubs. That's what burns me, to think those assholes would shoot him down.

Jack was a tough boy. He loved a fight. He would fight eight men if he had to, but

516

he never carried a gun or a knife. He may have been a bookie, I don't know. But he wasn't a killer.

His main ambition in life was to be an actor.

If I knew who actually killed my son I would run barefooted to the nearest police station.

If I did know, I'd put a gun on and go after them.

I'm a lot older than I was and I'm not going to strap on a gun and go looking for the guy who killed Jack. But I am going to see him in the gas chamber.

And I don't care whose toes I have to step on.

One newsman called him up and in conspiratorial tones asked for a meeting at Larry Potter's Supper Club. The newsman claimed to have the inside scoop. "We have proof he was killed by the police" — that nonsense again. Fred Whalen was hardly naive about cops, but he did not blame them. The very suggestion made him spell it out.

Mickey Cohen as good as pulled the trigger and everybody knows it.

The mob murdered my son.

Parker and Hamilton are fine honorable men. Chief of Police Parker knows who the murderer is.

I know these boys. I have ways of finding things out.

I know the Mickey Cohen mob. Mickey is surrounded by big guns — the Sicas, Dragna, and that type. But they will get theirs eventually.

The evening of December 14, 1959, Freddie went club-to-club in a rage along the Sunset Strip. One stop was at the Melody Room, where he found Tony Reno, the singer who was supposed to have been a friend of his boy's but had failed to stop Jack from entering the dining area of Rondelli's, as if that was possible. A couple of plainclothes cops were at the Melody Room, too, on that night. One was Roger Otis, who had been recruited to the Gangster Squad because he could scamper up a telephone pole like a pro. Perhaps he did tell Freddie where to find the crooner who had been part of Mickey's dinner crew on the fatal evening — that's what Tony Reno believed. A few minutes after midnight Freddie walked up to him and asked "Are you Reno?" Then he sent a right to his left ear, the second time in two weeks a Whalen had manhandled Tony Reno.

That was nothing. He come up on The Strip with two coppers. I remember it like it was yesterday. He come in the club on The Strip, I didn't see him, then he hit me on the

518

side, it was all bullshit. He was drunk, he come in with the two coppers, the two working on The Strip. They all worked for Chief Hamilton, was that his name? Another asshole. On The Strip, the Melody Room, everybody hung out there. I sang like Sinatra. It was just bullshit. You know, just to keep my nose clean. It was a nice piano bar. A lot of high-class whores would come in there. In those days $200, $300 is a lot of money for whores, and the maître d', he had the book. You know it was a hangout, a good place to hang out.

Never met the old man, knew he was a hustler, though. He just took a shot at me — it was like a faggot shot, hit me in the side and then they broke it up. He was with the two faggot coppers. They knew who I was — they pointed me out to him, those two assholes, because they knew I hung out in the Melody Room. Then he called and apologized.

When word reached Mickey Cohen that old man Whalen had gone trolling along Sunset and clocked Tony Reno, he was ready with a response. "Fifteen or twenty people told me Freddie was going around The Strip bragging he had an OK from the police department to kill me. He has my invitation to come out and see me," Mickey said. "Any time."

A day later, Freddie Whalen was in Municipal Court, all contrite as the judge fined him $25 for battery and placed him on six months' probation. Thirty-five years had passed since his visit to an L.A. courtroom with his wife for shoplifting, when he tried to sweet-talk his way out of trouble with an absurd story about a birthday shower. This time he said only, "I'm deeply sorry."

Jack O'Mara drove to the Big White House atop the hill in Los Feliz, the place Freddie let everyone believe was his but really was his daughter's. O'Mara had been there before, for one of Freddie holiday parties, the early portion, for the squares. He'd brought his daughter Maureen along that time. This time he came alone.

Freddie didn't seem drunk to him. He was in the basement, at his full-sized Brunswick table. He was dressed casually in a cardigan sweater but still had on his tie from court. He had grown a little mustache, one of those pencil-thin jobs like on the old silent movie actors. Either no one told him he looked like a relic, or he didn't care.

O'Mara had never seen what Freddie could do with a cue stick and didn't know what to expect. So much of what you saw and heard as a cop was bullshit and the old man served it up, too, without blinking. But the way he wielded the cue was no bull — Fred Whalen sent ball after ball into the pockets, working

his way around the table as he made his position clear.

The last thing I do O'Mara, I'm gonna get
that son of a bitch.

CHAPTER 36
MICKEY TAKES THE STAND

A week after the shooting in Rondelli's, the *Los Angeles Mirror-News* ran an editorial lamenting that the city had been transported back to the dismal days when Mickey was the cocky boss of The Strip. He had come out of prison offering comic relief as the harmless ex-hood but here he was making threats and tweaking the cops while, once again, "death was his handmaiden."

Mickey Cohen, assured and openly contemptuous, dominated the investigation of the Whalen gunning . . . From the standpoint of the mobsters, the boss was really living it up, giving the fuzz the brush-off, making them look silly . . . arrested on suspicion of murder, he walked out the next day, his prestige enhanced, strutting grandly.

Since his imprisonment for income tax evasion, Cohen has deliberately projected an image of himself as a half-comic pixie, a martyr to police prosecution, a lover swooning over a succession of stripteasers, a harmless eccentric ex-mobster.

That myth has now been exploded. The 1949 Mickey Cohen is back again, thumbing his nose at the LAPD gleefully, and murder walks in his wake, as it did 10 years ago when the Sunset Strip was a shooting gallery.

In sum: 1959 suddenly looked like 1949 all over.

At least the wheels of justice turned quickly. They were ready for trial in three months, by March 1960, and a bizarre trial it was given that Sam LoCigno was the only one charged. Prosecutors thought the whole night had been a plot by Mickey's lynch mob of human sewage to lure the bothersome Enforcer to his doom. But they couldn't be certain who pulled the trigger and had no witness to contradict LoCigno's confession that he did it, "I'm the man that shot Jack O'Hara in self-defense."

Typical was the testimony of Sandy Hagen, who was sitting next to Mickey but unfortunately reaching into her purse for a cigarette just as someone pulled out the .38 Special she never saw. Tony Reno kept to his story that he unfortunately was back in the bar, "Somebody says to me, 'Well they killed Jack,' so I went and I looked and I ran." About the only diner who now decided he had witnessed the action was the visiting (and squabbling) café owner Joe Friedman, a.k.a. Joe Mars, who had been tracked down by O'Mara the night of the killing and said his view had been blocked by Mickey's back. Now he declared, "I seen the shooting," and gave the exact account outlined by Mickey and his men.

One after another, the tablemates told of a menacing Jack Whalen barging in and going dago-this and dago-that, then punching out poor George Piscitelle who was sitting there eating his pasta, then lifting a chair and shouting "You're next!" to poor Sammy. The man was all but begging for a bullet, though none saw the gun that did it, or any gun. It often was a contest to see who could lie with the straightest face as the boys got up to testify that they had no inkling that the Mick would be at Rondelli's, even though they'd stopped to pick up his date. Then there was LoCigno saying he did it, yeah, but couldn't recall where he tossed his .38 Special afterward. "It's one of those foggy things."

Oh, he'd bought the gun for thirty-five bucks, loaded, from the boxing trainer Willie Ginsburg, who unfortunately had died since then of a heart attack, meaning Willie couldn't come in to confirm it . . .

. . . Oh, and he'd gone out with the .38 special packed in his right-side pocket because he was petrified by the threats from

The Enforcer, but that didn't deter him from schmoozing the girls at the bar and arranging a rendezvous at the comedy show later. "I don't stop living because I'm scared," Sammy said . . .

. . . Oh, and he couldn't recall who hid him up north for most of a week . . .

On it went.

Yet if the defense had its whoppers, the government had its innuendo, as when prosecutors harped on the nature of the crowd in Rondelli's, how so many there had two names and knew each other, so many belonging to this mysterious society of unemployed Cadillac owners. Sammy LoCigno was Exhibit A, eating at that joint three or four times a week while griping he couldn't get work as a bartender, but thank God his suit had a pocket just the right size for the .38 he got from a dead man.

Then there was how the two prosecutors asked witness after witness who had seen nothing if they at least had heard something — Mickey calling out, "Now, Sam, now!" right before the fatal shot. "Now, Sam, now!" It was like the plot of one of those boxing movies where the fighter is being clobbered for fourteen rounds until his corner gives him a secret signal to unleash an uppercut, then *KABOOM!* "Now, Sam, now!" The government's lawyers asked about those three words enough times that the jury must have thought that *someone* had heard them. But when pressed for the basis of the "Now, Sam, now!" the prosecutors finally revealed that an investigator had been told that by a prostitute, who'd heard it from the maître d', who wouldn't admit it now.

"You know it's false," Mickey said when given his turn to speak. "Listen, am I on trial here?"

Sure he was.

He was called as a defense witness, but that was only the preview. He did better with his name this time, not attempting the full Meyer Harris Cohen that had tripped him up at his tax trial. Sam LoCigno's chief lawyer, Norman Sugarman, led Mickey gently through the innocent events of the night, how he'd come early to meet the colored talent agent and his singing duo, and to see the former exterminator about the book and motion picture based on his life, and how the talk at his table was the usual trivia — none of the guys mentioned their spat with The Enforcer, or how he promised to break their skulls. Indeed, Mickey told the jury that while he had heard talk of the head-buster he'd never once met him. They might have been in the same club at some point but that was his only exposure to, "O'Hara or Whalen, whatever they call him." Mickey's testimony for the defense was done in a snap, filling merely twenty pages of trial transcript.

The cross-examination by Deputy District Attorney James C. Ford went nearly six times as long, filling 114 pages over two days in the Los Angeles Superior Court of Judge Clement D. Nye. It took that long to get through all the insults from Mickey and to ease Los Angeles' headline-happy hoodlum into the trap they had waiting.

Prosecutor Ford: You had an appointment to go there that night?

Mickey: I want to know with who you mean.

Judge Nye: That's an easy question to answer, isn't it?

Cohen: Yes, but I don't trust this man and I have a right to find out what he's doing to me.

Ford: The feeling is mutual . . . Did you use Rondelli's restaurant as a business headquarters?

Cohen: I did not.

Ford: Were you accustomed to making phone calls from the office . . . ?

Cohen: Not any more than any other customer.

Ford: You came to Rondelli's restaurant in your own automobile, didn't you?

Cohen: Yes.

Ford: What kind of car is that?

Cohen: Cadillac.

Ford: Were you driving . . . ?

Cohen: How else could I get there? The dog couldn't drive.

Ford: May the jury be instructed to disregard that?

Judge Nye: The jury is instructed to disregard the voluntary statement of the witness.

Cohen: What are these catchy questions? I don't understand, "How did I get there?" I drove myself . . . The man is trying to trip me up.

Judge Nye: Nobody is trying to trip you up . . .

Ford: Now about what time of the evening was it that you first saw Jack O'Hara . . . do you call him Jack O'Hara or Jack Whalen?

Cohen: I don't call him anything.

Ford: All right, we will call him Jack O'Hara.

Cohen: The only time I seen him was when he came over to the table.

Ford: Had you ever seen him before in your life?

Cohen: Not to my recollection.

Ford: Isn't it a fact that you had conversations with him prior to that night?

Cohen: That's absolutely untrue . . . I am positive of it. Not sure of it, but positive of it . . .

Ford: Did you ever have a conversation with Mr. O'Hara at the Formosa Café?

Cohen: Absolutely not.

Ford: . . . the Garden of Allah Hotel?

Cohen: Absolutely not.

Ford: Have you ever threatened Jack O'Hara?

Cohen: How could I threaten him, I never had no conversation with him.

Ford: You were looking at Mr. O'Hara at the time the shots were fired?

Cohen: When the shot was fired I didn't look at anybody, I ducked . . . the first BANG! I heard I ducked . . . I thought I heard three or four . . .

Ford: Well, were they bang, bang, bang, bang?

Cohen: I don't take no notes at a thing like that.

Ford: How long did you stay under the table?

Cohen: When I heard the stampeding and the running and all that and it sounded like there was nothing there, I got up.

Ford: You didn't see anything?

Cohen: I don't remember what I seen. It is dark, the restaurant is dark and I am under the table. I am trying to figure out if I got shot . . . I didn't see anybody except Sandra Hagen . . .

Ford: Did she come back to the table?

Cohen: She grabbed her purse or whatever was laying there . . . I walked her towards the front entrance . . . just told her to go on home so she shouldn't get mixed up with this thing.

Ford: Now after she went outside what was the next thing you did?

Cohen: The next thing, I went and washed my hands.

Ford: You did not call the operator or the police department or the fire department?

Cohen: I don't call the police department at no time.

Ford: Did you notice anyone cleaning off table 15?

Cohen: I did not.

Ford: How many years have you known Mr. LoCigno?

Cohen: I know him many, many years. I

knew him when I was boxing around Cleveland.

Ford: Do you know what his occupation was as of December 2, 1959?

Cohen: No. I knew that he made a bet here or there but I wouldn't consider it his occupation . . . I never discussed those things with Sammy . . .

Ford: Was he working for you?

Cohen: No. He has never worked for me.

Ford: What business are you in, Mr. Cohen?

Defense lawyer Sugarman: I object to that as being immaterial to the issues in this case . . .

Ford: After the police arrived there, Mr. Cohen, didn't you have a conversation with Deputy Chief of Police Thad Brown?

Cohen: The only conversation I had with deputy chief Thad Brown was in generalities.

Ford: And did he ask you in substance at that time whether you had shot O'Hara and

532

you said, "No"?

Cohen: I was asked that question forty times . . . I didn't give any answers, your honor.

Ford: Now, immediately after the shooting didn't you see Mr. LoCigno place a gun on the table?

Cohen: I didn't see any gun at all.

Ford: At the time Mr. O'Hara came up to the table, did you have a gun on you?

Cohen: I have never had a gun on me . . .

Ford: That night, December 2, 1959, did you see a gun at any time?

Cohen: I did not see any gun.

Ford: Did you hear any discussion of guns?

Cohen: There was absolutely no discussion of guns. It was a jovial party where people were supposed to go to another party.

Ford: Mr. Cohen, I will show you People's Exhibit No. 18, which is a long-barreled

Smith & Wesson .38 caliber revolver . . . and might be further described as having an ivory handle to it. Will you examine that and tell us if you ever saw that gun before?

Cohen: I don't trust you. I wouldn't put my hand on it for a million dollars. Are you kidding?

Ford: I move to strike that, Your Honor.

Judge Nye: Your motion to strike is granted.

Cohen: He is asking me to put my hands on it, sir.

Judge Nye: He is asking you, "Have you ever seen that gun before?"

Cohen: I don't know if I have . . . I have had many guns.

Ford: It seems to me he can use a handkerchief if he is really afraid to touch it.

Cohen: I don't care to touch it.

Judge Nye: You don't know if you have ever seen that or not?

Cohen: The only guns I have ever seen

were the guns that were auctioned off at the time before I went away on my income tax case . . . There was a group of them. I understand that they were bought up by the police department. I was a gun collector before I went away and all of my home furnishings and all of my guns and everything were auctioned off.

Ford: Have you owned numerous .38 caliber revolvers?

Cohen: I don't know the difference in the calibers. I just had a group of guns and I auctioned them . . .

Ford: DId you ever own a short-barreled .38 caliber revolver, Smith & Wesson?

Cohen: Well, I went away in 1950 . . . Every gun I possessed at that time was auctioned off . . .

Ford: At any time since that auction have you sold any guns?

Cohen: Absolutely not. I haven't had no guns.

Ford: At any time in the evening did you say the words, "Now, Sam, now"?

Cohen: How can you ask a man that question when it is absolutely false?

Ford: Mr. Cohen, what is your address?

Cohen: 705 South Barrington.

Ford: On December 2, 1959, did you have any place of business, any business address?

Cohen: No.

Ford: What is your occupation?

Cohen: I'm an associate author.

Ford: Are you engaged in bookmaking?

Cohen: No, I am not.

Ford: And you yourself have done some fighting, haven't you. You are familiar with the art of fisticuffs?

Cohen: I wasn't too much of a fighter.

Ford: Well, you have been a professional?

Cohen: Listen, am I on trial here or who is on trial? What is it that you want?

Judge Nye: Wait a minute, Mr. Cohen, there is no need of a voluntary statement of that kind.

Ford: Prior to the time that the police arrived on the morning of December 3, 1959, did you take any property from your pocket and give it to anyone else?

Cohen: I don't know what you are talking about Mr. Fart.

Judge Nye: Never mind the profanity Mr. Cohen. We can get along without that.

Cohen: I'm not using profanity. I'm not going to surrender my rights as a citizen, I'll tell you that right now, Judge Nye.

Judge Nye: Read the question . . .

Cohen: You mean did I loan somebody some money, or what are you talking about?

Judge Nye: Did you take anything out of your pocket and give something to somebody?

Cohen: I may have given somebody a five-dollar bill or ten-dollar bill or something.

So the star witness for the defense was an associate author who drove himself to Rondelli's because the dog couldn't drive and he didn't see no gun and didn't have no gun. They gave him a dozen opportunities to say something more about the three .38s sitting out on the table, but he passed each time. Mickey Cohen said, "I haven't had no guns," setting the stage for a pair of surprise rebuttal witnesses who would again draw the courtroom, and the city, back in time.

CHAPTER 37
O'MARA'S TURN

They were People's Exhibits 18, 19, and 20 and prosecutors kept them on display for the jury, next to the plastic bag in which they were found. But a Hollywood courtroom drama would have tweaked some details about the guns from the trash, making one the actual murder weapon. A Hollywood script might have had that gun be discovered with its barrel still hot and the last chamber conspicuously empty — zoom in on the empty chamber while the music swells.

In real life, the two bullets fired at Rondelli's had been found quickly, one embedded between the ceiling's acoustical tiles and the attic after it tore through the fake philodendron, and the other in the back of Whalen's skull. But by the time Sam LoCigno went to trial the gun that fired the bullets was nowhere to be seen, someone having tossed it who-knows-where. "It's one of those fuzzy things," LoCigno had said.

Still, the prosecution could show that

Mickey and his crew were heavily armed liars, arguably heavily armed liars lying in wait, if they could tie the .38s in the trash to him.

They knew almost right away that two of the three had been his — they were among the batch of handguns that O'Mara's mole had snuck out of Mickey Cohen's house in June 1950. The serial numbers alone revealed as much. O'Mara and his man Neal Hawkins had recorded them on the envelopes that also contained the test bullets fired from each gun. Ten years later, those envelopes were still in the LAPD's safe, but not the bullets.

Only a few members of the department — Chief Parker, Captain Hamilton, and a couple of lieutenants — knew originally of O'Mara's secret files. But he heard that one of the lieutenants might have inadvertently allowed Homicide to take the test bullets when it was desperate one time to tie a killing to Mickey. "The Homicide detectives came in because we had all the files. And some goddamned dipshit opens up the secret files and they get access to my report. Some of those guys didn't have too much allegiance to the police department." Or else it happened when the crime lab moved to the LAPD's new Glass House headquarters and his hidden cache was a victim of housekeeping. "They had all this old shit in there, ballistics, and they threw out my goddamned bullets." More infuriating to O'Mara was that word had leaked to Mickey over the years that his former security guard had been a police informant. Mickey might not have known exactly what Neal Hawkins had done at his house but Hawkins had to hide out after his cover was blown and then get the hell out of town. Now O'Mara had to find him.

So Joe Busch, he was the district attorney, and I knew Busch real well. So when they had the guns recovered and I told the Cap they could be the guns I took, Busch wanted Mickey the worst way. We wanted to get him. Joe called me over to meet him at the office and he says, "We've got to have our chain of evidence. Now we got to get a hold of Hawkins. Where's Hawkins?"

Shit, he disappeared years before, see. He no longer was an informant of mine. So we got to get him. Finally found he was in the desert, married with two kids, in the Lancaster area, working as an aircraft mechanic. I went up and did a lot of bird-dogging. I finally got an address and I went there about nine at night. I knock on the door. He opens the door. "Christ, O'Mara, where did you come from?"

"Neal, look-it, you and I gotta have a talk."

"What's it about, the Cohen deal? Oh, shit, no way."

"I know it's a lot to ask."

"Christ, they had a contract out on me, Mickey's boys."

"Is there somewhere we can go get a beer?"

They had a few and toasted the war, when O'Mara had it easy up in Alaska, intercepting Japanese communications, while Hawkins had been one of the risk takers, setting explosives on bridges behind enemy lines. Then they laughed about the time Mickey got his supposedly bombproof front door in Brentwood — the bottom was reinforced, but not the top with the porthole window. One of Hawkins's chores had been to go to the door when someone rang the bell so Mickey wasn't exposed. If Dragna's boys left another stack of dynamite he wouldn't have had his ass blown off, only his head.

O'Mara reassured Hawkins that if he came down to Los Angeles his testimony would be short and sweet, sticking to the basics — they wouldn't even say explicitly that he had been paid by the police to snitch on Mickey Cohen. O'Mara had to be careful not to sound too eager with his former informant, though, given what was at stake. This was a chance, at last, to get someone by the book. For thirteen years he had been operating far outside the police manual, as a shadow cop. Now there was hard evidence, a witness, a chain of custody, public testimony, and perhaps a suspect led off in handcuff s in the end, real cop stuff like they taught it in civics class. Still, he had to be straight with the man.

Without you, we got no case.

I've got to ask my wife.

Joe Busch handled the final questioning for the government after the defense rested and the prosecution got its chance to rebut the "seen no guns" fairy tale. Mickey's business about selling all his weapons at auction was poppycock too. He had sold some with his other possessions in 1951 but they were antiques, mostly old Colts. Los Angeles police hadn't bought any of them, but they had gotten the serial numbers — those weren't the guns found outside Rondelli's. As for the trio that were in the trash, the prosecution sprung that part of its rebuttal case March 21, the second day of spring, and it did go short and sweet for Mickey Cohen's former security man, often over the objections of a second lawyer for the defense, William Strong.

Deputy D.A. Busch: Mr. Hawkins, are you acquainted with a man by the name of Michael Cohen?

Hawkins: Yes, I am.

Busch: And in 1950 were you ever in his employ?

Defense attorney Strong: I object . . .

Judge Nye: Well, I presume it will be connected up.

Hawkins: I was employed as a guard. . . . at his home.

Busch: And in that capacity, sir, did you ever do any work on some guns for Mr. Cohen?

Strong: Objection to that as irrelevant, immaterial, and not within the issues of this case.

Judge Nye: The objection is overruled.

Strong: The mere fact that Mr. Cohen had these guns in 1950 has nothing to do with 1960, as to his credibility.

Judge Nye: Yes, it does.

Busch: Did you have more than two guns with you that night?

Hawkins: Yes. We had seven.

Busch: Where did you take them to?

Hawkins: To the West Los Angeles police range.

Busch: Upon arriving at that place did you meet Mr. O'Mara of the Los Angeles Police Department?

Hawkins: Yes I did . . .

Busch: Now what did you do with the guns, sir, after meeting with Mr. O'Mara?

Hawkins: I took them back with me and returned them to Mr. Cohen.

Busch: Did you hand them to him personally?

Hawkins: Yes, I did.

Strong: Have you seen any of these guns since?

Hawkins: No, I haven't.

Strong: You didn't put any guns in the trash barrel outside Rondelli's, did you?

Hawkins: No.

Strong: You don't know who did, either, do you?

Hawkins: No.

Strong: Just two more questions. You are talking about O'Mara? You are not talking about O'Hara?

Hawkins: Mr. O'Mara. Sergeant O'Mara.

Jack O'Mara picked out his own clothes when he had a public event. He wasn't one of those men who let their wives lay out their suit and tie or buy their clothing in the first place. He might joke about getting suits from J. C. Penney but he didn't — he was a faithful customer of Richards, a top men's shop in the San Gabriel Valley. Connie could look on from a distance while he dressed and he might ask, "OK, boss?" but that was it. He knew what made him look best, gray or blue, the colors that accentuated his piercing eyes. For a social occasion he might add a decorative handkerchief in the breast pocket, but not for an appearance on the witness stand. He went with the gray suit that second day of spring 1960, well aware that the city's most notorious clotheshorse might be eyeing him in court. He knew that Fred Whalen would be sitting in the courtroom for sure.

From day one, the rule for the foot soldiers had been to lay low, to remain as invisible as possible. If the bosses wanted to boast to the mayor (or a reporter) about how they had hidden a bug in Mickey's TV that was their prerogative, not yours. O'Mara had a healthy ego and would have loved to shout out how *he* did that . . . and how *he* had been able to plant a snitch inside Mickey's home at the peak of his power. But the rules of the job, and of the courtroom, said not to — like Hawkins before him he had to stick to the basics of the guns, specifically the two he could tie to that preening little punk. The pearl-handled .38 with dum-dum bullets had been registered to Johnny Stompanato before he was stabbed to death in Lana Turner's house. The .38 with the two-inch barrel had been sold originally in Nashville, Tennessee, and may once have been owned by a cop there. But Mickey had them in June 1950. They could show that most simply through the serial numbers. But there was a better way to convince the jury, far more theatrical, and that form of showing off just might be allowed.

Deputy D.A. Busch: How long have you been a police officer?

O'Mara: Over 19 years.

547

Busch: . . . did you know Mr. Neal Hawkins?

O'Mara: I did.

Busch: And sometime in 1950 . . . did he have any guns in his possession?

O'Mara: He did. Seven.

Busch: Now, did you do anything with the guns?

O'Mara: I myself marked these guns.

Busch: And where did you mark them?

O'Mara: I marked them inside the butt plate.

Busch: I will direct you attention to People's Exhibit 18 . . . would you have to take this gun apart to see the marks you put in it?

O'Mara: I would.

Defense attorney Strong: Did Mr. Hawkins say whose guns they were?

O'Mara: He told me they were Mickey Cohen's guns.

Strong: Did you ever see them after that?

O'Mara: Yes . . . the twenty-first of January up in the county clerk's office.

Strong: Ten years later?

O'Mara: That's correct.

Strong: Was there a particular reason you made a marking inside it?

O'Mara: Well, in checking these guns, none of these guns were registered to Mr. Cohen, and under these circumstances we believed that . . .

Strong: Not what you believed.

O'Mara: . . . these guns may be used in a future homicide or be thrown away and we could then check on them and trace the ownership back.

They went through that preliminary sparring right up to the noon hour, when everyone went to lunch and O'Mara went to find a screwdriver. When court resumed, the attorneys argued in chambers whether the jury should hear (or see) any more.

Prosecutor Busch: Now, we think that this

evidence goes to shed light, which is the test of relevancy, to determine whether or not Sam LoCigno truly acted in self defense or whether there was a concert of action up to and including an idea of conspiracy on the part of all the persons there that they should be armed and that Mr. O'Hara would be shot.

Prosecutor Ford: These guns were found in an ashcan at the rear of Rondelli's in the parking lot . . . Two of the three guns are shown to have belonged at one time to Mr. Cohen . . . Now that raises the inference that there were at least four guns at the table . . . It is a terrific coincidence for four men to be armed at the same table where a killing results and it being a surprise to each . . .

Defense lawyer Strong: Let's talk about reasonableness the way Mr. Ford does. Does Mr. Ford really think that Mr. Cohen, if he had been armed, would have put those guns in the trash can behind Rondelli's?

The police are always meticulous in their search. They obviously searched on the inside and the outside, but for some reason or the other they don't find the guns for five or six hours after the shooting. I just think it is just as reasonable to assume that somebody trying to create a case planted the guns.

I will say it would be a reasonable inference that the guns were planted there by the police.

With that, the policeman under oath returned to the stand for the prosecution.

Busch: Did you get a screwdriver of some kind during the lunch hour, Mr. O'Mara?

O'Mara: Yes.

Busch: Would you examine 18 and 19 for those marks you mentioned . . . ? For the record, he has removed the grips off People's Exhibit No. 18, Your Honor.

O'Mara: It is marked "K."

Judge Nye: Just "K"?

O'Mara: K.

Judge Nye: Is that your marking that you put there?

O'Mara: Yes, it is scratched in the middle of the surface of the gun.

Busch: Now would you take People's 19 apart and would you examine the gun, sir, please? What do you see there Mr. O'Mara?

O'Mara: CX.

Judge Nye: CX?

Strong: And "CX" for Cohen?

O'Mara: Pardon?

Strong: Was "CX" for Cohen?

O'Mara couldn't remember. He knew he had written his own initials *JOM* in the first of the guns taken from Mickey's house, but that .38 had never been found. Had the *K* been for Keeler? Or Jumbo Kennard? Was the *CX* for Connie, adding a kiss? After ten years, O'Mara couldn't remember. But he had to say something.

O'Mara: No, CX was just a random number.

There had been little attempt to humanize Jack Whalen during the trial. The closest may have been a deputy medical examiner's discussion of the wrinkles he noticed in the skin around the dead man's eyes, suggesting he may have clenched them for an instant after hearing the first shot that missed him. For that moment, at least, the jury was invited to stand in The Enforcer's shoes.

The prosecutors did not try to sanitize the victim in their closing statements to the jury. "The fact that Jack Whalen was killed that night doesn't affect us directly in any way. We lost nothing by it," Deputy District Attorney James C. Ford said, kicking off the government's pitch. "We do not grieve." The prosecutor said:

> Jack Whalen, Jack O'Hara, was a violent man. There is no denying that fact. He was a big man. He was a muscular man and . . . we may flatly state that Jack O'Hara was a tough, violent man . . . He could take somebody on, take almost anybody on, and lick him. That's the truth . . . one of the toughest guys in town. A real man and a half, and he stood tall and he weighed heavy . . . He could have been a contender for the heavyweight championship of the world . . .
>
> But he was not a gun carrier, not a knifer, but a man who . . . was at least manly enough to stand up with his own two fists and . . . he never killed anybody or ever used any weapon, including a chair . . .

In fact, the prosecutors had a theory of the fatal night built around Whalen's prowess: If he packed the wallop of a mule, how come George Piscitelle's face wasn't caved in or his teeth knocked out? Their answer: He wasn't knocked to the ground, he ducked, to clear the line of fire. And was Whalen really lifting the empty chair to bash poor Sammy? Or was he pulling it back, to take a seat? Why had Tony Reno rushed back to the bar after he was prodded into the dining area by the big man? He knew what was coming, that's why.

The prosecutors counted 310 lies by the defense witnesses, about 100 by Mickey Cohen, who never had a gun or saw a gun, including the three he'd had his boys rush out the back door. Joe Busch got to cap the prosecution's appeal for a guilty verdict by saying:

> If you had crimes committed in Hell, you wouldn't expect angels for witnesses, would you?
>
> It is pretty hard to get at the truth in this case with these liars that have testified here. It is like a bunch of human sewage passing through.
>
> As that man entered that restaurant that night, he went to his execution.

The defense offered a touch of philosophy in response. LoCigno's lawyer William Strong said, "You will find that there isn't any such thing as 'right is right and wrong is wrong.'

554

Everything is relative in this world, of course. And under certain circumstances . . ." Translation: you can kill a guy and it not be a crime. Strong said of the chief prosecutor, Busch:

He isn't trying Mr. LoCigno here at all. He is trying Mickey Cohen. I think he would be much happier, frankly, if the case were the people against Mickey Cohen. Then he could really stick his teeth into it. But he hasn't got a case like that . . . so he is doing the next best thing. He is making Sam LoCigno the whipping boy. He will beat him to death if he can because he can't establish a case against Mickey Cohen.

If Mr. Cohen hadn't been present I can tell you that there wouldn't have been any case here.

But I will say this, it makes a much more interesting case if you have three guns in a trash can on the outside . . . six hours later, ladies and gentlemen, they find them . . . that place, swarming with policemen . . . do you believe, really believe, they didn't bother going outside in the back and looking in the trash can?

O'Mara was sitting a couple of rows behind the prosecution table and you'd better believe he took it personally. The man had said, "I am not suggesting . . ." Really? There was no mistaking what he was suggesting — that Jack O'Mara, the young cop always looking to race, the code breaker in the war, the head church usher, the original member of the LAPD's Gangster Squad . . . that he must have planted those guns in the trash outside Rondelli's. Well, fuck you.

CHAPTER 38
JETHRO GIVES CHASE

The jury began deliberating Thursday, March 24, and the next night Mickey led his entourage to the Cloister, where his reservation to hear comedian Joey Bishop had gone unused on the fateful evening. This time he made the show but the damnedest thing happened — someone stole his dog. Actually, a drunk stole his Cadillac. Mickey Jr. was in the back. When the human Mickey and his hangers-on left the club at 2:45 A.M., they saw the car racing along Sunset. Luckily another Junior was around.

Max Baer Jr., son of the former heavyweight boxing champion, was a strapping lad who had not yet been discovered by Hollywood and become the *Beverly Hillbillies'* Jethro. He had just moved to town and almost instantly became part of Mickey's floating party, getting to know all the boys (and broads).

I was by myself, I was just a kid, just out of the service. I hadn't had a job yet. Oh, shit, he always got the good tables, he always had good-looking girls around, he always picked up the tab, so what's not to like if you're a young kid and don't have any money? In other words, I hate to say it, but I was a mooch.

Mickey had a whole bunch of people there and when we came out of the place early in the morning Mickey's car was gone and we were standing there wondering what the hell happened. It was a black '60 Cadillac Eldorado with a stainless steel floor. I had a Pontiac Chieftain, a blue one, two door, and so we were standing out there in front of the place and Mickey was not as upset about the car as he was about his dog, and all of a sudden the car comes driving right by the club. And I'm in my car and he yells at me, "Max! Hey, get that guy!" So I step on the gas, pull out of the thing, and go down following him. We must've been going a hundred miles an hour down The Strip and the guy for some reason, I can never figure it out, we turn on Wilcox, which dead-ends into the Hollywood police station. They got him there. I couldn't believe it. I'm looking right at the police station.

The drunken car thief and dog-napper had delivered himself right to the Hollywood lockup — a sign, if ever there was one, that the LAPD could get its man.

Three days later the Los Angeles Superior Court jury returned its verdict and declared Sam LoCigno guilty of first-degree murder. The jurors deliberated only eleven more minutes before recommending life in prison. The government had not pushed the death penalty for the killing of Jack Whalen. "He'd been flirting with the undertaker for a long time," the deputy police chief had noted.

Hours after the Tuesday, March 29, 1960, verdict, the *Mirror-News* was on the street with a banner headline that used the name of someone other than the man on trial.

COHEN PAL CONVICTED OF 1st-DEGREE MURDER

The public had to wait a day to learn the full significance of the moment. The follow-up head was a small one, inside the *Los Angeles Times*, and easy to miss. But it was on the record.

FIRST GANG CONVICTION IN 19 YEARS

In praising his deputies, Acting District Attorney Manley Bowler had pointed out that this was Los Angeles' first successful prosecution in a gangland killing in two decades. There was double reason to pop the champagne.

559

But it was more than that. The last conviction had stemmed from another killing of a gambling figure in an eatery, on October 25, 1937, when the pair of gunmen entered The Roost café and fired a barrage of shots at George "Les" Bruneman, who controlled the bookmaking by the beach but neglected to share with Bugsy Siegel or Jack Dragna. That was the case where it took two years for authorities to arrest the former jailbird Pete Pianezzi, based on an informant's tip and shaky but emotional eyewitness testimony by the café owner's wife. "His cold, steely eyes — I'll never forget them."

The Dragna crowd laughed for years about that poor sap rotting up in Folsom Prison for a shooting actually carried out by a real pro, Leo "Lips" Moceri, the hit man later caught putting slugs in a pay phone. It would take decades for Pianezzi to be exonerated, officially declared the wrong man. Had the District Attorney known that in 1960 he might have given his two prosecutors the complete credit they deserved — if you discounted the botched Pianezzi case, their conviction of Sam LoCigno stood as the twentieth century's first, and only, in a Los Angeles mob killing.

It was the perfect moment to toast the end of a long losing streak and of an era. A new decade, the '60s, had arrived. All they had to do was declare victory and go home before their own case, for the killing of Jack Whalen, went the way of noir.

CHAPTER 39
MICKEY'S BOAST

Appeals moved slowly, so it took a year for a higher court to lambaste their guilt-by-association prosecution as "extremely prejudicial," "utter unfairness," and "billingsgate," and to overturn the conviction of Sam LoCigno. He had been the defendant of record but you would never have known it from what transpired in Judge Nye's courtroom.

"The case we are reviewing could truly be called 'The trial of Mickey Cohen,' " the panel of three California appellate judges declared in a decision released June 26, 1961. Their unanimous sixty-page ruling made the tongue-lashing delivered in the *Cahan* case look like a mild tsk-tsk. The panel reviewing LoCigno's conviction couldn't get over the government's obsession with someone not on trial.

We may assume that the jurors in the course of the trial had learned enough about

562

Mickey Cohen to be able to classify him as a notorious ex-mobster and racketeer. His unsavory reputation was harped upon by the People as the most potent evidence that the killing of O'Hara was premeditated. In the brief of the attorney general it is said: "Mickey Cohen is a notorious figure . . . If we accept appellant's theory [the bad reputation of Cohen] then it becomes the thing for the 'bad man' to do, when he is planning a murder, to associate himself with a notorious gangster and carry out the killing when he is beside him . . ."

It is fair to say that throughout the trial the People treated Mickey Cohen as the central figure in the murder and the others, including LoCigno, as merely his henchmen, subject to his directions and control . . .

That was exactly what the cops and prosecutors believed. They thought it so obvious they put it in their sentencing memo: "This murder was committed pursuant to the purposes of organized crime." But the rules of the game were that you couldn't lock someone away based on what you believed, only what you could prove. The appellate judges did not appreciate the prosecutors' description of the crowd at Rondelli's as "a bunch of human sewage" or how they asked LoCigno, "Now, did you receive any money from anybody for shooting O'Hara?" The appellate panel also zeroed in on two trial tactics for extended condemnation. The first was the prosecution's insistence on asking witnesses whether Mickey had explicitly ordered the shooting by saying "Now, Sam, now!" — the damning statement based on a second-hand account from an unidentified prostitute.

The second fatal defect in the trial, the judges said, was the use of the three guns retrieved from the trash. The judges were not entirely naive — they acknowledged that the loaded .38s may well have been dumped by Mickey or his companions. But none had been used to kill the head-buster Jack Whalen, a.k.a. O'Hara, and what evidence tied them to the man on trial?

The evidence, both direct and circumstantial, indicated that defendant was on the defensive, that he was not only not looking for O'Hara, but that he had an intense desire to avoid an encounter with him . . . Mere evidence that defendant had friends who carried guns did not tend to prove any material or relevant fact and should not have been admitted . . . Although it warranted a strong suspicion that the several persons at the table were armed, it was not evidence of a conspiracy to shoot O'Hara . . . the shooting of O'Hara was being pictured as a "gangland" crime, the rub-bing out of one gangster by another in the course of underworld warfare . . .

The three guns were not admissible in evidence for any purpose.

Thus did Sergeant Jack O'Mara's prized accomplishment — the secret marking of Mickey's guns a decade before — help overturn their landmark guilty verdict and set the convicted man free.

Los Angeles authorities did not give up in the wake of the legal rebuke. If the judges complained that the trial of Sam LoCigno had seemed like a disguised prosecution of Mickey Cohen, why not lift the disguise and make it that for real? Four months after the conviction was tossed out they brought a new murder indictment that added a conspiracy count against Mickey, LoCigno, and three of their dinner companions: George Piscitelle from the drug store; Roger Leonard, the exterminator-turned-producer; and Joe De-Carlo, the man with the strippers.

The government did have one more piece of evidence to use this go-around. Sobered up by having started to serve a life sentence, LoCigno overcame his amnesia about the murder weapon and told prison authorities of a buddy who could lead them to it — the .38 Smith & Wesson had been tossed in the thick brush off Mulholland Drive, the winding road atop the hills where you got a perfect view of the city's lights, the jewels on the breast of the harlot.

By the time investigators for the D.A.'s office found the discarded weapon it was too rusted to be linked conclusively to the bullet in Whalen's brain. But on this point, they believed the imprisoned Sammy — it was the murder weapon, except it was not bought from a dead boxing trainer, as he had conveniently testified before. The .38 Special had been purchased in Arizona by another of the dinner crew, Leonard, who supposedly was at the restaurant to talk about making The Mickey Cohen Story. He apparently had sold or loaned the gun to LoCigno, except that Sammy had decided to change a second part of his story, as well. Now he wasn't the killer, after all — someone else pulled the trigger. He just wouldn't say who. He was only going semi-rat.

So the government finally had a key piece of the puzzle, the (presumed) murder weapon, but the entire case remained, more than ever, "one of those foggy things," to quote LoCigno's original accounting of his gun. The second trial thus proved to be a costly circus and waste of time — a hung jury — whose main highlight was a quip from Mickey as they waited for the verdict that would never come. He was at the barber shop getting the full treatment — a trim, manicure, and shine — while the radio offered updates on *the Mickey Cohen murder jury*, which had been sequestered for four days, arguing over the murky evidence.

"This is a crazy town," Mickey said. "They accuse me of bumping a guy off, so what do they do? They turn me loose and lock up the jury."

It still was one giant goof to him.

Only after that second exercise in courtroom futility did prosecutors settle for a face-saving deal under which LoCigno alone was tried before a new judge, without a jury and without additional testimony — Judge Lewis Drucker would base his verdict on the transcripts already in hand and on closing arguments by the lawyers. LoCigno was back to saying, yeah, he did it, but had no choice, and now all he wanted was to marry the girl from Rondelli's, Ona Rae, and whisk her back to Cleveland to operate a deli or candy store with his father. "I have," he told the judge, "gained something that I never possessed before, love . . . Her faith and love have kept me in good spirits and has given me at long last a way and desire to be a worthier citizen."

The lovebird looking for a worthier life came to court this time with a new attorney arguing his case for self-defense, the flamboyant Marvin Mitchelson, who would become famous (and infamous) as the Rolls-Royce–driving pioneer of "palimony" suits on behalf of spurned live-in lovers. But back then he was a young lawyer eager to take on a case that might get him some attention after being introduced to LoCigno by his friend at the drug store. Alas, Mitchelson did not encounter a client who seemed all that eager for a square's life behind a counter selling confections:

I lived up around Sunset and knew the guys at Turner's drug store. They were all threatening one another. I mean, this was a rough group and everyone carried a gun in those days. He came to my house once in a big, big hurry and very furtively looking around, you know. Then he left and he stashed a gun in the couch he was sitting on. In my house! Because he was trying to ditch it from the cops or something. I never got over it.

The defense was that he did it but he did it out of fear — big, burly tough guy just comes storming in. Sam knew that Whalen was going to come after him. Well, he was after both, actually. I also think that he was trying to protect Mickey. I think that was part of it, as well. They all tried to cover each other, that's what they do. I thought we got a good deal.

They got a very good deal. Under the new ground rules, the judge found LoCigno guilty merely of voluntary manslaughter and sentenced him to one to ten years in prison, the same term Jack Whalen had gotten for suckering $500 from a wannabe bookie.

Mickey Cohen had to wait until his end-of-life memoirs to boast how they'd worked the system.

"The first thing you got to understand is this: Sam LoCigno, who was accused of the hit, couldn't hit the wall of an auditorium," Mickey said in his last account of the night at Rondelli's. "The person that hit Whalen was an expert shot. This expert shot never missed before in whatever it was, you understand?" This account had Sam taking the rap for "$25,000 plus," though Mickey declined to say which expert shot really had done in Jack Whalen, that great big bullshit enforcer. Mickey did *suggest* who it was, however. He wanted the world to know. "I could shoot a gun pretty goddamned well . . . there's never a statute of limitations on murder, so I don't want to go no further."

How could the great Mickey Cohen not take credit for killing the fearsome Enforcer? That was Mickey's story, to be believed or not, as with anything he said.

To be fair, another of the dinner party eventually would back his account, albeit half a century after the shooting. Tony Reno, king of the Melody Room piano bar, swore in old age that he had lingered in the dining room at Rondelli's after Whalen pulled him out of the phone booth and prodded him around the fake philodendron — he lied, he said, when he told police and a jury that he rushed back into the lounge and saw nothing. A half century later, he insisted that he kept his eyes on big Jack walking toward his doom.

We're going back a lot of years now. The killing in the restaurant, that was 1959. Everybody thinks it was Sammy who killed him. That was all bullshit. Mickey Cohen shot him — who else could have shot him at that fucking table? The other guy, Sammy, he's a bookmaker, he couldn't hit the side of a barn. It was Mickey, who the fuck else would it be?

Sam LoCigno took the blame because we told him to take it for self-defense. He figured what a hero he'd be, he killed Jack the Enforcer. He'll take over the whole L.A. now, you know what I mean? But it didn't work out that way.

Jack was a good guy, he just got fucking goofy. He walked into the wrong restaurant at the wrong time. That's when all the shit started. Very, very good friend of mine, a nice guy, a stand-up guy, a powerful guy. But things were getting tough on him and

570

he decided to muscle in on Mickey Cohen and you can't do nothing with that little guy because he'll fucking shoot you.

When I was in the pay phone, that's when he came in. He came in through the back with a guy, Rocky Lombardi, that's another goof. Jack came in, he saw me in the phone booth, I was talking to my broad, and he says, "Where's the Jew and the dagos?" So that's when I tried to calm him down but you couldn't calm him down because he was drinking. He went in the back, the party was over. He got his brains blown out. Exactly what happened.

Sure they knew he was coming. Why do you think there were so many fucking guns at the table for?

One thing I'll tell you. If they missed that fucking shot between his eyes, that whole table would have went. That's how powerful he is. The whole table would have went. He was no pussycat. Powerful guy with his hands — are you kidding me? An unbelievable strong son of a bitch. Jack O'Hara, yeah. Good guy.

Why does he have to carry a gun for? Don't forget. It was, you know, a scumbag town, that's what it was. Yeah, bullshit. Mickey ran the whole place all them years. Just shows how bad they were — all the shit he did they could never put him in jail, they had to go back to the taxes.

Accounts of shootings are like family lore or anything Mickey said, and must be taken as such. By the time Tony Reno offered that version of the night at Rondelli's he was nearing eighty and looking for one last score before his time ran out. That's what it was about in their world, the score. Everything else was bullshit. So maybe someone would come up with some green and Anthony Amereno, a.k.a. Tony Reno, would tell all about how Mickey shot the big man between the eyes, and how they disposed of the gun — and while he was at it maybe the true story of who killed Bugsy . . .

As for Mickey Cohen, by the time he took half-assed credit for killing Jack Whalen . . . well, the Mick was a shell of a man by then, in no shape to be prosecuted for much of anything.

CHAPTER 40
DÉJÀ VU

Part of Tony Reno's account could not be questioned — the one way they could get Mickey was for taxes. Twice. When he landed back in prison it was not for Whalen or any violent crime, but again for his insistence on living a millionaire's life on pitifully little (reported) income. Just as Sammy LoCigno's first murder trial was ending, a federal grand jury began summoning Mickey's stripper consorts, gambling pals, evangelist dupes, and movie investors to testify to his lifestyle of Cadillacs and nightclubs that was hard to reconcile with the $1,200-a-year income he reported from his nursery and ice cream parlor since his release from prison. A disbelieving Mickey screamed double jeopardy — he'd already done time for telling a few white lies to the IRS. Didn't everyone do that? But law enforcement was like the criminal element. Once they found an MO that worked, they kept at it.

A show called *This Is Your Life* had been

running on television for a decade and Mickey had his equivalent in the trial that began May 2, 1961. One hundred eighty witnesses were called, filling 8,000 pages of transcript with testimony mostly about his earnings and spending since he stepped off the launch from McNeil Island. The squad had helped again by documenting his visits to (and bills from) Sunset Strip hotspots these recent years. But part of the thirteen-count indictment went back further than that, accusing him of continuing to avoid paying the hundreds of thousands of dollars in taxes and penalties he owed from as early as 1945, when he still was in Bugsy's shadow, taking bets in the back of his paint store and actually gunning down a rival bookie. The trial revisited his entire tenure as a showboating public nuisance in L.A.

Jim Vaus, the 304-pound electronics man who had swept Mickey's house for bugs in 1949 and gone to prison for perjury on his behalf, took the stand to describe his subsequent conversion to the ways of the Lord and the thousands he and other Billy Graham devotees advanced to bring Mickey to "a complete severance from the things of the past and a positive identification with God through Jesus Christ." Billy Gray, owner of the Band Box, the comedy club where Mickey met his wife Lavonne years before — and where Mickey often got his mail under the name O'Brien — testified to *loaning* him $69,000, some via checks to his sister, Lillian. The well-endowed Liz Renay told how someone would deposit money in her account so she could forward up to $3,500 at a pop to Mickey, similarly classified as personal loans.

A Texas private eye described Mickey giving him $800 from an envelope as a retainer for his work helping the stripper Candy Barr fight her marijuana conviction. Candy herself, fully clothed, testified that Mickey had given her $1,700 in cash along with a phony birth certificate and Social Security card so she could briefly go on the lam to Mexico. The Miami showman who hoped to get Candy ("a hot piece of property") to Florida told of placing bets with Mickey's recommended source, his flunky Sammy, then wiring his $800 loss to Mickey the night Jack Whalen was shot. A man from Western Union came in to detail eleven such money orders cashed by Mickey around the country.

The sweetest witness by far was a young singer from Cincinnati, Janet Schneider, who was just twelve when her father became convinced she could become the next Judy Garland with the right connections. A local boxing promoter knew somebody in Los Angeles who *knew people*, but the insider needed a token of appreciation, call it a loan, so her father dug deep for his little girl and

made three quick $500 payments. The box-
ing promoter wired the first two to Mickey at
the Waldorf Astoria in New York while he was
there talking with Billy Graham about the
future of his soul. That might have been the
end of it, just a few more hundreds for
Mickey's roll (and tough luck for the rubes)
except for the catch — he sort of came
through for the Cincinnati man and his innocent blonde daughter.

The girl drove to L.A. with her mom and
dad and was treated by their gentleman host
to meetings with agents and front-row tables
with his entourage to hear Bobby Darin sing
with Sammy Davis Jr. and Don Rickles do
insult comedy and Jerry Lewis open at the
Moulin Rouge. The stars all came over to
their party to say hello, with an extra touch
at the Villa Capri, where Frank Sinatra kissed
the little girl's hand. Janet visited the mansion of Red Skelton and met his parrot who
refused to talk ("he has a mind of his own,"
the comedian apologized) and she nearly got
a deal to appear on Red's TV show, and
Lewis's, too. The girl really could sing, but in
the end she drove back to Cincinnati with
only her memories and a photo of a casual
Mickey in a golf shirt (no tailored Italian suit)
and with a beaming smile (no scowl). The
photo was signed, "To my little girl, Janet,
and my little friend. I just know that you can't
miss reaching the absolute heights . . ."

But the federal prosecutors were less interested in this glimpse of a different Mickey, the kindly uncle, than in the dollars Janet's daddy had shelled out by the end: $2,350 to Mickey to promote his daughter and a $2,500 advance for the movie-to-be. The Schneider girl's proud father also volunteered to help Mickey with the book he was writing, *The Poison Has Left Me.*

All their payments came out in court along with a slew of accountings that went down to the penny, as in the $3,861.61 in custom carpeting and other improvements Mickey ordered for his post-prison apartment, from the louver windows ($260.03) to an ice bucket ($13). Mickey never did get around to paying that decorator but did have $7,500 to purchase U.S. Savings Bonds, purportedly for Lillian. "My sister is very patriotic," Mickey said.

The giant diamond ring figured in a series of witness accounts. It was 12.69 carats, the government disclosed, and served as Mickey's supposed collateral for a series of his self-described loans when it wasn't on the finger of one of the women at his side. The ring had finally passed to Sandy Hagen the night after the shooting at Rondelli's, when she had known Mickey all of eleven days. Their relationship had endured in the seventeen months since and Sandy was at Mickey's side throughout the forty-two-day tax trial in the spring of 1961. "I still plan to marry him," she said.

But how Mickey had sold his life was more pertinent to the proceedings than any of its soap opera details. Another group of witnesses testified to purchasing shares of "The Mickey Cohen Story," or whatever he called it at the moment, those investors ranging from the vending guy to the psychiatrist eager to get Mickey on his couch. The screenwriter Ben Hecht provided some expert perspective and a reminder of the gap between fiction and its opposite. In his 1932 gangster film *Scarface*, Hecht had to come up with a fitting ending for the title character based on Al Capone, who was still alive but about to go to Alcatraz, "The Rock," to serve his own sentence for tax evasion. The real-life Capone eventually would get out but never regain power — he'd waste away from syphilis. In the film, in contrast, his character goes out in a blaze of gunfire, shot down by the coppers under a travel agency's sign reading THE WORLD IS YOURS. Of course, when Hecht flirted with writing his Mickey Cohen book he'd feared the reform scenario, that Mickey would wind up just another dull Rotarian. Now Hecht was a witness at the trial that threatened to brand the man as just another (two-time) tax cheat, in part for raking in tens of thousands of dollars by selling percentages of his life story. On that point, Hecht told the federal court jury, "I couldn't believe anyone would be stupid enough to buy into a nonexistent property."

When an appeals court later took a look at this case, it, too, would be amazed by the foolishness of Mickey's benefactors:

> . . . during the years 1957 and 1958 he received very large sums of money from a remarkable variety of persons, rich and poor, prominent and obscure. It shows a studied attempt on his part to cast most of these transactions in the form of loans, many purportedly secured by "interests" in his life story . . . The particular brand of magic that he used in obtaining these moneys does not always appear. That there was fraud involved in many instances is plain.

That was putting it mildly, for the story of Mickey Cohen's sale of his story had a punch line worthy of one of Hecht's scripts — in reality, Mickey had nothing to sell. He had signed over all rights to his life story a decade earlier, on June 14, 1951, a week before he was convicted on tax charges the first time. He signed them over to a Henry Guttman, the decorator who did up his Brentwood house with the wonderful mirrored boudoir for Lavonne and the cute doggie bed for Tuffy. Meyer Harris Cohen, the boy from

Brooklyn or Boyle Heights — take your pick — had been selling shares of nothing.

"I'm not too good at business," was Mickey's basic defense at the 1961 tax trial that was a joke in many respects but hardly a goof, certainly not on the day he was sentenced.

The first time around, a kind judge had felt sorry for him as a hard-luck problem child of the urban melting pot. Not so U.S. District Judge George Boldt, who got to lecture Mickey this time after the jury of seven men and five women found him guilty on eight counts. In his own brief remarks on July 1, 1961, Mickey said, "Since my return from prison I have made every effort to live my life rightfully." Judge Boldt replied:

> Living on the luxury of the land, available to only a fortunate few of our people, Mr. Cohen has no notion of contributing anything to the cost of defending or maintaining the land affording him that luxury.
>
> In the present struggle for the continuance in the world of a free way of life, best and utmost effort is required. The obstruction and impeding weight of the collective Mickey Cohens in our national community conceivably could tip the balance to our doom.
>
> At least the menace of his conduct, for what I deem a reasonable season, will be curtailed.

For Judge Boldt, a reasonable season to put the menace of Mickey Cohen out of circulation was three consecutive terms of five years each, a stunning fifteen years for underpaying his taxes — far longer than the one-to-ten sentence Sam LoCigno had gotten for killing a man, and four years more than Al Capone himself had gotten for failing to report millions in income.

Perhaps equally startling was Mickey's age, just forty-seven. It seemed like he had been around forever.

CHAPTER 41
THE LEAD PIPE

Jack O'Mara was forty-four. He also was no longer a cop. He retired the day he hit twenty years on the LAPD, not long after his ill-fated turn on the witness stand. Captain Hamilton tried to talk him into staying with the force, and on the squad, to no avail. Hamilton then brought him in to see the chief, who was studying his file. Whiskey Bill Parker said, "Two degrees?"

"That's right, Chief."

O'Mara had just gotten his Masters in Public Service from Cal State L.A., three years after completing his undergraduate studies in Public Administration from USC. The degrees represented a decade's worth of part-time schooling for a fulltime cop and father of two.

"Is that your USC ring?" the chief asked.

It was. When you were a scrappy Depression kid from Manual Arts High, which specialized in shop classes, getting a college diploma meant you bought the ring and wore it — all the time — and attended graduation in a tasseled cap and gown, even at twice the age of most students.

"Are you sure you want to do this?" the chief asked.

"Yes, sir. It's a good job."

The Thoroughbred Racing Protective Bureau had invited him to oversee its uniformed security forces at the two L.A.-area tracks, Santa Anita and Hollywood Park. The bureau had been formed in 1946, the same year as the Gangster Squad, to combat the unsavory types and rampant cheating at the Thoroughbred Racing Association's thirty-seven venues around the country. From the onset it had been headed by a former top aide to J. Edgar Hoover, himself a big racing fan. Hoover may have resisted acknowledging the threat of organized crime to America but he saw the threat to horse racing — his man, Spencer Drayton, initiated the tattooing of IDs inside the animals' lips so scammers could not easily substitute a faster one for a certain loser. When it came to this security threat, the enmity between the FBI and LAPD was overlooked. Drayton personally solicited O'Mara to supervise almost eighty men in Los Angeles, including retired police captains, lieutenants, and federal agents, a larger force than you'd find in many city police departments. O'Mara would have his own office and secretary, as you'd expect of a chief.

His alternative was continuing to chase hoodlums such as Mickey Cohen, at all hours, and have their idiot lawyers accuse him of planting guns.

"I hope you understand," O'Mara told Los Angeles' police chief.

Then they squabbled over a trivial matter. O'Mara wanted to be sprung a couple of weeks early to begin his new job, using his unused leave days. Parker said no — like other veterans, O'Mara already was getting full credit for his time in the military. They couldn't let him retire a moment before twenty years from his join date.

"It doesn't look good," Chief Parker said.

O'Mara had heard that before often, "It doesn't look good," but he couldn't remember whether Chief Horrall or his deputy, Joe Reed, said it first. One of them was waving a headline, perhaps GANGSTERS IN GAMBLING WAR from 1946 or the editorial titled NO WINTER RESORT FOR RACKETEERS, which repeated an old fear in the city of sunshine: "This is the time of year when the chill winds and bleak skies of the East and Middle West remind people of the gentle atmosphere of Southern California, and they head this way, with a disproportionate number of crooks among the substantial citizens."

O'Mara never understood the preoccupation in Los Angeles with the notion that evil came from without, and with image. He was a simple man who saw the work as "I'm a cop, you're a bad guy, let's do our jobs." The politicians could worry about how things looked. The complicating factor was how they wanted you to defend the honor of their city. That was echoed in the editorial imagining another winter invasion of Mickeys — it openly evoked the name of one of L.A.'s iconic crime fighters. "Let it not be said that the spirit of Roughhouse Brown has vanished from the department!"

Ah, yes, Edward Daniel "Roughhouse" Brown, the cop who had become an overnight hero by giving Al Capone the boot in 1927. What they didn't tell you was that Roughhouse was banished from the police department two years after his famous encounter with Capone, accused of hanging around the speakeasy of a bootlegger. Roughhouse said he was only checking out the criminals there but they didn't let him back on the LAPD for six years. He was still on the force when O'Mara joined and could be found in the business office, the old guy shuffling papers with failing eyesight and telling tales about the wild old days.

It had been much the same with another iconic L.A. cop, Frank "Lefty" James, who was shot in 1913 after a week on the job, then headed the Gun Squad during Prohibition. Lefty quit the force a couple of times, only to return, before he finally was put out to pasture in the Valley and then the jail. They still called him a "fabled officer" when he died in 1959.

How lucky was O'Mara to have made it through two decades without a single complaint against him, unless you counted the drunk he pulled out of a car in '43?

I never was reprimanded. I never had anything against me. I just figured, you know, there are times to hold 'em and times to fold 'em. We were living on the sharp edge, you know. I was doing a lot of stuff that was very effective but with all the heat that was coming on — these so-called lawyers were givin' us a bad time and we were worried a little about undue force cases and tailing. They were trying to send out injunctions against tailing a person because you're invading their privacy, you're violating their civil rights, and a lot of the telephone company investigators were on our ass, to see if we were tapping lines. Finally it got to the point I figured, "Hell, I done my work, it's time to get the hell out." It just got to be no fun anymore.

Only two of the Gangster Squad's original eight remained on the job: rabbit-punching Archie Case, who was near retirement; and the bug man Con Keeler, Mr. Down the

Line, who figured to stay till he dropped. "Get the hell out," was O'Mara's advice. Their time was as past as Mickey's.

He followed Mickey's second tax trial as a civilian and took pleasure in the absurdity of the man getting fifteen years for fudging on his taxes. But O'Mara did not confuse that with justice. Real justice was what happened to Mickey behind bars.

Alcatraz had housed only one other tax cheat before: Capone. "It was a crumbling dungeon," Mickey later said of America's version of Devil's Island, where water dripped from the ceilings above cellblocks that lacked the usual prison amenities. No TVs, no playing cards, no commissary. "You never seen a bar of candy there, only on Christmas." About his only daily diversions were games of dominoes in the tiny prison yard but there he had to watch for inmates ready to slice him with a shiv for whatever offense, real or imagined. The whole place stank, literally and figuratively. One consolation was his job dispensing clothing — there still were advantages to having been a haberdasher — near where he could take hot showers for his sanity.

He also got one reprieve unique in Alcatraz's history, when the warden called him in and said, "Well, I guess you got the good news." Supreme Court Justice William O.

Douglas had approved his release on bond, pending his appeal. Mickey wrote the famous judge a thank-you — "I assured him that his faith in me wouldn't be abused" — and returned to Los Angeles to again enjoy the pleasures of freedom and the company of Sandy Hagen. But they were awoken at 6:55 A.M. on April 30, 1962, by a call with news from the East that was not good — the full Supreme Court would not overturn his conviction. Sandy cooked him scrambled eggs and bacon but he could manage only juice and coffee. "I gotta take care of some things," he said. He spent half an hour brushing his teeth with two brands of toothpaste and five brushes. He called his sister to calm her. He took off for a meeting at the Ambassador, where he once had one of his floating casinos. He saw his old Russian mother, still alive. He stopped by the ice cream parlor. He bought new T-shirts and socks. He went to the barber shop and said, "Manicure me extra short, so it will last me a few weeks." At 7 P.M. he did a TV interview, in which he made a virtue of his not running away. "I'm no lamster," he said. Then he and Sandy had dinner out, Italian, spaghetti, before the crowd gathered at their apartment one last time, into the morning, when his cruel taste of freedom had to end.

He had the honor of being one of the last inmates on The Rock, another institution whose time had passed — Alcatraz closed as a prison March 21, 1963, destined to become a tourist attraction and curiosity. Mickey was transferred to the federal pen in Atlanta, where he was assigned to work in the electronics shop and given the job that had been held by the New York mob boss Vito Genovese, dispensing tools to the inmate workers. Mickey was proud that "Don Vito" had left him his hot plate and heater in the small office there. Those things counted, you know?

The warden later said it was there in the shop that the crazed inmate Berl Estes McDonald bashed Mickey over the head with a lead pipe the morning of August 14, 1963. Mickey said that was wrong. "I know exactly where this ding-a-ling Estes McDonald got me. I was in the television room watching the noon news program with my back towards the corridor. I don't know if the fucking building fell on me or what happened, and the next thing I know, I came outa the coma I had been in for two weeks." Warden David Heritage said Mickey actually was out for six hours, but his injuries were real. His skull had been caved in, his brain damaged, and his left side largely paralyzed. He had been struck three times by the pipe, *BAM, BAM, BAM.* Inmate Berl McDonald "got in several good ones," the warden said.

Most every account had it as a random act by a deranged convict, with no good reason.

The thirty-three-year-old McDonald was a forger by profession, from rural South Carolina, but had a history of psychiatric problems and had knifed another prisoner at the federal prison at Leavenworth, Kansas — indeed, he'd been given ten more years for that assault and was supposed to have been in maximum security segregation in Atlanta. He was allowed into an exercise yard unsupervised, however, then climbed an eleven-foot brick wall and walked to the Radio-TV building, where Mickey was talking with an instructor. A prison guard who found McDonald holding the bloody pipe reported that he boasted "he had got one, and named Mickey Cohen."

Though McDonald was diagnosed to be in a "constitutional psycopathic state," federal authorities had to ponder the possibility that someone might have been after Mickey due to unfinished underworld business. The year before, the Atlanta pen had experienced a similar pipe bashing that was having continuing repercussions in that realm. A foot soldier from New York named Joe Valachi became convinced that another inmate in the yard was a hit man sent by mob higher-ups, and clobbered the guy to death. Facing a murder rap for the prison slaying, the fifty-eight-year-old Valachi was said now to be singing to the FBI, sharing hitherto unknown secrets of a national "La Cosa Nostra" and offering seemingly outlandish tidbits about blood oath initiations and kisses-of-death on the cheek . . .

Mickey himself pooh-poohed the notion that the attack might be tied to anything. The man who got him was a demented ding-a-ling, he said, "someone nobody in my walk of life knows about." Or as his stripper friend Liz Renay put it, while praying for Mickey's recovery, "They put a lot of kookie people in prison."

Back in Los Angeles, Jack O'Mara wasn't buying it. He was certain that Fred Whalen was behind the bashing of Mickey Cohen in prison.

O'Mara had been off on his August vacation, fishing for trout in the Sierra. He was far from the normal cares of life or the banner headline, MICKEY COHEN BEATEN IN PRISON, MAY DIE and the next day's smaller, MICKEY COHEN WILL LIVE. Only when he got back to civilization, and his job at the track, did he get a call from one of his old buddies from the squad, Jerry Greeley, now on Homicide, asking, "Did you hear?"

"Goddamn," O'Mara said.

He understood that it was another mind game, thinking Freddie the Thief had it done. It was like with Bugsy's murder ages before, or the Dahlia case, when O'Mara was sure, absolutely sure, he knew who did it. You could know things with dead certainty yet be wrong, or so people told you.

Yet didn't Freddie have connections all over from his life of scamming? Hadn't he spelled out what he'd do? "The last thing I do, O'Mara, I'm gonna get that son of a bitch. You won't nail me, but I'll have that done."

That was their world in a nutshell. The church usher Jack O'Mara may not have bought into their reality on paper, but he lived it: Truth was found not in the sunlight, but in the shadows, justice not in a courthouse but off Mulholland Drive, or in a prison radio shop. Jack O'Mara tied up his years on the Gangster Squad in a neat bow with this belief that the aging grifter Freddie the Thief Whalen had been able to reach across the continent into an Atlanta prison to have some dippy-do bash Mickey Cohen in the head for what he'd done to his boy — a pure noir fantasy if ever there was one. Except maybe it wasn't a fantasy.

CHAPTER 42
THE VISIT

If you were part of the Whalen clan you got an education in the rackets. John von Hurst just began his earlier than most, as the toddler taken on the walk by Grandpa Fred in 1948 when the kidnappers from Fresno threatened to drop Freddie from a plane. Years later, when the boy grew into a strapping football tight end, Grandpa Fred continued the tutorial by using him as a straight man when he would go to pool halls and pretend to be tipsy. Freddie would slur his words and stumble off the stool to slap his money on the table while taunting the young studs with their cue sticks, "Oh, you can't play," and one would snipe back, "Show me what you can do, old man." The grandkid's job was to keep nudging the wobbly Freddie, "C'mon, Grandpa, you've had enough!" thereby enticing more suckers into games of 8-ball they had no chance of winning.

So even if John von Hurst was destined to become a square in life — an architect and then a rancher up in Oregon — Freddie the Thief did not hide who he was from the boy. Grandpa Fred thus allowed him to hang around the time the two men came calling at their mansion atop the hill in Los Feliz soon after Mickey Cohen went to prison for taxes, not for what he'd done at Rondelli's. Young Johnny heard the bell and answered the door. Two visitors stood beneath the white-columned portico of the Big White House.

Yeah, I was there when the guys came to the house, yeah. I didn't know who those guys were. I'd never seen them before.

They came to the front door and I answered the door and they asked if Fred Whalen was at home and I said, "Yeah, just a second," and he came downstairs and sat in the living room, went from the entry to the living room and sat on the couch. They sat on two chairs near him and I stood on the other side of the room, I just stood there watching 'em. My grandfather was comfortable with them so I wasn't worried. I just listened.

They started out, "We haven't seen you for a long time. How you doing?"

My grandfather said "I'm doing fine."

They said, "You know Fred, we've never really gotten right about what happened with Jack. We would like to, you know, kind of even the score."

Then they asked my grandfather if he had a problem with it, with them doing something to Mickey Cohen. They probably figured my grandfather might have thought, "Why don't we just let him rot in jail?" I don't know.

I think the language they used was, "Do you mind if we have him taken care of?"

You knew what "take care of" meant. The idea was they were gonna kill him. Yeah, whack 'im. So they said, "Do you have a problem with this?" They felt it was my grandfather's business because it was his son. "Do you have a problem with this?"

My grandfather said, "Hell no, I don't care what you do to the son of a bitch." He said basically, "Let 'em kill the fat little fuck."

John von Hurst said his grandfather did not mention the visit again until they heard over the radio that Mickey Cohen had been bashed over the head in prison on August 14, 1963.

Freddie Whalen said then, "I guess those guys meant what they said."

CHAPTER 43
A SONG BY SINATRA

Sergeant Jerry Wooters, who had played the long odds all his life, ended his police career working the night shift at the Lincoln Heights Jail. "Couldn't get out," he said.

He couldn't get out even after the man who bounced him there, Captain James Hamilton, retired from the LAPD to take a plum job heading security for the National Football League, which had experienced a betting scandal and needed protection against its own Invasion of Undesirables. "He helped hook Mickey Cohen twice," one sports columnist wrote in touting Hamilton's qualifications. Chief Parker then appointed his former driver Daryl F. Gates to take over Intelligence, giving him a taste of the secretive unit before he, too, rose to chief. Sometimes it seemed like everyone else was getting ahead while you were going nowhere.

At least Jerry had a little clout as a watch commander at the jail. Once in a while he'd take his oldest son along so a trustee could give the boy a haircut. He'd march the kid by holding cells where inmates shouted catcalls and raked stuff across the bars, *BAM, BAM, BAM*, an experience Gerard Jr. would never forget.

> So we'd go around the corner and there was a little barber shop and the guy in there was crazy-eyed and pasty-faced and slamming a razor on one of those belts. He'd throw me in a barber chair and wrap one of those capes around me and my dad would say, "OK, give him a good cut there, Joe!"

Hey, the free buzz cut saved Jerry a few bucks.

He tried to find some respite by being a good suburban dad, enrolling one of his boys in an Indian Guides program that had fathers and sons rough it in the wilds. "The rest of us would be trying to sleep on the hard ground in the tepees with our feet hanging out," recalled Dr. Norm von Herzen, another of the parents, "and invariably Jerry would fudge a little bit. He would sneak out of the tepee after his kid was asleep and he'd go in the back of his station wagon on this soft mattress that he had. That's Jerry."

It was during those camping trips that Jerry confided to his doctor friend how apprehensive he was about life after police work. He recalled how the gangsters would mock cops like him as being suited to be security guards at best, minimum wage hacks. "You'll never make it, kid," they'd say. This was coming from pieces of shit like Mickey, but it got to him.

Then a Navy buddy pitched him on selling built-in vacuum systems for houses. Jerry and his wife had a vacation coming up in Hawaii, so he took a sample door-to-door there — he'd find the housewife and pretend he was back wooing nurses during the war. Why hadn't he realized he could sell anything? "Gosh, I made like $4,000 in a week. Came back, hocked the house, hocked the car, and got into the business." He started selling garage doors, also, and hooked up with a guy who made a "food center" gizmo with a spinner you built into the kitchen counter; a fancy blender, really. He began telling the developers of huge subdivisions, "Look, I'll take care of your intercom, garage door opener, build your alarm system." Before long, he was able to move his family into a house on the water in Newport Beach. He bought duplexes as investments and built an office park. You had to be an idiot not to get rich in the 1960s in booming Orange County, California.

He thankfully was out of police work and starting to make his fortune when the riots broke out in Watts in the summer of '65. Their generation of cops had come of age during the White Men Rule era when you could come back to the station house and joke about shooting a black man in the ass. *Those people* were not in the club, not close — they *got* the club. But O'Mara was right, their time had passed, and the changing realities caught up even with Chief William H. Parker. He had become a pioneer of professional policing by being a hard-ass but that didn't go over as well when the minority communities erupted and he said things like, "One person threw a rock and then, like monkeys in a zoo, others started throwing rocks."

However bitter Jerry Wooters remained about his last years in purgatory, he never held it against the chief. "An amazing man," Jerry called him, so it pained him to see Parker come under attack when he railed about some of the city's Latinos as being "not far removed from the wild tribes of Mexico" and how most of the blacks weren't from Los Angeles, either — they were from the South. "They came in and flooded a community that wasn't prepared to meet them," Parker declared. "We didn't ask these people to come here . . ." The riots, too, it seems, were an Invasion of Undesirables.

After that, the chief spent too much time defending himself when he needed to be nursing his health. He finally took a leave after undergoing surgery at the Mayo Clinic to remove an aortic aneurysm, but returned in time for the Second Marine Division Association to honor him at a banquet on July 16, 1966. After 1,000-plus vets gave him a standing ovation at the Statler Hilton, Parker returned to his table, sat down and collapsed. He was sixty-four.

His trusted right hand, Captain Hamilton, died four months later, a stroke cutting short his plum job keeping pro football honest. He was just fifty-seven.

Neither lived long enough to see the mob in Los Angeles come to be widely derided as a "Mickey Mouse Mafia" as the public gained an appreciation for how the city had never gone the way of Chicago or New York or Philly, where organized crime controlled whole ports and unions and construction trades. There were all sorts of reasons, but the Gangster Squad, for all its excesses — perhaps because of its excesses — was one. They *had* made life hell for Mickey Cohen and his ilk.

When they started out, eight men in two rusted cars, trying to remain invisible, it was nothing like later years when every third mob guy was wired up, getting the goods on the others. In their time, omerta was chillingly enforced. Joe Valachi did not break the mob's code of silence until 1963 and there wasn't a second great mob turncoat until 1978, when L.A.'s own Jimmy the Weasel 'fessed up to eleven killings. That was another thing — after Fratianno's confession you could rethink their long losing streak. You could go back over the city's half century of unsolved murders and declare many solved, after all.

"People today wouldn't understand what it was like," Jerry Wooters said one day. "You'd take 'em out to the desert, take their shoes away, take their clothes, and give 'em a paper sack. And the next day they'd be back."

In his later years he joked that he put his LAPD pension to good use, all $332 a week of it. "Pays my liquor bill," he said. He grew a wispy white beard like other multimillionaire beach bums who whiled away their days sipping drinks on the back patio and watching the California girls pass in their bikinis.

One afternoon in the fall of 1998 he showed up at the Newport offices where his son Gerard now ran the business. His son needed more time to talk with a pal so he said, "Hey, Dad, how about getting us a six-pack?"

He said, "Yeah, OK," so my friend and I just finished up and he rolled in, he has the beer, stood there and watched us crack a beer, and he says, "You know, I drank a fifth of whiskey a day for twenty years." And my buddy just looks at him and sings, "All my whiskey drinking friends are dead," and my dad lit up and started laughing, I mean a full belly laugh. Now, I don't know what was so funny about it, except that he was in hysterics to the point where he didn't say another word, got in his car, and as he drove out you could see his head bobbing as he laughed. He apparently thought it was so funny that he was still alive.

That Christmas, Jerry stumbled while putting on his pants before a holiday dinner. He told his wife Jean, the one-time stewardess, "I've got a headache." He had been shot down over the Pacific, drawn his gun on Mickey Cohen, and nearly walked into the wrong restaurant with Jack Whalen, but the brain hemorrhage took him out with little suffering for his sins.

The short obituary in *The Orange County Register* described Gerard "Jerry" Wooters, eighty-one, merely as president of Sea Coast Security and reported that services for the local businessman would not be at any church but at the Riverboat Café. His death certificate got it better: "Sergeant. Law Enforcement. Los Angeles Police Dept."

Two old cops were on the boat that took his ashes toward Catalina Island. One was Bert Phelps, whose police career had been stymied for being his partner. But Bert never blamed him, nor was he jealous of Jerry's later-life success, for he had not done badly himself. After law school Bert had become more than another cop-turned-lawyer — the old bug man became a judge, Superior Court Judge Beauford H. Phelps. He studied jurisprudence at Oxford. He tried murder cases.

Also onboard was Robert Peinado, who worked for the LAPD from 1951 to 1963 and also became a lawyer. He lived near the beach, too, and Jerry loved to hear him sing. Peinado performed "Danny Boy" at Wooters's eightieth birthday and afterward Jerry asked a favor, for when his time came. Jerry had another song in mind, made famous by Sinatra.

The boat was halfway to Catalina when they began struggling with the box of ashes, had to get pliers to rip it open. When they did get the ashes out, a wind gust blew some back into their faces. Jerry was causing trouble to the end. But the wind finally calmed and they sprinkled the remaining ashes on the waves as Peinado sang the man's last request, "My Way."

CHAPTER 44
FREDDIE'S LAST LAUGH

Fred Whalen drank heavily through the '60s — he couldn't much enjoy the years after his son was killed. But he was out of his funk by the time he received a proclamation from Mayor Sam Yorty declaring February 1971, "Billiards Month" in Los Angeles. The embossed certificate acknowledged how Fred had begun promoting a "World Pocket Billiards Championship" in the city, though there actually were three competitions — in straight pool, 9-ball, and one-pocket — offering $40,500 in prizes. Many of the players wore tuxedos, and off-duty LAPD cops provided security. World champ Irving "The Deacon" Crane was entered, as were several contestants from Japan. The program had a "Thank You Los Angeles" note from Freddie and two photos of his face with the salesman's smile.

The event was held at the Elks Building (Lodge No. 99) an imposing neo-Gothic edifice at the upper end of what used to be

Westlake Park, near where Freddie's clan had settled and opened their small dry goods store in 1922. The park had since been renamed for General Douglas MacArthur, but the Elks tower dated to the time of the mass migration that brought the Whalens and the Wooters and the O'Maras to Los Angeles. The front of the building was engraved with wisdom from Matthew 7:12:

All things Whatsoever Ye
Would That Men Should Do
To You, Do Ye Even So to Them

That was the Bible's best statement of the Golden Rule ("Do unto others . . .") but anyone so inclined might stretch it a bit to sanction "An eye for an eye," as well.

Freddie the Thief would have loved for his son to be around when Disney cast him a few years later in *The Cat from Outer Space*, playing a pool shark named Sarasota Slim. The next year, at eighty-one, he returned to his hometown of Alton, Illinois, where the local paper did a local-boy-makes-good feature, quoting him puffing, "I'm a millionaire today." While it mentioned his pool promotions, the piece reported "Fred credits his success to the cleaning business from which he recently retired." He was still telling that story, bless him.

Back in L.A., he continued to give exhibitions with his cue stick, making the rounds of taverns and VFW halls and hitting balls off the top of Coke bottles, like he had as a kid. After people gathered 'round to see the show, he would go out to his Cadillac and get merchandise from the trunk, boxes of steak knives for the men and bottles of Chanel No. 5 for their wives. He'd wink at the absurdly low price for the world's most famous fragrance, $5 a bottle, and they got the gist — it was hot, stolen, had to be.

Freddie told a different story to the professional pool players he recruited to sell the stuff for him. That was a way to get on his good side and guarantee favorable draws in his tournaments — sell for Freddie. He confided to the pool whizzes that the perfume wasn't stolen at all. "Mixed it in the bathtub," he whispered. Of course, that wasn't true either.

Freddie's favorite place to be toward the end of his life was a warehouse in Hollywood once used by Charlie Chaplin to shoot silent films. It was called Associated Consumers now and run by an old Brooklyn boy, Alan Grahm, who recognized the potential, decades ahead of most, of counterfeit goods. He sold fake watches and lighters and Mont Blanc pens and Majorica pearls, on it went. But the perfume was the favorite of Freddie Whalen. He had never gotten over being nabbed in the '30s for failing to have tax stamps on the cheap whiskey he poured into fake Johnny Walker bottles. He still loved that scheme, loved it. The warehouse sold the fake Chanel and White Christmas to regulars for $2 a bottle and they'd resell it to the suckers for $5 or $10 or whatever.

Freddie would be the first one at the warehouse in the morning but the regular crew soon joined him for coffee and donuts at a stand run by a Greek guy across the street. It was a convention of grifters. One guy would go to massage parlors and show the girls pearls with a $250 price tag and say, "Look, gimme twenty dollars and take care of me and I'll give you the necklace." He got a lot of free massages (and more) for that phony strand that cost him $3. A regular from Detroit had never driven a semi in his life but dressed like a trucker and told people he had this load of unclaimed freight. "Listen, it's worth a thousand but I'll give it to you for a couple a hundred, take it off my hands." An operator from Vegas pretended to be in the Navy and in need of money for a bus ticket back to his base. If you loaned him $25, he'd let you keep his $300 watch, "I'll pay you back when I get there." There even were a couple of police detectives who bought the fake goods, then let their marks believe it was real thing they'd confiscated from robbers. These were Freddie's people indeed, among the first invitees to his annual holiday party in the Big White House.

He got a second proclamation from the mayor when he and Lillian were married for seventy years, but she was sick by then. Freddie appeared at a charity exhibition while she was in the hospital and did his ball-in-the-handkerchief trick where he'd announce "I'm going to cheat you," but mostly he reminisced about the former Lillian Wunderlich, "such a wonderful girl." After she passed, he moved to Oregon to be close to his daughter Bobie and her kids, including his grandson Johnny. Freddie started showing up at a bar there that had 8-ball competitions each Sunday until they told him to stay away — no one else had a chance, never mind that he was over ninety. He told his family he was thinking of doing the *scamus* again, going to hospitals in his white coat and stethoscope. They said, "No, Grandpa."

The night before he died, he played cards with his daughter, then in her seventies. She had tried the *scamus* herself in her younger days, posing as a nurse, and pulled it off. She was clever like her dad, a true Whalen. So she saw what he was doing as they played gin for the last time, dealing himself cards from the bottom of the deck. She said nothing, the daughter of Freddie the Thief. His life had spanned the century when Los Angeles came of age. Why not let him end it the way he he'd begun it, by cheating?

CHAPTER 45
THE EULOGY

Jack O'Mara did not take a day off between his last shift at the LAPD and his first heading up security at Los Angeles' two horse tracks. That provided one of two work photos he hung on his wall the rest of his life. The first was of the Gangster Squad at its picnic, circa 1948 — fifteen plainclothes bruisers, a few squinting under hats, a couple with cigars in hand. In the second photo O'Mara was the only one in a suit standing amid dozens of uniformed guards in front of the Santa Anita grandstand.

"I think you're a dummy that you didn't go for chief," his wife Connie said one day, speaking of the LAPD.

"I had more fun than the chief."

But she could get him going by noting how his contemporaries Tom Reddin and Ed Davis had risen that far. Hadn't he done as well as them at the Academy, or as Tom Bradley, his 1940 classmate who became mayor? "Hell no, higher!" O'Mara said, and she had him.

They all were part of a generation that was supposed to remake the LAPD. But none of the others had been given the chore that had been an obsession in Los Angeles for a century, of protecting this paradise from the evil outsiders of the underworld. Every decade or so, another shadowy unit was formed to take on the job that promised to make you a hero only to leave even the most celebrated foot soldiers tarnished in the end.

"Somebody's gotta do the dirty work," O'Mara said, and for him it meant settling for being the chief of two racetracks, where he still had to watch for crooks and scammers but also escorted dignitaries to see the stables' most famous resident, "Mr. Ed," television's talking horse.

Crazy Jerry Wooters came to the track a few times with business associates and Jack set him up in a box and then a table in the Turf Club, good perks for impressing clients. They didn't say much about the old days, just kept their secrets with a firm handshake. Fred Whalen came by also and O'Mara was pleased to see that Freddie had gotten over his vengeful anger. He even had some pearls to sell at amazing prices. Connie O'Mara was suspicious, for some reason, when Jack gave her that necklace as a present — she had picked up a little horse sense over the decades married to a cop.

O'Mara's daughters were sharp too. He

taught the youngest to drive in Santa Anita's vast parking lot and she was a whiz, Martha (Marti) O'Mara. Blessed with the looks of her mom, she was invited at sixteen to be a bachelorette contestant on TV's *The Dating Game* on a night when the other girl featured was Maureen Reagan, Ronnie's daughter. Bitten by the quiz-show bug, the whole O'Mara clan got on *Family Feud*, where Jack gave host Richard Dawson a whip used by Willie Shoemaker, the famous jockey. Then Marti got on *Tic-Tac-Dough* and won $6,000. Smart? O'Mara's youngest got a scholarship to study sociology in college and earned a Ph.D. from Harvard, where she then taught in its business and design schools while doing consulting around the country. The oldest, Maureen, merely got a master's in health administration and taught maternal and prenatal nursing at Azusa Pacific University. He had quite some girls there.

Maybe all that was justice, though — what O'Mara and the other Gangster Squad alumni had done with the rest of their lives. It wasn't merely their bug man who became a judge. Lindo Giacopuzzi, the burly first-generation Italian American whose family ran a dairy? He became about as rich as Wooters by developing a shopping center on their ten acres. Jack Horrall, the chief's son, became military liaison to the governor. Some of the others headed security for recluse Howard

612

Hughes in Vegas — an oddball, but the man could pay. O'Mara's big Irish buddy Jerry Greeley hadn't gotten enough action as a Navy commander and LAPD lieutenant, so he took off for Southeast Asia amid the war there, supposedly working as a civilian advisor to South Vietnamese police. Everyone knew Greeley really was CIA, especially after his helicopter was shot down over Burma. He survived, made it home and became active in a group called The Spies Who Wouldn't Die.

They all lived to see a crippled Mickey Cohen die in 1976, at sixty-two, leaving an estate valued at $3,000. Mickey had shuffled out of prison four years earlier, hunched over and needing a three-pronged cane, a moist towel over the handle to protect his hand from germs. But his injuries weren't why he left the media crowd outside the penitentiary waiting. "He's taking three hours to get dressed," his brother Harry explained.

After the brutal beating nearly killed him in Atlanta, Mickey had been moved to the federal prison system's medical center in Springfield, Missouri, where he went through delicate brain operations and painful therapy to regain partial use of his legs. He won a moral victory when a federal judge in Atlanta ordered the Unites States of America to pay him $110,000 as damages for his prison beating. Of course, all that money went right back to the government to cover some of his unpaid taxes.

After his release, Mickey spent most of his time at home, in his pajamas. But he did earn his way back into the headlines from time to time, most notably when he claimed to have an inside track on finding newspaper heiress Patricia Hearst, who had been abducted by the radical Symbionese Liberation Army and brainwashed into helping the group rob banks. Hearst's parents actually flew to Los Angeles to meet Mickey at one of his new favorite restaurants. "While we were having dinner," he said later, "the owner came over and told me the police Intelligence squad was in the restaurant. I said I didn't give a damn — they could sit at the table if they wanted."

He did finally get to tell his story, though not with the masterful help of a Ben Hecht. It was one of those as-told-to autobiographies, *Mickey Cohen: In My Own Words*, and never reached the bestseller status of the two confessionals penned by his onetime stripper consort Liz Renay. But Liz did list him in the "Most Exciting Men" section of one memoir and she was one of the old crowd who stuck with him to the end, through his hospitalization for stomach cancer at UCLA Medical Center. "I'm on my way out. Too bad," he told her. "We could have been so happy." The flamboyant redhead concluded that Mickey

614

possessed the power to destroy, himself and others, but she also wrote "He lived with a flourish and he died like a man."

Mickey was buried by his sisters as Meyer H. Cohen ("Our Beloved Brother") in the Alcove of Love section of Hillside Memorial Park, surrounded by other of Los Angeles' over-the-top performers: Al Jolson, Eddie Cantor, and George Jessel.

After his retirement from his second career, at the track, O'Mara tended the roses in his garden and fished the Sierras. He also decided it was time to tell the tales of the Gangster Squad, though his wife thought that was a mistake.

"I think sometimes you talk too much and you might put your foot in it," Connie O'Mara said, as if they would haul him off to jail for having taken some hit man into the hills for a chat in 1949. "Oh, Daddy, don't go into that."

"Leave it alone a minute, will you, boss? I still got my marbles."

"Sometimes I wonder," she said.

When Connie had her stroke he cared for her at home, lifting her in and out of bed and keeping her clean, doing everything, until he got weak, too, with lymphoma. Only then did he allow her to be taken to a nursing home, where he visited every day. He years before had picked out their gravesite in a Catholic cemetery in the San Gabriel Valley, on a hillside with a tree that shaded visitors in the afternoon.

That's where his daughter read his eulogy after he died in June 2003, at eighty-six.

Marti O'Mara went into a brief panic when she gazed about the rolling lawns before the graveside ceremony. She knew it probably was her own mind game but she found herself studying the other headstones. Some had disturbingly young faces etched into the marble, a smiling fellow in a T-shirt, dead at seventeen, or an eighteen-year-old with a mustache. "It's the gangbanger cemetery," she said, fretting for an instant that her dad would be surrounded for eternity by a newer era's bad guys. Los Angeles' street gangs now claimed hundred of victims a year and no one could say this menace came from without. The *inner city*, that's what they called it.

Then she realized it didn't matter if those were gangbangers buried on that bucolic hillside. Her dad could handle those guys.

Marti O'Mara titled her eulogy, "A Good Life."

"My father loved being a cop," she said. "He was part of the team that really did keep organized crime out of Southern California."

"For my father, there was good, there was evil. He fought evil."

616

AFTERWORD: MACHINE GUN SHOOT-OUTS ON THE BIG SCREEN

Gangster Squad, both the book and the film, began with a phone call twenty years ago. An article in the *Los Angeles Times* on July 26, 1992, reported on a controversy over sensitive information in the police department's files — dirt, in essence, on politicians, celebrities, and hoodlums. The unit keeping the files was known then as the Organized Crime Intelligence Division (OCID), but the article said it had its roots in the Intelligence Division formed in the early 1950s by the legendary Chief William H. Parker. Then the phone rang that morning and the voice on the other end — clearly of an older man — said that was wrong. The roots went back further, to just after World War II, and something called the Gangster Squad. When I asked how he knew, the caller paused and said, "Well, I was on it."

The next day I was in the San Gabriel Valley living room of long-retired Sergeant John J. O'Mara, going through his fitness reports from when he joined the LAPD in 1940. His wife, Connie, lurked a safe distance away by the kitchen, cooking a pot of chili for us, but always listening in. At one point Jack railed against modern political correctness, with all these women charging sexual harassment.

"Sure a bunch of boys will be boys and get out of hand, play a little grab-ass," the faithful church usher said.

And the voice from the kitchen piped in, "Don't you feel honored to talk to such an intelligent man?"

Of course, she mostly worried about him getting into other sensitive matters, for as he said, "We'd be indicted today for things we did every day then."

Another LAPD unit of the era, a robbery trio known as the Hat Squad, had gotten a lot of attention over the years — its members were remarkable too, but also good self-promoters. The Gangster Squad had remained virtually invisible, in contrast, as its founders intended. Some of the men, particularly the original bugging expert Conwell Keeler, embraced almost the same code of silence as the mob, omerta. But O'Mara loved telling the tales, to a point where his family tuned them out, "Oh, that again." Or else they wondered, reasonably, whether he might have embellished some of the stories, even the mundane ones. After the former LAPD lieutenant Tom Bradley was elected mayor in 1973, the first black to hold the post, O'Mara spoke often of his rookie rivalry with the former UCLA track star. Such I-knew-him-when claims are commonly stretched and some of O'Mara's relatives thought they might catch Jack on this one years later when they took him to a show at the Ahmanson Theatre and noticed another old man being helped across the plaza, Tom Bradley, then long out of office. A nephew, Jim O'Mara, recalled prodding his gray-haired uncle to say hello, a classic "now we'll see" moment. But Bradley beat them to it. Spotting the familiar face, he called out "OOOOO MARA!" and the two geezers all but got down into their racing stances right there.

Over the months (then years) after our initial chili lunch, O'Mara helped steer me toward other surviving members of the secretive squad convened by Lieutenant Willie Burns. But even then only one other of the original eight was still alive, bug man Keeler. "I don't think he'd say shit if he had a mouthful," warned the subsequent bugging genius (Judge) Bert Phelps, and he was right. A series of visits, notes, and knocks on Keeler's door produced one curt response. "We had a job to do and we did it. Those are, how do you say, bodies that are buried." That went on for a decade.

Judge Phelps was the first to say I *had* to

see Jerry Wooters. As with Bert becoming a judge, the arc of Wooters's life alone presented a novelty — he was the renegade cop who became a millionaire by the beach, though I did have to pick up the check every time we met. The grizzled Sergeant Wooters would reach for it and get there just a moment late, "That's Jerry," as they say. But it was more than his unlikely success. Most all these old cops were children of the Depression and veterans of the War — they'd been through a lot — and their storytelling bore little resemblance to what you encounter in today's age of puffery and (instant) celebrity, when people don't hesitate to tout their own (invented) heroism. The Gangster Squad cops, in contrast, were modest and self-deprecating, and Jerry was at the extreme of the latter, portraying himself as a screw-up in virtually every story he told. Forget the medals he'd won in the war, he was a draft-dodger at heart. Forget the descriptions of him as Mickey Cohen's pursuing "Javert" — they both wound up in some damn jail, didn't they?

I naturally wondered about some of Jerry's stories too, even if he came out on the wrong end in them. I loved his tale of getting a watchdog as a gift from the fearsome Jack Whalen after trying in vain to turn down the animal. "They die on you, then you're miserable." With many of the stories told by the cops, thousands of pages of dusty records could be found to check them out — grand jury transcripts on the Gangster Squad's role in the Black Dahlia case, for instance, or testimony of a former guard at Mickey's home, confirming how he snuck the guns to O'Mara. But how do you check whether a cop got a gift dog from "The Enforcer," a man killed a half century before? Well, I recalled Jerry mentioning in passing that Whalen's sister was the one who raised the Great Danes, so I tracked down the colorful Bobie von Hurst in Oregon. With some trepidation I asked the woman, then nearing ninety, if she remembered the episode and that particular animal. She said, "Yes, sure, Thor," and that was the start of long sessions with the daughter of "Freddie the Thief," and then other family members who could help piece together his journey across America, conning all the way.

Yet even as notebooks and cassette tapes filled with the details of Fred Whalen's trek and the Gangster Squad's missions, I still was not sure of what to do with the material — it wasn't easy to see how it fit into a daily newspaper. But when the fiftieth anniversary of the squad's founding approached I decided with my editors that the story needed to be told, however outside the box. So I set out to see Jack O'Mara one last time.

I had kept in touch through Connie's illness and death, convinced that his caring for her was his finest act as a man — far beyond anything he did with a gun. But with his own lymphoma taking its toll, his family moved him into an upscale senior residence down in the Laguna Beach area. That was a story in itself. The other men there tended to be doctors and lawyers, etc., but the blue-eyed Irish cop quickly became cock of the walk, winning their competitions in pitch-and-putt golf and lawn croquet, everyone dressed in white for that. No doctor or lawyer could match his stories either, that's a given. The widower Jack O'Mara perked up and had a couple of attractive girlfriends, you better believe it, before his health failed again. At that point I was living in New York, so I flew out, hoping for one final visit that didn't happen — Jack O'Mara died that week, with three younger generations around him, a great-grandson curled up at his side.

Two days later in June 2003, I decided to make one last call before I flew back East. I wanted to try Con Keeler again, after a decade of rebuffs. I was at a barbecue at an old friend's house and at sundown called on my cell phone and got a "Hello?" Then I simply asked a question, with no preliminaries, about the squad's roster in 1946 — and Con answered. He talked a while about tough little Willie Burns then went down the list of the originals for three hours, burning out the cell phone's battery. When I informed him that O'Mara had died, he said, "I guess I'm the only one left."

After that, we spoke or met close to one hundred times. Con had the best memory of anyone for dates, addresses, or names — or exactly how Lieutenant Burns showed off his Tommy gun at their first meeting. He never hesitated to question someone else's memory of a detail, either. "Noooo, I don't think so," he'd say. He never said why he had decided to talk after all those years.

It defied logic that he was the last of the originals alive. During World War II, he had become infected amid routine surgery in an operating room that had sawdust in it and they left him in a "dark room" to die. After the war, during an operation to remove his scar tissue, an anesthesiologist overjuiced him and he went into a coma for two days — other squad members dropped by to say good-bye before he fooled 'em again. He was supposed to die in 1965 also, from a heart attack the last day of the Watts riots. That ended his police career, but on he lived.

Unlike other squad members, Keeler did not become a millionaire or a judge or a racetrack honcho. He dabbled in private debugging, then decided he could make do on his pension. Having been a policeman was enough for him. He hung a rendering of his sergeant's badge, #2763, in his living room, across from the 1883 clock his grandparents had carted in a covered wagon from Iowa. "It ticks away," he said as he neared his ninetieth birthday, miraculously still ticking himself.

That was about the time he said, "I want to show you something," and got out the little notebook that started their files, his fine-point pen recording the basics on "Accardo, Anthony," "Cornero, Tony," and "Cohen, Mickey," with his "46 Cad. Sed Blk. Shiny 3T9 364."

But Con was taking seven pills in the morning for his thyroid and strokes and to control the timing of his heart. Sometimes he'd collapse and a rescue crew would rush him to the hospital. Back home, he'd go to the garage to get a tool and forget why he was there. It went on that way for several years until his family, like O'Mara's, moved their old warrior to assisted living.

That's where I hoped to see him one last time when I came west this past fall for the filming of *Gangster Squad*.

I was nervous, I must admit, because of my trip out to see O'Mara eight years earlier, when Jack died. I didn't want to jinx Con, now a month from his ninety-seventh birthday. The producers of the Warner Bros. film hoped to get him to the set, but that was unrealistic. I had been speaking with his daughter Kathleen, retired after working for the LAPD's crime lab, and her husband, Don Irvine, a retired lieutenant. Empty nesters since their son took off to attend Harvard — I don't have to tell you how proud they were — they had taken on the wrenching task of moving Con out of the house he built with the help of Benny Williams, another Gangster Squad original, now long gone.

We met at Con's group care residence, where an aide helped him from his room. Con, neat in gray slacks and a gray shirt, stood almost erect, if not quite to his six-foot-one of old. We hugged and took seats at a table next to a framed display of shells atop sand.

"You're a character in a movie," the son-in-law, Don, kicked us off.

"I was in one before," Keeler replied, "Webb's."

He then recalled how *Dragnet*'s Jack Webb had given him a shotgun not for the 1954 movie, but for serving as technical adviser on several episodes of the TV series.

"We still have the shotgun," Don told him.

Con was at the stage where not a day was guaranteed, but we were sure to get a couple of the old stories. They would likely be ones I had heard several times, because he'd evolved from omerta to thirsting to talk. But you never knew when a new story would pop out and one did that day, November 7, 2011, though it had nothing at all to do with Mickey Cohen. It was about how Chief Parker, like his predecessors, could not resist using the squad for *other chores* . . . in this case helping to protect a dignitary, President John F. Kennedy. Con Keeler's final story, then:

Parker always was fearful that something might happen in L.A. and embarrass the city, though this attitude was rare in the era before the Kennedy assassination. So Kennedy himself comes to town and they assign a car to watch him. I was like a supervisor then and the guys are reporting in to me. So he goes to his hotel where he checks into a bungalow and then they see him crawl out a window and get a cab. A cab — the president of the United States. Oh, my. So they call me, "What should we do?"

"Follow him."

So they do . . . to Kim Novak's house.

I call the Secret Service, which is supposed to be protecting him. "Do you know where your man is?"

"He's asleep."

"You'd better check where."

The film *Gangster Squad* was shot "on location," as they say, and that week the location was the north end of what used to be fashionable Westlake Park, now MacArthur Park, and in a neighborhood that's changed. But the building being used was a remnant of the area's peak, the neo-Gothic tower that originally housed the Elks Lodge, then a hotel (the Park Plaza), which now is used mostly for catered events and film shoots. It was to be the setting for the climactic showdown between Mickey and his men and the Gangster Squad led in the film by Jack O'Mara and Jerry Wooters. There would be bullets flying back and forth all week, both on the street outside the hotel, amid vintage Cadillacs, and inside the enormous lobby, which was decorated for Christmas. In a gangster film, you can't have the Tommy guns kept under the overcoats at the big confrontation.

"Boys with toys!" declared Dan Lin, the producer who led the transformation of the real story into a film geared toward multiplexes, meaning a dozen antique Tommies would be rat-a-tat-tatting all week, some old enough to have been under O'Mara's bed. Actor Ryan Gosling, playing Wooters, was getting ready to charge the hotel where Sean Penn, the film's Mickey, was holed up.

"Did any of these guys get killed?" Gosling asked.

I explained that two of the original eight had been shot, and one had a partner killed, but early in their careers. Jumbo Kennard was killed, but not by a gun.

Gosling had already been visited on the set

by the sons of the real Jerry Wooters, Gerard, and David, along with their dad's old partner, Judge Phelps, very much still kicking. All had pestered the actor on the small things he had to do — or stop doing — to be true to the real Jerry. "You've got to ash your cigarette *into your cuff*," one of the boys told him. "That's how the old man did it." Then the trio of visitors went nuts when Gosling, in the bar scene, ordered a Nehi, or something as tame.

"I never saw your dad drink a soda pop in his life!" the judge told the boys. And Jerry in *spats*?

Relishing the interplay, Gosling explained that *his* Wooters is the hard drinker they knew when we first see him in the film. But Gosling saw going on the wagon was a way of signaling the character's shedding of cynicism as he gets with the mission of getting Mickey Cohen.

Actors make decisions like that. Sean Penn no doubt considered many ways to play Mickey, who was a different person in different eras, going from the don't-mess-with-me heist man to the showman of his last years. Were he alive today, he'd have a reality TV series, without question. But the film is set in 1949, when he was causing serious havoc in the city and the bullets *were* flying, even if mostly in his direction. Penn decided that the key to that Mickey lay earlier in his life, when he had to measure his opponent, strategize, and inflict pain a different way. "It's all about boxing," explained the director Ruben Fleischer, watching the action on a bank of monitors as Gosling and Josh Brolin finally stormed the hotel, Tommies blazin'. Brolin was doing O'Mara as a Berserker, one of those Norse fighters who charged forward without much concern for their safety.

During a break, I jotted a note to myself to calculate how close we were to where the Whalens opened their little store in 1922. I guessed eight blocks. The imposing old Elks lodge being shot up was where Freddie the Thief staged his pool championships in later years, with L.A. cops providing security.

Another intersection between fiction and reality was delicious: The film crews recreated *Slapsy Maxie's* to stage the scene in which Wooters first eyes Mickey and meets the woman who will be caught between them, a fictionalized character played by the young actress Emma Stone, who dyed her hair from its natural blond to red for the role — Caddies and redheads, that too was their world. Anyway, during this part of the shoot, they ran into an old-time fireman who had been around in the restaurant's glory days, so Gosling started questioning him.

He said a couple of times he saw the real Mickey Cohen there so I asked what that was like. The man said, "He was right at that table," and pointed. He said, "He was telling these lame jokes but everybody was laughing."

Then Emma Stone came out of a trailer, getting ready for her scene, and Gosling greeted her with a question.

I asked Emma, "How's it going at the trailer?" She said, "Oh, Sean's telling all these lame jokes and everyone's laughing."

Two days later, the filming by the park drew more visitors from the real story. One was Lindo Giacopuzzi, the Gangster Squad's first addition after the original eight, who became the resident Italian. Now ninety-five, the old football lineman had been driven to the shoot by a granddaughter, but looked like he still could knock your block off. He carried a scrapbook with clippings of some of his cases, including the 1947 roust of six Midwesterners in the Caddy owned by one of Mickey's henchman. With perfect timing, two of the actors playing Mickey's thugs came over and plopped themselves in directors chairs next to Jaco. He told them then how he had been transferred out of the squad without explanation when Chief Parker took office and put Captain James Hamilton in charge.

"He thought I'd be clannish," Jaco told the

actors. "I was *put on* because I was Italian and spoke Italian and I was *put off* because I was Italian."

"How come men were tougher in your day?" asked Holt McCallany, a rugged guy who in the film was trying to kill Jaco's old buddies.

"We used to say 'half-tough.' We'd say 'That Jumbo Kennard, he's half-tough.' "

On the monitors everywhere, Sean Penn was running through the scene in which he puts on his coat and heads out from his suite for the showdown with O'Mara and company. In another reality-meets-fiction, the script was written by cop-turned-novelist Will Beall, who worked out of the LAPD's 77th Street Division a half century after the Gangster Squad was formed there. But you hire an actor such as Penn knowing he's going to make the script his own — he'll try things a few ways once he inhabits a character. So one time he heads off to the showdown without uttering a line, it's all in his stride. Another time he says just a single word, "Unbelievable." A third time he gets ready for the shootout — you know bodies will fall — by muttering, "Gotta fix my tie — I can't go out in public with my tie like this." A fourth time he goes for melodrama, "This is it. This is the end."

Jack O'Mara's older daughter also came by that night, but that was no surprise. Maureen

O'Mara Stevens had been showing up several times a week, like a groupie. "I know they think I'm nuts, but I don't care," she said. "How often do they make a movie with your father in it?"

The two O'Mara girls represent a classic divide. The youngest, Marti, was the prodigal, picked for those TV quiz shows and then off to Harvard for three advanced degrees. Dr. O'Mara still lives in Cambridge, Massachusetts, and is an expert in corporate real estate, traveling the country as head of her own consulting company when she isn't home, as a mother of three. The older daughter, Maureen, stayed closer to the original nest. While teaching nursing and tending her family — she's a grandma already — Maureen took on the dutiful care of their parents. After her father's death, she refused to cooperate with my research for several years — the loss of her dad was too much for her — while Marti was eager to see her father's life shared with the world. Now the two sisters saw the filming entirely differently.

In Cambridge, Marti was bothered by the violence. She had not known her father to ever use his gun. He had once, but he spared his daughters the details. She was bothered too by the casting of the buffed, ripped Brolin as her smaller dad. Even hearing that he wore a brown suit got to her — her dad went for blue and gray, to go with his eyes. But mostly it was all the shoot-'em-up scenes she heard about, ones her older sister invariably witnessed. "I kept telling her, 'It's a movie,' " Maureen said during yet another day of shooting.

> She doesn't think my father was very violent but, you know, I'm sorry, I saw all those guns under my dad's bed and in the closet, because I was very fascinated with them and they had to keep moving them. I know they don't look like Mom and Dad. Yes, he's wearing a wedding ring and Dad didn't. But it's a movie."

That said, the elder sister was disappointed herself at one tweaking of reality: when Jack and Connie O'Mara have a child in the film, the baby's room in their post-war American Dream house is *blue*. "That's me being born, except it's a boy," she told the actors playing Mickey's henchman.

Then came the miracle. She was watching that scene being shot and one take brought chills to her body. Brolin was playing her dad, actress Mireille Enos her mom. Enos said, "Oh, Jack," and the (fictional) couple exchanged a look and suddenly it was *them*, her real parents.

From then on the filming became an opportunity for her to make peace, finally, with her father's death. Maureen O'Mara Stevens started visiting all the places of their lives, and her own, then went to the cemetery for the first time since her father's burial.

I made a little map of all these places I wanted to go visit. I wanted to see the houses where we lived. I just wanted to see everything again. The house on Pedley, the house in El Monte. Then we went to their grave and I realized why my parents bought a grave there — the cemetery is not even five minutes away from where they bought their first house. It's the same beautiful view of the foothills. They bought their burial plot when they bought their first house. Dad was looking ahead, I guess, to what might happen.

I went by my dad's grave and my mom's grave and told them about it, the film. My dad, I think, he's not going to care that anybody made him look tougher than he was. But you hear about him taking those guys up into the hills, you know, I think he was pretty tough.

The capper for Maureen came at Halloween when her grandson was given his choice of costumes. He got himself one of those hats and trick-or-treated as Jack O'Mara of the Gangster Squad.

The expected e-mail from the son-in-law arrived January 31, 2012. A massive stroke did it. Don Irvine sent a notice to the police department, "Sorry to report that retired Sergeant Con Keeler, one of the last men standing . . ."

The last of the original eight was gone. Only their stories remained.

ACKNOWLEDGMENTS

Thanks must start with Jack O'Mara, for making a phone call in 1992, then to Connie O'Mara, for graciously putting up with so many hours of war stories; to the O'Mara daughters, Maureen and Marti, for offering loving yet honest perspective on their parents; and to other members of their extended family for filling in details back to the 1920s. The Wooters's sons, Gerard and David, deserve similar thanks for their candid guidance in advancing the research on "the old man" after Jerry Wooters was no longer around to tell stories himself.

I wish Con Keeler had lived to be one hundred, when he finally might have revealed why he decided to talk after a decade of silence, but I'm indebted to him for remembering the trivia of 1946 a full sixty-five years later. The two LAPD veterans who may yet break the century mark, Lindo Giacopuzzi and Judge Phelps, kept their good humor while being prodded to go over the same ground time and again. Other Gangster Squad members shared their stories with equal fervor — thanks especially to Jack Horrall, William Unland, and John Olsen — even if they are secondary figures in the final narrative. Many family members helped bring back to life other of the old cops no longer with us. Thanks to the three Greeley kids, Jumbo Kennard's sister, Willie Burns's grandson, and Buzz Williams, a policeman himself who had both a grandfather (Benny) and father (Dick) on the Gangster Squad.

Many in the extended Whalen-Wunderlich clan helped as well, but the thanks there must start with Bobie von Hurst, who as a child was part of the family's trek West in 1922 and lived until the fall of 2011. She set the tone with her willingness to discuss the extraordinary (and often extralegal) antics of her father, Fred Whalen. Her son, John von Hurst, may have been the square of the clan, but thank goodness he was willing to endure endless questions in his role as the unofficial Whalen family historian.

Thanks also to those readers who shared their own experiences with the Gangster Squad, or with Mickey Cohen and the other hoodlums, following publication of the seven-part "Tales from the Gangster Squad" in the *Los Angeles Times*. Musician Bill Peterson volunteered a telling Sunset Strip encounter from his own memoir, "Show Biz from the

Back Row," while the Grahm family shared the inner workings of the Hollywood warehouse that supplied Fred Whalen and other of L.A.'s colorful con men. Thanks, too, to Chicago's Newberry Library for access to the Ben Hecht Papers.

On the sausage-making side, two editors at the *Los Angeles Times*, Marc Duvoisin and Rick Meyer, helped shape the first telling of this story. But the most valuable players at the newspaper were researchers Tracy Thomas and Maloy Moore, who dug up thousands of pages of documents that made it possible to check and amplify the oral histories. Nona Yates then carried on that same high calling with professionalism and zeal while helping to track down more witnesses and documents essential to the writing of this book.

In Los Angeles, Peter Nelson helped figure out how to give this material additional life, and Jim Ehrich made it happen, while Dan Lin and Jon Silk turned the words into moving pictures, albeit with a lot more rat-a-tat-tat. In New York, Jake Elwell helped make this book happen while Peter Wolverton and Anne Bensson labored under extraordinary deadlines to get it ready for the presses at Thomas Dunne Books.

Finally, thanks for moral support to the usual suspects, Joan, M.T., and Dr. C., and to the saintly Heidi, of course, for putting up with the obsessed soul laboring on the computer down in the Man Cave.

ABOUT THE AUTHOR

Paul Lieberman worked for 24 years as a writer and editor at the *Los Angeles Times.* He has won dozens of journalism honors, including the Robert F. Kennedy Awards Grand Prize. Lieberman is a graduate of Williams College and was a Nieman Fellow at Harvard.

The employees of Thorndike Press hope you have enjoyed this Large Print book. All our Thorndike, Wheeler, and Kennebec Large Print titles are designed for easy reading, and all our books are made to last. Other Thorndike Press Large Print books are available at your library, through selected bookstores, or directly from us.

For information about titles, please call:

(800) 223-1244

or visit our Web site at:

http://gale.cengage.com/thorndike

To share your comments, please write:

Publisher
Thorndike Press
10 Water St., Suite 310
Waterville, ME 04901